War Experiences in Rural Germany
1914–1923

BENJAMIN ZIEMANN

Translated by
Alex Skinner

Oxford • New York

English Edition
First published in 2007 by
Berg
Editorial offices:
1st Floor, Angel Court, 81 St Clements Street, Oxford, OX4 1AW, UK
175 Fifth Avenue, New York, NY 10010, USA

Berg is the imprint of Oxford International Publishers Ltd.

First published in 1997 as *Front und Heimat: Ländliche Kriegserfahrungen im südlichen Bayern 1914–1923* by Klartext Verlag, Essen

Library of Congress Cataloguing-in-Publication Data

Ziemann, Benjamin.
[Front und Heimat. English]
War experiences in rural Germany, 1914–1923 / Benjamin Ziemann
; translated by Alex Skinner.—English ed.
p. cm.—(The legacy of the Great War)
Includes bibliographical references and index.
ISBN-13: 978-1-84520-244-6 (cloth)
ISBN-10: 1-84520-244-9 (cloth)
ISBN-13: 978-1-84520-245-3 (pbk.)
ISBN-10: 1-84520-245-7 (pbk.)
1. World War, 1914–1918—Germany—Bavaria. 2. Soldiers—Germany—Bavaria—History—20th century. 3. Rural population—Germany-Bavaria—History—20th century. 4. Bavaria (Germany)—Rural conditions. 5. Bavaria (Germany)—History—20th century.
I. Title.
D534.Z5413 2007
940.3'433091734—dc22

2006032830

British Library Cataloguing-in-Publication Data
A catalogue record for this book is available from the British Library.

ISBN-13 978 1 84520 244 6 (Cloth)
ISBN-10 1 84520 244 9 (Cloth)

ISBN-13 978 1 84520 245 3 (Paper)
ISBN-10 1 84520 245 7 (Paper)

Typeset by JS Typesetting Ltd, Porthcawl, Mid Glamorgan

www.bergpublishers.com

Contents

List of Tables

List of Abbreviations

ABA	Archiv des Bistums Augsburg
ABP	Archiv des Bistums Passau
AEM	Archiv des Erzbistums München und Freising
AfS	*Archiv für Sozialgeschichte*
AK	Armeekorps (army corps)
AOK	Armeeoberkommando (army supreme command)
BA	Bezirksamt (district administration)
BArch	Bundesarchiv Berlin-Lichterfelde (Federal Archive Berlin-Lichterfelde)
BA/MA	Bundesarchiv/Militärarchiv Freiburg (Federal Military Archive Freiburg)
BBB	Bayerischer Bauernbund (Bavarian Peasants' League)
BfZ	Bibliothek für Zeitgeschichte Stuttgart
BHStA/II	Bayerisches Hauptstaatsarchiv München, Abt. II
BHStA/IV	Bayerisches Hauptstaatsarchiv München, Abt. IV: Kriegsarchiv
BKZ	*Bayerische Krieger Zeitung* (Bavarian Warrior's Newspaper)
BSB	Bayerische Staatsbibliothek München, Handschriftenabteilung, Schinnereriana
Btl.	Batallion
BVP	Bayerische Volkspartei (Bavarian People's Party)
BZAR	Bischöfliches Zentralarchiv Regensburg
DDVP	Deutsche Demokratische Volkspartei
Div.	Division
E./Ers.	'Ersatz' (unit situated in Bavaria, sending replacements to the related unit at the front)
E.W.	Einwohnerwehr (Citizens' militia)
GG	*Geschichte und Gesellschaft*

GK	Generalkommando (general command of an army corps)
HMB	Halbmonatsbericht (fortnightly report)
Inf.	Infantry
I.R.	Infantry regiment
JMH	*Journal of Modern History*
K.M.	Kriegsministerium (War Ministry)
Ldw.	Landwehr (units of the territorial army, consisting of conscripts aged 30–45)
Ldst.	Landsturm
L.I.R.	Landwehr-Infanterie-Regiment
MA	Ministerium des Königlichen Hauses und des Äußern (Bavarian Ministry of the Royal House and the Exterior)
MdL	Mitglied des Landtags (Member of the Bavarian Diet)
MdR	Mitglied des Reichstags (Member of the Imperial Diet)
MInn	Ministerium des Innern (Bavarian Home Office)
MK	Ministerium für Kultus und Unterricht (Bavarian Ministry for Culture and Schools)
ML	Ministerium für Landwirtschaft (Bavarian Ministry for Agriculture)
MSPD	Majority Social Democratic Party
Ndb.	Niederbayern (Lower Bavaria)
Obb.	Oberbayern (Upper Bavaria)
OHL	Oberste Heeresleitung (German Army Supreme Command)
R./Res.	Reserve
Rgt.	Regiment
RP	Regierungspräsident (head of regional administration in Upper Bavaria, etc.)
Schw.	Bayerisch Schwaben (Bavarian Swabia)
SHStAD	Sächsisches Hauptstaatsarchiv Dresden
SPD	Sozialdemokratische Partei Deutschlands (Social Democratic Party of Germany)
StAA	Staatsarchiv Augsburg
StAL	Staatsarchiv Landshut
StAM	Staatsarchiv München
StaA	Stadtarchiv
stv.	stellvertretend (deputy; related to units of the replacement army)
Uffz.	Unteroffizier (non-commissioned officer)
USPD	Independent Social Democratic Party of Germany
WB	Wochenbericht (weekly report)

WUA	Das Werk des Untersuchungsausschusses der Verfassunggebenden Deutschen Nationalversammlung und des Deutschen Reichstages 1919–1930, Vierte Reihe: Die Ursachen des Deutschen Zusammenbruches im Jahre 1918
ZBLG	*Zeitschrift für Bayerische Landesgeschichte*
ZBSL	*Zeitschrift des Bayerischen Statistischen Landesamtes*

Foreword

Belinda Davis was the first to suggest that my work about the First World War and its consequences should be translated into English, and she gave helpful advice on how to change the presentation of my argument for an anglophone readership. Jay Winter accepted my manuscript for publication in this series and offered help at a crucial moment. Richard Bessel has provided intellectual inspiration, hospitality and - most crucially - friendship, and not only during my stay at the University of York in 2003/4. I wish to express my gratitude to these persons and to the Alexander von Humboldt Foundation, which funded my year in York with a Feodor Lynen fellowship.

Over the years I have accumulated a great debt of gratitude to several friends who have always been supportive and ready to share their insights into the history of violence in the twentieth century. My thanks go to Christine Brocks, Christa Hämmerle, Christian Jansen, Frank Kebbedies, Thomas Mergel, Josef Mooser, Dirk Schumann, Bernd Ulrich and particularly to Thomas Kühne.

Alex Skinner has translated my manuscript with verve and professionalism. Many of the quotations from war letters and diaries, written by ordinary peasants and their wives, are crafted in a peculiar style, very often without any punctuation and in blatant breach of the rules of grammar. For the convenience of the reader and because the specific flavour of the original is almost impossible to convey, these quotations have been translated into grammatically correct English.

Benjamin Ziemann
Sheffield, May 2006

Introduction

The notion that the First World War was an important, if not *the* most important, turning point in twentieth-century German and European history has become a commonplace in historical research. Between 1914 and 1918, in economics, science, politics and culture, traditional structures were transformed or destroyed, models of a new social order were introduced and the knowledge passed from one generation to the next was radically devalued.[1] In Germany and other European countries, front-line soldiers constitute the key symbol of the First World War's drastic consequences. As early as the 1920s, they were seen as embodying the discontinuity produced by the experience of war, as a model of uprooting, brutalisation and the aggressive reordering of social relations, epitomised by front-line camaraderie. Soldiers' experience of violence, and how this was processed, passed down and symbolised in the inter-war period, provides an excellent basis upon which to discuss and evaluate theories asserting that the First World War was a profound turning point. Did the experience of war, particularly that of German soldiers, facilitate the breakthrough of a semantics rooted in the symbolic world of artistic modernity, as Modris Eksteins has claimed? Is there evidence of a 'war culture' among soldiers, a system of collective representations, intimately bound up with a 'powerful hatred of the opponent'?[2] Questions such as these, discussed in recent studies, have yet to be answered in empirically grounded fashion.

1. Recent research, however, has stressed continuities rather than the dramatic change previously assumed. See especially Jay Winter, *Sites of Memory, Sites of Mourning. The Great War in European Cultural History*, Cambridge: Cambridge University Press 1996.

2. Eksteins, *Rites of Spring*; Audoin-Rouzeau/Becker, *Understanding*, quote pp. 102–3. The best general discussion of the First World War as a caesura is Jay Winter/Geoffrey Parker/Mary Habeck (eds), *The Great War and the Twentieth Century*, New Haven: Yale University Press 2000.

The way many historians use the example of German soldiers from 1914-18 to back up their hypotheses stands in marked contrast with the current state of empirical research. We still lack a comprehensive social and experiential history of German soldiers between 1914 and 1918. Klaus Latzel, Anne Lipp, Aribert Reimann and Bernd Ulrich have presented key initial findings on the content of letters written by German soldiers and of trench newspapers.[3] None of these studies, however, has attempted to link the experiences of war as a history of mentalities with the analysis of structural factors, as Richard Bessel and Ute Daniel have done in their pioneering studies of wartime German society on the home front.[4] In order to examine the effects and repercussions of the war and how people dealt with these experiences after 11 November 1918, we must in any case look beyond the end of the war. Researchers studying how specific social groups or milieus experienced the Great War and how they came to terms with this in the Weimar Republic tend to work in isolation from one another, however, failing to examine how their research ties in with other work. Some recent studies have furnished us with significant insights into the aestheticisation and symbolisation of wartime violence in the 1920s. Only Sven Reichardt, however, has succeeded in linking the symbolisation of war experiences with the models of social order characteristic of a specific social group in his innovative study on the group culture of SA storm troopers.[5] Most studies of the

3. Klaus Latzel, *Deutsche Soldaten - nationalsozialistischer Krieg? Kriegserlebnis-Kriegserfahrung 1939-1945*, Paderborn: Ferdinand Schöningh 1998; Lipp, *Meinungslenkung*; Aribert Reimann, *Der Große Krieg der Sprachen. Untersuchungen zur historischen Semantik in Deutschland und England zur Zeit des Ersten Weltkriegs*, Essen: Klartext 2000; Ulrich, *Augenzeugen*; see the review article by Belinda Davis, Experience, Identity, and Memory: The Legacy of World War I, *JMH* 75 (2003), pp. 111-31. A still valuable account on German soldiers during the First World War is the expert report by liberal historian Martin Hobohm for the parliamentary committee of investigation into the causes of the German collapse in 1918, published in 1928. See WUA, vol. 11/1. For more information on Hobohm see Hans Schleier, *Die bürgerliche deutsche Geschichtsschreibung der Weimarer Republik*, Berlin: Akademie Verlag 1975, pp. 531-74.

4. Bessel, *Germany*; Daniel, *Arbeiterfrauen*. See also the brilliant study by Leonard V. Smith, *Between Mutiny and Obedience. The Case of the French Fifth Infantry Division during World War I*, Princeton: Princeton University Press 1994.

5. Sabine Behrenbeck, *Der Kult um die toten Helden. Nationalsozialistische Mythen, Riten und Symbole 1923 bis 1945*, Vierow: SH-Verlag 1996; Sven

collective representation of wartime experiences, moreover, focus on representatives of elite culture or bourgeois social groups. Very few deal with the symbolism of memories of war among the lower classes such as urban workers, most of whom were members of the Social Democratic Party and its veterans' association, the *Reichsbanner Schwarz-Rot-Gold,* with a membership of more than one million one of the largest veterans' associations during the Weimar Republic.[6]

The present work tackles some of these issues through a regional study. The aim here is to produce empirically robust findings by focusing on a specific region and social group. Future researchers will then be in a position to compare these findings with those for other regions or groups. I have chosen to study the rural inhabitants of southern Bavaria: peasant farmers, their wives and sons, farm labourers and maids (female rural workers and servants) from the districts (*Regierungsbezirke*) of Upper and Lower Bavaria and Bavarian Swabia, a region dominated by medium-sized farms of up to 20 hectares. This choice may appear random and artificial, but it is anchored in the significance of this social group and its spatial origins to the history of the First World War in Germany.

This significance is, first of all, quantitative in nature. Unlike the student volunteers and middle-class intellectuals whose letters home have so often been quoted and interpreted as representative of wartime experience, soldiers from a rural background were by no means a marginal group. Large numbers of such men served in the Bavarian or German army.[7] From 1914 to 1918 around half the soldiers in the Bavarian army and about a third of those in the German army as a whole worked in agriculture in civilian life. Students and other soldiers

---

Reichardt, *Faschistische Kampfbünde. Gewalt und Gemeinschaft im italienischen Squadrismus und in der deutschen SA*, Cologne: Böhlau 2002, chapter 5. For an overview of recent research, see Ziemann, Erinnerung.

6. See Ziemann, Republikanische Kriegserinnerung.

7. Until 1918 the German army consisted of contingents from Bavaria, Prussia, Saxony and Württemberg, under a common Imperial Supreme Command. Bavaria, like the other contingents, had a war ministry of its own, but the Prussian War Ministry was in charge of all matters and decisions of major importance. Unless otherwise stated, all references in the main text and footnotes refer to Bavarian army units. On the use of war letters written by students, see Manfred Hettling/Michael Jeismann, Der Weltkrieg als Epos. Philipp Witkops 'Kriegsbriefe gefallener Studenten', in: Gerhard Hirschfeld/Gerd Krumeich (eds), *Keiner fühlt sich hier mehr als Mensch... Erlebnis und Wirkung des Ersten Weltkriegs*, Essen: Klartext 1993, pp. 175–98.

and officers from the educated middle class, meanwhile, made up no more than about 2 per cent of all army personnel. Among the rural-agrarian regions of the German Empire, Bavaria was a special case in certain respects. By 1914 agricultural modernisation had had a far greater impact on other major farming regions in Schleswig-Holstein, Lower Saxony or Westphalia. Peasants there had already been subject to partial embourgeoisement. Bavarian peasants' life-world and culture was vastly more traditional in character.[8]

Religion also played an important role here. Almost the entire rural population of southern Bavaria was Catholic. Alongside Baden, the Rhineland, Westphalia and Silesia, 'Altbayern' (old Bavaria) was one of the core Catholic regions of the German Empire. The Catholicism of Altbayern diverged somewhat from its socio-politically active, bourgeois counterpart, which dominated in the industrialised parts of the Rhineland and Westphalia. Traditional rituals and symbols, such as family prayers, pilgrimages and pictures of saints, continued to play a far greater role in rural Bavaria. Popular piety was more vigorous and imbued the culture more than in other Catholic regions. Nonetheless, the Catholics of Altbayern were not completely untypical of German Catholics as a whole, who made up roughly one-third of the country's population in 1914.[9] The differences and similarities with other social groups can be discussed further. What I want to bring out here is that Bavarian soldiers from a rural background were not a marginal group. They made up around half of all Bavarian and roughly 5 per cent of all German soldiers called up between 1914 and 1918. This was a significantly larger group than all the students, professors, writers, artists and doctors who served in the German army taken together. Yet to this day it is the latter group which tends to serve as material for academic discussions of the front-line experiences during the Great War. The voices of rural soldiers have as yet scarcely been heard in the research. In future, rather than privileging the middle class, researchers should produce more comparative analyses of the wartime experience of soldiers drawn from the ranks of industrial workers, the other major group within the German army alongside peasants.[10]

8. See Chapter 1 and the comparative research in Jacobeit, *Idylle*.

9. See Chapter 4.2; Thomas Mergel, Mapping Milieus. On the Spatial Rootedness of Collective Identities in the 19th Century, in: Jim Retallack (ed.), *Saxony in German History. Culture, Society, and Politics, 1830-1933*, Ann Arbor, MI: University of Michigan Press 2000, pp. 77-95.

10. See the evidence in Kruse, Klassenheer; idem, *Krieg und nationale Integration*; Cohen, *The War Come Home*.

Within the Bavarian army, soldiers from a rural background formed a group with a unique social profile and specific behaviour patterns and interpretive models, through which they came to terms with the experience of total war. Some of these models were unique to them, at least some important characteristics. This applies, for instance, to the significance of piety to soldiers' psychological stability in the face of the death and destruction at the front, or to the 'hatred of Prussia' which lays bare the limits of national integration within the German Empire. Other interpretive models, meanwhile, were also common among soldiers from other social groups. This applies to soldiers' complete rejection of aggressive nationalism, as advocated, for instance, by the German Fatherland Party, founded in 1917.[11] Bavarian peasant soldiers are, however, highly significant to the history of the First World War in another respect. In recent years, historians have put under scrutiny the connections and continuities in the exercise of violence from the First to the Second World War. Michael Geyer has analysed this as an increasing 'societalisation of violence'.[12] The primary focus here is the readiness of *Wehrmacht* soldiers to use extreme violence in the war against the Soviet Union from 1941 until 1945. Was the violent mentality of German soldiers in Operation Barbarossa anchored in a substantial prehistory during the First World War, particularly as far as German troops on the Eastern Front are concerned? Such questions are important and legitimate. Vejas G. Liulevicius' study of the German occupation regime of the Commander *Ober-Ost* during the First World War has already produced major findings.[13]

Interest in continuities, however, should not cause us to take autobiographical accounts by soldiers during the First World War seriously only insofar as they reveal the aggressive self-image of decidedly nationalist and racist actors and thus point directly to the Second World War.[14] Such material exists; from August 1914 on, it is in

11. See Reimann, *Große Krieg*, pp. 167–222; Kruse, Klassenheer.

12. See the discussion in Ziemann, 'Vergesellschaftung der Gewalt'; for a general discussion of recent trends in military history see Kühne/Ziemann, *Was ist Militärgeschichte?*

13. Vejas G. Liulevicius, *War Land on the Eastern Front. Culture, National Identity, and German Occupation in World War I*, Cambridge: Cambridge University Press 2000.

14. See Robert L. Nelson, 'Ordinary Men' in the First World War? German Soldiers as Victims and Participants, *Journal of Contemporary History* 39 (2004), pp. 425–35.

fact largely to be found among soldiers at the Eastern Front.[15] However, we are not indulging in misconceived 'historicism' when we stress the clear limits of such constructions of continuity. To do so is to strive to achieve a balanced understanding of the structure of violence typical of the First World War. The great majority of all German soldiers, after all, served on the Western Front. On average, from 1914 to 1918 the field army (*Feldheer*) in the West comprised some 2.78 million men, compared to 1.3 million on the Eastern Front.[16] This applies to Bavarian soldiers as well, the vast majority of whom served in Belgium and France; only a minority was posted on the front in Russia. Most thus fought within the system of violence typical of the First World War, based around stationary trench warfare. This reduced the individual initiative of infantrymen to a minimum and made killing at a distance by means of artillery the predominant form of killing and thus also of culpability.[17] To grasp the wartime experience of German soldiers in the First World War and its symbolic representation in the post-war period, the first essential is to analyse this system of violence and its structural peculiarities.

The first key aim of this study is thus to analyse the social configurations of the army, the wartime experience of regular soldiers and the models they used to interpret their lived experience of the front, taking rural soldiers from southern Bavaria as an example. One of the central aims here is to evaluate the assertion that front-line soldiers were generally 'brutalised' by their experience of the destructiveness and indifference to human life at the front. George L. Mosse, and in a different way Omer Bartov as well, have advocated this theory to explain why the paramilitary defence associations (*Wehrverbände*) in the Weimar Republic, particularly the National Socialist 'storm troopers', were so attractive and why their members were so keen to fight. They rely, however, not on the empirical reconstruction of German soldiers' wartime experiences, but on the ideological self-stylisation of the *Freikorps* ('free corps') and SA fighters.[18] Recent research has, however, already pointed to the fact that within the National Socialist

15. See the examples in Ziemann, German Soldiers, p. 263–4.

16. *Sanitätsbericht*, p. 5*.

17. See Chapter 2.2.; Ziemann, Soldaten; Bernd Hüppauf, Räume der Destruktion und Konstruktion von Raum. Landschaft, Sehen, Raum und der Erste Weltkrieg, *Krieg und Literatur/War and Literature* 3 (1991), pp. 105–23.

18. Mosse, *Fallen Soldiers*, pp. 159–181; Omer Bartov, *Murder in Our Midst: The Holocaust, Industrial Killing, and Representation*, New York, Oxford:

movement it was above all the younger generation, born from 1900 on, who derived this violent cultural style from the 'experience of the front'. They had in fact experienced the war merely as young victory watchers and grew into this violence-prone tradition via their elders' accounts of wartime experience.[19]

The present work, however, aims to go beyond a mere history of the mentalities of ordinary German soldiers. It also intends to bring out the inner connections and interactions between wartime experiences at the front and at home and thus to analyse both settings as one all-embracing context. Previous work in this vein is thin on the ground. To what extent front and home front were related and integrated is thus still perhaps 'the most important question on the historical agenda' in relation to the First World War.[20] The understanding of this issue has long been hampered by the fact that the literary topos of the front-line soldier alienated from his home and family, found in the work of Erich Maria Remarque and many other authors of the 1920s and 1930s, is still extremely influential. This issue thus requires separate empirical examination.[21] The links and interactions between front and home front were generally a result of the totalisation of warfare, which reached its first peak from 1914 to 1918. 'From above', that is, from the vantage point of the military leadership, this link consisted above all in the fact that the popular mood at both front and home front became an important resource for waging war. To mobilise the population, the war required adequate ideological legitimation. To counter the growing war weariness, the German authorities deployed censorship and propaganda. This involved trying to stem the exchange of anti-war opinions which came about as a result of the 'wailing letters' sent by women at home and the stories told by men on furlough in

---

Oxford University Press 1996, pp. 15–50. For a general conceptual critique of this argument see Ziemann, Violent Society?

19. Patrick Krassnitzer, Die Geburt des Nationalsozialismus im Schützengraben. Formen der Brutalisierung in den Autobiographien von nationalsozialistischen Frontsoldaten, in: Jost Dülffer/Gerd Krumeich (eds), *Der verlorene Frieden. Politik und Kriegskultur nach 1918*, Essen: Klartext 2002, pp. 119–48.

20. See the contributions in Gerhard Hirschfeld/Gerd Krumeich/Dieter Langewiesche/Hans-Peter Ullmann (eds), *Kriegserfahrungen. Studien zur Sozial- und Mentalitätsgeschichte des Ersten Weltkrieges*, Essen: Klartext 1997; Jay M. Winter, Catastrophe and Culture. Recent Trends in the Historiography of the First World War, *JMH* 64 (1992), pp. 525–32, quote p. 531.

21. See chapters 2.2. and 4.1.

their villages.[22] 'From below', from the perspective of rural soldiers and their wives and friends in the villages, this connection between front and home front arose from the attention each side paid to the other's personal situation and the social developments marking each sphere. Interpretations of these realities were exchanged in letters or while men were home on leave; the rural population tended to develop a shared experience of war on the basis of this exchange of interpretations. For women and 'war wives' (*Kriegerfrauen*) in particular, however, gender-specific perceptions and interpretations of the war and their personal situation were in many respects inconsistent with this tendency.[23]

The dynamics of rural society on the home front and the experiences of those living there were largely shaped by state control of the agrarian economy, which began in 1915 and lasted to varying degrees until late 1923. What is more, farmers' wives were largely powerless in the face of this system of maximum prices, farm inspections and confiscation.[24] The present work asserts that circumstances on the home front imbued the wartime experiences of peasant soldiers at least as much as their lived experience at the front. The command economy was accompanied by inflation, which also began during the war, peaking in the hyperinflation of 1922/23. Money as a means of payment was increasingly withdrawn from circulation and people sought refuge in physical assets (*Sachwerte*). Inflation triggered a wave of political irrationalism, not only in cities such as Munich but also in the countryside. It changed political discourse as well as the values and moral conceptions of the people; it thus moulded their experience long term. In choosing to focus in the present work on the inflation decade from 1914 to 1923, I follow a periodisation which has already proved its value in many earlier studies.[25]

How veterans came to terms with their experience of war and violence has as yet hardly been examined for Germany as a whole. The seminal study of demobilisation in Richard Bessel's book on

22. See Chapter 2.3.

23. See Chapter 5.1., and for a more general interpretation Ziemann, Geschlechterbeziehungen.

24. The key account dealing with these developments is the regional study of the Rhineland and Westphalia by Moeller, *Peasants*.

25. See Chapter 5, and the important study by Martin H. Geyer, *Verkehrte Welt. Revolution, Inflation und Moderne. München 1914-1924*, Göttingen: Vandenhoeck & Ruprecht 1998, which can be read as a parallel to my description of events in the Bavarian countryside.

Germany after the First World War is one exception. Yet we still lack work on Germany of the kind produced by Antoine Prost, who has furnished us with an in-depth study of the organisational culture, ideology and symbolic representation in war memorials of the French 'anciens combattants'. These issues are examined here empirically with reference to four thematic fields for the 1918-23 period.[26] We look first at the technological, social and social-moral aspects of demobilisation, probing how men returning home from the war fit back into post-war society. We then turn to the citizens' militias (*Einwohnerwehren*), an important paramilitary organisation, and investigate whether former front-line experiences encouraged or hampered their development and militancy. The *Einwohnerwehren* thus also serve as a litmus test of the theory that soldiers were 'brutalised'. The key forum for the representation of soldiers' wartime experiences at the local level was the veterans' association, whose organisational culture we examine on the basis of a somewhat patchy source material. Finally, we look at the construction and symbolism of war memorials in provincial rural villages. Among other things, I discuss whether the memorials' symbolic messages were largely shaped by the aggressive suppression of defeat and revanchism, as researchers have claimed for the vast majority of German war memorials.[27]

The present work is a history of experience (*Erfahrungsgeschichte*). This simply means, first of all, that it concentrates on how individuals subjectively constitute, interpret and reinterpret social reality in a ceaseless process of communication. The concept of experience used here involves three distinctions.[28] The first can be expressed better in German than in English parlance, because the former has two words for the English 'experience'. *Erfahrung* (experience) is distinct from *Erlebnis*, the immediate sensory impressions with which we are

26. See Chapter 6; Bessel, *Germany*; Prost, *War*. By way of contrast, see the important regional study of the Prussian province of Saxony: Schumann, *Politische Gewalt*.

27. See Jeismann/Westheider, *Bürger*. On the denial of Germany's defeat and the stab-in-the-back legend, see Boris Barth, *Dolchstoßlegenden und politische Desintegration. Das Trauma der deutschen Niederlage im Ersten Weltkrieg 1914-1933*, Düsseldorf: Droste 2003.

28. See the useful reflections in Nikolaus Buschmann/Horst Carl (eds), *Die Erfahrung des Krieges. Erfahrungsgeschichtliche Perspektiven von der Französischen Revolution bis zum Zweiten Weltkrieg*, Paderborn: Ferdinand Schöningh 2001; Koselleck, Einfluß.

constantly bombarded. As understood in the sociology of knowledge, experiences are those impressions to which individuals pay attention. Through this process of interpretation, sensory impressions can be passed on in the medium or even long term, allowing people to fit new impressions into a pre-existing framework and endow them with meaning. In this process, the second distinction, between experiential space and horizon of expectations (Reinhart Koselleck), is of key importance. This distinction brings out the divergent temporal structures within which experiences are accumulated, changed or devalued.[29] The third distinction, important to understanding the present work, is between experiences and discourses. The concept of experience stresses the subjective aspect of the construction of social reality and how communicative acts of speaking and writing can mould and change such constructions. It is related to the life-worlds and socialisation processes of specific social groups. The concept of discourse, meanwhile, emphasises the objective and often inflexible aspect of this construction of reality, that is, the limits of what may be said and written about certain subjects within the public sphere.[30]

The dominant media involved in the communicative construction of experience were letters and private conversations, whether in a dugout at the front, a train compartment or the village tavern. The public discourse on the reality of the war at the front and how to remember its horrors in appropriate fashion drew its strength above all from media with extensive reach: regimental histories with their huge print run, war novels and war films, both of tremendous importance for the self-descriptions of Weimar society, and numerous printed collections of war letters, which allegedly bore witness to the 'real', 'genuine' front-line experience.[31] During the war itself, the military authorities took steps to mould the public *discourse* on the 'experience of the front' to stem the negative effect of soldiers' *actual experiences* of the war on

29. The key text is Koselleck, *Space of Experience*.

30. For a helpful conceptualisation see Kathleen Canning, Feminist History After the Linguistic Turn: Historicizing Discourse and Experience, *Signs* 19 (1994), pp. 368–404.

31. See, for example, Bernadette Kester, *Film Front Weimar. Representations of the First World War in German Films of the Weimar Period (1919-1933)*, Amsterdam: Amsterdam University Press 2003; Markus Pöhlmann, *Kriegsgeschichte und Geschichtspolitik: Der Erste Weltkrieg. Die amtliche deutsche Militärgeschichtsschreibung 1914-1956*, Paderborn: Ferdinand Schöningh 2002, chapter 5; Ulrich, *Augenzeugen*.

public opinion. Until November 1918, they failed almost entirely in this. Whether they managed to do so in the Weimar Republic and, if they did, to what extent are reconsidered at the end of this study.[32]

Finally, some comments on the sources. Since the loss of the files of the Prussian army in the spring of 1945, the holdings of Section IV of the Bavarian Hauptstaatsarchiv in Munich offer by far the most comprehensive and varied military source materials for the period from 1914 to 1918.[33] The present work has drawn extensively on these holdings, particularly files of the Bavarian War Ministry and the Deputy General Command of the 1st Bavarian Army Corps. Another important source genre, scarcely used as yet in studies about the First World War, is represented by court-martial files. They often include highly informative war letters (*Feldpostbriefe*), which can be linked with the soldier's biography and the event which led to their being put on record. Moreover, the statements and interrogation transcripts from the court proceedings also offer a variety of evidence related to everyday realities, conflicts and behaviour patterns at the front.

This study thus relies by no means only on evaluation of war letters. Accounts by military chaplains, for instance, are fertile sources of information on the front-line experience, as are the war diaries kept by rural soldiers. Soldiers' letters are, however, the best source for analysing the subjective interpretive models of soldiers. The letters used in this work come from two sources above all. The first comprises series of letters from archival or private collections. They cover extended periods of up to a year, in rare cases much longer than that; they often include the other side of the story, letters from friends and relatives. Correspondence such as this does allow us to trace personal developments and analyse individual backgrounds, though this information could not always be integrated into the present book.

Another treasure trove of war letters are the reports produced by the postal surveillance offices established from April 1916 in divisions and army high commands (*Armee-Ober-Kommandos*). These carried out random checks and summarised their findings in monthly reports featuring selected excerpts. These reports are interesting because they

32. This distinction is a major topic in the innovative study by Lipp, *Meinungslenkung*. See the Conclusion below.

33. The most important source for the home front are the weekly or fortnightly reports on the general mood of the population (hereafter: WB and HMB) by the district administrations or the head of the regional administration in Upper and Lower Bavaria and Bavarian Swabia (hereafter: BA and RP).

were intended to convey the mood among the troops in representative fashion. The surviving evidence, however, in contrast to that for the French army, is patchy.[34] I was, however, able to analyse and evaluate for the first time one source containing excerpts of letters under surveillance, sent from both the front and home front. From March 1917 on, art historian Adolf Schinnerer scrutinised letters passing through Railway Post Office Munich I. As well as summing up the mood among the population in representative fashion, he wished to document statements relevant to cultural history. This makes this material, which comprises somewhat more than 1,000 excerpts, most of them fairly lengthy, particularly interesting for the historian.[35]

Any researcher using war letters for a history of wartime mentalities must pay attention to the relevant source criticism. These relate, first of all, to how much we may generalise on the basis of the interpretations in these letters. We cannot hope to achieve statistical certainty. Nonetheless, the reports produced by the postal surveillance offices do in fact support many generalisations. Censorship is another problem. The external censorship of letters was carried out by military authorities, by officers in companies or regiments until 1916 and then by the postal surveillance offices. Given that around 28 billion war letters were sent during the First World War, however, it was impossible to check everything.[36] Self-censorship is a more serious problem. Most soldiers' letters were addressed to parents, or wives in the case of married soldiers. Some topics were taboo, especially when soldiers wrote to their wives, such as extra-marital sexual relations at the front. These were mentioned only when a Catholic soldier expressed his outrage at the behaviour of many of his comrades.[37]

34. See the important study by Annick Cochet, L'opinion et le moral des soldats en 1916 d'après les archives du contrôle postal, 2 vols, Thèse du doctorat, Paris 1986.

35. Adolf Schinnerer, Leitsätze für die Briefabschriften, n.d.: BHStA/IV, stv. GK I. AK. The excerpts are located in the Bayerische Staatsbibliothek München, Handschriftenabteilung, Schinnereriana (BSB).

36. For details of military censorship see Ulrich, *Augenzeugen*, pp. 78-105.

37. See the example in Chapter 4.1. Useful methodological reflections on the use of war letters can be found in Klaus Latzel, Vom Kriegserlebnis zur Kriegserfahrung. Theoretische und methodische Überlegungen zur erfahrun gsgeschichtlichen Untersuchung von Feldpostbriefen, *Militärgeschichtliche Mitteilungen* 56 (1997), pp. 1-30.

It is, however, methodologically pointless to search war letters for subjects such as the exploitation and maltreatment of Belgian and French civilians by the occupying German forces and then to complain when it proves impossible to locate them.[38] The fact that such things were not mentioned does not mean that they did not happen. It does indicate, however, that they were only marginally relevant, if at all, to how the soldiers subjectively constructed their experience, even bearing in mind the possible impact of self-censorship. It is solely for this purpose that the present work draws on soldiers' letters. I do not deploy them as evidence of the 'objective' facts and events which shaped the course of the war, which can be studied through many other sources. Their value lies in how they reflect the subjective construction of a wartime reality that moulded the collective experience of rural soldiers and their families.

To mention another example: letters sent by Bavarian peasants from the front are almost entirely free of passages alluding proudly to the pleasure of killing, of the kind Joanna Bourke has presented in her *Intimate History of Killing* from British and American examples.[39] This finding is surely due, first of all, to the fact that letters to one's wife do not seem like the best place to boast of such a flagrant offence against the Fifth Commandment, and not only for pious Catholics. Such passages, however, are also missing in letters to male relatives, in which soldiers express their abhorrence at the 'murder' at the front in many different ways and invoke at length the victimisation of the soldiers through the wartime violence.[40] This does not of course mean that soldiers from a rural background did not kill deliberately, knowing exactly what they were doing; some may have enjoyed it. If they did, such pleasure found no place in the subjective construction of identity to which the letters and diaries bear witness.[41] But how Bavarian peasants constructed their subjective war experience is what this book aims to uncover.

38. This point is misunderstood by Nelson, 'Ordinary Men', p. 428.

39. Joanna Bourke, *An Intimate History of Killing. Face-to-Face Killing in Twentieth-century Warfare*, London: Granta Books 1999; see my critique in *Mittelweg 36* 9 (2000), 1, pp. 58–9. The arguments about a 'killing instinct' in Niall Ferguson, *The Pity of War*, London: Penguin 1999, chapter 11, are out of touch with the historical reality.

40. See chapters 3 and 4.

41. For general reflections on this problem see Peter Gleichmann/Thomas Kühne (eds), *Massenhaftes Töten. Kriege und Genozide im 20. Jahrhundert*, Essen: Klartext 2004.

1

Depression, August 1914

Upper and Lower Bavaria, the Upper Palatinate - all areas of Altbayern - and Swabia are commonly referred to as southern Bavaria. Here, however, this term is used for the area within the responsibility of the Deputy General Command (*stellvertretendes Generalkommando*) of the 1st Bavarian Army Corps. A range of responsibilities and tasks fell to this institution and the military commanders in charge of it after the declaration of the state of siege on 1 August 1914. These initially comprised genuine military issues such as ensuring that the front-line units recruited in this district were supplied with soldiers and resources, and commanding the subordinate units of the replacement army (*Besatzungsheer*). This competence soon expanded to the regulation of labour policy, food supply and press censorship. Geographically, the 1st Army Corps took in the *Regierungsbezirke* (the largest administrative division of a *Land*) of Upper Bavaria - minus the districts of Ingolstadt, Schrobenhausen and Pfaffenhofen - and Swabia, along with the southern half of the districts of Lower Bavaria with ten of its district authorities.[1]

Before the war, most southern Bavarians still worked in agriculture. In 1907 agriculture occupied almost 70 per cent of the economically active population in Lower Bavaria, about 53 per cent in Swabia and around 59 per cent in Upper Bavaria - excluding the flourishing city of Munich.[2] The rural population lived in numerous scattered villages and small market towns, the number of isolated farms and small hamlets increasing as one neared the Alps. While only around a third of the German population lived in rural communities in 1925, more than 50 per cent of Bavarians lived in settlements of fewer than 2,000 people, and almost 20 per cent

1. See the map in Deist, *Militär und Innenpolitik*, pp. 1530-1. On the remit of the Deputy General Commands see ibid., pp. XL-XLIV.

2. The figure for Upper Bavaria as a whole was almost 40 per cent. Calculated on the basis of *Die Kriegs-Volkszählungen vom Jahre 1916 und 1917 in Bayern*, Munich: Lindauer 1919, p. 164.

in those with fewer than 500 inhabitants.[3] In line with industrialisation, apart from the few cities, urbanisation in Altbayern remained a 'selective phenomenon' until well into the 1920s, generally concentrated in small, monostructural industrial towns. It was thus only from the turn of the century that people developed a pronounced awareness of the differences between urban and rural ways of life. The migration of rural workers to the towns meant that peasants saw urbanisation as something negative.[4] Experientially, the lives of those remaining in the villages were restricted to the local area and a highly circumscribed sphere of influence; they were integrated very little into national structures of communication. This horizon was expanded only occasionally during festivals, pilgrimages or when visiting markets. Even these activities, though, were firmly embedded in the regional setting.[5]

In contrast to the Rhenish Palatinate and Lower Franconia, where the division of inheritance fragmented ownership, the inheritance law which dominated in Altbayern passed on everything to a sole heir, favouring the continuity of peasant farms, almost all of which worked their own land.[6] Southern Bavaria was a classical farming region. The largest group, both in terms of the number of farms and the area under cultivation, was made up of medium-sized farms of 5-20 ha.[7] Such farms worked around 42 per cent of the land in Upper Bavaria and 45 per cent in Lower Bavaria; in Swabia the figure was about 56 per cent. In southern Bavaria, this group of farms lay more often than elsewhere in the German Empire at the upper limit of 20 ha. Large estates of over 100 ha meanwhile were few and far between in Altbayern.

How did rural Bavarians respond to the outbreak of the First World War? Recent studies have shown that, in many cities and towns of the German Empire, the notion, popular for so long, of an all-embracing enthusiasm for war in August 1914 is a myth. By thoroughly checking

3. Schulte, *Dorf*, p. 32; figures in Bergmann, *Bauernbund*, p. 12.

4. Klaus Tenfelde, Stadt und Land in Krisenzeiten. München und das Münchener Umland zwischen Revolution und Inflation 1918-1923, in: Wolfgang Hardtwig/ Klaus Tenfelde (eds), *Soziale Räume in der Urbanisierung*, Munich: C.H. Beck 1990, pp. 37-57, quote p. 42.

5. Blessing, Umwelt.

6. Axel Schnorbus, Die ländlichen Unterschichten in der bayerischen Gesellschaft am Ausgang des 19. Jahrhunderts, *ZBLG* 30 (1967), pp. 824-52, p. 831.

7. *Die Landwirtschaft in Bayern. Nach der Betriebszählung vom 12. Juni 1907*, Munich: Lindauer 1910, pp. 15-36.

the available evidence, they have shown that the masses who approved of the war consisted largely of members of the nationalistic middle-class, particularly supporters of the youth movement and members of the student fraternities. The vast majority of the working class, meanwhile, was despondent about the war.[8] Setting the record straight for rural areas is a hard task, particularly because the provincial press, which stoked popular belligerence through its biased reporting, cannot be drawn upon as a source, particularly for the highly censored period following declaration of the state of siege. These publications tended to focus on events in Berlin and paid little heed to those in the countryside because of the dearth of spectacular mass gatherings; they simply took it for granted that the nation could 'rely' on the rural population. Even some of the small number of available memoirs have been distorted by the successful myth of enthusiasm for war. A Franconian peasant thus disseminates the image of widespread enthusiasm in his notes. Drawing on his own experience, however, he relates how, when mobilisation began, his sister came running to harvesters working in a field in tears to tell one of the young men that he had been called up. The harvesters 'seemed to have turned to stone'. It was only when soldiers began to depart that a certain enthusiasm kicked in.[9] Nevertheless, there are plenty of accounts which provide us with a detailed picture of the rural state of mind shortly before and after mobilisation. In October 1914 the state counsellor in the Ministry of the Interior, Gustav von Kahr, called on the district bailiffs to produce war chronicles to record events related to mobilisation. Some district authorities, apparently in response to this appeal, then requested that teachers and priests produce such reports.[10] Such accounts, produced at the level of the boroughs, are essential to precise historical reconstruction.

In most rural communities an increasingly tense atmosphere had developed in the weeks of the July crisis. Particularly after Austria's ultimatum to Serbia on 23 July, there was 'serious concern about the war for the first time' in many places, as reported for the village of Walda by the Neuburg district authority.[11] This news stoked the 'tension, even

8. See Verhey, *Spirit of 1914*; Christian Geinitz, *Kriegsfurcht und Kampfbereitschaft. Das Augusterlebnis in Freiburg. Eine Studie zum Kriegsbeginn 1914*, Essen: Klartext 1998; Kruse, *Krieg*, pp. 54–61, 91–8.

9. Peter Högler (ed.), *Konrad Dürr, Erinnerungen und Gedanken aus meinem Leben*, Öllingen: Gelchsheim 1987, p. 51.

10. Gustav von Kahr, 6.10.1914: StAM, LRA 82665.

11. Catholic parish of Walda, 29.11.1914: StAA, BA Neuburg 7214.

agitation', in the villages, and fears now began to grow that Germany would be caught up in a war between Austria and Serbia.[12] The declaration of war by Austria-Hungary on Serbia on 28 July further 'intensified these concerns' about the possibility of war.[13] Such presentiments of war may have been further intensified by the fact that some conscripts, granted furlough to help out with the harvest, were recalled to the barracks even before the proclamation of impending war on 31 July.[14]

The anxieties and fears inspired by the possibility of war had thus built up steadily in the weeks before mobilisation. In just a few communities, people were so preoccupied with harvest work that mobilisation came like a 'bolt from the blue'.[15] There is very little evidence that mobilisation was experienced as the end of a 'state of uncertainty' following weeks of increasing tension. In such places, a general 'dismay' was usually the first response to such news.[16] To interpret the outbreak of war as a positive route out of the uncertainty which had built up during the weeks of the July crisis, as contemporaries did for the cities, thus fails to capture the realities of rural Bavaria.

Before mobilisation, the 'state of war' or state of siege was declared on 31 July. In Bavaria, executive power was now transferred to the commanders of the three army corps.[17] The final threshold had been crossed; mobilisation and war had become inevitable. 'As everywhere,' it was reported from one village at the time, 'here too the declaration of a state of war has caused great dismay in every quarter.' A 'very fearful atmosphere' sometimes developed when the domestic state of war was confused with a declaration of war on another country.[18] The news that the first day of mobilisation was set for Sunday 2 August 1914 reached most villages during the evening of 1 August.

Only two accounts which refer to the response immediately after mobilisation was announced reflect general resoluteness in the face of war. In the parish of Karlskron people were of the opinion that 'we

12. Head teacher Wagner from Neuschwetzingen, 21.12.1914: StAA, BA Neuburg 7214.

13. Primary school teacher Ganshorn from Karlshuld, 4.12.1914: StAA, BA Neuburg 7214.

14. Catholic parish of Dezenacker, 27.11.1914: StAA, BA Neuburg 7214.

15. Körber, a teacher from Oberhausen, n.d.: StAA, BA Neuburg 7214.

16. Head teacher from Obermaxfeld, 3.12.1914: StAA, BA Neuburg 7214.

17. Albrecht, *Landtag*, pp. 74-8.

18. Ihlmeider, a teacher from Bertoldsheim, 5.12.1914: StAA, BA Neuburg 7214.

have to take action. The French won't leave us in peace unless we give them a good hiding.' An 'enthusiastic' mood 'always' prevailed in the Lower Bavarian parish of Baumgarten.[19] The juxtaposition of 'dismay and the pain of saying goodbye and on the other hand great enthusiasm for the Fatherland' is reported for other villages as well.[20] All other accounts suggest that people responded to the announcement of German mobilisation with much despondency and pessimism. The following is one of many examples:

> When the declaration of mobilisation was hung upon the community noticeboard and announced on 1 August 1914, the locals were highly agitated and dismayed. The community noticeboard was surrounded by a large number of people for several hours and the wives of men liable for military service expressed their misery in no uncertain terms.[21]

Almost nowhere in the countryside was the start of the war greeted with enthusiasm. The exact opposite often applied. The fact that the war became a reality only with the German Empire's subsequent declarations of war on Russia on 1 August and on France on 3 August was irrelevant. Popular perception saw the war as a given from the point of mobilisation onwards. This was usually followed immediately by a declaration of war, and 'experienced soldiers in particular were aware of this'.[22]

There are four key reasons why the rural population responded to the outbreak of war in this way. The first and most important is that nationalistic explanations of the war and negative conceptions of the 'enemy' were thin on the ground in rural areas. There are no indications that such conceptual models prevailed in any rural community at any point during the July crisis or the outbreak of the war. People lacked positive expectations of the nation state that could be related to the war. In rural Bavaria, the engineering of the Wilhelmine Imperial cult succeeded in matching the importance of regional loyalties and the cult surrounding the Wittelsbachs only in the Rhenish Palatinate and in Protestant areas of Franconia.[23]

19. Head teacher Kriß from Karlskron, 29.11.1914: StAA, BA Neuburg 7214.
20. Parish of Niederschönenfeld to BA Neuburg, 29.11.1914: StAA, BA Neuburg 7214.
21. Parish of Walburgskirchen, 25.1.1919: StAL, Rep. 164/14, 8724.
22. Head teacher Genzner from Untermaxfeld, 31.12.1914: StAA, BA Neuburg 7214.
23. Blessing, *Staat und Kirche*, pp. 228–35.

Farmers also worried about how the farms would be run and how the current harvest would be brought in now that so many men were at war. The farm and those working on it were inseparably linked in farmers' minds. Should they be forced apart, there were bound to be severe economic consequences. After mobilisation, many people in the district of Kempten, for example, lamented that 'men and Russians have to go away now, so the harvest can't be brought in and is rotting in the fields and many lives have been ruined'.[24] Such fears were also fuelled by the purchase of horses for the army, which began immediately. Some of these young horses had already been inspected by the military authorities before the war. They were now given a final seal of approval by special commissions and taken away. Despite the handsome payments, these forced sales were at times a tearful affair for the farmers.[25]

Another reason why people were anxious and concerned about the outbreak of war was their awareness that there would be many victims and much devastation. Even if the 'outcome' was 'good' for Germany, it would be a 'terrible affliction'.[26] These fears were connected with distressing tales of the Napoleonic wars handed down from one generation to the next, which emphasised that every campaign might mean billeting and devastation in one's own country. In the first few weeks after the war began, villagers thus afforded the troops recognition for 'having protected the homeland from destruction by the enemy'.[27] Soldiers also touched on such fears when they described the destruction in Belgium and France in their letters, telling their nearest and dearest to be pleased that the war had not devastated their own country.[28] In the first weeks of the war, cash was hoarded in some places out of fear of an enemy invasion.[29]

Ultimately, it was straightforward concern for the lives of the soldiers which underlay the pessimistic response to the war. Mothers and wives were particularly affected when their sons and husbands were called up, and accounts from many places mention the 'weeping mothers, wives and sisters', particularly when it was time to say goodbye.[30] Such

24. WB BA Kempten, 14.8.1914: StAA, BA Kempten 6224.
25. Pfarrkirchen police station, 19.2.1915: StAL, Rep. 164/14, 8724.
26. Catholic parish of Illdorf, 25.11.1914: StAA, BA Neuburg 7214.
27. Teacher Braun from Karlshuld, 14.12.1914: StAA, BA Neuburg 7214.
28. Teacher Herzog from Unterhausen, 6.12.1914: StAA, BA Neuburg 7214.
29. MInn, 9.10.1914: BHStA/II, MInn 54013.
30. Parish of Walburgskirchen, 25.1.1919: StAL, Rep. 164/14, 8724.

statements entail a degree of stylisation in line with the stereotypes circulating about the tasks appropriate to women in wartime, which were mainly seen as revolving around charitable support for the soldiers. In an appeal to women intended to move them to 'relieve the distress of those brave men', the Bavarian queen, Maria Theresia, stated: 'Out there, blood is flowing. Here tears are flowing. Such tears are at their most bitter wherever troubled souls are joined by bodily suffering.'[31]

In accounts from villages, however, this stylisation tended to relate to the men, whose readiness to rally round the flag and sense of duty was to be underlined in contrast to the weeping women. Amidst the general despondency of rural dwellers, the negative reaction of farmers' wives and servant girls was gender-specific and particularly intense.[32] The village public sphere was marked by far-reaching gender-specific segregation. The women of the village had no share in the exchange of experiences of army life in which men engaged in the tavern, or in the prestige associated with it.[33] For farmers' wives, one of the central concerns was how they were now to cope with the harvest work without their husbands.

They also knew, moreover, that their husbands' absence would lower their status in the village and cause them significant difficulties in asserting their economic rights within the community. One peasant referred to such realities when he wrote to his wife from the field about a dispute over obtaining the financial support for families to which soldiers' wives were entitled: 'Don't sign anything you don't understand. Ask father or if not, say you don't understand and my husband can do that when he comes, even if the mayor comes to see you. Tell him to go into battle, then he'll know what it's like. They try to put pressure on women whose men are away.'[34]

Farmers' wives were unprepared for this new situation in which they had to struggle alone for recognition in the village with respect to a large number of everyday problems. Their first response was a sense of tremendous uncertainty. Their tears and the expressions of mutual

31. Appeal by Queen Maria Theresia to the women and young maids of Bavaria, 2.8.1914: Kriegs-Beilage 1914 des Amtsblattes der K. Staatsministerien des Königlichen Hauses und des Äußern und des Innern, Munich 1914, pp. 47–8.

32. Teacher Körber from Oberhausen, n.d.: StAA, BA Neuburg 7214.

33. On the segregation of the village public sphere according to gender, see Schulte, *Dorf*, pp. 166–72.

34. Jakob Eberhard, 26.5.1915: private possession.

affection in letters composed by spouses also suggest, however, that their emotional ties to their husbands made their departure a serious source of dismay. In the atmosphere which prevailed at the beginning of the war, churned up by worrying news and rumours, some wives even committed suicide after their husbands were called up.[35] In the days after 2 August, the reservists and territorial reservists were assembled by the district commander and assigned to their units. This began immediately for many riflemen and cavalrymen, and after three to six days following mobilisation for the other reservists and territorial reservists.[36] During this week, therefore, rural communities saw soldiers depart on several occasions, heading for the nearest railway station or leaving from their local station.

It was above all on such occasions that pessimism waned. Another facet of this complex totality was also visible, already apparent to some extent immediately after mobilisation had been declared. When marching off from their communities, soldiers showed that 'devotion to the Fatherland and martial spirit' was alive within them. They answered 'the call to the flag cheerfully, though saying goodbye was painful for some'.[37] This phenomenon was concentrated on the railway stations, because communities were determined to give their soldiers an impressive send-off and thus lend them courage. Stations and trains were decorated; a festive atmosphere prevailed as the reservists were bid farewell.[38] Here at the railway stations was the nearest thing to a rural counterpart to the festive urban mass gatherings, which were a prerequisite for the effusive scenes of enthusiasm seen there. Nonetheless, many tears were shed over the pain of departure, though the only men to weep were married ones worried about their families.[39] Those between 20 and 30 years old, who had completed their military service but were as yet unmarried, again showed, as they had done already to some degree after the declaration of mobilisation, that they harboured positive expectations of the war. These were not overlain with anxiety about business or family.[40] They announced their enthusiasm at leaving parties in taverns and later when marching off.

35. Ulrich/Ziemann, *Frontalltag*, p. 30.

36. For the technical details of mobilisation see Bayerisches Kriegsarchiv (ed.), *Die Bayern*, vol. 1, pp. 5-9.

37. Ering police station, 7.2.1915: StAL, Rep. 164/14, 8724.

38. Teacher Körber from Oberhausen, n.d.: StAA, BA Neuburg 7214.

39. Karlshuld parish, 2.12.1914: StAA, BA Neuburg 7214.

40. Pfarrkirchen police station, 19.2.1915: StAL Rep. 164/14, 8724.

Such behaviour was rooted in the tremendous significance of the military service the young men had just completed for their personal recognition within the village public sphere. The latter was dominated by established farmers whose status rested on marriage and property. For such young men, military service meant respect and initiation into this sphere.[41] Regardless of the frequently denigrating treatment of soldiers, the two-year stint in the garrison towns removed local restrictions and furnished men with practical skills and knowledge of ways of life new to them through both their training and their everyday interaction with their comrades.[42] Looking back, Bavarian Peasants' League (*Bayerischer Bauernbund*) leader Georg Eisenberger, a farmer's son from near Ruhpolding, regretted the fact that his father had prevented him from being called up through the information he had submitted to the authorities: 'I myself was unhappy with the fact that I was not called up to perform active duty, because I was always keen to learn more and to see something of the world.'[43]

With the knowledge and respect attained during one's stint in the armed forces, one could hold one's own in conversation in the tavern and market square. The outbreak of war thus raised men's hopes that their newly gained prestige, associated with the completion of military service, could be further enhanced if they took part in the war. Among young men, these hopes were anchored in popular notions of what the war would be like, clearly discernible in available accounts. They embraced the interpretation propagated by the Imperial leadership and read out by the Bavarian bishops from the pulpits in their pastoral letters at the start of the war, which asserted that this was a defensive war forced upon the German Empire.[44] The common idea that the war would be over by Christmas at the latest was also important.[45] This was bound up with the hopes of victory cultivated by many young men. People knew, of course, that even a rapid victory would claim many victims, and many

41. Dennis E. Showalter, Army, State and Society in Germany 1871-1914. An Interpretation, in: Jack R. Dukes/James Remak (eds), *Another Germany. A Reconsideration of the Imperial Era*, London, Boulder: Westview Press 1988, pp. 1-18, pp. 8-10.

42. Blessing, Disziplinierung und Qualifizierung, pp. 461-4.

43. From memoirs quoted in Georg Eisenberger (ed.), *Georg Eisenberger. Der Hutzenauer 1863-1945. Ein Porträt des Bauernbundführers*, Ruhpolding: Selbstverlag 1988, no page.

44. Parish of Ortlfing, 2.12.1914: StAA, BA Neuburg 7214.

45. Bauer, *Kopfsteinpflaster*, p. 27.

reservists 'who used to talk about the war in a high-spirited way' now felt uneasy.[46]

However, the prevailing concept of war among the soldiers was informed by the typical depictions of the war of 1870/71. School books and the popular pictorial broadsheets - which achieved circulation figures of three million with this motif - painted a picture of warfare that emphasised the individual heroism of attacking cavalrymen or direct man to man combat between bayonet-wielding infantrymen.[47] Such reminiscences of the last war, which played down the inevitable victims and basically extended the experience of village brawls to the field of battle, gave them confidence in their ability to 'give the Frenchmen and Russians such a beating that there will be peace again soon'.[48] This notion of war, soon to prove antiquated, was bound up with the expectation that war would expand horizons formerly limited to the village and its surrounding area and thus endow men with a certain worldliness. Though it may be hard to relate to this today, the war had a touristic aspect, especially for young soldiers. In Zweikirchen, in Lower Bavaria, they welcomed the outbreak of war with the words 'Now's our chance to get out!'[49] The rhetoric of the 'fortress peace' (*Burgfrieden*), fuelled by the SPD's approval of war loans, rarely motivated soldiers.[50] The expectations of young unmarried men, linked with the notion of service in the armed forces as a source of social prestige, are best understood as martial enthusiasm, rather than enthusiasm for war as such.

However, the enthusiasm of departing individual reservists could cover up the despondent mood of other villagers for a short time only; it tended to improve the overall mood primarily during farewells at the railway station.[51] For those left behind, Great Britain's declaration of war on Germany on 4 August, followed by Japan's on 23 August, pushed all hopes of victory far into the future and intensified the prevailing atmosphere of 'dismay' and 'deep despondency'. The popular mood stabilised only when hopes of victory began to grow again, along with hopes of a speedy end to the war as a result of successes in the Battle

46. Teacher Neumaier from Seibersdorf, 19.4.1916: StAL, Rep. 164/14, 8724.

47. Blessing, *Staat und Kirche*, pp. 212–15.

48. Walburgskirchen parish, 25.1.1919: StAL, Rep. 164/14, 8724.

49. Maria Hartl, *Damals zu meiner Zeit. Bäuerliches Leben im Jahresverlauf*, Munich: Süddeutscher Verlag 1988, p. 53.

50. Head teacher Genzner from Untermaxfeld, 31.12.1914: StAA, BA Neuburg 7214.

51. Diary of the priest Karl Heichele, 4.8.1914: ABA, Pfa 6/I.

of Lorraine (20 to 22 August) - in which the Bavarian troops brought together in the 6th Army were the main protagonists - and at Tannenberg (26 to 31 August).[52] With flags flying from houses and bells ringing to report victories, there was now to some extent a rural equivalent of the euphoric victory celebrations in the towns. The optimistic mood of the last days of August also played a significant role in propagating the myth of enthusiasm for war. This myth of the *Augusterlebnis* (August experience) frequently glossed over in people's memories the initially very negative response to the outbreak of war.[53] Even further tearful farewells did nothing to change the overall optimism, when the remaining *Landsturm* soldiers were called up at the end of August.[54]

The initiation of hostilities also had an impact on popular piety. A war theology quickly evolved. In public declarations, bishops and priests outdid one another in emphasising that the nation could rely on the Catholics. Church elites and the leading figures within socially active Catholicism joined in the press's invocation of national enthusiasm for war; they took the chance to dismantle prejudices about Catholic ultramontanism.[55] More important than such ideological freight, however, is the matter of whether and how the religious upturn asserted within war theology was manifested in rural areas as a result of the war.

On Sunday 2 August practically all the parishioners were at church. The priests' main task on this day was to deal with the depressive mood of the faithful, apparent in church in the form of 'frequent, bitter sobbing'. This continued over the coming days, as the vast majority of conscripted soldiers attended confession, usually in tears.[56] Religious life took on a new intensity which may be described as a specific form of war piety. The war, as an exceptional, emergency situation shattering the realities of everyday life, reinforced people's need for certainty in their beliefs and thus religious ways of understanding the world and consolation in religion. Immediately after the war began, this was apparent in the rogation processions to nearby pilgrimage churches which took place in many locations. Even some soldiers made their way to pilgrimage sites

52. Dietersburg police station, 8.2.1915: StAL, Rep. 164/14, 8724.

53. Walburgskirchen parish, 25.1.1919, an BA Pfarrkirchen: StAL, Rep. 164/14, 8724.

54. Events of the war in the parish of Tann, n.d.: StAL, Rep. 164/14, 8724.

55. Heinrich Missalla, *'Gott mit uns'. Die deutsche katholische Kriegspredigt 1914-1918*, Munich: Kösel 1968.

56. L. Bobinger, Kriegsarbeit des Klerus in der Heimat, *Theologisch-praktische Monats-Schrift* 27 (1917), pp. 314-21, p. 315.

before they departed for the barracks.[57] In the subsequent weeks and months it was women and children who begged for a happy and speedy end to the war in many well-attended pilgrimages.[58] Villagers formerly uninvolved in religious life also took part. Wartime prayer meetings, often combined with saying rosaries, were the main events dedicated to prayers requesting that the war end quickly and victoriously; these were a sometimes daily event.[59]

It is hard to pin down which particular religious symbols people turned to in response to the war. In their sermons, bishops and priests tended to interpret the war as a religious test or divine judgment inspired by the decline in popular morality.[60] The bishops encouraged the Sacred Heart of Jesus cult as a 'specific cult for dealing with the war'. The cult came to be seen as a guarantee of victory; the faithful had to make atonement to the Heart for past neglect of their religious duties. The cult experienced a major boom during the first year of the war, particularly in connection with the national Sacred Heart of Jesus dedication on 10 January 1915.[61] Such interpretations met with a positive response in rural areas, as reports of an increasing number of Sacred Heart of Jesus prayer meetings following the start of the war and the diffusion of the notion that the 'war [was] divine punishment' attest.[62]

The extent to which people took advantage of the pastoral care offered by the Church clearly increased after the war had begun. The number of communicants provides an excellent indication of this. Comprehensive statistics on numbers of communicants were compiled only once the Office for Church Statistics had been founded in 1915, and a general comparison with the pre-war period is thus impossible.[63] The pastoral reports compiled by the parish offices, however, offer several pieces of evidence, both general remarks and specific figures, suggesting that the number of people taking communion had increased rapidly since the start of the war, despite the absence of large numbers of men.[64] Many men not yet called up got more actively involved in the Church than they

57. Parish of Neukirchen, 1.12.1914: StAA, BA Neuburg 7214.

58. Parish of Friesenried, 19.7.1919: ABA, DA 6, Karton 13.

59. Parish of Bidingen, 1.9.1919: ABA, DA 6, Karton 13.

60. Missalla, *Kriegspredigt*, pp. 52-6.

61. Busch, *Katholische Frömmigkeit*, pp. 101-15, quote p. 112.

62. Parish of Waldhof, 28.5.1915: ABP, DekA II, Pfarrkirchen 12/I.

63. Oswin Rutz, *Obrigkeitliche Seelsorge. Die Pastoral im Bistum Passau von 1800 bis 1918*, Passau: Passavia-Universitätsverlag 1984, pp. 320-1.

64. Material in: ABP, DekA II, Pfarrkirchen 12/I.

had been before the war, a fact which received a good deal of attention. Yet the frequency with which they received the sacrament tailed off again during the first year of the war. People's piety was, however, only shaken seriously from 1916 or 1917 on.[65]

In contrast to the cities, where conscription had brought many factories to a standstill, causing a rapid increase in unemployment,[66] there were scarcely any major economic problems in rural areas during the initial stages of the war. The authorities managed to dispel farmers' fears relating to bringing in the harvest. They also stopped cattle dealers from trying to obtain livestock at a knockdown price by deluding farmers' wives into believing that it would be confiscated by the armed forces anyway.[67] Official schemes brought the urban unemployed briefly to many rural locations to do harvest work.[68] Most communities, however, managed to get the harvest in on time by means of mutual support and help with the teams of draught animals and by making maximum use of the energies of all available workers.[69] The mood had been stabilised by the time the first reports of victory came in. From the autumn of 1914 on, rumours spread by soldiers on leave about major losses, soon to be confirmed in every village, caused a decline in the popular mood as lasting as it was rapid.[70] Before Christmas 1914, the postal authorities were instructed to deliver new reports of losses from the field only via the local clergy.[71] The war and its destructive consequences had quickly become an oppressive normality.

65. Parish of Biessenhofen, 1.8.1919: ABA, DA 6, Karton 13.
66. Albrecht, *Landtag*, pp. 82–7.
67. Stv. GK I.AK, 11.8.1914: StAA, BA Donauwörth n.S. 5403.
68. RP Obb., 14.9.1914: BHStA/II, MInn 66134.
69. WB BA Nördlingen, 19.12.1914: StAA, Regierung 9761.
70. BA Erding, 8.10.1914: BHStA/IV, stv. GK I.AK 948.
71. Ministry of Transport, 16.12.1914: BHStA/II, MInn 54032.

2

Military Cohesion, 1914–18

Contemporary observers may struggle to grasp what inspired soldiers in the First World War to hold out at the front for long periods of time or even return there after suffering injury. No one at the time knew how destructive industrial warfare would prove to be. A stint in the trenches must have been an extreme experience requiring tremendous emotional resources. This makes it all the more vital to understand the reasons for the cohesion of the troops. In seeking to cast light on this, we should avoid rushing to privilege subjective motivations and perceptual models. The first essential is a subtle analysis of the wartime social configurations of the military that gets to grips with the factors promoting the stability or instability of the army. It is crucial here to bear in mind the exteriority of such ascriptions. Factors identified as stabilising a priori functioned as such only if they in fact 'meshed' with soldiers' socially specific interpretive models. Because they were generally limited in scope, they might also heighten the subjective perception of injustice and thus have a destabilising effect. By the same token, conflicts by no means automatically morphed into forms of protest directly opposed to the military hierarchy. By systematically exploring the central issue, the reasons for the stability or instability of the troops, we can tease out the most important factors underpinning military socialisation during the war. This chapter investigates how rural soldiers fit into the matrix of factors reinforcing the cohesion of the army. Chapter 3 probes their role in conflicts within the armed forces. It is not always possible to pin down specific differences in the patterns of response and behaviour of troops of a particular class, age or urban or rural background. Issues affecting those who had worked in agriculture as a clearly defined group of soldiers are therefore explicitly identified as such. A large number of interests and behaviour patterns were common to the majority of soldiers.

The social history of ordinary soldiers, however, goes beyond a description of the war 'from below'. If we wish to grasp the structural and subjective reasons for the internal cohesion of the army, we need to do more than examine soldiers' attitudes and strategies. Cohesion depended on the interplay of soldiers' actions and the intended and unintended consequences that decisions taken by the military leadership had on their living conditions. To shed light on this level, we will have to shift the perspective respectively, taking also the behaviour of officers and higher military authorities into account.

2.1 Fluctuation

The social configuration of the army was determined, first of all, by the social composition of the units and particularly by their fluctuating nature as soldiers arrived and departed. For the forms of wartime military service and the risks involved in it were initially dependent on structural conditions, which determined where troops would be deployed and for how long. Here, factors emerge which worked to spread risks such as death or injury, faced by all front-line soldiers in principle, unevenly between the various units and age and professional groups. This distribution depended on how hard specific units had to fight and the exigencies of the war economy. The stability of the military as a social collective depended to a significant degree on the scale and distribution of lives lost. Their quantitative distribution also affected how soldiers perceived the quality of their mission. Military mass mobilisation attained previously unheard-of dimensions between 1914 and 1918. The peacetime strength of the Bavarian army was 4,089 officers and officials and 83,125 NCOs and ordinary soldiers. The planned wartime strength of 12,753 officers, officials, doctors and vets and 406,000 NCOs and ordinary soldiers had been slightly exceeded by 20 August 1914.[1] Over the next few years, the Bavarian army grew to more than ten times the size of its peacetime equivalent.

Apart from a brief period in early 1915, more than a third of soldiers spent the war in the replacement army, in other words within the borders of Bavaria.[2] On average, of the entire German army, about 4.18 million soldiers served in the field army (including the back area, or *Etappe*, and occupied territories) and 2.19 million in the replacement army from 1914 to 1918.[3] By 1 November 1918, a total of 1.43 million Bavarian

1. Bayerisches Kriegsarchiv (ed.), *Die Bayern im Großen Kriege*, vol. 1, pp. 5, 7.

2. *Sanitätsbericht*, p. 32.

3. Ibid., p. 5.

Table 2.1 Number of ordinary soldiers and NCOs in the Bavarian army (field and replacement army)

	Field	*Replacement*	*Total*
20.8.1914	270,000	137,000	407,000
20.1.1915	382,550	107,500	490,050
1.10.1915	440,000	256,000	696,000
1.9.1917	530,000	350,000	880,000
Early 1918	550,000	360,000	910,000

Source: Bayerisches Kriegsarchiv (ed.), *Die Bayern im Großen Kriege*, vol. 1, p. 9, vol. 2, p. 46.

soldiers had been sent into battle, two-thirds of them in the infantry.[4] A total of 1.4 million men were conscripted in Bavaria during the war. The figure for the German army as a whole was 13.38 million, of which 10.57 million served in the field army at one time or another.[5]

Around a fifth of the entire population of Germany thus served in the armed forces. The age cohorts born between 1869 and 1900 became liable for military service during the 1914-18 period. Of this group of men, aged from 18 to 49 in 1918, around 85 per cent were called up at some point during the war.[6] Military involvement in the war thus moulded the experience of an entire generation of men. Nonetheless, conscription took many different forms for this generation. Nothing could be wider of the mark than the notion of hordes of men in their millions marching off to battle in August 1914 and returning home in November 1918. In fact, only a small number of soldiers served in the field army over the entire course of the war, which lasted almost 52 months. Of the soldiers who put in a claim for a pension as a result of general nervous ailments at the benefits office (*Versorgungsamt*) in Munich, half were called up at the beginning of the war and could thus have served from beginning to end. The average length of service in the field army was,

4. Compilation by the *Kriegsamtsstelle* Munich, n.d.: BHStA/IV, MKr 17114.

5. Gerhard Heyl, Militärwesen, in: Wilhelm Volkert (ed.), *Handbuch der bayerischen Ämter, Gerichte und Gemeinden (1799-1980)*, Munich: C.H. Beck 1983, pp. 330-93, p. 382; *Sanitätsbericht*, p. 31.

6. Whalen, *Bitter Wounds*, p. 39.

however, only 15 months, and a mere 2.7 per cent of applicants were on active duty for the duration of the war.[7]

The nature and number of losses were a key factor in inequality among soldiers. Almost 200,000 soldiers, NCOs and officers in the Bavarian army died in the war.[8] Being taken prisoner meant a premature end to the fighting, but tended to make the war longer for those involved, a total of 0.93 million soldiers in the Empire as a whole.[9] Of men serving in the German field army, 4.8 million wounded and almost 14.7 million cases of illness were registered. Many of these were admitted for treatment in Bavarian hospitals.[10] Around 345,000 sick or wounded Bavarian soldiers returned one or more times to the field after a period at home.[11] For every 100 soldiers in the field army, 60 had to be replaced entirely or for long periods over the course of the war, half by new replacement troops and half by men considered to have regained their fitness to serve. During each year of the war, the field army lost a third of its men through death, injury or illness.[12]

Losses were distributed very unevenly across the various stages of the war. The first three months of the war in particular, characterised by the war of movement, saw average casualty rates for the entire army in the West that were never to be reached again on this stretch of the front, even during the battles of matériel in 1916. The total number of losses on the Western Front was 12.4 per cent in August and 16.8 per cent in September 1914. The average monthly figure for 1915/16 was 2.9 per cent and for the war as a whole, until July 1918, 3.5 per cent.[13] The spring offensive of 1918 and, on a yet greater scale, the rearguard action during the last few months of the war led to a rise in the number of losses for the armies taking part equal to that of the first months of the war.[14] The losses suffered during the battles of matériel in 1916 were concentrated on the armies deployed to fight them. These suffered massive losses. The

7. Karl Weiler, *Nervöse und seelische Störungen bei Teilnehmern am Weltkriege, ihre ärztliche und rechtliche Beurteilung*, Leipzig: Thieme 1933, pp. 106, 217.

8. Ibid., p. 71.

9. *Sanitätsbericht*, p. 13.

10. Ibid., pp. 20, 31.

11. Bayerisches Kriegsarchiv (ed.), *Die Bayern im Großen Kriege*, vol. 2, p. 46.

12. *Sanitätsbericht*, p. 33.

13. The calculation here refers to the fallen, missing, sick and wounded on a fairly long-term basis: ibid., p. 140.

14. Deist, Militärstreik, pp. 149-53.

5th Army at Verdun, for instance, ultimately lost around 350,000 men or 60 per cent of actual strength and the 1st and 2nd Army at the Somme each lost around half of actual strength.[15] The dangers posed by enemy fire were greatest among the infantry, and smaller for the artillery and MG (machine-gun) units.[16]

One key parameter of the army's social configuration during the war, the high degree of troop fluctuation, was due largely to the high rate of losses. A number of factors intensified this tendency. Many sick and injured men were transferred to a new unit once they had regained their health, where they had to 'repeatedly prove their competence anew in a completely unfamiliar set of circumstances, among unknown comrades and superiors'.[17] A certain percentage of soldiers was always at home on leave, though leave was banned before major offensives. Individual soldiers were transferred between units on an ongoing basis.[18]

Some units were affected by this situation more than others. Divisions responsible for quiet sections of the front featured a good deal of continuity, both in terms of personnel and in contrast to the high level of geographical mobility typical of the most efficient, powerful units. A unit such as the Bavarian 20th Infantry Regiment, meanwhile, part of one of the best German attack divisions according to the Allies, had to replace losses equal to its full initial complement over the course of the war. The total throughput of troops in this unit was around six times the index-value strength.[19] Different age groups were also affected unequally, a disproportionate number of younger soldiers being lost. The 15 to 18-year-olds made up only 2.26 per cent of fatalities. Almost half of all losses thus involved soldiers from 19 to 24 years of age, while those aged 35 and above made up only a tenth of the dead. Different age groups were affected differently over the course of the war. For example, 25 to 29-year-olds, who comprised the majority of troops at the beginning of the war, made up a good 30 per cent of the fallen in the bloodiest period of

15. But the overall number of dead and missing at Verdun was only 81,668: *Sanitätsbericht*, p. 49.

16. Günther Hebert, *Das Alpenkorps. Aufbau, Organisation und Einsatz einer Gebirgstruppe im Ersten Weltkrieg*, Boppard: Boldt 1988, p. 47.

17. Albrecht Thaer, *Generalstabsdienst an der Front und in der O.H.L. Aus Briefen und Tagebuchaufzeichnungen 1915-1919* (ed. by Siegfried A. Kaehler), Göttingen: Vandenhoeck & Ruprecht 1958, p. 122.

18. Hebert, *Alpenkorps*, pp. 45, 53.

19. Hugo Höfl, *Das K.-B. 20. Infanterie-Regiment Prinz Franz*, Munich: Verlag Max Schick 1929, p. 304.

Table 2.2 Deaths among Bavarian military personnel according to age group, 1914-18

Age	*15-19*	*20-24*	*25-29*	*30-34*	*35-39*	*40-44*	*>44*
%	8.43	41.98	23.61	14.61	8.15	2.6	0.62

Source: *Statistik des Deutschen Reichs*, vol. 276, p. LVII.

1914. However, their share had fallen by 10 percentage points by the end of the war; similar applied to the next youngest cohort. By contrast, 18 to 20-year-olds made up only 7.6 per cent of fatalities in 1914, but in 1917 and 1918 their share rocketed to almost one quarter.[20] Conscripts newly deployed during the war were thus exposed to a particularly high risk of losing their lives.

This was the result of restructuring carried out by the military authorities when allocating soldiers to specific types of troops and in planning their deployment. Most of the troops mobilised at the beginning of the war consisted of units made up of conscripts who had already served for some time; these units were brought up to war strength by bringing in 46 per cent worth of reservists. On a smaller scale, reserve troops made up of one-third reservists and two-thirds territorial army (*Landwehr*) of the first contingent were also mobilised, as were territorial army units. As early as October 1914 and January 1915, these were joined by two more Bavarian reserve divisions.[21]

When putting together other formations, all conscripts had to be brought in regardless of age, including large numbers of untrained *Landsturm* soldiers until 1916. In that year, the difficulties of obtaining replacement troops made it necessary to begin exchanging soldiers of different age groups between units. In response to the great demands made on many replacement and reserve divisions, in August 1916 the War Ministry stipulated that the *k.v.*- troops (*kriegsverwendungsfähige*, liable fo field duty)[22] born in 1876 or later were to be used solely in the

20. Statistik des Deutschen Reichs, vol. 276: *Bewegung der Bevölkerung in den Jahren 1914 bis 1919*, Berlin: Verlag für Sozialpolitik 1919, p. LVII.

21. Bayerisches Kriegsarchiv (ed.), *Die Bayern im Großen Kriege*, vol. 1, pp 6-8.

22. From February 1915, in line with their physical capacities, men liable for military service and soldiers were classified by the military doctors as *k.v.*

replacement units of the field and reserve divisions.[23] In April 1917 the Supreme Command (*Oberste Heeresleitung*) concluded that infantrymen and particularly soldiers serving in the Pioneers on the Western Front who were older than 35 were no longer up to the tasks facing them. They were to be transferred to field and reserve divisions only if they were in 'good physical condition'.[24] To balance things out, from the summer of 1916 onwards younger soldiers were removed from the territorial and reserve divisions responsible for quiet sections of the front. Initially, the 30th and 39th Reserve Division had to hand over a total of 6,000 troops under 35 years of age to the replacement army, their places being taken by older substitutes.[25] In October 1916 this procedure was extended to the 1st and 6th *Landwehr* Divisions.[26]

The figures on age distribution submitted on such occasions show clearly the extent to which these divisions were characterised by an increasing proportion of older men in the second half of the war. For example, 89 per cent of the 1st Territorial Division was aged over 35, while the proportion of *Landsturm* men with no experience of military service was still 40 per cent.[27] Around 47 per cent of the 39th Reserve Division was between 30 and 40 years of age, and about 25 per cent were even over 40.[28] Finally, to prepare for the spring offensive of 1918, most of the remaining younger soldiers were taken from the positional divisions (*Stellungsdivisionen*) basically meant to hold a quiet sector at the front.[29] For the same reason, younger soldiers under 35 were moved from the Eastern to the Western Front during the second half of 1917.[30] The younger soldiers served in units constantly redeployed to different battlefields, particularly during the second half of the war. After the first major replacement convoys had arrived, they made up a significant proportion of the troops in such units. From the middle of 1916 on, in three companies of different types from the Alpine Corps, those born

(*kriegsverwendungsfähig* or liable to field duty), *g.v.* (*garnisonsverwendungsfähig* or liable to garrison duty) or *a.v.* (*arbeitsverwendungsfähig* or liable to work duty): BA/MA, W-10/50900, fol. 18.

23. K.M., 8.11.1916: BHStA/IV, stv. GK I.AK 277.
24. K.M., 20.11.1917: BHStA/IV, stv. GK I.AK 277.
25. K.M., 29.8.1916: BHStA/IV, MKr 1802.
26. K.M., 19.10.1916: BHStA/IV, MKr 1802.
27. 1. Ldw.-Div., 26.1.1917: BHStA/IV, MKr 1803.
28. 39. Res.-Div., 31.12.1916: BHStA/IV, MKr 1803.
29. *Histories*, pp. 143, 441.
30. Excerpt from a letter, 7.12.1917: BSB.

in 1894 and later made up around 50 per cent of soldiers.[31] The attack divisions wanted soldiers under 35. From as early as 1917, however, there were not enough of these to cover their need for replacement troops.[32]

Younger soldiers thus mainly served in units which saw a lot of heavy fighting; inevitably, many of them died. Single soldiers thus made up 75 per cent of the dead from Bavaria.[33] In total, however, a little over half of the soldiers were married. The census of 1 December 1916 provides an insight into the age distribution of soldiers serving in the replacement army. These figures probably provide a rough idea of the age distribution of men serving in the field and replacement army as a whole. Even from those replacement units which constantly assigned soldiers to the front, around a third of the troops were over the age of 35 in 1917.[34] The social composition of the troops also had a major impact on the distribution of risk at the front. Only the wartime muster rolls of individual units provide reliable information on the number of soldiers belonging to various professional groups. These include an entry on the 'job' done by individual soldiers and list all the soldiers detailed to each unit from mobilisation until the end of the war, unless they were permanently transferred to another unit.[35]

Muster roll data from various units of the Alpine Corps for a total of 6,186 NCOs and soldiers show that around half of them worked in agriculture. Artisans also made up a significant group.[36] Soldiers working in agriculture made up almost 45 per cent of male workers in southern

Table 2.3 Military personnel living in Bavaria on 1 December 1916 according to age group

Age	*16-19*	*20-24*	*25-29*	*30-34*	*35-39*	*40-44*	*>44*
%	13.2	21.1	17.6	17.0	16.0	12.6	2.5

Source: Kriegs-Volkszählungen, p. 100.

31. Hebert, *Alpenkorps*, p. 44.
32. Stv. GK I.AK 20.6.1917: BHStA/IV, 2. Inf.-Div. Bund 109.
33. Statistik des Deutschen Reichs, vol. 276, p. LVII.
34. Documents in: BHStA/IV, stv. GK I.AK 431.
35. Gerhard Böhn, Die Kriegsstammrollen und Kriegsranglisten der Königlich Bayerischen Armee aus der Zeit des 1. Weltkrieges, *Mitteilungen für die Archivpflege in Bayern* 9 (1963), pp. 35-41, p. 36.
36. Hebert, *Alpenkorps*, p. 45.

Bavaria and only a slightly larger proportion of the troops in the Alpine Corps.[37] Alongside this isolated census, global estimations made during demobilisation also cast doubt on the notion that a disproportionately large number of agricultural workers was called up. These assumed that a total of around 3 to 4 million agricultural workers were conscripted in Germany during the war.[38] Why, then, was the proportion of agricultural workers in the field army not higher, given that large numbers of skilled workers were recalled to work in the armaments industry? To answer this question, we would have to systematically analyse the interplay of labour policy and the provision of replacement troops, a task beyond the scope of the present work. Nonetheless, we shall briefly survey four key reasons.

The first is the unequal distribution of the male agricultural or industrial workers within the various age groups. The 20 to 40-year-old age group, which includes the vast majority of conscripts serving in the war, made up 52 per cent of economically active male industrial workers in the Empire in 1907, but only 36.3 per cent of their agricultural counterparts. This was due to the steady migration of the young, productive age cohorts from the countryside to the cities. During the war, this meant that a proportionately larger reservoir of men old enough to be called up was available among industrial workers.[39] Secondly, regardless of the struggle to obtain the scarcest human resource needed for waging war - skilled workers - the army was furnished with new reserves by means, for example, of the repeated medical examination for service of conscripts from September 1915. These measures alone produced 500,000 new men fit for service. In addition, regulations governing fitness for service were relaxed, and *k.v.*-soldiers in the back area and replacement army were released for service. Furthermore, the struggle going on between the army and industry over skilled workers was institutionalised through the Auxiliary Service Law (*Hilfsdienstgesetz*) in December 1916. From then on, if not before, skilled workers were no longer recalled permanently from the front. Instead, the military authorities detailed a certain number of workers to the front on a month-by-month basis only; at the same time,

37. Calculated on the basis of the figures for 1907: *Bayerische Berufsstatistik 1907. Berufliche und soziale Gliederung*, Munich: Lindauer 1908, pp. 158, 160, 178, 180, 304, 306.

38. Statistik des Deutschen Reichs, vol. 202, p. 4.

39. G. Neuhaus, Die berufliche und soziale Gliederung der Bevölkerung im Zeitalter des Kapitalismus, in: *Grundriß der Sozialökonomik*, IX. Abt., I. Teil, Tübingen: Mohr 1926, pp. 360–459, p. 399.

a similar number went home.[40] Finally, the recalling of workers from the field army had to be stopped entirely as early as March 1917. The Supreme Command issued a decree on 25 September 1917 confirming this. Front-line soldiers born in 1876 or later were to be recalled only in exceptional cases. A large proportion of recalled skilled workers was thus probably taken from the replacement army and the back area.[41]

Yet even in the immediate post-war period, commentators worked on the basis that a disproportionate number of rural workers had been called up. In line with this, such men were thought to have made up an outsize chunk of soldiers and casualties. Alongside rural inhabitants' greater fitness for military service, this was explained as a result of the large number of workers recalled to work in the armaments industry.[42] However, insufficient efforts were made to assess the meaningfulness of the available data. Rudolf Meerwarth compared how many soldiers died as a percentage of the male population liable for military service in the Prussian provinces and the other *Länder* of the Empire. This produced maximum values in certain Prussian provinces which may be classified as predominately agrarian. The figure for 'agrarian' Bavaria of 12.7 per cent, meanwhile, was below the average for the Empire of 12.9 per cent and only slightly above that of the 'industrial' Kingdom of Saxony at 11.9 per cent.[43]

The values calculated by Meerwarth were of negligible range. This suggests, first, that regional disparities still present at the beginning of the war, because rural men were recruited more often than their urban counterparts before 1914, levelled out over the course of the war. Regional differences in casualty statistics are thus unsuitable for determining the social composition of the army. The slight discrepancy between the number of casualties for Saxony and Bavaria, for example, in fact indicates that agricultural workers were *less* exposed to the risk of death at the front than one would expect given their share of troops in the field. Study of the employment details of the fallen in selected units

40. Dieter Dreetz, Methoden der Ersatzgewinnung für das deutsche Heer 1914 bis 1918, *Militärgeschichte* 16 (1977), pp. 700-7, pp. 702-5.

41. Feldman, *Armee*, pp. 243, 336.

42. Weiler, *Störungen*, p. 66.

43. Rudolf Meerwarth, Die Entwicklung der Bevölkerung in Deutschland während der Kriegs- und Nachkriegszeit, in: Rudolf Meerwarth/Adolf Günther/Waldemar Zimmermann (eds), *Die Einwirkung des Krieges auf Bevölkerungsbewegung, Einkommen und Lebenshaltung in Deutschland*, Stuttgart, Berlin, Leipzig: Deutsche Verlags-Anstalt 1932, pp. 1-97, p. 69.

of the Alpine Corps confirms this. Soldiers working in agriculture made up only 31.3 per cent of this group.[44] The fact that soldiers working in agriculture made up a smaller share of the fallen suggests that they were deployed less and less to serve on the front line. This was a result of the mechanisation of warfare, which made far greater intellectual and technical demands on soldiers. As discipline declined, complaints from the field that replacement troops lacked training underlined troops' inability to use equipment efficiently in line with changes in the technology of battle.[45]

Replacement units had trouble training recruits because, first, training personnel were of poor quality and their turnover rate was high. Few of them were officers or NCOs with experience of war. Yet it was precisely front-line experience that troops respected.[46] Moreover, the available training period of twelve weeks for basic infantry training and the compulsory special training in small-calibre machine-guns, trench mortars and telephones was far too short. The training of agricultural troops was often interrupted after only a few weeks by harvest leave. These were subsequently 'hobbled' and continued to underperform despite repetition of the training stages they had missed.[47] Rural recruits understood less because they had less practice in handling abstract contexts, hampering their training. They required lengthy instruction even to memorise the names and ranks of officers.[48]

In response to such educational shortcomings, many unit commanders at the front must have assigned replacement troops to rearward duties, at least to some extent, rather than the trenches. Farmers and farmers' sons tended to be assigned to the field artillery regiments, which required several hundred horses and almost as many drivers and grooms to transport artillery. Their expertise with the animals could be made good use of here and, like working with horses in civilian life, the farmers enjoyed great prestige because of it. The opportunity to gain professional qualifications inherent in military service thus took on a familiar form among rural recruits in particular and had no modernising effect. The *Landsturm* battalions deployed at the rear to carry out guard duty and labour service also had no trouble taking on large numbers of

44. Hebert, *Alpenkorps*, p. 48.
45. BA/MA, W-10/50900, fol. 15.
46. K.M., 8.1.1918: BHStA/IV, stv. GK I.AK 451.
47. E./1.I.R. 23.8.1917: BHStA/IV, stv. GK I.AK 452.
48. Klemperer, *Curriculum Vitae*, p. 301.

farmers.[49] Meanwhile, special units requiring soldiers with a high degree of technical understanding, machine-gun troops being a prime example, were recruited mainly from industrial workers.[50] Other than for troops requiring technical expertise, the age composition of replacements was, however, far more important to maintaining overall fighting strength than professional make-up.

Many more agricultural workers served in the replacement army than would be expected according to their share of the gainfully employed population. A survey in June 1917 suggested a figure of 65.5 per cent, though this includes only the 32,891 men available as replacement troops in the sector covered by the 1st Army Corps when the survey was carried out.[51] The true number of farmers was most likely higher. Along with the sick, soldiers on detention and those assigned elsewhere, other units also included the large number of farmers classified as *g.v.* (*garnisonsverwen dungsfähige*) already on leave for the hay harvest. Reports from 1917 and 1918 by liaison officers responsible for educating the troops also provide plenty of evidence of replacement units consisting largely or almost entirely of farmers, particularly those territorial and reserve regiments with older troops.[52]

The replacement army contained so many farmers because the military authorities were attempting to secure the agricultural labour force. In early 1915, at least in the case of replacement reservists and those liable to serve with the *Landsturm*, the district commander was instructed to call up farmers in these categories only if the district offices confirmed that this would not hamper the tilling of the fields. This guideline was followed until 1918, as made apparent by the fact that some *Landsturm* troops were not called up; older soldiers were always the last to be conscripted. In 1916 recruits from cereal growing areas were called up only once harvesting was over.[53] Only a few rural soldiers were, however, recalled for longer periods, as industrial workers took priority.[54]

The labour needs of the agricultural economy followed a seasonal rhythm. It thus made sense to grant leave three times a year, particularly to farmers and rural workers serving in the field and replacement army. The latter in particular were systematically used as a reservoir of agricultural

49. Ldst.-Btl. I B, 14 28.6.1918: BHStA/IV, MKr 2419.
50. WUA, vol. 11/1, p. 423.
51. Documents in: BHStA/IV, stv. GK I.AK 620.
52. BHStA/IV, stv. GK I.AK 2401.
53. K.M., 18.7.1916: BHStA/IV, MKr 2451.
54. Stv. GK I.AK 22.7.1918: BHStA/IV, MKr 622.

labour.[55] If possible, those classified as *g.v.* were moved to a unit near their home area immediately after being called up, so they could be sent home on leave as efficiently as possible. The War Ministry had been pushing since 1915 for troops classified as *g.v.* and *a.v.* who were surplus to the army's requirements to be sent home for good. Yet they made up an ever larger share of the replacement army. In the spring of 1915, 50,000 NCOs and ordinary soldiers in this category were counted in the Bavarian replacement army. In March 1916 this had climbed to around 134,000, almost half the troops on home territory.[56] Replacement units were forced in 'ruthless' fashion to give up skilled workers and other industrial workers in this category to industry from 1916 on. As a result, farmers classified as *g.v.*, who were indispensable while on harvest leave, made up the majority of those remaining in the garrisons.[57]

It was the authorities back home responsible for the war economy who were most interested in skilled workers. For the military authorities in the field, meanwhile, the troops' age composition was of key importance, hence their constant struggle to obtain the youngest possible replacement troops. The distribution pattern produced by these divergent interests and the external realities of battle had certain motivating consequences. The large number of troops retained on home territory and the high turnover rate of units within the field army both helped ensure that soldiers generally experienced periods of heavy fighting and the extreme strains this involved for relatively short periods only. Younger conscripts were disproportionately affected by this, the very group which tended to be more willing to do military service than were older soldiers.[58] These structural factors provide our first clue as to why morale among the troops was seriously shaken only towards the end of the war, despite heavy fighting over long periods of time.

2.2 Routines of Everyday Life

Everyday life at the front did not differ fundamentally from civilian life; it too consisted of temporal segments of varying length. Periods of extreme exertion and danger alternated with those of relative calm and relaxation. These recurrent and overlapping rhythms divided a stint at the front into various stretches of time, offering soldiers a manageable

55. See Chapter 2.2.
56. K.M., 15.5.1915: BHStA/IV, stv. GK I.AK 2865.
57. Ernst v. Wrisberg, *Heer und Heimat*, Leipzig: Koehler 1921, p. 91.
58. See Chapter 3.3.

horizon of expectations. Given the imponderables of life at the front, the regular repetition of certain procedures and actions provided a sense of behavioural security that promoted stability among the troops.

In positional warfare, one phase of deployment was rapidly followed by another. The soldiers in an infantry battalion usually spent between five and seven and sometimes up to ten days in the trenches closest to the front. This was followed by standby duty of the same length in a trench not far from the front line or temporary quarters. This cycle concluded with three to five days in a billet a few kilometres behind the front line.[59] Particularly during the initial stages of the war, periods of rest alternated with standby or trench duty, each lasting only two days.[60] This proved necessary in later years too, particularly when troops came under heavy artillery fire and had to repulse attacks. Wherever fighting was particularly intense, it was also advisable to establish another line with troops at the ready, and to keep a regiment in reserve from the outset. This made it possible to move entire regiments to a quiet area free of artillery fire for several days. If two reserve positions were to be established behind the front line, however, the section of the front occupied had to be kept short.[61]

Towards the end of the war, troops generally fought for longer. After the initiation of rearguard action in July 1918, even divisions known to require rest could not be withdrawn from the front.[62] Instead, relieved divisions were immediately transported to other battle zones or had to make their own way there by marching for several days, an exhausting prospect.[63] Towards the end of the war, many units thus fought without rest for weeks. Together with the heavy rearguard battles, this exhausted the troops physically and psychologically.[64] Most front-line activities took place at night. The darkness required the trenches to be fitted with a dense array of listening posts. Depending how far away the enemy was, these were placed every 20 to 50 metres and were usually relieved after two hours.[65] The troops also worked on improvements to the trenches and fortifications at night. The constant activity provided little opportunity for sleep and combatants were thus generally overtired. Even in the

59. Relief survey 2. Inf.-Div., 1.-31.5.1916: BHStA/IV, 2. Inf.-Div. Bund 68.
60. Stefan Schimmer, 18.10.1914: BHStA/IV, Amtsbibliothek 9584.
61. Höfl, *20. Infanterie-Regiment*, p. 63.
62. WUA, vol. 11/1, p. 397.
63. Hans Spieß, 3.7.1918: BHStA/IV, Kriegsbriefe 340.
64. WUA, vol. 11/1, p. 329.
65. BHStA/IV, MilGer 6394, 6465; Militärgericht 6. Ldw.-Div. B 50.

absence of fighting, those manning the listening posts were constantly exposed to uncertainty at night. Both sides regularly undertook patrols to identify changes in fortifications and take prisoners who could provide information on the identity, strength and intentions of the enemy.[66] The reserve positions were not plagued by constant danger, but troops were sometimes exposed to artillery fire when advancing to or retreating from them.[67]

It was thus a tremendous weight off soldiers' minds when they were relieved and left the trenches for the rearward positions. They were now free from harm for a while and had a welcome opportunity to relax after the exertions of the previous days. Their first priority was to resume their accustomed daily routine and have a good long sleep.[68] Even during the rest period, however, soldiers were unable to recuperate undisturbed by the demands of duty. Depending on the habits of the company and regimental commanders, the time remaining to the individual soldier was interrupted by frequent roll calls and drills:

> Am on 8 days at rest at the moment, but it's pretty strict, with drills. At 6 in the morning it all starts up again. This damned swindle, I've had my fill of it. You're no sooner back than it all starts up again, they don't even let you have a rest. We just had 16 days in position without a break. We came back full of mud and *speck*, early in the morning at 6.30 am and they scarcely allowed us five hours of sleep. In the trench there was nothing to sleep on at night in the first place and we had to keep a constant lookout for the enemy because of raids. We have a load of lieutenants in the company, but you don't see any of them going into the trench position; an NCO has to take over the platoon. He can certainly hold his head high, but when you're back in to rest, there they are grinding [*schleifen*] and exercising you properly, they're good at that. They're just a bunch of young lieutenants, an older one would be more sensible and would be ashamed in front of the troops. They have no respect at all.[69]

From the troops' perspective it was anything but clear why the period of quiet, in any case meagre and desperately needed, had to be disturbed by marching in parade step and other drills unnecessary to trench warfare. They thus vented their outrage at unreasonable demands during quiet periods in grumbling, complaints and insubordination, and by

66. BHStA/IV, MilGer 6250, 6274, 6436, 6465.
67. BHStA/IV, MilGer 6412.
68. Joseph Reininger, 18.3.1917: private possession.
69. O.H., 12.9.1917: local authority of Kochel.

complaining to their relatives in letters.[70] Some higher authorities in the field did issue decrees stipulating that periods of quiet should not be disturbed by drills and labour service and that troops should be allowed a full day of rest on a regular basis to have a good sleep.[71] Despite this, many officers behind the front persisted with drills, believing that they reinforced discipline and wanting to show their superior officers the martial 'strictness' of the men under their command.[72] The third Supreme Command also pressed for drills to be reduced in favour of weapons training in its new educational guidelines published in early 1917. Nonetheless, there was no let-up in the complaints about pointless drills until the summer of 1918.[73] Quiet periods thus provided relief only in that there was no immediate threat to life and limb.

Deployment in a unit not stationed in the trenches was generally desirable. In December 1917 one soldier thus stated ironically: 'The war is like a cinema. The action's at the front and the best seats are at the back.'[74] Even in the artillery units, the risk of casualties was lower than in the infantry. When they talked about the infantrymen, whom they called 'Schniggel', artillerymen thus alternated between 'mild contempt' and 'shivering empathy and honest admiration'.[75] Soldiers who served in rearward positions rather than manning weapons were permanently excluded from the oscillation between danger and relaxation. This included, for instance, soldiers in the baggage train responsible for supplies of ammunition and food, which was budgeted for around 5,500 troops and NCOs in each army corps.[76] Of these, only men in the ammunition columns were exposed to artillery fire and then only rarely, when they had to advance close to positions subject to heavy bombardment. Serving with the *Bagage*, as it was popularly known, was thus generally regarded as relatively pleasant.[77]

The post of batman was even more highly prized. Agricultural labourers or farmers' sons were often chosen because of their aptitude

70. BA/MA, W-10/50794, fol. 31, 65-6.

71. Armee-Abteilung C, 20.4.1917: BHStA/IV, HS 2348.

72. WUA, vol. 11/1, p. 239.

73. Karl Gandorfer, 17.6.1918: BHStA/IV, MKr 13359.

74. Excerpt from a letter by a soldier in the field, 24.9.1917: BSB.

75. Klemperer, *Curriculum Vitae*, p. 334.

76. Calculated on the basis of the information in Edgar Graf von Matuschka, Organisationsgeschichte des Heeres 1890-1918, in: Militärgeschichtliches Forschungsamt (ed.), *Handbuch zur deutschen Militärgeschichte*, vol. 3, Frankfurt/M.: Bernhard & Graefe 1968, pp. 246, 264.

77. Diary entry by Josef Ullrich, 14.7.1916: BHStA/IV, HS 3262.

with horses.[78] They could show themselves willing to oblige their 'master' by furnishing him with food packages from back home, reducing the risk that they might lose their post.[79] The 'shovellers' (*Schipper*) or reinforcement soldiers, as they were called officially, were also exposed to enemy fire only rarely. They were brought in to help expand the rearward fortifications, which had become ever more necessary during the war of immobility, and dig trenches behind the first line. Around 200,000 older troops served in the 217 reinforcement battalions of the German army.[80]

For all soldiers, going home on leave was the main opportunity for periodic liberation from the stresses and strains of everyday life at the front. Other than rations, there was probably no topic to which they devoted more attention in their correspondence or which had a greater impact on the mood of the troops. At the same time, the unequal distribution of leave and restrictions on the length of leave entailed significant potential for conflict: 'It looks like there will be no more leave for the foreseeable future. The new orders couldn't make it any clearer. No orders could be more demoralising. What else does a field soldier have other than the hope of going home on leave twice a year?'[81]

From the spring of 1915, between 3 and 7 per cent of the field troops were regularly on leave at the same time. The aim was to allow every soldier furlough at least once a year. Before and during major offensives, however, leave was cancelled. On the Western Front the ban on leave from 11 February 1918 was the main reason for the dark mood of the men stationed there. Farmers were excepted from this ban. At the insistence of the Christian Peasants' Association, the Bavarian War Ministry managed to persuade the Supreme Command that, with the exception, from 5 April 1918, of a number of armies on the Western Front, farmers should be allowed furlough again.[82] This exceptional rule, formulated at a time of rapidly declining troop strength in all units was the culmination of a policy which had made leave in the field and replacement army a tool for securing agricultural labour needs since 1915. Requests for furlough from soldiers serving in front-line units were given the fullest possible consideration as early as the spring of 1915. Here, and in the following wave of leave for the harvest of 1915, it was, however, obvious that commanders would grant leave from the field army only insofar as this

78. B.G., 27.6.1915: local authority of Kochel.
79. Hans Spieß, 7.1.1917: BHStA/IV, Kriegsbriefe 340.
80. Matuschka, Organisationsgeschichte, pp. 269–70.
81. Letter from 30.10.1917: WUA, vol. 5, p. 275.
82. Sebastian Schlittenbauer, 1.3.1918: BHStA/IV, MKr 2418.

was in accord with tactical exigencies.[83] The authorities in the field also needed yardsticks by which they could assess the urgency of the many requests made, some of them at the front itself. Many soldiers who missed out on furlough complained that it was granted in an irregular fashion.[84]

A uniform approval procedure was thus established in January of 1916. It was based on a questionnaire to be filled out by every farm of more than two hectares requesting information about the size of the farm and how many people worked on it.[85] This was handed in by the local authority, along with notification of the period when leave was likely to be necessary, at the district office, which passed it on to the unit if it considered a request well-founded. In assessing how urgently leave was needed, farm heads, especially of large farms, took precedence over agricultural workers. In the field and replacement army, requests for leave by agricultural workers were to be prioritised over those of all other groups during harvest time and the tilling of the fields in spring and autumn.[86] Soldiers not involved in agriculture thus observed their rural 'comrades' being granted furlough several times a year, though many of the former had never been home in two years of active service. They believed that the farmers were preventing this highly desirable commodity from being shared out more fairly. This led to a persistent worsening of soldiers' mood, deep antipathy and 'spiteful criticism' of this privileged professional group.[87] The farmers were also suspected of buying the cooperation of the officers responsible for granting leave by bribing them with food packages brought back from their villages.[88]

As a consequence of this, exceeding one's leave was one of the offences most often tried by court martial.[89] Significantly, almost no farmers exceeded their leave. The main reason for this was probably that they were well catered for in this respect. The military authorities were aware that the meagre amount of furlough was making absence without leave more likely.[90] However, the accused also typically expressed their anger

83. K.M., 17.4.1915: BHStA/IV, MKr 2417.
84. Stefan Schimmer, n.d.: BHStA/IV, Amtsbibliothek 9584.
85. Minn, 29.1.1916: BHStA/IV, stv. GK I.AK 849.
86. War Ministry decree issued on 28.1.1916: BHStA/IV, MKr 2450.
87. Letter excerpts in BA/MA, W-10/50794, fol. 31.
88. Memorandum K.M.-Abt.A II, 23.6.1918: BHStA/IV, MKr 13359.
89. This does not come close to reflecting the frequency with which soldiers exceeded their furlough, as less serious cases of absence without leave were also subject to punishment by disciplinary means at times.
90. WUA, vol. 11/1, p. 400.

about lack of furlough, or the lack of consideration shown by the officers responsible for granting it, to explain their behaviour in relation to other offences, such as refusal to obey orders, cowardice or self-inflicted injury. They clearly hoped that this would be considered an especially exculpatory motive, given that it was generally acknowledged how important leave was to soldiers.[91]

In the replacement army there was no need to take the tactical situation into account when granting leave, as there was in the field. As early as the summer of 1915, the War Ministry urged the replacement units to organise military service more efficiently, to free up more troops for leave.[92] In the following years, the commanders were repeatedly warned to retain only the number of men strictly necessary for replacement, to restrict office duty as much as possible and to reduce the number of nights on which there was no guard duty.[93] The number of days' leave granted climbed continuously from 1915 on, but this merely reflected the increasing strength of the replacement army. The percentage figures for 1917 reveal how many farmers left the replacement army three times a year. On 30 April 1917, 43 per cent of regular soldiers and NCOs in the 1st Army Corps were on leave.[94]

More and more craftsmen and other members of the commercial middle class complained about the persistently preferential treatment of farmers. Especially against the background of the promotion of war loans, they complained that their economic welfare was being damaged, as they were unable to work regularly in their firms, while the farmers, they felt, were generating profits. The perception that the farmers were hardly soldiers any longer because they were constantly on leave, while they themselves were brought in to do guard duty and labour service in the barracks with increasing frequency, also depressed them:

> The best thing would be for all the lads to become farmers if the war goes on much longer, because here at least they're not soldiers so much as constant paid leave-takers. And they laugh at you because you can do your duty for them no trouble as a craftsman and they let things go to wrack and ruin rather than give you a bit of money. To witness all of this, to taste it, is really not the best way to get you into a hopeful state of mind. Now you know why I've been in such ill humour recently.[95]

91. BHStA/IV, MilGer 6270, 6279.
92. K.M., 19.7.1915: BHStA/IV, MKr 2417.
93. Stv. GK I.AK, 25.5.1916: BHStA/IV, stv. GK I.AK 849.
94. Undated surveys: BHStA/IV, MKr 2452.
95. Letter by a territorial reservist, 9.9.1917: BSB.

In the consciousness of their 'comrades', the peasants in the replacement army, even more than those at the front, were thus identified as *the* group of soldiers constantly granted leave. Nonetheless, for soldiers in the field army, even the numerous hardships and injustices bound up with the granting of leave were unable to destroy the subjectively relieving function of hopes of a limited period at home. The expectation that one would be able, in the foreseeable future, to escape from the front at least for a while divided the temporal continuum of the mission into a succession of manageable segments. Most soldiers lived, to some extent, from one period of leave to the next. For them, nothing seemed more promising than peace.[96]

The prospect of leave was generally associated with the desire for a cluster of closely related opportunities rarely available at the front. Soldiers could escape the risk of being killed for a time, even on the front line. The safety of life back home was thus not their main concern. They were more preoccupied by the desire for a series of days during which they could relax without interruption and, if possible, eat their fill and enjoy a break from the monotony of everyday life at the front.[97] Whatever their prejudiced urban 'comrades' and some military authorities might think, farmers used their leave to work on their own or neighbouring farms. Furlough thus periodically confirmed their civilian identity as farmers. It was also attractive because of soldiers' need to be free of the unceasing constraints of military hierarchy, at least for a while. In 1915 the farmer and *Landsturm* soldier Jakob Eberhard vividly depicted the feeling of liberation bound up with a stay in one's home village: 'From 27 July until 9 August I was on furlough for the harvest. It was lovely. I felt like a bird let out of its cage.'[98]

Soldiers wished to go home on leave mainly because they longed to see their family and friends. Single young men took the opportunity to meet up with their girlfriends. Married men looked forward to seeing their wives and children. They were affected most by homesickness; in the face of a great deal of 'indescribable violence', it was the all-embracing reason for going home on leave, taking in 'all other motives'.[99] After a lengthy period of worrying and hoping, such soldiers were thus hugely relieved to have arrived home at last and be able to enjoy seeing their loved ones again. Shock at their wives' poor state of health and meagre

96. Letter excerpt from 25.6.1917: BSB.
97. Josef Thalmeier, 10.6.1916: AEM, Kriegschronik Altenerding B 1837.
98. War diary of Jakob Eberhard: private possession.
99. WUA, vol. 11/1, p. 97.

diet, however, sometimes made leave a depressing experience. Soldiers from urban centres were not the only ones to encounter shortages at home, as a letter by a farmer from the Rhenish Palatinate, probably the owner of a fairly modest property, attests:

> After three years of war, I was allowed to visit my dear wife and children for the third time. In the nine months that I've been away from them the children have grown so much that I hardly recognised them, but I hardly knew even my own dear wife, for she has lost so much weight that there's almost nothing left of her but skin and bones.[100]

Such impressions, of course, tended to intensify soldiers' persistent anxiety about their loved ones once they returned to the front. Apart from the restrictions imposed by the command economy, rural soldiers home on leave felt that normality reigned back home, largely undisturbed by the war.[101] On the other hand, they were enraged by the material prosperity of the well-to-do in the towns and by the 'armchair strategists' who felt that every offensive was proceeding too slowly. Most soldiers on furlough took the opportunity to relate to their families an unvarnished picture of the realities of the front. A minority preferred to keep quiet about their experiences because they were 'happy' 'not to have to think about them'.[102] The time spent back home passed by quickly and soldiers always felt that their leave was too short. The most difficult moment soon arrived. For soldiers on leave and their wives, against the stereotype of the front-line soldier alienated from his home ground, this was saying goodbye. For both, this moment was overshadowed by the agonising fact that it was by no means certain that they would ever see each other again:

> Prayed for furlough on 1 March 1915. Off-duty on the 2nd. Collected my shoes on March 15. Left on leave at two in the afternoon until the 12.III.15. Leaving wasn't difficult but saying goodbye and the reverence [expressed by the family], that's hard. To get through that, it brings you to tears and burdens your heart, because I don't know if I'll come home again.[103]

This problem was made even worse by a succession of periods on leave, as it became more and more difficult to part. While the significance of

100. Letter excerpt from 26.8.1917: BSB.
101. Letter excerpt by a soldier on leave from Osterhofen, 20.3.1918: ibid.
102. Fritz Einert, 8.12.1916: BArch, 92, 275, fol. 18.
103. War diary of Jakob Eberhard: private possession.

leave as a short-term liberation from physical strain tended to increase over the course of the war, the pain of parting increasingly diminished its function as psychological outlet. Repeated contact with their accustomed life-world in fact made soldiers all the keener for peace. The more men were 'tied' to the 'natural environment' of their civilian past, the greater this effect was. This applied particularly to peasants, while the educated and unionised workers had learned to abstract from their own needs and situation.[104]

For farmers, however, this effect was offset by their privileged position in relation to the granting of leave. Even during the most wearing periods of deployment at the front, they generally had good reason to expect that they would be granted leave soon. If not, they might urge their nearest and dearest to submit a request for leave themselves, especially if a stint in the field loomed.[105] They provided family members with detailed instructions to enhance the prospects of their request being granted, though well aware how their 'comrades' complained about farmers' special treatment. The happiness inspired by a promising request was sometimes succeeded by bitterness, when their commanding officers turned down their requests despite the seal of approval from the authorities back home.[106] The men in the replacement army longed for peace. Because the farmers serving in it enjoyed a disproportionate share of leave, their mood often brightened, at least over the short term, right up to the end of the war. Farmers classified as *g.v.*, however, were increasingly impatient to know why they could not take up their civilian work again full-time. Even a short period living in civilian circumstances had consequences that were apparent for a considerable time after the men had returned to the field. The pain of departure remained palpable:

> Only now, so long after a hard farewell, although I didn't let my feelings show, can I tell you that I left with a heavy heart. It's been such a long time now and we haven't seen each other, but I believe the Mother of God will not abandon us. But I wanted to say, let's go on the pilgrimage as soon as possible when I'm allowed to return back home to you.[107]

It was only with difficulty, and after a few weeks had passed, that the soldiers grew accustomed once more to the rhythm of everyday life on

104. WUA, vol. 4, p. 131.
105. L.R., 30.3.1918: BfZ, Slg. Schüling, vol. 5, Nr. 88.
106. Hans Spieß, 12.3.1917: BHStA/IV, Kriegsbriefe 340.
107. Johann Baptist Blehle, 8.5.1915: StAA, Amtsgericht Immenstadt, Zivilsachen E 29/1920.

the front. They described their apathy and lack of appetite during this period and their persistent memories of home.

Alongside the short-term alternation between trenches and rest position behind the front and periodic leave, everyday life at the front featured a longer-term rhythm of strain and relaxation. After the transition to the war of immobility in October and November 1914 on the Western Front, and during 1915 in the East, the intensity of fighting varied from one section of the front to another. The active infantry divisions, which existed from the very beginning of the war, were exposed to the most horrendous strain and were constantly being redeployed throughout the war. This also applied to some reserve divisions, particularly those established in autumn 1914, consisting of large numbers of volunteers.[108] Such attack divisions were deployed repeatedly in the battles of matériel from 1916 on, which involved heavy losses. Here, as the General Staff officers cynically put it, 'whole divisions are reduced to ashes in a few hours'.[109]

On days when fighting was particularly intense, hours of constant artillery barrage of a specific sector wore down the infantrymen. The artillery's consumption of ammunition conveys an impression of the varying degrees of exposure to enemy fire. During two relatively quiet periods, the second quarter of 1915 and the first quarter of 1916, the twenty-four guns of the six batteries of the 9th Field Artillery Regiment used a total of 8,288 and 13,217 rounds of ammunition. In the Battle of the Somme, on the other hand, a single battery fired between 800 and 1,200 and sometimes even as many as 2,000 mortars or shrapnel shells per day.[110] To recover their strength and replace losses after such battles, these divisions, which had been subjected to intense strain, were transferred to a quiet sector of the front for anything from a few days to several months.[111]

108. Of the divisions recruited entirely or partly in the southern Bavarian region, this includes the 1st, 2nd and 11th Infantry Divisions, the 6th Reserve Division, the 1st Reserve Division at least for a time (until early 1917) and the 8th Reserve Division: *Histories*, pp. 40–1, 43–4, 65–8, 139–42, 164–5, 208–10.

109. Diary entry, 31.7.1917: Thaer, *Generalstabsdienst*, p. 130.

110. Lorenz Kuchtner, *Das K.B. 9. Feld-Artillerie-Regiment*, Munich: Lindauer 1927, pp. 83, 118.

111. The 2nd Infantry Division's history of military engagements, for example, features such phases: in the summer of 1915, from July to October 1916 after deployment at Verdun, from January to April 1917 after deployment at the Somme, for fourteen days in June 1917 after the battles at Chemin des Dames and for another fourteen days in early 1918, and for almost four weeks in 1918 from early May and a full month from the end of June. *Histories*, pp. 65–8.

Soldiers on the Eastern and Western Fronts generally faced different demands and different degrees of danger. While more men died in the fighting in the East than in the West during the first year of the war, the balance shifted in favour of the East in subsequent years. Particularly from the spring of 1917 on, when Russian troops slipped free of government control once the revolutionary transformation was under way in Russia, the fighting there was highly sporadic. The German military leadership reinforced this tendency by initiating fraternisation. This made it possible to dispatch officers responsible for spreading propaganda in order to further weaken the enemy's fighting strength.[112] Quite apart from this, some units such as the 8th Reserve Division had achieved an informal 'separate peace' with the Russian units.[113] This situation was finally sanctioned by the cease-fire of 7 December 1917 and the armistice of 15 December 1917. Units in the East thus suffered far fewer losses than their Western counterparts during the second half of the war (see Table 2.4). The soldiers, aware of this situation, thus responded positively when their unit was moved to the Eastern Front. An unsettled mood prevailed whenever a unit had to travel in the opposite direction.[114] This is the

Table 2.4 Average monthly losses among German troops (fallen and missing) on the Western and Eastern Front (per thousand of total strength)

Year	West	East
1914/15	14.5	17.1
1915/16	6.5	5.8
1916/17	8.8	3.3
1917/18	8.4	0.7

Source: *Sanitätsbericht*, vol. III, pp. 140*-3*.

112. Benjamin Ziemann, Verweigerungsformen von Frontsoldaten in der deutschen Armee 1914-1918, in: Andreas Gestrich (ed.), *Gewalt im Krieg. Ausübung, Erfahrung und Verweigerung von Gewalt in Kriegen des 20. Jahrhunderts*, Münster: Lit 1996, pp. 99-122, p. 107.

113. Hans Carossa, *Briefe I. 1886-1918* (ed. by Eva Kampmann-Carossa), Frankfurt/M.: Insel 1978, pp. 145, 147.

114. *Histories*, p. 28.

main reason that so many soldiers - sometimes up to 10 per cent of the train convoys - fled in autumn 1917 when units were transferred to the Western Front, and explains the numerous violent episodes in some convoys.[115]

There is no evidence that the troops' behaviour was a result of a politicisation of the Eastern army in the wake of the October Revolution. This is apparent in an account describing acts of violence among a trainload of 600 soldiers serving in the 4th and 15th Bavarian Reserve Infantry Regiments on their way to the Western Front in November 1917.[116] While there was no problem getting the men into the wagons, the meagre rations inspired them to fire shots and call out 'hungry' on several occasions during the five-day journey to the German border. The trainload was thus reported as 'out of control'. As a result, a ring of soldiers had surrounded the station in Bebra, though the troops had been calm while travelling through Germany. As is clear from the cordoning off of the station, the station commandant, acting on orders from above, clearly distrusted them. The angry men responded with shouts of 'We're not criminals, we're defending the Fatherland'. After a lengthy stay in Frankfurt am Main, a number of soldiers left the train there. The soldiers in one of the battalions had obviously been assured before the journey began that the convoy was destined for the replacement battalion in Germersheim. In Frankfurt they learned the true destination. The men therefore announced that they were determined 'never again' to cross the Rhine. One of the ringleaders wanted to organise sentinels in the train, so that everyone would leave the train in the Rhenish Palatinate.[117]

Soldiers in the positional divisions saw little fighting. These were territorial and reserve divisions which occupied the same quiet sector of the front for the duration of the war. In the case of the Bavarian army, this applied to the 1st and 6th Territorial Divisions and the 30th and 39th Reserve Divisions. These units occupied passive sectors in the Vosges and Lorraine at the beginning of the war of position - or from February 1915, when the 39th Reserve Division was created. Here, both sides were concerned only with defending the front line.[118] The only changes to affect these units during the war involved subordinate regiments, some of

115. Order issued by the Chief of the General Staff of the Regular Army, 19.11.1917: BHStA/IV, MKr 2324.

116. Report by the train driver, 2.12.1917: BHStA/IV, MKr 2324.

117. Ibid.

118. Bayerisches Staatsarchiv (ed.), *Die Bayern im Großen Kriege*, vol. 1, p. 585.

which were replaced, and the removal of younger men in 1916. From this point on, troops here were mainly occupied with extending the positions, which made it impossible for them to learn how to fight a modern war of position. From autumn 1915 these divisions saw no more heavy fighting.[119] They were engaged only in securing through guard posts the sector of front with which they had been entrusted.

Special attack units were available to divisions for special tasks from the spring of 1916. From September 1915 Captain Willy Rohr worked with the 'Rohr attack battalion', of which he was in charge, to develop new techniques and tactics to overcome the ossified fortification systems characteristic of the war of position. The massed, combined deployment of hand grenades, machine-guns and mortars was intended to enable the shock troops to penetrate the enemy trenches and beat a path for the infantry.[120] Successful tests inspired the Supreme Command to instruct divisions to establish their own attack units for special offensive missions in May 1916. Physically suitable unmarried volunteers aged under 25 were brought in for this. They received separate meals and were released from normal trench duty.[121] The positional divisions also tended to have their own attack companies. Because the ageing troops were in poor physical condition, these took over all tasks other than guard duty and maintaining the positions. This mainly involved periodic patrols to establish the strength and position of the enemy, above all by taking prisoners.[122]

Soldiers' stock comment on short- or long-term postings to quiet sectors was that they had it 'pretty good at the moment'.[123] Beyond this, soldiers had ways of making their sector of the front 'quiet'. During the first weeks of the war of immobility opposing troops fraternised at various sectors of the front and agreed to stop fighting for a while.[124] During the Christmas period of 1914, a cease-fire was generally observed. Troops, particularly German and British ones, met in no man's land.[125]

119. *Histories*, p. 441.

120. Helmuth Gruss, *Aufbau und Verwendung der deutschen Sturmbataillone im Weltkrieg*, Berlin: Junker & Dünnhaupt 1939, pp. 13–35.

121. Ibid., pp. 43, 62, 87.

122. Hans Jordan, *Das K.-B. Landwehr-Infanterie-Regiment Nr. 3*, Munich: Bayerisches Kriegsarchiv 1925, pp. 64, 80.

123. G.T., 17.6.1917: private possession.

124. Decree by the Chief of the General Staff of the Field Army, 28.11.1914: BHStA/IV, GK I.AK Bund 96.

125. Malcolm Brown/Shirley Seaton, *Christmas Truce*, London: Cooper 1984, pp. IX, 210–11.

There were further attempts to fraternise at Christmas 1915. Victor Klemperer, an artilleryman sent to observe in the trenches, described how he incurred the wrath of the infantrymen when a sergeant of the 5th Infantry Division prevented the opposing British troops from visiting the Bavarian trenches.[126]

Soldiers did not immediately fire on every 'enemy' that appeared, despite being ordered to. In February 1916 one infantryman did nothing when he saw an NCO, who had been carrying out repairs on the barbed wire defences, disappearing into the enemy trenches with two Frenchmen. It was unclear whether he was being taken prisoner or deserting. Following this incident, soldiers were ordered to shoot comrades who made contact with the enemy.[127] The two sides also stopped firing in order to recover the wounded or dead from the no man's land between the trenches. The main aim of tacitly agreed, informal cease-fires was, however, to minimise aggressive action. Infantrymen on both sides wished to avoid unnecessary losses and fired less or stopped entirely:

> Dear Martin, things are pretty good again here, we have nice conversations with the Frenchmen. Our boys take cigarettes over there and the Frenchmen bring wine over here. It goes on like this all night. The infantry stops firing all day long, just an officer now and then. If it wasn't for the artillery, we'd soon be out of here. The big-headed (*Groß Köpfigen*) should also serve in the trenches, then the war would soon be over. But there's no sign of them here.[128]

Newly arrived units were informed about such agreements. Even officers serving in the trenches, who generally urged their men to fire on the enemy, did not necessarily report friendly contact. One informal cease-fire, for example, was recorded only when an NCO made use of it to desert late one evening towards the end of May 1917. A lieutenant had rebuked the troops that afternoon, but they continued to exchange cigarettes with the enemy.[129] Tacit agreements evolved into longer-term arrangements, particularly when troops on both sides were forced by adverse weather conditions, above all constant rain, to leave the trenches in order to advance to their positions and expose themselves to the enemy on open ground. If the same units were stationed opposite one another for a lengthy period, such a 'peace of mud' sometimes featured

126. Klemperer, *Curriculum Vitae*, pp. 388–91.
127. BHStA/IV, Militärgericht 6. Ldw.-Div. K 12.
128. Letter from 24.12.1915: private possession.
129. BHStA/IV, MilGer 3361.

fraternisation.[130] Tacit agreements initiated by the infantry were often interrupted or ruined by artillery fire. Yet even those manning the guns could satisfy their superior officers that they were actively engaging the enemy by 'ritualising' their barrages. These were so regular that the other side knew exactly when they would occur:

> Every day at 11am about a dozen shrapnel shells are fired punctually over our weapons. We're used to it. We know which enemy guns are going to target us. We fire back in response an hour later. The French shells do our cannons no harm, the German shells do the French cannons no harm. You fire as a sign that we are still at war, that they are over there, and we are over here.[131]

If, on the other hand, a quiet period was wantonly disturbed by enemy artillery, the response was a 'punitive barrage'.[132] While it is impossible to determine precisely how often tacit agreements were reached, they prove that troops on both sides, regardless of their social background, were generally keen to minimise the violence, in sharp contrast to nationalistic conceptions of the enemy.[133] By making use of the spatial and temporal variations in the intensity of the fighting, the soldiers were in a position to actively help reduce the risk to life and limb, as long as their superiors in the trenches tolerated this.

On the whole, soldiers were not constantly engaged in fighting, nor was this generally as extreme as in the famous battles of matériel. Even among troops serving at the front, a certain number of men were in fact never involved in fighting for long. The extent of enemy fire varied dramatically between different sections of the front or the units usually posted there. If the notion that all soldiers saw active duty between 1914 and 1918 is wrong, the idea that the war at the front was nothing but an unbroken chain of battles is even less correct. Because fighting always subjected the social integration of the military to the most extreme test, the rhythms and distribution of risk were thus central to the cohesion of units.

130. *Der Dolchstoß-Prozeß in München Oktober-November 1925. Eine Ehrenrettung des deutschen Volkes*, Munich: Birk 1925, p. 362.

131. Ernst Toller, *Eine Jugend in Deutschland (1933)*, Reinbek: Rowohlt 1990, p. 50.

132. Jordan, *Landwehr-Infanterie-Regiment Nr. 3*, p. 47.

133. Tony Ashworth, *Trench Warfare 1914-1918. The Live and Let Live System*, London: Macmillan 1980, pp. 129-52, 153-75.

2.3 Discipline and Ideology

The cohesion of the units depended, however, not only on the structures and temporal rhythms characteristic of the social configuration at the front. The military authorities also intervened purposefully to force soldiers to show obedience. The two key means of achieving this were disciplinary measures intended to prevent breaches of duty and open resistance, and the inculcation of ideology by means of propaganda, intended to legitimise the war in the eyes of the soldiers. Disciplinary measures took a variety of forms. These were anchored in the deterrent effect of penalties imposed by court martial and less severe punishment and in the social control exercised by family, neighbours and comrades. The following section explores these measures, ranging from simple warnings by superiors all the way up to death sentences.

To instil discipline, officers were repeatedly urged to make sure that their subordinates conscientiously saluted them, maintained the usual marching discipline and kept their uniforms and items of equipment in order, especially when close to the front.[134] Complaints voiced in the summer of 1918 about undone uniform buttons, an unbuckled belt or failure to stand to attention when officers drove past may seem banal to the point of absurdity given the state the troops were in at the time.[135] However, the insistence on such details shows that superiors thought that they could discipline soldiers by bringing home to them how permanent the control exercised over them was and that they had no choice but to show their superiors respect.

This is also why NCOs were urged not to use the familiar 'du' when addressing the troops, which they often did when interacting with older soldiers, at least when off-duty and sometimes in the trenches.[136] The frequent reading out of the articles of war (*Kriegsartikel*) had a highly intimidating effect. As well as functioning to inform soldiers of their duties, these also listed the severe penalties for offences committed 'in the field' - including the death penalty in extreme cases.[137] This brought home to soldiers their 'lack of free will and powerlessness'.[138] The war

134. GK I. bayer.AK, 22.3.1915: BHStA/IV, GK I.AK Bund 104.

135. AOK 6, 8.5.1918: BHStA/IV, AOK 6 Bund 22.

136. 2. Inf.-Div., 12.12.1917: BHStA/IV, 2. Inf.-Div. Bund 110.

137. Siegfried Pelz, *Die Preussischen und Reichsdeutschen Kriegsartikel. Historische Entwicklung und rechtliche Einordnung*, Hamburg: Selbstverlag 1979, pp. 246-7.

138. Richert, *Beste Gelegenheit*, pp. 135-6.

articles included the specific threat that officers could ensure obedience by using weapons, making soldiers feel highly insecure. In relation to the hardships he had experienced, this made the journeyman-butcher Michael Kappelmeier think that informing a deputy was more likely to help than making a complaint himself: 'Please ask Möggenried whether he could talk to a deputy, nothing has changed with the soldiers' letters. Of course, the sergeant hands them over when he sees fit. We can't do anything about it, they immediately threaten to shoot us.'[139]

Officers and NCOs had a wide range of disciplinary tools at their disposal when dealing with ordinary soldiers on an everyday basis. Many soldiers were intimidated by officers shouting at them, a far from rare event which inspired one miner to comment that, in his experience, 'the secret of military education [consisted of] snarling, snarling and snarling once again'.[140] Before penalising the men in their charge, understanding superior officers first issued paternalistic warnings, urging them 'not to make things difficult' for themselves. They could often obtain the men's obedience by treating them justly.[141] According to a maxim widely accepted among the soldiers, it was advisable to keep as low a profile as possible and to ensure the goodwill of one's superiors through good conduct. Soldiers' trust in this bargain diminished when the authorities failed to keep their side of it: 'I have to tell you that I didn't get furlough. It is sad, being the oldest in the company. My conduct has been good, no penalties as yet. You're poorly rewarded for that in the armed forces.'[142]

Officers could be as flexible and thus unpredictable in using their disciplinary authority as in alternating between threats and warnings. The company, battery and squadron leaders, who were primarily responsible for taking disciplinary action, had a completely free hand when deciding which actions should be categorised as breaches of duty, what kind of punishment was appropriate and how severe it should be. It might take the form of disciplinary measures (withdrawal of privileges such as leave), imposition of special duties (guard duty, drills) or detention.[143] Officers were generally advised to start off with milder forms of punishment and to use more severe forms only if soldiers repeated the offence. In practice, though, many officers tended to impose the severest possible

139. Michael Kappelmeier, 11.10.1914: BHStA/IV, MilGer 6313.

140. Theodor Wagner, 25.12.1916: BArch, 92, 271, fol. 257.

141. Klemperer, *Curriculum Vitae*, p. 406.

142. Stefan Schimmer, 6.6.1915: BHStA/IV, Amtsbibliothek 9584.

143. Heinrich Dietz, *Disziplinarstrafrecht, Beschwerderecht, Ehrengerichtsbarkeit. Grundriß für Krieg und Frieden*, Rastatt: Greiser 1917, pp. 13, 23, 36.

penalties even for minor offences. They thus rapidly undermined the intended 'educational' character of punishment and lost authority among the troops, who felt bitter about unjustifiably stiff penalties. Some soldiers became indifferent to the threat of disciplinary action because they had received humiliating treatment from their superiors:

> I have enough trouble to run away. I don't know which way to turn. You're not a human being at all, you would think we were dogs or pi ... you're simply not a free man here. It's dreadful to think that you can be a soldier for five years and be treated like this for 5.30 marks [a soldier's pay, paid every ten days]. If things go on like this I don't know what will happen, then it's quite possible that I'll be punished. But it makes no difference in a war like this. When you see the young lads that are being promoted and want to put us older men through the mill, and we're supposed to accept that. It makes you want to get out of here. When I get back to the world, I'm going to put on a pince-nez and play the gentleman. We have duty as in the barracks and nothing.[144]

Generally, however, disciplinary action continued to have a deterrent effect. It is very difficult to pin down its extent or how it may have impacted on men from differing social backgrounds, because soldiers rarely articulated their attitude towards it. Tying up was, however, an exception and is a good example of the difficulties involved in exercising disciplinary power. If while at war no suitable place of detention was available, and it appeared inappropriate to postpone punishment, instead of placing soldiers in detention they were tethered to a wall or tree in a standing position for two hours a day.[145] Officers used this form of punishment primarily during the war of movement of 1914, but sometimes thereafter. Soldiers found this punishment extremely humiliating. Some even committed suicide as soon as they had been tethered.[146]

A few months after the war began, the War Ministry therefore received numerous complaints about soldiers tied up because of minor breaches of discipline, even during spells of inclement weather. In December 1915 a survey was carried out among field units asking whether tying up ought to continue. The majority regarded it as useful precisely because of its humiliating character. Tying up was 'generally feared' and thus

144. Letter by a front-line soldier, 1.7.1917: BSB.

145. Heinrich Dietz, *Die Disziplinarstrafordnung für das Heer vom 31. Oktober 1872*, Mannheim: Bensheimer 1909, pp. 239–40.

146. Ulrich/Ziemann, *Frontalltag*, pp. 121–2.

had a deterrent effect because of the injury to one's sense of honour that was associated with it.[147] The War Ministry thus declared itself in favour of going on as before. It did, however, propose that the military authorities be involved as little as possible and that battalion commanders should be empowered to impose such penalties rather than company commanders.[148] Such arguments elucidate the ambivalent nature of tying up. Its powerful deterrent effect stemmed from the fact that most soldiers feared the damage to personal integrity suffered by individuals exposed to the sympathy and mockery of their comrades and superiors while they stood there helpless and motionless. On the other hand, when young, inexperienced officers ordered men to be tied up in an ill-considered, malicious way, this destroyed the frame of reference within which a sense of moral honour made sense, and upon whose validity the effectiveness of tying up, and of the penal system as a whole, ultimately rested.

The war ministries in Berlin and Munich agreed in March 1917 that the tying up of soldiers would be enforced without admitting the public, even the military public, while high-ranking commanding officers would be supervised more closely, thus making this type of punishment less severe.[149] Parliamentarians in the Imperial Diet were persistently critical of such punishment, finally causing the military authorities to abolish it entirely in May 1917. In August 1918 Hindenburg pushed for the reintroduction of the measure, in line with the supposed wishes of the army leadership. The Prussian war minister, responsible for disciplinary measures, rejected this request.[150]

Alongside the threat of punishment, families also exercised social control, making serious disciplinary offences less likely. Directly and indirectly, their relatives prevented soldiers from committing crimes. Parents and wives sometimes urged soldiers absent without leave to return to their units. The families of soldiers known to have been placed in detention or sentenced to a lengthy spell in prison were gravely ashamed, particularly in rural areas. The relatives of such soldiers often lectured them about their duties and the moral taint which they had caused. In August 1917, for example, a basket-maker from a village background, who had refused to take his position after repeatedly reporting sick, was warned by his sister in a letter:

147. 6. Ldw.-Div., 25.12.1915: BHStA/IV, MKr 11231.

148. K.M., 18.1.1916: BHStA/IV, MKr 11231.

149. Decree of 21.3.1917: BHStA/IV, MKr 11232.

150. WUA, vol. 11/1, pp. 393–6.

> Dear Ludwig, what are you thinking of? Please don't do anything like that, do your duty like anyone else and write more often too. You're better off taking your position than being locked up. Mother is up all night worrying about you because of these things you're doing. The others have to do it too. We feel ashamed. So dear Ludwig do as we say. The convulsion won't last for ever.[151]

Their mothers' reaction, which presumably consisted of a mixture of concern and accusations, was a particularly awkward problem for younger soldiers. Farm labourer Jakob Wirth, arrested in December 1915 for absence without leave, frankly admitted to his brother, who had also been called up, that even a lengthy sentence was 'fine' by him, as he had had his 'fill' of being at the front. Meanwhile, he assured his sister, whom he authorised specially to explain things to their mother, that it was 'not so bad' and that other soldiers were also in detention.[152]

Alongside disciplinary procedures, offences and crimes liable for punishment according to the military penal code were dealt with by the court martial. Long prison sentences had a significantly greater deterrent effect than disciplinary measures, especially because soldiers could never be sure during the war whether an amnesty would smooth their way out of prison or not once the war was over. The Eisner government and the Council of People's Representatives (*Rat der Volksbeauftragten*) did in fact announce two comprehensive amnesties shortly after the war ended.[153] As with disciplinary procedures, the preventive effect of judicial punishment also diminished over time. For individual soldiers who were caught up in the machinery of military justice because of what they felt were minor offences, arrest and the prospect of a lengthy prison sentence were disheartening experiences that laid bare their powerlessness *vis-à-vis* the system of repression within the armed forces:

> My dear wife! This is to let you know that I entered the prison of the county court on Saturday and indeed in such a way that the people in Kaiserslautern spent a lot of time on it with an NCO and two men. I was treated just like a common criminal - that's my reward for risking my stupid neck. But, my dear wife, don't worry yourself about it, it's not so bad. I should have been returning to the field on Friday, but I want nothing to do with it. They wanted to shut me in like an animal and I don't want that. Let them do as they see fit, it's becoming a bloody scandal.[154]

151. Marie Blunder, 20.8.1917: BHStA/IV, Militärgericht 1. Res.-Div. B 32.
152. Jakob Wirth, 9.12.1915: Ulrich/Ziemann, *Frontalltag*, p. 165.
153. *Armee-Verordnungsblatt* 52 (1918), pp. 717-22, 731-5.
154. Josef Wahl, 1.9.1918: BHStA/IV, MilGer 7365.

For a large number of soldiers, prison sentences lost their deterrent effect as the war dragged on. Towards the end of 1915, during disputes over duties or when soldiers were put in detention while awaiting trial, commanding officers and officers involved in judicial proceedings were confronted for the first time by men who openly declared that they would not mind in the least 'doing some solid time'.[155] Shortly after serving their sentence or while in detention awaiting trial, some soldiers also stated candidly in letters that their punishment would offer them the welcome opportunity to escape the dangers of the front line for a lengthy period.[156] This view was expressed in June 1917 by a soldier stationed at the Eastern Front. His letter demonstrates once again that the loss of honour associated with punishment declined during the second half of the war. Even then, though, some soldiers still found a long stint in prison an awful prospect, fearing that it would make them 'miserable for the rest of our lives':

> Let them do what they want, I'll accept any punishment. It's no dishonour to be punished by the armed forces and no sentence could be harder than the one we've been serving all this time - life in the trenches. You stop caring about anything here and would be glad of a couple of weeks in detention just to get away from this unbelievable, unnecessary grind for a while, and not to see the outrageous injustices that we have to suffer, all of which you have to accept without a word, because all the institutions and laws are used against us and after all we don't want to be miserable for the rest of our lives. What sort of slavery have we ended up in, we who used to feel like free men and would never have thought that we'd let even the slightest insult or other injustice pass without doing something about it. How much longer?[157]

In any event, the judicial authorities, especially of active divisions under a great deal of pressure, often gave soldiers a deferred sentence to avoid unnecessarily depriving units of men fit for service. From April 1915 it was possible to defer sentences on the condition that the soldiers involved proved themselves by resuming front-line service and on pain of further punishment. The authorities, however, feared that those whose lack of discipline had already been noted would negatively influence their fellows if they remained in the unit. Sentences were thus deferred in ever fewer cases.[158]

155. III./Inf.-Leib-Rgt. 20.7.1917: BHStA/IV, MKr 14160.

156. Georg Heinle, 28.7.1917: Ulrich/Ziemann, *Frontalltag*, p. 165.

157. Soldier's letter from the field, 25.6.1917: BSB.

158. Decree issued by the War Ministry on 18.8.1918: BHStA/IV, GK I.AK, Bund 104.

Towards the end of the war, officers often stepped up their threats of punishment and punished their subordinates more harshly. Even this, though, could no longer stop the army from disintegrating. In the summer of 1918, a quick succession of brief decrees from the war ministries in Berlin and Munich urged field commanders to use the means of coercion at their disposal 'ruthlessly'. Should soldiers refuse to take their positions or march back into the field, officers were to make use of their right to use a weapon. Particularly in cases of explicit insubordination when fighting the enemy, the courts should not hesitate to sentence men to death. It is impossible to reconstruct precisely how the commanders in the field responded to these instructions or how many executions they carried out. The Imperial Archive of the *Reichswehr* announced during the Weimar Republic that 150 death sentences were imposed in the German army as a whole, of which forty-eight were carried out.[159] However, an array of scattered evidence shows that soldiers were indeed sentenced to death or executed, suggesting that this figure is far too low. In October 1918, for example, the commander *Ober-Ost* in occupied Russia recounted a mutiny in a convoy of the 1st Bavarian *Landsturm* infantry regiment in Luck bound for the Western Front, during which superior officers were physically attacked. Two NCOs and two of the regular soldiers involved were condemned to death.[160] In the summer and autumn of 1918, however, most commanders must have realised that trying to force soldiers to obey by shooting some of them would make open rebellion more rather than less likely. Nonetheless, to intimidate troops officers would sometimes announce that in cases of collective resistance 'the most likely candidate would be singled out and shot'.[161]

The disciplinary system probably intimidated soldiers a great deal, though the evidence for this is generally indirect, consisting of the fact that the system had less and less impact over time. Soldiers were probably increasingly less afraid of a term of imprisonment imposed by the court martial than of disciplinary punishment of offences. A lengthy stint in prison initially had a powerful deterrent effect, in part because it was impossible to judge what the consequences for civilian life would be. From 1917 on, however, as mentioned above, an increasing number of soldiers saw it as a sure-fire way to escape the dangers of front-line deployment. Meanwhile, the small number of officers genuinely concerned

159. WUA, vol. 11/2, pp. 63, 385–7.

160. Telegramm Ober-Ost, 20.10.1918: BHStA/IV, MKr 2325; see Ziemann, Fahnenflucht, p. 123.

161. WUA, vol. 11/1, p. 329.

about the well-being of their subordinates and keen to win their trust had a major advantage: they could implement their disciplinary authority as they saw fit. Punishment was not the only means of discipline available to them. Officers had a whole range of options at their disposal, such as warnings, intimidation and ultimately punishment; these they could deploy in a flexible and sometimes unpredictable way to maintain their authority. In this way, at least some soldiers could be forced to respect their superiors and obey their orders for a considerable time.[162] The disciplinary straitjacket constraining the troops offered them almost no opportunity to express themselves and the right of appeal was largely ineffective. Together, these factors effectively nipped serious resistance in the bud for a long time.

Officers and the military authorities strove to prevent disciplinary offences by threatening to punish soldiers and indeed doing so. This, however, was just one, more traditional, aspect of attempts to secure hegemony within the armed forces. Warfare was becoming increasingly mechanised, while there was an intimate 'interaction between home front and field army'.[163] It was thus no longer enough for soldiers to obey their superiors' commands more or less willingly. The popular mood at the front and home front was itself a vital resource for fighting the war. If mobilisation was to succeed, people in general had to be willing to face further hardships. Discipline had for long been maintained unquestioningly. Yet front-line soldiers began to reject the regime's conception of the war, underpinning increasing discontent. The beginnings of this discord and its consequences had in fact been apparent since early 1916, triggering the first counter-measures. The third Supreme Command was first to acknowledge the seriousness of the situation. In 1917, with the goal of a victorious peace in mind, it attempted to counter the politicisation of the longing for peace, which also affected front-line soldiers, by means of increased propaganda. It hoped to promote the 'victory consciousness' which would smooth the transition to offensive activities.[164]

162. In a brilliant synthesis, Ulrich Bröckling, *Disziplin. Soziologie und Geschichte militärischer Gehorsamsproduktion*, Munich: Wilhelm Fink 1997, pp. 199–240, has rightly stressed the importance of psychiatric methods as a means of enhancing discipline during the First World War. Yet these new approaches did not, I would argue, make traditional methods like exercise dispensable.

163. Decree issued by the War Ministry on 1.2.1916: Deist, *Militär*, pp. 300–2.

164. Ibid., p. 845.

Soldiers' increasingly critical view of the war first influenced those back home when they went home on leave. In February 1916 the war minister felt it necessary, in the light of soldiers' descriptions of the shortcomings of army life, which 'poisoned the atmosphere of entire villages', to urge commanders in the field to help by holding talks, educating soldiers and warning them not to criticise.[165] Yet front-line commanders were quite unwilling to acknowledge this problem. Most insisted that it was people back home who were having a bad influence on front-line soldiers. They claimed that replacement troops and those home on leave were returning to the front in a bad state of mind because of their relatives' dire economic situation and 'deliberate stirring', making it more relevant to educate those at home.[166] The military authorities back home and attentive observers of the popular mood were, however, in no doubt: 'You can't separate the mood at the front from that at home.'[167]

The War Ministry continued to be disturbed by the negative impact of the tales told by soldiers on leave. In August 1917 they again urged Bavarian units in the field to warn soldiers, before they departed for home, against making such statements and to encourage reliable soldiers to try to improve the mood back home through positive stories.[168] Despite these efforts, the unrest that front-line soldiers brought with them was a problem that refused to go away for the civilian authorities; educational work failed to solve it.[169] Soldiers' letters were supervised by censors. When home on leave, they could say what they liked about their feelings and the negative aspects of military service without having to worry about possible disciplinary measures. These accounts had an enormous impact. People 'accepted and believed them like gospel' because soldiers had first-hand experience and they distrusted official reports.[170] Civilians told one village priest in Lower Bavaria who criticised the stories told by men home on leave that 'he knew nothing and should stand by the Lord.'[171]

Soldiers on leave talked about what they had experienced first-hand. People were captivated by tales of serious tensions between Prussian and

165. Decree issued by the War Ministry on 1.2.1916: Deist, *Militär*, pp. 300-2, quote p. 300.

166. GK I.AK, 23.9.1917: BHStA/IV, MKr 2337.

167. Press Office of the War Ministry, 1.8.1918: BHStA/IV, MKr 2338.

168. Decree issued by the War Ministry on 11.8.1917: Deist, *Militär*, pp. 855-7.

169. WUA, vol. 11/1, pp. 56-8.

170. Letter by a priest from Middle Fra`nconia, 20.7.1916: BHStA/IV, HS 2348.

171. Sulzbach parish office, 12.6.1916: ABP, DekA II, Fürstenzell 12/I.

Bavarian troops and rumours of massive casualties.[172] Soldiers on leave 'whipped up class hatred',[173] corroding loyalty towards the traditional civilian authorities. Aside from being aimed at priests, criticisms initially focused on official measures to control the agricultural economy. Soldiers on furlough also cast doubt on the need for a Bavarian or Imperial monarch. In addition to disseminating the view, common in the autumn of 1918, that victory was impossible and the war already lost, soldiers on leave created a 'revolutionary mood' in the countryside.[174] Their unvarnished accounts, which had a long-term impact, and their special authority in all matters relating to the war, thus contributed substantially to undermining the legitimacy of the state among the rural populace.

Soldiers also fuelled dissatisfaction among the civilian population about war loans, triggering efforts to instruct the troops by means of 'enlightening work' (*Aufklärungsarbeit*), as the official euphemism had it. Subscription forms were issued twice a year from September 1914; because the Imperial government had refrained from raising taxes drastically, these loans were the key means of financing the war. In addition, over the course of the war the success of the loans became symbolic of the general population's willingness to stay the course and identify with the national war effort. In line with their financial importance and potential to mobilise, the subscription periods were from the outset often accompanied by comprehensive propaganda measures, implemented with the help of the daily press, posters and public presentations.[175]

The loans were thus anchored in the popular consciousness as symbols of the German people's will to stay the course. Yet this caused problems for the authorities. At the front, where the consequences of ongoing war were most palpable on a daily basis, most soldiers became critical of the war and thus rejected the loans. When subscriptions were being issued for the fourth loan in March 1916, the civilian administrative authorities reported that in a number of rural districts front-line soldiers' letters were urging their relatives not to subscribe so that the war would end soon.[176] In the run-up to the fifth loan, the Ministry of the Interior thus requested that the War Ministry help alleviate this problem by censoring soldiers' letters and educating the troops. The War Ministry responded by referring

172. Garrison Eldest Bad Reichenhall, 23.5.1918: BHStA/IV, stv. GK I.AK 1965.
173. BA Tölz, 27.10.1916: BHStA/IV, stv. GK I.AK 1946.
174. WB BA Miesbach, 20.10.1918: BHStA/IV, stv. GK I.AK 1970.
175. Albrecht, *Landtag*, pp. 199-206.
176. Minn, 15.3.1916: BHStA/IV, MKr 2330.

to the letter censorship already being carried out and the measures ordained at the start of the year intended to influence those home on leave. At the same time, the Deputy General Commands were asked to identify those spreading such views, in collaboration with the civilian authorities. Instruction within the replacement army was intended to encourage soldiers to oppose rumours critical of war loans.[177]

Soldiers in the field were also instructed in the importance of the fifth war loan in the autumn of 1916, in one army division at least.[178] The Bavarian War Ministry was, however, unable to decide which measures to ordain in relation to the loans in the field army, suspecting that conditions there made it highly unlikely that education would meet with success.[179] The authorities in the field saw references to the gloomy mood among the troops in their charge as unwelcome interference in their affairs.[180] Further measures in the replacement army seemed more promising. These were ordained in September 1916 for the fifth loan, since soldiers back home had also agitated against the war loans.[181]

Nonetheless, in autumn 1916 many NCOs and soldiers continued to urge their relatives to refuse to subscribe for a war loan, either in letters or while on furlough. Particularly among the prosperous farmers of the Rottal in Lower Bavaria, communication from the field helped ensure almost total rejection of war loans until the end of the war. The military authorities, however, believed that their promotional work was having some impact and thus decided to institutionalise it.[182] A liaison officer was assigned to every section of the replacement army able to appoint suitable assistants. Every Deputy General Command and the three technical inspectorates were furnished with a representative. While loans were being issued, lectures were to be held each week, before a civilian audience if desired. Any person or soldier's letter criticising the loans was to be reported to the War Ministry immediately. The Bavarian units in the field were also informed of these measures. A War Ministry

177. K.M., 1.9.1916: BHStA/IV, stv. GK I. AK 916.

178. Decree by the Armee-Abteilung B, 19.9.1916: BHStA/IV, 6. Ldw.-Div. Bund 56.

179. Memorandum by Press Office of the War Ministry, 15.9.1916: BHStA/IV, MKr 2330.

180. Memorandum of the Armee-Abteilung I K.M., 6.6.1916: BHStA/IV, MKr 2330.

181. Decree issued by the War Ministry on 12.9.1916: BHStA/IV, stv. GK I. AK 916.

182. K.M., 27.12.1916: BHStA/IV, stv. GK I. AK 916.

declaration underlined that it would be 'of tremendous value if instructive promotional work could be initiated at this stage among field units as well'. How best to carry out such educational work and what form it should take were, however, left to the authorities in the field.[183] Deputy General Commands in Baden, Württemberg and Prussia started educating replacement army troops as early as spring 1917. The organisation created in Bavaria in early 1917 for the sixth loan was smoothly converted into the 'Patriotic Instruction' programme (*Vaterländischer Unterricht*) in the summer of the same year.[184]

'Patriotic Instruction' was finally institutionalised across the board in the summer of 1917 at the instigation of the Supreme Command.[185] From this point forward, Section IIIb of the Supreme Command was in charge of propaganda among the troops. It made use of the War Press Office (*Kriegspresseamt*), established in October 1915, to pursue its aims. The Army Supreme Commands (*Armeeoberkommandos*) in the field and the Deputy General Commands back home were responsible for implementation and budgeted for full-time workers.[186] The Bavarian military attempted to prevent superior Prussian authorities from interfering in practical activities within the divisions.[187] By the middle of October 1918, every division had been furnished with an instructional officer. Lectures, films and plays, sermons by military chaplains and a vast array of printed material were all used to instruct soldiers.[188]

In practice, instructional activities in the field army faced a whole range of obstacles and ultimately failed. Embedding such activities in military service made them feel like 'orders', causing soldiers to reject them.[189] In any case, brochures and instructional officers who travelled around as 'itinerant preachers' made 'no impression' on soldiers.[190] To

183. Decree issued by the War Ministry on 13.1.1917: BHStA/IV, stv. GK I. AK 916.

184. K.M., 30.7.1917: BHStA/IV, stv. GK I. AK 916.

185. Deist, *Militär*, pp. 835-7, 841-8, 861.

186. In Bavaria, the instructional work of the Deputy General Commands was under the overall control of the War Ministry (Press Office): Doris Fischer, *Die Münchener Zensurstelle während des Ersten Weltkrieges. Alfons Falkner von Sonneburg als Pressereferent im bayerischen Kriegsministerium in den Jahren 1914-1918/19*, Munich: Selbstverlag 1973, pp. 90, 103.

187. Note by the Press Office of the War Ministry, 3.10.1917: BHStA/IV, MKr 2335.

188. 'Guiding principles' laid down on 29.7.1917: Deist, *Militär*, p. 844.

189. 6. Inf.-Div., 3.11.1917: BHStA/IV, MKr 2338.

190. Press Office of the War Ministry, 3.10.1917: BHStA/IV, MKr 2335.

help them identify emerging rumours and critical opinions among the troops, officers charged with instructional work made use of ordinary soldiers or NCO liaison officers. If the latter belonged to the educated classes, however, they ran the risk of being seen as 'informers' or simply being ignored by their comrades.[191] Because so many soldiers in the field wanted a peace of understanding, Patriotic Instruction, which propagated offensive war aims until the last months of the war in many units, was bound to be rejected. In the 9th Army, soldiers 'very often asked' about war aims. They were told that 'every officer and musketeer [must] be satisfied' with the peace that Hindenburg wanted.[192] Yet it seems that front-line troops' indifference and disinterest were the greatest obstacles to educational work, as is apparent *ex negativo* in soldiers' letters: 'Soldiers criticise every military institution. Yet there is almost no criticism of the activities of the instructional or educational officers (*Aufklärungsoffiziere*) in soldiers' letters. It thus seems that this institution is failing to connect properly with the common man.'[193]

The instructional activities within the replacement army are well documented and provide a nuanced insight into why propaganda failed to sway the troops; the reasons were partly social in nature, and partly anchored in the realities of military life. Military instructors' reports also elucidate how the mood among the soldiers developed over time.[194] The social background of the liaison officers within individual units posed a problem. Practical qualifications were needed to promote war loans among the troops and explain how to apply for one, and most liaison officers were thus bank employees, lawyers or businessmen. Their bourgeois origins distanced them from the troops. On top of the problematic relations between the ranks - most liaison officers were reserve officers - this made it harder to have an open discussion and thus to recognise and challenge critical voices.[195] Many liaison officers thus used liaison assistants who were ordinary soldiers. Because they knew Bavarian dialect, they were thought most likely to gain soldiers' trust, particularly in units with many farmers.[196]

191. Officer with responsibility for instruction in the Prussian 18th Infantry Division, 7.6.1918: BHStA/IV, AOK 6 Bund 121.

192. Chief of the General Staff of the Field Army IIIb, 4 November 1917: BHStA/IV, MKr 2336.

193. BA/MA, W-10/50794, fol. 78.

194. Documents in: BHStA/IV, stv. GK I.AK 1980, 1981, 2400-2412.

195. K.M., 13.1.1917: BHStA/IV, stv. GK I.AK 916.

196. Liaison officer, Augsburg *Landsturm* Infantry Replacement Battalion I B, 18, 29.9.1917: BHStA/IV, stv. GK I.AK 2401.

Instructional efforts were most likely to bear fruit through private conversations, and instructors' lack of familiarity with the troops thus had negative consequences. When the subject of loans was discussed in large groups, the few soldiers willing to subscribe were prevented from openly expressing their views by the 'gibes and teasing' of their comrades.[197] For this reason, and because textual and visual materials were used very little - some promotional posters were torn down - the focus was necessarily on conversations with individual soldiers during the subscription period.[198] As with official announcements and military communiqués generally, soldiers placed little trust in the reliability of the information they received.[199]

Soldiers were also granted leave in order to get them to subscribe for war loans. The authorities issued instructions stating that leave must not be granted to reward soldiers for voluntarily subscribing, but only to consult with relatives and carry out the necessary financial transactions. This was, however, a purely formal distinction. One liaison officer openly complained that in his unit 'leave could [not] be granted in line with how many men subscribed as in other units'.[200] Leave was the one sure means of repeatedly mobilising soldiers to subscribe for war loans.[201] The many farmers in the replacement army, however, could not be enticed by the prospect of leave; they were already well provided for as far as this valuable commodity was concerned, especially in spring and autumn, the very periods when attempts to get soldiers to subscribe for war loans were in full swing. The farmers thus escaped being 'worked on' by the liaison officers; the number of those interested in 'Patriotic Instruction' was very small.[202]

The liaison officers' work was also hampered by the fact that the slogans they uttered urging the men to stay the course could easily be associated with the goals of the Fatherland Party. If liaison officers failed to proceed with the 'utmost caution', they might quickly arouse

197. Liaison officer, Landsberg Reserve Field Hospital, 27.3.1918: BHStA/IV, stv. GK I.AK 2407.

198. Liaison officer, Neuburg Reserve Field Hospital, 27.6.1918: BHStA/IV, stv. GK I.AK 2410.

199. Liaison officer, E./R.I.R. 12, 11.12.1917: BHStA/IV, stv. GK I.AK 2378.

200. Liaison officer, Ingolstadt Anti-aircraft Section, 23.8.1917: BHStA/IV, stv. GK I.AK 2400.

201. Minutes of the liaison officers' meeting in Kempten, 29.9.1917: BHStA/IV, stv. GK I.AK 2396.

202. E./L.I.R. 3, 29.9.1917: BHStA/IV, stv. GK I.AK 2401.

suspicions of political bias.[203] Though officers tasked with instructional work were expressly forbidden from agitating for the Fatherland Party or discussing war aims, some still did so.[204] Given that soldiers tended to reject annexationist viewpoints, this could destroy their authority entirely. Even the retention of Alsace and Lorraine had to be argued for in lectures. It seemed superfluous to the troops.[205] Influences flowing from the front line caused trust in the war loans and rural civilians' willingness to subscribe for them to fall steadily. When subscribed for on a large scale in the countryside, they were generally transacted by the loan societies (*Darlehenskassen*), at times over the heads of their members. Some farmers withdrew their deposits as a result.[206]

The younger troops were generally more receptive to attempts to educate them, while the older farmers in particular proved both ignorant of abstract economic realities and generally unteachable.[207] On the whole, the propagation of ideological aims and convictions failed to motivate soldiers. The fact that those tasked with educational work used straightforward force or material benefits to win cooperation demonstrates that attempts to adapt the military system to the exigencies of modern ideological warfare succeeded only in part. Patriotic Instruction was irrelevant to farmers' interests, except for practical problems. In the field army, in particular, a lack of interest prevailed. This suggests that, for the soldiers, grappling with topical political issues - their decisive rejection of annexationist views aside - was of merely secondary significance.

203. Liaison officer, 1. E./1. I.R., 28.1.1918: BHStA/IV, stv. GK I.AK 2405.

204. Deist, *Militär*, pp. 862, 872.

205. Liaison officer, Reserve-Lazarett Munich P, 2.12.1917: BHStA/IV, stv. GK I. AK 2403.

206. Stv. GK I.AK, 8.10.1917: BHStA/IV, MKr 2336.

207. Liaison officer, E./9. Field Artillery Regiment, 27.8.1918: BHStA/IV, stv. GK I.AK 1980.

3

War Weariness, 1914–18

A war lasting more than four years inevitably made great physical and psychological demands on soldiers. The extent to which such burdens undermined the legitimacy of military authority depended largely on the professional skills of the officer corps and military leaders' willingness to tackle the potential for conflict as thoroughly as possible.[1] The inevitability of the German army's defeat can no doubt be explained by reference to the superior material resources enjoyed by the Entente powers.[2] The following analyses, however, are best understood in the light of political forces within the Wilhelmine Empire which opposed and obstructed the reform of outmoded military structures and remits. The hardships and discontent in the army, which peaked in 1918, arose within this framework. During the course of the war, some high-ranking Bavarian officers and the war ministers Kreß von Kressenstein and, later, von Hellingrath recognised that the people would make sacrifices only if they were given greater opportunities to participate politically and the burdens were shared out fairly.[3] Such views were not reflected in the lives of ordinary soldiers, which continued to be shaped by the approach of the Supreme Command. In any case, given the powers enjoyed by the Supreme Command, efforts to maintain the pretence that Bavaria enjoyed sovereign rights over troops in the field seemed quite out of touch.

1. Comparison with the reforms introduced in the French army in response to the crisis of 1917, intended to deal with the shortcomings attacked by the mutineers, is illuminating. See Guy Pedroncini, *Les Mutineries de 1917*, Paris: PUF 1967, pp. 234–9.

2. Baldur Kaulisch, Strategie der Niederlage. Betrachtungen zur deutschen Frühjahrsoffensive 1918, *Zeitschrift für Militärgeschichte* 7 (1968), pp. 661–75.

3. Deist, *Militär*, pp. 492–7, 700–2.

3.1 Injustice

The division of the army into officers and ordinary soldiers threw up much potential for social conflict, destabilising the social configuration of the military. This conflict was rooted, first of all, in the fact that the borderline between the two groups could be crossed only rarely, even in war. The active officer corps suffered major losses in the first year of the war. Yet while the military authorities were aware how useful it could be to promote NCOs with front-line experience, it remained very difficult to rise to the rank of reserve lieutenant without a one-year-volunteer certificate (*Einjährig-Freiwilligen Zeugnis*), which required completion of secondary education.[4] A mere ninety-one NCOs without this certificate were promoted to the rank of officer in 1914-18 in the Bavarian army, mostly for bravery.[5] Instead, NCOs performing the duties of officers without the certificate were made *Feldwebelleutnant*. They still ranked below the lowest rank of reserve officer and were 'second-class officers' only.[6]

Officers enjoyed not only the power of command, but also a range of quotidian privileges. The major sacrifices and dangers which front-line service entailed made ordinary soldiers all the more aware that their relationship with officers was an unequal one. The social exclusivity of the officer corps persisted during the war, encouraging them to seal themselves off from their subordinates' dire circumstances and to make blatant use of their privileges. Ordinary soldiers condemned officers for abusing their position in a huge number of different ways. Some offences, however, riled them more than others. They felt bitter about their wages, very low in comparison with those of officers. An ordinary soldier received 15.90 marks per month, while even a lieutenant got 310 marks.[7] Rural soldiers also complained about this disparity, especially when they felt that officers were failing to earn their pay by performing their duties well or shining on the field of battle.[8] The 'issue of food and drink' played the 'most important role in the life of the soldier' by a long way.[9] Following the advance of autumn 1914, during which the troops

4. WUA, vol. 11/1, pp. 108-10.

5. WUA, vol. 11/2, p. 36.

6. Wiegand Schmidt-Richberg, Die Regierungszeit Wilhelms II., in: Militärgeschichtliches Forschungsamt (ed.), *Handbuch zur deutschen Militärgeschichte*, vol. 3, Frankfurt/M. 1968, pp. 9-155; quote in WUA, vol. 11/2, p. 36.

7. WUA, vol. 11/1, pp. 111-13; vol. 11/2, pp. 85-6.

8. Michael Kitzelmann, 21.4.1918: StaA Regensburg, NL Heim 1316.

9. Report by postal surveillance office of the 5th Army, 12.7.1917: BA/MA, W-10/50794, fol. 14.

could still requisition large quantities of food from the occupied area, the army depended almost entirely on deliveries from home. The soldiers' state of nutrition thus worsened to the same extent that it did at home. However, because the army took priority, soldiers' rations were always more generous than those of civilians entitled to assistance from the state.[10]

Soldiers began to complain about insufficient rations as early as 1915 and 1916.[11] A survey of post carried out in the 6th Army in spring 1916 showed that 'the majority of complaints [related] to lack of food'.[12] From the end of March 1917, the daily bread ration was reduced by almost a third.[13] This measure laid bare the general lack of food in the army. It inspired soldiers to make particularly malicious remarks about social inequality, which the war had intensified, and to analyse it critically:

> I also have to tell you that our rations have been cut again. Earlier we got half a slice of bread every day and now we get one third, but I don't think they'll treat us like this for long otherwise it's going all wrong. The men are already raging about it. They should stop the war if they aren't up to it any more. We would be truly happy if the pain was over at last. It's not as if they're achieving anything, apart from getting rid of the poor, and the poor soldiers are the ones who suffer. They're getting so done in that soon none will be left standing. And why? Because they're getting nothing to eat while the rich and powerful eat as they want and laugh themselves silly. That's what the war is now, because the rich are lining their pockets and the little people do the dirty work. But they'll see when the war's finally over, what's happening then, because we're not so stupid now, charging into the fire so idiotically like we did at first. The war has made us smarter.[14]

Meals were monotonous and of low nutritional value, making soldiers' experience of food still less edifying.[15] The 'jam' provided for evening meals from 1915 on in place of butter or other types of fat was notorious and often satirised in soldiers' songs. From 1917 many soldiers serving in the field army on both the Eastern and Western Front were constantly

10. Daniel, *Arbeiterfrauen*, pp. 200–1.

11. Georg Saam, 22.4.1915: BHStA/IV, MilGer 6409.

12. GK XXVII. Res.-Korps, 15.5.1916: SHStAD, Kriegsarchiv (P) 20155, fol. 16.

13. Erich Ludendorff (ed.), *Urkunden der Obersten Heeresleitung über ihre Tätigkeit 1916/18*, Berlin: Mittler 1921, pp. 195–6.

14. Letter of 17.4.1917: BSB.

15. Wolfgang Steinitz, *Deutsche Volkslieder demokratischen Charakters aus sechs Jahrhunderten*, vol. 2, Berlin: Akademie-Verlag 1963, pp. 363–7.

hungry. This is clearly apparent in reports by the postal surveillance offices as well as numerous soldiers' letters. Soldiers were exhausted much of the time as a result of this poor nutrition and because of the severe physical strains they were under, particularly when constructing positions. For the spring offensive of 1918, assault divisions were thus furnished with extra food and drink and tobacco.[16] The persistent lack of food made inequalities in provisioning stand out all the more. Soldiers were particularly bitter about the way officers made use of their privileges without a second thought. As early as the war of movement, soldiers complained that their superiors took the lion's share of charitable gifts, as well as food requisitioned or sent from home.[17] Such practices began seriously to damage officers' reputations, however, only from 1916, when there was an overall lack of food. Towards the end of 1916, the quartermaster-general felt compelled to issue a decree to stop the common practice of kitchen staff preparing larger and better portions for officers, exceeding even the field rations to which they were entitled.[18]

Soldiers were not critical only of officers' rations, however. Farmers were also targets of their ire. Peasant soldiers in the field received large food packages from their relatives on a regular basis; up to one pound in weight could be posted free of charge.[19] Butter was sent in such quantities that senders fell foul of the delivery quotas in the controlled economy (*Zwangswirtschaft*). Soldiers from farming families wrote home requesting a food package whenever rations were scanty. These regular deliveries were all the more valuable given that the personal goods which troops could buy to supplement their rations were very expensive.[20] Weekly food packages helped farmers compensate for the meagre fat rations in particular, especially those who received such packages even more frequently.[21] Given how serious the shortages were, soldiers were greatly concerned that the unfair provision of food be rectified. Farmers, however, occupied a fairly privileged position within the struggle for food. They were thus criticised by their 'comrades', furious about the provisions they received from home:

16. WUA, vol. 11/1, p. 124.
17. Michael Kappelmeier, 11.10.1914: BHStA/IV, MilGer 6313.
18. Decree issued by the quartermaster-general, 26.12.1916: BHStA/IV, HS 2348.
19. Garrison Eldest Kaufbeuren, 17.12.1916: BHStA/IV, stv. GK I.AK 1948.
20. Joseph Reininger, 3.11.1916: private possession.
21. Stefan Schimmer, 15.2.1915: BHStA/IV, Amtsbibliothek 9584.

> I know what it means to be hungry. I've exchanged my things for bread and potatoes so I could have a decent meal now and then, and here a decent meal means a banquet. How painful it is to watch while others open up their packages full of good things and gobble them down, while I have no hope of receiving a package like that. I have a special idea of what comradeship means. Worst of all are the rich farmers who stuff themselves full. If there was anything edible to be bought, they are ready to snatch it away from the poor devils' mouths at a moment's notice. I would never have expected such a low cast of mind.[22]

Both at the front and in the replacement army, their fellow soldiers commonly responded to farmers' uncomradely behaviour by stealing food from them.[23] While farmers managed to avoid the problem of food shortages by drawing on their family resources, they could do very little about the inconsiderate and even abusive behaviour meted out by many of their superiors. Farmers as a professional group were denigrated by training staff and officers from their training days in the replacement units onwards. Insults included 'peasant pig', 'stinking peasant' and 'peasant head'.[24] Some officers punished unpopular soldiers or those who had made a bad impression while on duty in a particularly humiliating way by making them step forward. Soldiers then had to report for duty by stating 'I am an ass' or 'I am a sleepyhead'.[25] At the front, too, ordinary soldiers were 'addressed and insulted in a disheartening manner' by the officers. Given how close they were to danger, this made them all the more bitter.[26]

Officers continued not only to insult and offend soldiers once the war had started, but also to physically abuse them. In the replacement army, officers 'repeatedly' set about soldiers with a riding crop or whip while on duty.[27] Even at the front, soldiers were physically assaulted by officers and NCOs.[28] It was above all their fear that officers would object to their approach that inspired NCOs to force men to perform drills with all the - often extreme - bullying that this involved. Especially before units were inspected by the commander or other high-ranking officers, soldiers

22. Letter by a reinforcement soldier, 22.1.1918: BSB.
23. Klemperer, *Curriculum Vitae*, pp. 403-4.
24. MdR Matzinger, 28.1.1916: BHStA/IV, MKr 13348.
25. Stv. GK I.AK, 9.12.1915: BHStA/IV, MKr 11104.
26. Johann Preisinger, 31.10.1914: BHStA/IV, MilGer 6382.
27. K.M., 13.12.1916: BHStA/IV, MKr 11100.
28. BHStA/IV, MilGer 6235, 6372, 6449, 6489.

were forced to perform drills until they were 'wringing with sweat'.[29] It was often NCOs and lance corporals who misused their authority. Within the hierarchy of command, however, the superior officers ultimately bore responsibility for this; they failed to take action to stamp out unfair treatment as requested by their own superiors. In 1918 the War Ministry also underlined the connection between the military authorities' demand for discipline and increasing attacks by superiors. A decree intended to 'improve discipline' impressed upon the replacement army authorities the need to counter the resulting increase in improper treatment.[30]

Soldiers had the right to complain about unjust or even degrading treatment or abuse by their superiors. However, the regulations governing how to make a formally correct complaint were extremely complex. Soldiers could, moreover, be punished if their complaint was thought to be ill-considered, negligent or incorrectly presented, or if it was handed in late.[31] The War Ministry soon instructed company commanders to hold lectures on the right of complaint.[32] Their total dependence on the commanding officers' goodwill, however, put many soldiers off. Towards the end of 1915, after the finance committee of the Bavarian Diet had heard numerous cases of improper treatment of soldiers, the war minister thus felt compelled to impress upon commanding officers the importance of ensuring that the right of complaint did not exist 'on paper only'. The war minister took this step because he rightly suspected that soldiers who made complaints were 'exposed to torment or intangible snide remarks'.[33]

The inadequate right of complaint in a way incapacitated soldiers, a circumstance they deplored. This is evident from the fact that one of the demands made at the first revolutionary rally on 7 November 1918 on the Theresienwiese in Munich was that soldiers be guaranteed their right of complaint.[34] During the war, however, the difficulties involved in making a complaint tended to make soldiers feel powerless and thus had a disciplining effect. This applied particularly to rural soldiers unpractised in the arts of conflict. It did not defuse the potential for conflict

29. Christoph Erhardt, 12.7.1916: BfZ, Slg. Knoch.

30. Decree issued by the War Ministry, 8.1.1918: BHStA/IV, stv. GK I.AK 451.

31. Heinrich Dietz (ed.), *Die Beschwerdeordnungen für das Heer und für die Kaiserliche Marine*, Rastatt: Greiser 1911, pp. 65–140.

32. Decree issued by the War Ministry, 7.9.1915: BHStA/IV, stv. GK I.AK 591.

33. Decree issued by the War Ministry, 9.11.1915: BHStA/IV, stv. GK I.AK 591.

34. Hans Beyer, *Die Revolution in Bayern 1918-1919*, Berlin: Deutscher Verlag der Wissenschaften 1988, pp. 161–2.

underpinning the complaint, but simply caused soldiers to bottle it up. This is likely to have accelerated the transition to mass protest, ultimately triggered by the hopelessness of the war, in the summer of 1918.

Along with the insulting and degrading approach adopted by many officers, the hardships and injustices of army life made ordinary soldiers increasingly bitter. A small proportion of officers no doubt strove to treat soldiers fairly. Even if these considerate officers were prepared to behave differently from their fellows, however, they would be very hard pushed to escape the prevailing *esprit de corps*. Attending the officers' mess, for instance, was generally vital to furthering one's career.[35] Approachable officers could thus do little to change the deep sense of bitterness that ordinary soldiers felt towards officers. Victor Klemperer has described the troops' opinion of the few obliging officers: 'On the whole, for every hundred critical remarks about officers there was no more than one good one. This was inevitably followed by: "He's not like the others".'[36] The soldiers were, however, very aware of the internal differentiation of the officer corps. The active officers who had already served before 1914 (*Friedensstand*) were highly regarded. They won recognition, particularly in the initial stages of the war, for striving to treat their subordinates fairly and considerately in the light of the everyday realities of life at the front. Because of the heavy losses incurred early in the war and the increased need for officers caused by an expanding army, however, active officers made up less than one-sixth of officers serving in infantry regiments in 1918.[37]

Most of the 'lower-ranking officers', up to and including company commanders, were thus recruited from the officers 'off-duty' (the *Beurlaubtenstand*, not on active duty before 1914) and the 'war lieutenants' first promoted during the conflict. These officers, most of whom were only 19 or 20 years old, were particularly inept at treating older, married soldiers with the smallest degree of sensitivity. Young company commanders were poor at dealing with the provisioning of food and quarters, so central to soldiers' well-being. The 'NCO economy' which burgeoned as a result made it difficult for soldiers to advance their interests.[38] Soldiers, particularly older ones, responded negatively to this state of affairs, partly because of the generational conflict which

35. WUA, vol. 11/1, pp. 45-6.

36. Klemperer, *Curriculum Vitae*, p. 372.

37. WUA, vol. 11/2, S. 33, p. 111.

38. *Armee und Revolution, Entwicklung und Zusammenhänge. Von einem deutschen Generalstabsoffizier*, Berlin: Mittler 1919, p. 17.

it involved. For soldiers long established in their civilian lives and accustomed to a respect appropriate to their age, it was highly troubling to be subordinate to a man up to twenty years one's junior. A farmer from Baden mentioned this to his wife in relation to his poor prospects of leave: 'The company commander is not like the last one. I have a lot to do and have to hold my tongue. It's hard to be so old and to have to obey these youngsters. My dear wife, the dear Lord will surely take pity on us as we face these injustices and a time will come when we no longer have to take orders.'[39]

The intention here is not to make sweeping judgements, which are in any case impossible to prove. Nonetheless, the various accusations made against officers added up to a widespread 'hatred of officers'.[40] While most soldiers felt this way, the conclusions it inspired varied a great deal according to their social background. Urban workers, especially members of the SPD or the Social Democratic trade unions, interpreted officers' privileged position as confirming insights into the class character of Wilhelmine society which they had already gained before the war.[41]

Aware of the censorship of letters, the many soldiers from a rural background who belonged to no political party tended to wait until they were home on leave to tell people about injustices such as officers' superior rations and their poor treatment of ordinary soldiers. Soldiers found to have insulted officers in their letters faced harsh punishment. In some cases of humiliating treatment, however, soldiers' outrage at their superior officers burst forth suddenly and with tremendous force. A farmer's son who wished to report sick after coming into contact with toxic substances during a gas attack is a good example:

> Because I did that, the company commander refused to let me see the doctor and locked me up instead. That shows you what they're like, he'd be glad if I was dead. He then scolded me in a way no one has done before, calling me a coward and shirker and refusing to let me see the doctor. My dearest Mother, am I supposed to put up with this, if it wasn't for you I would take my own life. No matter how many requests for leave he grants, he won't let me go home. I can't think of a word bad enough for him, a man like that really deserves to be shot.[42]

39. Josef Beigel, 20.3.1917: BHStA/IV, Militärgericht 6. Ldw.-Div. B 11.

40. Hermann Kantorowicz, *Der Offiziershaß im deutschen Heer*, Freiburg/Br.: Bielefeld 1919, pp. 11-23.

41. WUA, vol. 11/1, p. 266.

42. Infantryman Birzer, 20.8.1917: BHStA/IV, 6. Inf.-Div., Bund 81.

For rural soldiers, another aspect of officers' behaviour also took centre stage. They were keenly aware of officers' moral failings and of any statements they made insulting the intimate life of the ordinary soldiers. The same went for the provocative flaunting of irreligious views, sometimes bound up with criticisms of Catholic priests. Because anyone wishing to enter the officer corps needed to gain the *Abitur* (school-leaving certificate), a condition which applied strictly only in Bavaria, it was 40 per cent Protestant before the war.[43] This in itself may have created an impression of faithlessness among pious Catholic soldiers. Observers such as military chaplains stated that Catholic officers were generally religiously inactive and claimed that most were highly 'averse to attending church'.[44] Highly religious soldiers such as Stefan Schimmer strove to be moderate. He thus drank water rather than wine 'for God's sake'.[45] For any soldier determined to live a morally impeccable life, the behaviour of some officers, who often drunk to excess or had relationships with women in the occupied areas, must have been hugely disappointing:

> From 12 midday off duty. During the evening it was *Bismarkfeier* and the company assembled to sing songs. At 7 o'clock the general came and gave a speech. Then the campfire was lit and shots were fired. The fine officers drank until three in the morning, shouting their heads off and firing shots, setting a good example. Then they brought two donkeys from the stable and had the male mount the female. They do that every time they're drunk.[46]

The injustices which soldiers experienced became bound up with sobering images of their superiors' moral failings; this lent them their explosive power. Ultimately, apart from the active officers of the *Friedensstand*, most soldiers became disillusioned with the moral qualities of this elite. Its members failed to act like the role models much acclaimed in the press before and during the war:

> Pictures of naked Frenchwomen hanging in a dug-out in the Vosges? Who did that? The officers, who are supposed to set a good example, who you are meant to regard as saints, indeed as infallible gods, and that's why there's nothing left

43. Hermann Rumschöttel, *Das bayerische Offizierskorps, 1866-1914*, Berlin: Duncker & Humblot 1973, pp. 45-54, 237.

44. Pastoral report by Josef Holzner, priest at the commandant's HQ, 31.8.1916: AEM, Akten des DK Buchberger.

45. Stefan Schimmer, 2.1.1915: BHStA/IV, Amtsbibliothek 9584.

46. War diary by Jakob Eberhard, 1.4.1915: private possession.

> for the one infallible God. And who is to blame for this unbelief, which is becoming a habit, for this immorality, this revolt against the regulations? The officer class, which has never had a faith or religion, the treatment meted out to the ordinary soldiers, the immorality of the superior officers, the subordinates' lack of rights, the striving for medals and decoration, no matter how many men pointlessly come to grief because of it.[47]

Views such as this, which focused on the officers' moral responsibility for injustices and hardships, offered only limited scope for the politicisation of the hatred soldiers felt for officers. As with interpretations privileging class-based models of inequality, the legitimacy of military authority diminished. Soldiers did not, however, necessarily make a direct connection with the Social Democratic Party's critical stance on the war or their programme of action. This demonstrates that social shortcomings did not automatically challenge the system of domination within the army. This happened only to the extent that soldiers interpreted them within a conceptual framework that underlined the unbridgeable divide between rulers and ruled within society.

Southern Bavarian soldiers from a rural background were, however, shaped by Catholic social teaching, which postulated a structured system of mutually dependent and complementary 'corporations', bound in principle to uphold the common good, as the basis of social order.[48] Rural Catholics found moral interpretations of social realities privileging convictions persuasive. In relation to the shortcomings of army life, they thus focused less on the structurally unfair and unequal distribution of opportunities built into the system of military domination than on the subjective responsibility of those officers whose behaviour they found immoral and unjust. Social Democratic interpretations of the war, including the dire social realities of army life, came to seem plausible only to the extent that the hold of religious interpretive models over some peasant soldiers slackened as the war progressed.

3.2 Expectations and Disappointments

Soldiers' expectations shifted several times over the four years of the war. Initial hopes that the war would be over quickly were disappointed. The more the prospects for peace in the near future were overtaken by

47. Michael Stapfer, n.d. [1918]: StaA Regensburg, NL Heim 1316.

48. Hermann Sacher (ed.), *Staatslexikon*, vol. IV, Freiburg/Br.: Herder 1931, pp. 1673–80, quote p. 1676.

events, the more soldiers longed for peace. Short-term fluctuations in the overall mood were a constant feature of soldiers' lives, anchored in the rhythms of strain and relaxation and the temporary impressions of the extent of artillery fire coming from either side. Impressions perceived as stressful were at times rapidly compensated for by positive events. In 1917 the press officer of the Bavarian War Ministry correctly stated with reference to soldiers' horizon of expectations: 'The man at the front has got used to living for the moment and being influenced by the moment - it is therefore extremely difficult to pin down his mood.'[49]

However, the build-up of negative experiences of fighting and the shortcomings of life within the army paved the way for a long-term, inexorable decline in soldiers' willingness to go on with the war. This process also found expression in the increase in various forms of disobedience through which soldiers could escape the sacrifices of everyday life at the front. Soldiers' readiness for disobedient behaviour is an indirect indication of their declining motivation to fight. There was, however, no automatic connection between the two phenomena; a worsening mood was not always immediately manifest in disobedience.

When analysing how the prevailing mood developed over time, far-reaching generalisations are best avoided. Even within a single unit, at the same moment, the atmosphere could vary tremendously.[50] Bearing this in mind, we can nonetheless sketch how the atmosphere tended to worsen, in stages, by scrutinising some of the many surviving war letters and other evidence. In the first weeks and months of the war, many young soldiers from the educated classes were particularly likely to show a readiness to make sacrifices and a strong motivation to fight, rooted in a positive view of the war. Many young soldiers from a rural background shared this attitude. As early as August 1914, however, some took a more sober view of things, especially after experiencing the first fighting. The diary entries by the journeyman-carpenter Georg Schenk are symptomatic of this process of rapid disillusionment. Towards the end of August, having experienced his 'baptism of fire' and another battle during the preceding ten days, he continued to express a basically positive view of life as a soldier, though this was already shaken by the negative attendant circumstances of the war: 'The soldier's life is quite nice when there are no battles, though we have a leader who ought to have stayed at home, because he has made

49. Memorandum by the War Ministry Press Office, 16.9.1917: BHStA/IV, MKr 2334.

50. Field postal station surveillance office 50, 4.2.1918: SHStAD, Kriegsarchiv (P) 21133, fol. 90.

our company worse. If we'd had nothing but fighting, everything would have been grand, but we've had not a moment's peace. They couldn't stand to see us doing nothing.'[51]

Just one week later, however, after another battle in which Schenk had observed the consequences of enemy as well as 'friendly' artillery fire, his initial assessment had given way to a fundamental insight into the destructiveness of the war:

> The 8th Company was at the front and came under such heavy fire from our own artillery that of the 1st column not a single man could maintain his position. Anyone who was not dead or wounded went back of his own accord. It was dreadful to witness the wounded returning, 3, 4 or 5 often came together. In the night between 6 and 7 [September], Remereville was ablaze. Another four villages were set alight by our artillery fire and the whole area was lit up. Remereville is now a place of devastation, there are almost no houses left intact. Anyone who really thinks about it has to admit that there is nothing more terrible than war. About 300m ahead of us the dead from yesterday now lie, most of them shot by our own unit, that is, the artillery.[52]

From September until the end of 1914, an increasing number of letters were sent from the field expressing a deeply felt longing for peace.[53] Many soldiers were thus already disillusioned about the reality of war during the war of movement and in the subsequent period of transition to the war of position.[54] The enormous losses and difficult battles of the first few months of the war utterly exhausted the troops and made them long for a break. This underpinned both the upholding of Christmas and the fraternisation which occurred during the Christmas period of 1914. From the end of 1914, more and more soldiers came to understand that the war would be longer and more stationary than expected. Alongside the first wave of furlough in the following spring, which caused soldiers to wonder when they might return to their civilian lives, this brought about the transition to a 'general longing for peace' during 1915.[55]

At this stage, the desire for peace was generally unelaborated and was thus linked neither with political nor territorial conceptions. It most often found expression in soldiers' asking mantra-like when it would all 'be

51. War diary by Lance Corporal Georg Schenk, 31.8.1914: BHStA/IV, HS 3410.
52. War diary by Georg Schenk, 7.9.1914: BHStA/IV, HS 3410.
53. Stefan Schimmer, 20.11.1914: BHStA/IV, Amtsbibliothek 9584.
54. Thimme, *Weltkrieg*, p. 164.
55. Cron, *Sekretariat*, p. 28.

over' at last.[56] From 1915 on, soldiers frequently expressed their rejection of the war by calling it a 'swindle'. In addition to their displeasure at their situation, they thus expressed in a 'playful' manner their suspicion that the people had been fooled about the true nature of the war by key opinion-forming authorities.[57] In October 1915, in a letter from western Flanders, a Social Democratic miner stated: 'I can tell you with absolute certainty that out here among the troops the mood is such that with the best will in the world I cannot imagine that we can fight successfully through another winter. I've heard too much in this vein and thoughtless opinions expressed by soldiers, which I myself was surprised by.'[58]

In sharp contrast to these predictions, however, the troops fought for almost three more years with at least enough success to hold off enemy offensives. From 1916 on, most of the troops longed for peace. This and the steady worsening of their mood by no means automatically undermined their ability to face the demands made of their fighting power and discipline. In fact, from 1915 until early 1918, as the liberal historian Ludwig Bergsträsser stated after the war, 'doing one's duty and longing for peace' were 'linked, and in a certain sense in fact determined' one another.[59] These realities, out of synch with the chronological progression of the war, are investigated in what follows in the form of an excursus.

Initially, the combination of these two factors could take on an aggressive tenor. This was the case among soldiers who welcomed imminent offensive action in the expectation that every military success would bring them closer to peace. For the same reason, they were delighted to hear any news of victories. Soldiers also wanted to win the war as soon as possible because this would prevent more lives from being lost.[60] Workers in the SPD or the Social Democratic 'free trade unions' (*Freie Gewerkschaften*), who made up around one-sixth of the troops in the German army, were reinforced in their willingness to stay the course by the party leadership. Until the party split and its conception of peace was modified in the spring of 1917, and apart from a few members who failed to toe the party line and with the exception of the radical left, the debates within the SPD all assumed that the country had to be defended. Both wings of the party leadership thus furnished members with the same advice, which was disseminated throughout the party and trade

56. O.H., 3.9.1915: local authority of Kochel.
57. Testimony by von Rudolph: *Dolchstoß-Prozeß*, p. 447.
58. Richard Schiller, 13.10.1915: BArch, 92, 271, fol. 228.
59. WUA, vol. 5, pp. 257-61, p. 258.
60. NCO E.H., 12.3.1915: BfZ, Slg. Schüling, vol. 20, no. 2.

union press. This reinforced the determination of workers at the front to stay the course.

This is particularly evident in a series of war letters written by miners who were members of the miner's union *Alter Verband*. However, in interpreting these it is important to bear in mind that, unlike most politically organised workers, mine workers from the Ruhr region had shown a fair degree of enthusiasm from the very beginning of the war; the leaders of the union were among the resolute champions of the 'fortress peace' policy (*Burgfriedenspolitik*).[61] Anti-tsarism, traditional within the SPD and reactivated when the Imperial leadership shifted the blame for the war onto Russia at the beginning of the war, was also widespread among workers in the field.[62] Some trade union members were quite convinced of the aggressive war aims of the Entente powers. A derogatory view of the impoverishment of the Russian people, often found among middle-class soldiers as well, sometimes flowed into this interpretation, lending it renewed vigour:

> We have one concern only: defending the country against invasion by Russia. This means you must approve whatever is necessary to wage war. We have to rid the Russians of their desire to return to Germany for ever more. Every German with even the most superficial knowledge of the situation here will and must support this. As for those who wish to give the German workers other so-called 'good' advice, they should go to *their* fatherland; there is much work to be done here, much indeed! We trade union members must not be tainted by these elements, even at the risk of having abuse heaped upon us. This applies, first of all, to those remaining at home. Should we return, we shall certainly do our share.[63]

From as early as 1915, increasing numbers of urban workers in the SPD demanded that the party pursue an active policy aimed at ending the war. After voting against further funding for the war in the *Reichstag* vote of December 1914, Karl Liebknecht quickly attained a certain popularity among the workers at war. In assessing this factor, however, we need to bear in mind that the anti-war minority in the SPD remained a minority, particularly following the organisational split in 1917.[64]

The acceptance of the SPD's interpretation of the war among politically organised workers prevailed over the critique which it inspired,

61. Kruse, *Krieg*, p. 189.
62. Ibid., pp. 65–76.
63. August Balke, 8.8.1915: BArch, 92, 271, fol. 98.
64. Kruse, *Krieg*, pp. 188, 194–5.

at least until 1917, in part because it was reinforced by a very specific mechanism. This was the organisational discipline characteristic of the labour movement. Before the war, it had to some extent suppressed independent and spontaneous activities among the workers in favour of the long-term strategies pursued by the elite of functionaries. The trade unions in particular propagated a concept of discipline quite comparable with that of the armed forces.[65] For soldiers moulded by such discipline, their intense longing for peace was fused with their willingness to fight on to victory. This is apparent in several letters by miners who were members of the *Alter Verband*:

> With any luck this terrible war will be over soon and I can get back to my family and my old job as soon as possible. But for the time being the thing is to stay the course and do your bounden duty like everyone else. To do all you can to defeat the enemy so we can make peace as soon as possible. Most people at home have no idea what it means to be at war. The people at home owe our brave soldiers a tremendous debt of gratitude. The strains and sacrifices which the soldiers have to bear are great indeed. These things are borne by the soldiers, including us politically organised workers in uniform; they are borne on the condition that the comrades in the party and trade unions who stayed at home continue to do their duty to their organisations.[66]

Once the Majority SPD had adopted the peace formula produced by the Petrograd Soviet in April 1917, it publicly pursued the peace for which so many longed. After the *Reichstag* had passed the Peace Resolution, however, the goal of defending the country again took priority. From the summer of 1917, the Majority SPD 'gradually' converted its propaganda for peace back into an 'endurance campaign'.[67] Many politically organised workers were thus still willing to do their duty, as the Majority SPD *Landtag* deputy and Munich workers' secretary Johannes Timm stated in November 1917.[68] In contrast to those soldiers whose willingness to do their duty had an aggressive slant, others were prepared to stay the course on the basis of a more passive attitude. These soldiers remained in position and continued to hope that the war would be over soon. As long

65. Friedhelm Boll, *Frieden ohne Revolution? Friedensstrategien der deutschen Sozialdemokratie vom Erfurter Programm 1891 bis zur Revolution 1918*, Bonn: J.H.W. Dietz 1980, pp. 69–75.

66. Friedrich Husemann, 23.3.1915: BArch, 92, 271, fol. 9.

67. Boll, *Frieden*, pp. 221–30, quote p. 227.

68. Niederschrift über die Sitzung des Beirats für Aufklärungsfragen, 3.11.1917: BHStA/II, MK 19289.

as the war showed no sign of changing course decisively, soldiers had no choice but to repeatedly abandon hopes that peace was no more than a few months away. Other soldiers, meanwhile, thought in terms of shorter periods of time. In February 1917, when it seemed to him 'as if the war is never going to end', a farmer wrote to his wife: 'You don't hear anything about peace these days. How, I wonder, will this hard struggle turn out? Our hopes extend no further than the day at hand. What we have to deal with never varies. We don't know where the offensive will be launched, but wherever it is, thousands of lives will be lost.'[69]

Ultimately, soldiers' willingness to do their duty was also fused with a longing for peace as long as they had a reasonable chance of 'making it through' in more or less one piece and returning home. If the burdens of war remained fairly manageable and the risks associated with individual forms of protest were unappealing, many soldiers could plausibly link their expectations to a passive waiting for the chance to return home. This, however, had at least to seem possible given how the war as a whole was going. After the failure of the German spring offensive of 1918, many soldiers who had 'hoped' that the fighting might allow them 'to go home soon' were therefore 'dispirited and despairing'.[70]

This attitude was very common among rural soldiers. Because it emphasised one's own survival, the willingness to hold out which it inspired was not automatically shaken even by the death or injury of one's comrades. All that mattered was that one had 'got out OK' oneself.[71] Many soldiers newly arrived at the front were reinforced in this attitude because they did not believe that they themselves would be killed or injured.[72] This belief was undergirded by an instinctive psychological mechanism: it was easier to deal with the danger of sudden, random death, not subject to rational control, by suppressing it. Belief in one's own invulnerability - should one survive the first few weeks in the field unscathed - could in fact become more plausible over time, as soldiers with experience of the front became increasingly confident of their ability to assess the risks they faced:

> We've been through a lot. We've been deployed in all the major battles raging on the Western Front since 16 August, and I've always made it through in one piece - a miracle. I haven't been injured yet so I've become very relaxed

69. G.T., 25.2.1917: private possession.
70. WUA, vol. 5, p. 293.
71. Joseph Reininger, 18.3.1917: private possession.
72. Ulrich/Ziemann, *Frontalltag*, pp. 77-9.

> when under fire. That spares me a lot of frayed nerves. The greater the mess, the calmer I become. So far I've had a good nose for evading enemy fire - it's impossible to remain in position when under heavy artillery fire.[73]

The first few days at the front were the most difficult for soldiers to get through, particularly their 'baptism of fire', but also after returning from leave. However, after two to three weeks' experience of the rules of conduct and the precautionary measures necessary to a stint at the front, or after a mere two days in the case of some soldiers, the worst 'feelings of anxiety passed'.[74] Subsequently, service in the field increasingly developed into a routine. Soldiers performed their tasks with reluctance but initially found them increasingly easy to cope with for a certain time. The combatants grew accustomed to the strains of everyday living. It made it easier to deal subjectively with risks if these were shared equally by the men in a unit, that is, if the others were 'no better' off.[75] The pressure to adapt within one's primary group tended to ensure that this was the case. In any event, farmers and farmers' sons in particular saw no cause for excessive daring, which simply increased risk for no good reason. They refrained from volunteering for high-risk ventures and thus gave up the chance to obtain 'Iron Crosses', because they would 'rather be alive'.[76] The connections between a longing for peace and the performance of one's duty in the field summarised here applied from early 1915 until the spring offensive of 1918. The mood among different groups of soldiers also diverged, sometimes dramatically, throughout the war. In what follows, these differences are discussed in another excursus, with separate treatment of the replacement and field army.

At the front, living through heavy fighting always had a significant influence on troops' motivation levels. In the replacement army, meanwhile, the danger to one's own life had an indirect impact on the overall mood whenever replacement units were assigned. Units such as those responsible for garrison administration or prison camps, which did not provide replacement troops, were of course unaffected by the negative effects of imminent deployment to the front.[77] In replacement units, soldiers about to be assigned had an unsettling effect, though this quickly subsided after their departure.[78] Real or imagined injustices in the

73. Letter by a front-line soldier, 14.9.1917: BSB.
74. War diary by Josef Ullrich, 9.4.1916: BHStA/IV, HS 3262.
75. Hans Spieß, 26.10.1916: BHStA/IV, Kriegsbriefe 340.
76. Hans Spieß, 12.2.1918: BHStA/IV, Kriegsbriefe 340.
77. Liaison officer, E./3.I.R., 21.6.1918: BHStA/IV, stv. GK I.AK 2410.
78. Liaison officer, E./Ldst.-Btl. I B 17, 1.8.1918: BHStA/IV, stv. GK I.AK 1980.

selection of the soldiers to be sent to the front worsened soldiers' mood for lengthy periods. Many company sergeants, who were in practice in charge of selecting troops, were suspected of letting their personal goodwill towards individuals or actual bribery influence their judgement. To deal with this distrust, the military authorities forbade company commanders from leaving selection to sergeants as early as 1916 - though clearly without much success.[79]

In the replacement army, groups of soldiers shielded from assignment to the front for lengthy periods were regarded with a mixture of contempt and outrage. Alongside farmers periodically allowed home on leave, these mainly consisted of conscripts recalled to work in the armaments industry. Those still serving in the forces were envious not only of their freedom from personal risk but also of their pay, which was far higher than that of soldiers.[80] Soldiers in the replacement army were connected to their civilian milieu even more closely than those in the field army. As a result, the prospects of a good or bad harvest and the associated work immediately changed farmers' mood. Until the very end of the war, positive expectations had the power to lift their spirits.[81] Finally, the mood among soldiers of different ages tended to diverge greatly. Married soldiers over thirty years of age, in particular, became physically weaker as they got older and worried constantly about their families:

> A lot of officers have been assigned recently, so there are now only two instead of twelve. That's still not enough unfortunately and all *K.V.* have been ordered to the front by the 15th, which includes me. But the worst thing is that I am going to be in the infantry, in the trenches - cannon fodder. This is my seventh year in the army, I'm 42 years old, I've always done my duty - but now I'm being sent back into the line of fire again, though I had my fill of that in the first year. "If he can take it, he's healthy, if he can't he's finished." My dear Mr A.! It makes you want to howl and weep with rage, the fourth year and you have to struggle through - a bag of bones is all that's left of me, I've gone from 150 pounds to barely 120. Where is all this supposed to lead? Many of my friends are still at home and so many thousands of others. You daren't even think about your family - everything is coming to grief - if they're not starving to death they're dying of sorrow and anxiety. Leave is permanently banned and you just have to get on with your duty, and subscribe for a war loan if possible. In any case I'm sick to death of the whole thing like millions of others.[82]

79. Stv. GK I.AK, 1.11.1916: BHStA/IV, stv. GK I.AK 311.

80. Liaison officer, 4. Ers.-MG-Komp., 23.9.1918: BHStA/IV, stv. GK I.AK 1981.

81. Liaison officer, *Landsturm* replacement battalion I B 17, 29.8.1917: BHStA/IV, stv. GK I.AK 2400.

82. Letter by an NCO, 10.10.1917: BSB.

Young recruits of 18 or 19, meanwhile, generally had a positive attitude. Out of a mixture of thirst for adventure, inexperience and genuine willingness to fight, some soldiers in this age group volunteered to serve in the field even after the failure of the spring offensive of 1918.[83]

In the field army, too, the mood of younger and older soldiers diverged significantly. Even extreme strains and sacrifices did not necessarily diminish for long unmarried soldiers' willingness to do their duty. Some young soldiers wished to prove themselves, while some even took part in dangerous ventures such as patrols for 'the hell of it'. One of the reasons for this attitude was the sense of liberation which young men hoped to experience, and which some perhaps did experience, during their stint in the field. One married farmer rubbished such expectations as illusory in 1918: 'Hans should leave off his big talk about becoming a soldier. He would soon hold his tongue if he was here. You can't say, if I don't like it I'll leave. They'd soon teach him.'[84]

Married soldiers above the age of 30, meanwhile, quickly began to suffer under the strains of deployment at the front. The distribution of complaints submitted to the War Ministry from the field provides reliable evidence that their mood was much worse than that of their younger fellows. Most were written by soldiers in territorial reserve and *Landsturm* units or 'formations' which, like the reinforcement troops for example, 'contained physically deficient material'.[85] For 1918, it was reported that the mood among the mainly older soldiers serving in the 6th Territorial Reserve Division, stationed on one of the quietest sectors of the Western Front, was extremely poor, and that they openly admitted their moroseness *vis-à-vis* the war to the officers.[86]

Older soldiers struggled particularly with the physical strains of the war of immobility, such as strenuous work on the positions, in the absence of sufficient sleep and sustenance. Married soldiers were also constantly anxious about the well-being of their wives and children. Soldiers from an urban background, whose families were starving and whose wives had to queue up day after day to obtain meagre provisions, 'were sometimes out of their minds with worry'.[87] From late 1915 on, the 'wailing letters' sent by the wives of urban workers began to have a

83. Liaison officer, Ers.-MG-Trupp, 30.5.1918: BHStA/IV, stv. GK I.AK 2409.

84. L.R., 8.6.1918: BfZ, Slg. Schüling, vol. 5, Nr. 89.

85. Undated document [1928] drawn up by the Bavarian War Archive on material in the files involving 'complaints and laments': BHStA/IV, HS 2348.

86. *Histories*, p. 143.

87. Soldier's letter from 16.8.1917: BHStA/IV, MKr 2334.

negative impact on front-line soldiers' mood which the authorities were unable to control.[88] The mood of farmers serving in the field army, meanwhile, was darkened by their wives' accounts of their excessive workload, the aggressive behaviour of hoarders and how the command economy was being managed.

In both the field and replacement army, soldiers' mood varied above all in line with their status as young and unmarried or older and married. In this respect, one consequence of the total exhaustion of the pool of potential conscripts is apparent in soldiers' subjective perceptions. Ultimately, the army leadership could usefully deploy older units only at quiet sectors of the front. As a result, they tended to experience a quite different war from younger soldiers. There is little evidence of open inter-generational tensions.[89] Nonetheless, only those soldiers born in the 1890s can properly be described as a 'front generation' moulded by a common 'strata of experiences'. For them, the lived experience of the front, associated with tremendous strains, occurred during a formative phase of personality development. Most soldiers born in the previous decade, meanwhile, were already married and established when the war began.[90] This qualification holds good, even if we view the idea of a front generation primarily as a mythical construct of the post-war era created to impose meaning on what had occurred.[91] In the symbolic representation of 'the' front-line soldier during the Weimar period, the bearded, portly territorial reservist or *Landsturm* soldier played no role whatsoever.

Having looked at the factors shaping the mood among the troops over the long term, our analytical focus now shifts back to the changes which occurred as the war progressed. During the course of 1916, it was above all the major battles of matériel at Verdun and the Somme which caused a massive worsening of the mood. Here, the terrible intensity of artillery fire was the key factor depleting the energies of the infantrymen. Soldiers were already aware and very afraid of the effects of artillery, used to keep fraternisation in check and taking the form of barrages lasting

88. Daniel, *Arbeiterfrauen*, pp. 149-51.

89. Ernst Müller-Meiningen, *Aus Bayerns schwersten Tagen. Erinnerungen und Betrachtungen aus der Revolutionszeit*, Berlin, Leipzig: Vereinigung wissenschaftlicher Verlage 1924, p. 326.

90. Erich Weniger, Das Bild des Krieges. Erlebnis, Erinnerung, Überlieferung, *Die Erziehung* 5 (1929), no. 1, pp. 1-21, p. 16.

91. Richard Bessel, The 'Front Generation' and the Politics of Weimar Germany, in: Mark Roseman (ed.), *Generations in Conflict*, Cambridge: Cambridge University Press 1995, pp. 121-36, p. 126.

several hours from 1915 on. At Verdun and the Somme, however, troops encountered 'a quite different war'.[92] The seven days of intensive artillery barrage at the Somme, which was carried out to prepare the ground for the Allied offensive and in which weapons of various calibres were used, were on a quite new scale. Some of the soldiers holding out in their dug-outs were worn down more by the crippling uncertainty of their fate than by the impact of the enemy fire itself.[93] At Verdun and the Somme, arriving troops and replacement units were told of the horrors of artillery fire before they had even been deployed, putting them in a state of fear: 'When we reached the Somme, it was terrible. I met some comrades who were already in position there, and they told me what was happening at the front, that there are lots of seriously wounded men lying there who can't be brought back because of the terrible artillery fire, and are thus hopelessly lost, and other terrible stories.'[94]

The troops deployed in the battles of matériel were soon depressed and exhausted; their desire for peace became yet more urgent.[95] Soldiers' letters from 1916 mention for the first time the notion that the war might be followed by 'revolution'.[96] The Supreme Command and higher-ranking officers were also aware that the men's mood had taken a turn for the worse as a result of the battles at Verdun and the Somme; it worried them. The tremendous demands made on the divisions which took part were reflected in isolated mutinies but, above all, in an increase in individual forms of disobedience. For the first time, a significant number of soldiers who had lost contact with their units was noted. These men absented themselves during the advance to the front and then went into hiding for a few days until the unit returned.[97]

The highly mechanised battles of 1916 saw tens of thousands of men in a single location used as objectified 'material' which, now damaged to a greater or lesser extent, had to be rapidly replaced. This laid bare the absurdity of the war of position. A war which continued to be waged in the absence of significant changes or consequences - other than

92. Josef Uebele, Kriegserlebnisse eines Pionier-Unteroffiziers: BHStA/IV, HS 1984.

93. John Keegan, *Das Antlitz des Krieges. Die Schlachten von Azincourt 1415, Waterloo 1815 und an der Somme 1916*, Frankfurt/M., New York: Campus 1991, pp. 269-81.

94. Statement by Georg Karr: BHStA/IV, MilGer 3454.

95. Thimme, *Weltkrieg*, p. 165.

96. Cron, *Studentendienst*, p. 33.

97. *Armee und Revolution*, p. 25.

destructive ones - year in and year out was not a war in the traditional sense of a limited engagement leading to a definite outcome. Soldiers came to see it as mere 'killing':

> All human justice has ceased to exist. And all of it just to satisfy the wishes of big capitalism, and Prussian militarism, for which the poor *Volk* has to suffer so terribly. Again and again, new reserves are brought in to this public slaughterhouse, where they are slaughtered in the most dreadful manner. Where is this absolute butchery supposed to get us? It's not hard to find the answer. The rich and powerful want to be alone with the stolen money they've extorted from the people with their profiteering hands, so they can say, 'We're free to do as we please again and our lives are free of danger.' There were simply too many people and they said to themselves, 'We need to show them that we're strong. In order to annihilate them we have to pursue policies that will lead to war.'[98]

In 1916 the war seemed increasingly meaningless and looked set to drag on. From that year onwards, soldiers often expressed their feelings about the conflict in stereotypical fashion by referring to it as 'killing' or a 'slaughterhouse'. The Social Democrat Wilhelm Lamszus had used such language as early as 1912 in his visionary description of the coming war.[99] The peace initiative of 12 December 1916 put forward by the Central Powers, soon rejected by the Allies, awoke new hopes - as did all such initiatives. Disappointed that the initiative had failed, the longing for peace among war-weary soldiers again increased as a result of the official offer. For soldiers with patriotic leanings determined to stay the course, meanwhile, this rejection strengthened their resolve.[100]

Over the course of 1917, the soldiers' mood initially darkened further. The tone in which they expressed their war-weariness in letters became generally more aggressive. In June the Majority Social Democrat Paul Löbe detected a widespread 'rage towards one's own country', up to and including the 'wish' that 'Germany is defeated', even among front-line soldiers such as farmers and businessmen not close to the SPD.[101] Yet in

98. Matthäus Birner, 4.12.1916: BHStA/IV, Militärgericht 1. Res.-Div. B 20.

99. Wilhelm Platta, 19.5.1915: BArch, 92, 271, fol. 196; Wilhelm Lamszus, *Das Menschenschlachthaus. Bilder vom kommenden Krieg (1912)*, Munich: Weismann 1980.

100. Ulrich/Ziemann, *Frontalltag*, p. 126.

101. Meeting of the party committee of the SPD, 26.6.1917: Dieter Dowe (ed.), *Protokolle der Sitzungen des Parteiausschusses der SPD 1912 bis 1921*, Bonn: J.H.W. Dietz 1980, vol. I, p. 535.

1917, as happened at the Somme, the German troops' resolve to stay the course was bolstered by the fact that they were fighting from a defensive position. This applied particularly to the French attempt to break through in April 1917 in Artois and Champagne. This poorly prepared offensive, in which many lives were lost, led to a massive crisis of discipline in the French army, reflected in the large number of mutinies.[102] Among the troops defending themselves on the German side, no such serious crisis occurred. In fact, some of the soldiers, imbued with a sense of duty, found their will to repulse the enemy fortified.[103]

During 1917 soldiers' war-weariness not only intensified but became more clearly fleshed out. This was due to the heating up of domestic political debates on the question of peace. As opposing positions hardened, these debates became more clearly defined in the perception of the troops in the field. Soldiers had no time for the advocates of annexationist views who had formed the Fatherland Party in the autumn of that year. In general, troops were sharply critical of the ruling elites and influential interest groups, who were suspected of having an interest in extending the war.[104] The prevailing desire for peace in fact became politicised in 1917 in line with the notion of a peace 'without annexations or contributions' now advocated by the Majority SPD.

From late autumn of 1917, however, the overall military situation fuelled soldiers' hopes that a decisive engagement on the Western Front would occur in the near future, paving the way for peace. Such ideas were initially inspired by German and Austrian successes against Italy in late October 1917 at Isonzo, in which the Alpine Corps, a Bavarian unit, played a decisive role, and in the wake of which the soldiers' mood improved markedly.[105] Soldiers unanimously regarded the armistice with Russia and the subsequent peace negotiations in December 1917 as an important turning point in the war. These events were 'greeted with tremendous enthusiasm' at the front. Now 'a fair number felt able to predict that the war would be over in a few months'. Soldiers generally expected a 'great clash' in the West that would resolve things once and for all.[106]

The expectation that they would soon be engaging in a war of movement awoke memories of 1914 among soldiers who had grown weary

102. Pedroncini, *Les Mutineries*.

103. Cron, *Sekretariat*, p. 30.

104. Soldier's letter of 21.10.1917: BSB.

105. Representative for Patriotic Instruction, 6.12.1917: BHStA/IV, MKr 2339.

106. Report by the postal surveillance office of the 5th Army, 10.1.1918: BA/MA, W-10/50794, fol. 35.

of immobility. These were bound up, to some extent, with the determination to prove once again one's own military strike power in a decisive and 'titanic struggle' after years of stagnation.[107] As a result of the widespread 'intoxication with victory' immediately before, and in the initial stages of, the advance, some soldiers even came to embrace the notion of territorial expansion and of a peace advantageous to Germany for a limited period.[108] Soldiers' emotional state, churned up by the imminent events and fluctuating between fear and anticipation, found expression in February 1918 in an unheard of number 'of mystical prophecies, *Schutzbriefen*, quotations from the Book of Daniel and the Apocalypse'.[109]

In advance of the spring offensive, however, a political event shook the confidence of the soldiers in the field. The massive wave of strike action affecting many German industrial areas for a brief period towards the end of January 1918 - in Munich alone around 9,000 workers took part - met with a mixed response.[110] A small minority of soldiers expressed approval of the strikes. The majority of men at the front, however, felt that the strikes were providing succour to the enemy, in light of the imminent offensive. Some were sharply critical of such action, which they felt was likely to lengthen the war. While many soldiers shared the strikers' desire for peace, they felt bitter about the generous wages enjoyed by recalled workers. 'Darling,' wrote one front-line soldier to his wife about the strikers, 'they have no idea what a good life they have back home.' Many soldiers, he added, 'would return home to work at a moment's notice'.[111]

Once the offensive had begun on 21 March 1918, however, the soldiers concentrated on the progress of the fighting, hoping it would bring the longed-for peace at last after one final push. Past sacrifices receded into the background for a short time; most soldiers had a confident outlook: 'Here on the Western Front spiritual matters have taken a back seat since the offensive began. I have seen such unanimous urgency und eagerness for the fray only in the August of 1914. The oppressive tension has finally left us and we are at last able to hope that after a final battle we will soon be returning home.'[112] Perceptive observers, however, quickly recognised

107. BA/MA, W-10/50794, fol. 63.
108. Heinrich Aufderstrasse, 1.5.1918: BArch, 92, 271, fol. 88-91.
109. Adolf Schinnerer, Eindrücke aus der Briefzensur, February 1918: BSB.
110. Albrecht, *Landtag*, pp. 297-301; Ay, *Entstehung*, pp. 196-200.
111. BA/MA, W-10/50794, fol. 47-61, quote fol. 54.
112. Soldier's letter from 30.3.1918: Cron, *Studentendienst*, p. 35.

that the soldiers would 'plunge into depression' if the offensive failed. Once soldiers understood that there was no prospect of achieving victory, they thought, their readiness to defend their positions was bound to dissolve and their desire for immediate peace would grow.[113] These predictions proved correct, when the phase of mobile warfare came to an end 'like a dream' after a short time.[114] Despite the great initial successes, the advancing troops were soon confronted with impressions that were devastating in their effect. Units repeatedly came across supply depots left behind by the Allies containing food reserves of a scale and quality which the poorly provisioned German soldiers could only dream of. While some soldiers were pleased to receive this short-term boost to their provisions, the overriding effect of these experiences was to make them aware of their opponent's material superiority.[115]

By June 1918 the poor state of provisions, the extremely high losses and the palpable superiority of the enemy in terms of resources and personnel had already severely impaired soldiers' morale. After the failure within a few days of a new offensive launched on 15 July, the German troops found themselves in a defensive position until the end of the war. From early August on, this could be maintained only through rearguard action in which many lives were lost.[116] From around the beginning of August, these realities triggered a final and irreversible change of mood. The soldiers had been robbed of their 'last hopes' that the war might end successfully. Peace could now be attained only through a frank and official German admission of defeat. Soldiers in the field were now prepared to pay any political or financial price and to abandon all territorial claims. With defeat clearly inevitable, the vast majority of soldiers had resigned themselves to 'insurmountable fatalism'.[117] Tentative diplomatic manoeuvres towards peace were now incapable of resolving the situation, especially given that trust in the skills of diplomats and politicians, who had supposedly been appointed to their posts through patronage, had reached rock bottom. Most soldiers regarded the Austrian offer of separate peace negotiations of 14 September 1918 as nothing more than a means of keeping the people waiting and making them more likely to subscribe for the ninth war loan.[118] Soldiers were more

113. Ulrich/Ziemann, *Frontalltag*, pp. 198-9.
114. Kurt Raschig, 25.4.1918: WUA, vol. 5, p. 292.
115. BA/MA, W-10/50794, fol. 72.
116. Deist, *Militärstreik*, pp. 148-56.
117. Cron, *Sekretariat*, pp. 32-3.
118. BA/MA, W-10/50794, fol. 94-105.

likely to place their trust, despite the peace terms which he personified, in American president Woodrow Wilson. Towards the end of October, troops to be transported from Donauwörth to Ulm adorned the railway carriages with the words 'Down with the Kaiser, up with the Revolution, up with Wilson'. It took persistent pressure from the officers present to get these removed.[119]

In the months between August and the armistice, two things mattered above all to the exhausted and war-weary troops. The armistice, now within reach, became fused with the desire to return home at last to one's family. This, however, meant staying out of harm's way during the final stretch of the war. Most soldiers were therefore no longer prepared 'to place their life on the line for no good reason'.[120] This attitude casts light on the factors still hampering the transition from extreme war-weariness to collective protest shortly before the end of the war. Soldiers were still primarily concerned with ensuring their own survival, encouraging them to opt for individual forms of protest that involved the least amount of risk. Particularly among soldiers from a rural background, moreover, a passive and defensive attitude was common in the face of the worsening realities of everyday life at the front. As a result, until July 1918 many of them hung 'desperately' on each and every turn of events that held out the prospect of a speedy end to the war.[121]

Particularly in 1917, 'supposed and genuine' efforts to achieve peace - such as the Peace Note produced by Pope Benedict XV - 'stirred up [soldiers'] emotions throughout the year. The merest hint of peace', as one soldier put it early in 1918, had unleashed 'a great storm of hopeful enthusiasm'.[122] Though soldiers' mood as a whole had steadily darkened from the autumn of 1914, such short-term political manoeuvres repeatedly opened up the prospect of a positive outcome, preventing their motivation from withering away entirely. After the failure of the spring offensive, however, of which soldiers had expected much, such periodic improvements in mood ceased to be viable, as the response to the Austrian peace proposal lays bare. Analysis of soldiers' deteriorating mood thus lends credence to explanations of the 'covert military strike' - both in terms of its character and its extent - in the summer and autumn of 1918 that privilege the troops' general exhaustion and their recognition that further exertions would be pointless.[123]

119. WB BA Donauwörth, 31.10.1918: BHStA/IV, MKr 2325.
120. BA/MA, W-10/50794, fol. 106.
121. Ulrich/Ziemann, *Frontalltag*, pp. 206-7.
122. WUA, vol. 5, p. 281.
123. See Deist, Military Collapse.

3.3 Disobedience

Soldiers' increasing dissatisfaction with the burdens of everyday life at the front was not limited to spoken or written statements referring to their war-weariness. A whole range of forms of disobedience was in fact available to them, through which they could permanently or at least temporarily escape the danger of death. The factors underpinning disobedience comprised fairly long-term motivations, short-term triggers inspiring men to take action, and the presence of a more or less risk-free opportunity. The primary reason for refusal was the unwillingness, which steadily mounted as the war wore on, to be exposed to massive and potentially deadly fire for a moment longer. Most soldiers, however, had additional reasons for their refusal. These tended to include dissatisfaction with the realities of army life or private motives unique to the individual. Soldiers were rarely motivated by a rejection of the use of violence against the enemy.[124] Tacit agreements with the enemy certainly embodied a willingness to cooperate to minimise the dangers faced equally by both sides. Soldiers' own experience of violence, however, was so extreme that it provided them with more than enough motivation to refuse.

The first few weeks of the war were in any case much influenced by escalating violence perpetrated by soldiers in the German army. In August 1914, during the advance through Belgium and France, they committed atrocities against the civilian population which cost the lives of around 6,000 people. A complex cluster of reasons can be identified for this, the most important being the idea, widespread among the soldiers, that armed civilians were carrying out a 'franctireur' war.[125] The escalation of violence apparent in crimes against the civilian population and the atrocities suffered by prisoners, but also the careless attitude towards violence shown in uncovered advances in the face of superior enemy fire power, were linked with the specific conditions of the war of movement.[126] The nature of the war of position offered even infantrymen little opportunity for direct contact with the enemy. As they gained experience, soldiers adapted to the new circumstances and fought in such a way as to keep the number of losses to a minimum.[127] From late 1916, the hand grenade

124. See, for example, Richert, *Beste Gelegenheit*, pp. 36-8.

125. See the brilliant analysis in John Horne/Alan Kramer, *German Atrocities, 1914. A History of Denial*, New Haven, London: Yale University Press 2001.

126. WUA, vol. 11/1, p. 304.

127. Here, we should note the fact, first confirmed by interviews with American soldiers during the Second World War, that even in elite units engaged in active combat no more than 25 per cent of the soldiers make use of their weapons. This

thus became the key weapon in the infantryman's arsenal, as it could be hurled from the trenches. To use a rifle, meanwhile, soldiers had to break cover in jerry-built trenches.[128] In the spring of 1918 during the battles on the Western Front, observers noted, infantrymen made 'almost no use' of their rifles. For them, the chattering of an enemy machine-gun was a signal to seek 'total cover' and to wait until the machine-gun positions were destroyed by the artillery.[129]

Making one's own body unfit for further service, or pretending that it was, constituted the first key form of disobedience. There were a number of options open to soldiers wishing to deliberately injure themselves. Guard duty regularly offered soldiers, who were posted individually in the first line of trenches, a particularly good opportunity for this. The most frequent approach was to shoot oneself in the foot or hand with one's own weapon. Right-handed soldiers tended to injure their left hand, as this seemed most likely to allow them to work once they had returned to their civilian lives. Deliberately infecting oneself with a venereal disease offered another route to temporary exemption from duty; prostitutes in the back area and at railway stations back home were the key means of achieving this.[130] Towards the end of the war, soldiers became more willing to mutilate themselves. Some soldiers even mentioned the intention to do so in their letters.[131] In its 1928 assessment of the court-martial statistics of the Bavarian contingent, the War Archive in Munich described self-injury as something which happened 'relatively often'. The archive did not, however, provide figures on this specific group of offenders.[132] This evidence, which relates to the number of sentences passed, allows us to conclude that it was a common offence: of twenty-eight soldiers of the

---

is not a matter of straightforward refusal - soldiers would try to abscond if this was their aim. Such behaviour is in fact anchored in the fear of drawing attention to oneself unnecessarily by firing one's weapon on the field of battle and thus attracting enemy fire. Soldiers are generally unaware of the aggressive potential of their own weapon's fire and its capacity to confuse the enemy. See the key text, confirmed by many subsequent studies: S.L.A. Marshall, *Men against Fire. The Problem of Battle Command in Future War*, Washington, New York: Morrow 1947, pp. 50-63.

128. Ulrich/Ziemann, *Frontalltag*, pp. 54-5.

129. K.M., 17.5.1918: BHStA/IV, stv. GK I.AK 451.

130. Prussian War Ministry, 16.3.1917: BHStA/IV, stv. GK I.AK 967.

131. Letter of 23.7.1918: BHStA/IV, Inf.-Leib-Rgt. Bund 21.

132. Undated compilation [1928] by the Bavarian War Archive: BHStA/IV, HS 2348.

2nd Infantry Division for which the archive mentions the existence of a report filed on self-injury, only seven were sentenced.[133]

A number of obstacles hampered the court-martialling of self-mutilation. First, medical service personnel had to be encouraged to keep an eye out for suspicious injuries and report them to the soldier's commanding officer. After being alerted by a doctor, or when the soldier involved was being treated in his unit, the commanding officer could choose to file a report. It was to the accused's own statement that most importance was attached in the legal proceedings, as most injuries occurred while the soldier was alone in the trench or observation post. In such cases, everything depended on how believable his story was in the light of the circumstances. It was also necessary that he repeated the story unchanged in further interrogations.[134] Circumstantial evidence such as traces of powder was rarely sufficient to condemn a man. This was because any evidence which suggested a shot had been fired from one's own weapon merely triggered the scarcely refutable claim that this had happened while cleaning one's weapon. The only sure way of achieving a successful prosecution was thus to get the accused to admit to his crime.[135]

It is very difficult to come to any firm conclusions about why soldiers decided to mutilate themselves, other than the obvious desire to be permanently released from duty. However, it is striking that almost a third of suspects belonged to a single employment group, agricultural servants and day labourers.[136] This suggests that we should view self-mutilation as a form of disobedience selected mainly by a passive type of soldier inexperienced in the 'art' of skilful refusal and highly intimidated by the risk of punishment. The moral and legal risks of this form of disobedience were low, given how close self-mutilation was to the widespread incidents of careless handling of weapons and to the equally frequent *Heimatschuß*, a 'lucky shot' in a non-vital limb bringing the soldier home and off-duty. It is true that a good deal of determination was necessary for an act of self-mutilation. Several of the convicted offenders, however, had been in the field only a short time when they acted, or did so immediately following a

133. BHStA/IV, MilGer 6200, 6208, 6220, 6268, 6318, 6336, 6425.

134. BHStA/IV, MilGer 6268, 6318.

135. BHStA/IV, MilGer 6200, 6220, 6336.

136. In the British army, which consisted mainly of industrial workers, self-mutilation was a marginal phenomenon: David Englander/James Osborne, Jack, Tommy and Henry Dubb. The Armed Forces and the Working Class, *Historical Journal* 21 (1978), pp. 593-621, p. 598.

disheartening experience. This points to a spontaneous decision by men less afraid of physical damage than of the certainty of punishment should they refuse in other ways.[137]

By far the most important type of disobedience, both in terms of frequency and the negative consequences for military organisation, was desertion.[138] The personal risk involved in going over to the enemy was high, varying in line with the intensity of artillery fire at the time. In extreme cases, soldiers had to go back to their own lines and thus face a certain sentence. There was, moreover, no way for a soldier to know for sure whether the enemy was interested in taking prisoners in the first place. Less beset with difficulties was the option taken up by many soldiers to flee to the neutral Netherlands, Switzerland or Denmark while at home on leave or from the back area or replacement army. Even then, soldiers had to be prepared to spend several years under unknown circumstances away from their family in a foreign country. To go through with desertion thus required a high degree of single-mindedness, self-confidence and self-assertion.

Desertion was practised above all by members of the national minorities. These comprised soldiers hailing from Alsace-Lorraine, Poles (particularly from Poznań and West Prussia) and Danes from North Schleswig. They were less keen to fight in the German army from the outset. Moreover, particularly among soldiers from Alsace-Lorraine and the Poles, the willingness to defect was reinforced by the harassment and discrimination to which they were exposed in the Prussian-German army. The Prussian military authorities thus helped create the group of soldiers most dissatisfied and most willing to go over to the enemy. There were, however, very few men from Alsace-Lorraine in the Bavarian army. The military authorities' indiscriminate, distrustful treatment of Alsatian soldiers met with their fellow soldiers' disapproval. A relatively small number of workers involved in the USPD or the Spartacus Group, who continued their political work at home or in a neutral foreign country, were inspired to desert primarily for political reasons. There is no overall indication that certain social groups were more likely to desert than

137. BHStA/IV, MilGer 3565, 6220, 6268.

138. For a comprehensive treatment of desertion in the German army see Ziemann, Fahnenflucht; Christoph Jahr, *Gewöhnliche Soldaten. Desertion und Deserteure im deutschen und britischen Heer 1914-1918*, Göttingen: Vandenhoeck & Ruprecht 1998, tends to underestimate the quantitative dimensions and the negative consequences of desertion for the German armed forces.

others. In any event, very few soldiers working in agriculture resorted to this form of refusal. They made up less than 4 per cent of convicted deserters.[139]

Over the course of the war, the number of ordinary soldiers and NCOs who deserted became a heavy burden for the military apparatus. This phenomenon is reflected only very imperfectly in the extent of convictions by courts martial, as it was impossible to prosecute if soldiers succeeded in deserting to the enemy or absconding to neutral foreign countries. The number of convictions increased particularly during the last year of the war, though they had already risen substantially in 1917. The total number of deserters in the German army before the 'covert military strike' commenced in mid-July 1918 was probably around 90,000-100,000. Only a few thousand of these deserted to the enemy. Around 30,000 fled to neutral countries. In addition to this, tens of thousands of soldiers were listed as wanted from January to July 1918 on the Western Front; these men are likely to have remained in hiding until the end of the war in the French and Belgian back area.[140] From mid-July 1918 until the armistice on 11 November, within the context of the 'covert military strike' (Wilhelm Deist), from 750,000 to 1,000,000 soldiers serving in the German field army on the Western Front absconded and poured towards the German border. The military authorities could do nothing to control this process. Desertion had finally become a mass phenomenon, fatally undermining the system of authority within the German army.[141]

Finally, apart from self-mutilation and desertion, soldiers could openly refuse to obey orders. Individual cases of insubordination by one or two soldiers were far from uncommon, as the number of convictions by courts martial attests.[142] This enabled particularly discontented soldiers to vent their annoyance to some extent. Individual acts of insubordination, however, tended to work against the development of collective protest. This also applies to more minor rebellious actions by a group of soldiers. Georg Schenk, NCO in the 2nd company of the newly formed 32nd Infantry Regiment, which carried out exercises from January 1917 in Murnau, describes in his war diary how a lance corporal threw down his weapon after hours of group exercises. A number of soldiers then refused to perform rifle practice and to salute a major.

139. Jahr, *Gewöhnliche Soldaten*, p. 132.

140. Ziemann, *Fahnenflucht*, pp. 116-17.

141. On the covert strike in the armed forces see Deist, Military Collapse, and below.

142. See the statistics in: BHStA/IV, HS 2348.

Vociferous complaints marked the subsequent march through Murnau. Presumably in part because the captain and company commander 'got a right earful' afterwards and subsequently improved his conduct, Schenk described this as the 'best day we ever had, 12 February, the day of mutiny and rebellion'.[143]

Genuine mutinies, the collective insubordination of entire units, occurred only very rarely and never involved more than one unit at a time. The first incidents occurred during the battles of matériel of 1916 and 1917, particularly at Verdun and the Somme and during the Battle of Ypres in the autumn of 1917. Smallish groups of soldiers, never more than a whole company, refused to advance to the front.[144] In the last few months of the war, soldiers collectively refused to do so on many occasions. Towards the end of October 1918, the units of an entire territorial reserve division at Metz refused to advance to the front.[145] Even these events, though, pale into insignificance given the individual acts of disobedience which occurred on a massive scale at this time.

Mutinies were few and far between and never became greatly significant within the overall framework of soldiers' disobedience. There are a number of reasons why collective protest happened so rarely. First, soldiers voiced their indignation at unreasonable strains and unfair treatment immediately after returning to the rest position in no uncertain terms. This allowed them to let off steam and generally exhausted their outrage. Friedrich Lutz, *Landtag* deputy for the Bavarian Peasants' League, recognised this in 1917. 'As long', he stated, as the soldiers 'grumble, there's no problem at all. When they stop grumbling, then there's a problem.'[146] If a soldier wished to instigate collective insubordination, he had to be sure of his comrades' determination to follow through. In contrast to civilian working life, the men who came together at the front were from the most varied social backgrounds and their motivations and views differed greatly. Even if many soldiers in one unit were prepared to act on their anti-war sentiments, this did not necessarily lead them to discuss together the possible opportunities or risks involved. The rough tone typical of army life and the fear of being branded a coward caused some soldiers to hide their real feelings.[147]

143. War diary by Georg Schenk: BHStA/IV, HS 3410.

144. Thaer, *Generalstabsdienst*, p. 92.

145. *Dolchstoß-Prozeß*, p. 213.

146. Verhandlungen der Kammer der Abgeordneten des Bayerischen Landtages, Stenographische Berichte, Vol. 16, Munich 1917, p. 717.

147. Letter from the field, 9.7.1918: BSB.

Yet even among those soldiers who complained vociferously about the war to their comrades, those who thought about resisting were surely few in number. Individual and socially specific interpretive models facilitated soldiers' passive and conflict-avoiding insertion within the constraining matrix of subordination. This included a fatalism with religious roots particularly common among soldiers from rural areas.[148] A number of such soldiers expressed a general sense of powerlessness in the face of the pressure to conform that prevailed within the armed forces. Regardless of concrete disciplinary practices, they were convinced that one 'can't do as one pleases in the army'.[149] The idea of disobedience was thus beyond rural soldiers' horizon of imagination, the result of a collective habitus moulded by the experience of highly patriarchal forms of social dependency and a low degree of social and horizontal mobility.[150]

There were, however, differences among rural soldiers in this respect that depended on their social background. In 1914 a village priest from Swabia described a well-off farmer used to the 'good life' who entered the field as an untrained reservist and therefore complained about the 'strict command' in the armed forces. Agricultural servants, meanwhile, who were used to privation, found it far easier to deal with the strains of the campaign than other soldiers, as the priest went on to relate: 'All such men and youngsters, who have to labour at home or for others, cope easily with the campaign. They do not complain about the food. There could scarcely be hardier soldiers.'[151]

The impact of these various strategies for coping with army life was further reinforced by the high rate of fluctuation among the troops. This ensured that soldiers faced short cycles of strain, particularly in those units on which the greatest demands were made. Moreover, the high number of losses made it difficult for soldiers to build up a stock of collective experience within the units, hampering any social bonds between the soldiers that might have encouraged them to oppose the war. The fairly long-term and equal distribution of burdens on the soldiers, meanwhile, made it easier for them to come to terms with the system of military domination collectively and with solidarity. This is particularly apparent in comparison with the German navy. As a result of the strategic constraints

148. See Chapter 4.2.

149. Christoph Erhardt, n.d. [June 1917]: BfZ, Slg. Knoch.

150. Wolfgang Kaschuba, *Lebenswelt und Kultur der unterbürgerlichen Schichten im 19. und frühen 20. Jahrhundert*, Munich: Oldenbourg 1990, pp. 34-8.

151. Neukirchen parish office, 1.12.1914: StAA, BA Neuburg 7214.

of the war at sea, the navy was largely condemned to inactivity, with the exception of the Battle of Jutland in May 1916. A far greater proportion of the navy consisted of workers involved in trade unions than was the case in the army. Their dissatisfaction mounted with the poor treatment they received from officers; this was clearly an even greater problem than in the army because of the lack of active engagement in battle. Their vastly superior meals were also a point of contention. The relatively homogeneous composition of the crews and the fact that they often served on the ships continuously for several years caused their displeasure at the hardships and injustices and their desire for an immediate peace to boil over in July and August 1917 in a number of cases of collective protest. Around 5,000 soldiers in the fleet signed a document expressing their support for the USPD and its peace aims. The sailors even notched up successes with the creation of the rationing committees, whose recommendations the commanders were slow at implementing despite orders from the Imperial Naval Office (*Reichsmarineamt*). The sailors' collective resistance was broken only by the imposition of the death penalty on a number of occasions, lengthy prison sentences and other repressive measures.[152]

While the high rate of fluctuation among the troops had worked against collective protest at the front, it came to encourage such protest at a nodal point of the system of military discipline during the second half of the war. This involved convoys of replacement troops travelling to the front from garrisons back home. Towards the end of September 1916 a replacement convoy destined for the Alpine Corps was hit by disciplinary problems while troops were being loaded into the carriages at the railway station; some of the men loudly expressed their demand for leave.[153] From February 1917 until September 1918 units of the Bavarian replacement army were involved in a total of twenty-three further generally serious cases of collective refusal to obey orders.[154]

A typical example of incidents of this kind is the violence which took place on 28/29 May 1918 in Neu-Ulm. Over the course of 27 May troops from various replacement units from Munich and Augsburg arrived in Neu-Ulm. These were earmarked for a marching battalion of around

152. See Daniel Horn, *The German Naval Mutinies of World War I*, New Brunswick: Rutgers University Press 1969, pp. 10-168.

153. Immenstadt Mountain Infantry Replacement Battalion, 16.10.1916: BHStA/IV, stv. GK I.AK 557.

154. Compilation by the War Ministry, n.d.: BHStA/IV, MKr 2324.

500 men with replacement troops for the 2nd Infantry Division.[155] The majority of these soldiers had learned only the day before departing for Neu-Ulm that they would be heading into the field and received meagre rations when they arrived.

The soldiers were ordered to march to the parade ground on the morning of 29 May, where they were to be instructed in how to conduct themselves in the convoy. As had occurred the day before, however, early on the 29th around 200 soldiers made their way to Ulm after a rumour of imminent drills had been doing the rounds. While crossing the bridge over the Danube, policemen and the castle constabulary (*Festungsgendarmerie*) were unable to stop their progress; some scuffles occurred. In the light of the soldiers' threatening behaviour, it was impossible to force them to obey by means of armed force, especially given that civilians would have been in the line of fire. Around 180 soldiers then forced the owner of a tavern to provide them with beer before returning, whistling, to Neu-Ulm that same morning. Questioned about their motives on the barrack square, they mentioned their indignation about possible drills and above all their displeasure at the fact that they had been assigned to the field after discharge from the field hospital without being granted any leave beforehand.

On the afternoon of 29 May the commander of the replacement battalion in charge of the convoy managed to get the men to fall in only by making concessions. Some soldiers openly refused to accept assignment. The major guaranteed them a further health check as well as a judicial investigation. The soldiers also made sure that troops from Württemberg stationed in Ulm, ordered to secure the convoy, pulled back far enough so that they could not be seen by the troops marching to the station. Once there, a few soldiers from Munich tried to prevent the loading of the troops into the carriages. After lengthy delays, the convoy was finally able to depart. Although a search for ammunition had already been carried out upon arrival in Neu-Ulm, several shots were fired in the air when the convoy departed and stones were hurled from the train. When the convoy stopped near Göppingen, the soldiers stormed several taverns.[156]

Some of the soldiers involved in acts of violence in the relief convoys committed offences mainly in order to evade front-line service. Most soldiers committed such acts, however, because they wanted a short

155. Stv. 4. Inf.-Brigade, 31.5.1918: BHStA/IV, MKr 2324.
156. Stv. GK I. AK, 15.6.1918: BHStA/IV, MKr 2324.

period of leave before returning to the front.[157] Regulations laid down in 1917 in fact stipulated that soldiers must be granted sufficient leave before being assigned to the front. The lack of replacement troops in 1918, however, made it necessary to bring in soldiers discharged from the field hospital only a few days before transportation. This was essential to ensure that troops were deployed on time whenever urgent requests were made. The desire for leave was accompanied by the perception of injustices in the selection of the troops allowed to go home, already discussed in relation to the evolution of soldiers' mood. Officers, moreover, were unable to get to know their subordinates well because the former were transferred with such frequency within the replacement army.[158] Over the course of 1918 an increasing number of soldiers and NCOs absconded from replacement convoys; up to 20 per cent of the initial fighting force could be missing upon arrival in the field.[159]

Up to 1918 only a small percentage of front-line soldiers ever tried to evade their military service by means of the various forms of disobedience. Particularly from 1917, the frequency and intensity of disobedience did indeed increase, as is apparent from the growing number of deserters. Yet even this development did not seriously jeopardise the stability of the system of military domination as a whole. It was only when it became apparent from mid-July 1918 how hopeless it was to battle on that the ground was laid for the widespread anti-war mood among the soldiers to evolve into individual disobedience on a massive scale. The pattern of the forms of disobedience used indicates that the aims of the soldiers did not differ fundamentally from those prevalent during earlier stages of the war, even in the last few months of the war. Cases of open, collective insubordination remained thin on the ground and ultimately meaningless. Soldiers were more focused on finding ways to minimise the risk of fatal injury. In addition to allowing themselves to be captured or, on a lesser scale, defecting, soldiers often opted for 'shirking'. This option was available in the back area to fleeing front-line soldiers, those on leave, those discharged from the field hospital or replacement troops unwilling to report to their unit. Because troops were relocated so frequently, it was relatively easy for individuals to roam around in the back area. Even the

157. Field court official of the 2nd Infantry Division, 28.6.1918: BHStA/IV, MKr 2325.

158. Memorandum by Section A II of the War Ministry, 1.7.1918: BHStA/IV, MKr 2325.

159. Heeresgruppe Kronprinz Rupprecht, 27.6.1918: BHStA/IV, Heeresgruppe Kronprinz Rupprecht Bund 30.

establishment of 'assembly points for scattered soldiers' (*Versprengten-Sammelstellen*) and the erection of barricades against 'shirkers' by the military police failed to curb this.[160] The looting of food depots and the use of the kitchens of other units allowed fleeing soldiers to survive in the rearward areas.[161]

The fear of imminent death at the front was the main reason for disobedience during the last few months of the war. With defeat now foreseeable, this could trigger individual disobedience on a massive scale, because the majority of soldiers were no longer prepared to put their lives on the line just before the end of the war.[162] For a very small proportion of urban soldiers, the refusal to carry out orders at the front became bound up with an increasing willingness to pursue revolutionary aims. However, this mass movement among soldiers was 'revolutionary', as Wilhelm Deist has rightly stated, 'only to the extent' that it 'undermined the very basis [of the army] as the guarantor of the existing power structure [in Imperial Germany]'. The covert strike in the armed forces, rather than being a coherent collective protest resting on shared aims and convictions, was a form of mass action by individuals.[163] We should beware of overestimating the degree of politicisation among the soldiers, especially as the political dynamics back home played almost no role in the events of autumn 1918. Nonetheless, the extent and results of the soldiers' movement were considerable. They demonstrate that the collapse of the state's legitimacy had reached a level in the armed forces similar to that in civilian society.

The pattern of the forms of protest, to repeat, also supports the cautious interpretation of Wilhelm Deist. Acts of protest by war-weary soldiers were only rarely directed at the command authority as such. They tended, rather, to make use of the fault lines and lacunae in the system of discipline arising from the huge increase in soldiers' mobility during these months. The ordinary soldiers did not turn against the officers – though they often disgorged the rage which had accumulated within them in the form of invective. The many injured and those suffering from influenza simply poured back home. From August 1918 until 11 November, up to one million German soldiers on the Western Front thus ended the war on their own initiative and headed back home. At the time of the

160. Documents in: BHStA/IV, AOK 6, Bund 22.

161. AOK 6, 29.10.1918: BHStA/IV, AOK 6, Bund 22.

162. WUA, vol. 4, pp. 135–6.

163. Deist, Militärstreik, p. 160; for a different interpretation see Kruse, Klassenheer.

armistice, according to contemporary estimates, no more than 750,000 soldiers were in the front combat line of the German army on the Western Front.[164] It is not possible to identify the social groups to which soldiers willing to serve until the end of the war belonged. In any case, we have no reason to assume that particular groups predominated. It seems more likely that those involved comprised the 'hard core' of nationalistic soldiers. Some evidence suggests that units which remained intact until the end tended to be led by officers with outstanding leadership qualities who had a core of 'proven fighters' at hand.[165] Given the huge scale of protest in autumn 1918, which crossed the lines of social class, we have to assume that many soldiers from a rural background also took the opportunity to bring their war to an early close.

On the whole, however, this major social group had rather hampered the mobilisation of soldiers against the war. Rural soldiers were privileged in terms of leave and rations, so important to the state of mind among the troops. These privileges facilitated their passive insertion into the constraints of military subordination. Rural soldiers had a somewhat fatalistic attitude towards the burdens of everyday life at the front. A prison sentence, on the other hand, was a major moral blemish in tightly knit village communities. As a result of these two factors, rural soldiers tended to do what they could to ensure their own survival within the niches of the military system. They preferred the 'small-scale escapes' from the front before considering disobedience as an option. Before the hopelessness of Germany's military situation became fully apparent, disobedience was in any case - with the exception of deserters from the national minorities - overwhelmingly a situational tactic pursued when the opportunity presented itself or because it dramatically improved one's chances of survival.

164. Deist, Militärstreik, p. 151.

165. Eugen Neter, Der seelische Zusammenbruch der deutschen Kampffront. Betrachtungen eines Frontarztes, *Süddeutsche Monatshefte* 22 (1924/5), no. 10, pp. 1-47, p. 23.

4

Mentalities, 1914–18

Soldiers and other contemporary observers who struggled through the four long years of the Great War interpreted their experiences in a variety of different ways. While keeping this in mind, it is possible to identify three broad themes common to how soldiers perceived the war and constructed their own identity. The first essential is to probe the extent to which soldiers were able to identify with their role as military men. Did they experience the 'comradeship at the front', much acclaimed by contemporaries, as an alternative to their civilian lives? Secondly, how significant was religiosity as a factor in how soldiers interpreted the war? To what extent did it bolster their emotional stability? This issue is particularly pertinent in relation to soldiers from rural areas. Finally, how successful were nationalistic concepts and campaigns against the enemy in motivating soldiers and giving meaning to their experiences? Or were the troops in the field and at home more affected by other political ideas?

4.1 Homesickness

The 'community of the front' allegedly formed in the trenches has become a symbol of the widespread acceptance of a new kind of militaristic social order and system of values among the troops. Later generations used the idea of comradeship, thought to embrace all classes and ranks, to their own ideological ends, presenting it as a model for a new type of social configuration transferable to civilian life. The myths of comradeship generated by the National Socialist movement are a prime example. The term implied not only a 'community of necessity' responding to external constraints, but also a 'community of fate' that soldiers entered into on a free, subjective basis.[1] If we wish to reconstruct the reality of experiences

1. Günther Lutz, *Die Frontgemeinschaft. Das Gemeinschaftserlebnis in der Kriegsliteratur*, Greifswald: Hans Adler 1936, p. 86. For a critical discussion of the idea of comradeship in the German armed forces during the twentieth century see Kühne, *Comradeship*.

of community through a critical lens, however, we need to work from a sober definition that underlines the compulsion inherent in cooperation. Thus, it is in the

> nature of comradeship, notwithstanding its positive sides, that it is *not* based on the other's personal or individual characteristics, but is determined by the given situation of the group, by its particular 'mission' and is granted to each 'member' of the group in uniform fashion. Comradeship is a codex and duty. Far from requiring people to take on board others' special, individual traits as does friendship, it applies without respect of persons.[2]

The hierarchical relationship between officers and ordinary soldiers entailed social hardships that hindered the development of comradeship. With respect to their living conditions - of key significance to how ordinary soldiers perceived deployment at the front - these two groups were worlds apart. The changes in tactics introduced by the third Supreme Command provided a basis for ordinary soldiers and their superiors to move closer together in combat units, fuelling subsequent stylisation. Those on the lower rungs of the command structure saw their responsibilities enhanced, first within the framework of the regulations on 'defensive action within positional warfare' which came into effect at the end of 1916, and later through decrees on offensive action. Within groups more deeply staggered when the terrain allowed, the officers in charge could now evade an attack and decide when to launch a counter-attack.[3] Lower-ranking unit officers thus became more self-confident when dealing with those higher up the chain of command. A small number of soldiers felt a sense of pride in combat. For them, common soldiers and their commanding officers moved closer together. This was in contrast to the back area (*Etappe*), which was seen as a hotbed of corruption, and to the higher-ranking military staff posted there, far away from the fighting:

> I am studying here in the back area for a short while on my way back from the military hospital to the front. I tell you - it'd be better if I said nothing at all.

2. Martin Broszat, Einleitung, in: idem (ed.), *Kommandant in Auschwitz. Autobiographische Aufzeichnungen von Rudolf Höß*, Stuttgart: Deutsche Verlags-Anstalt 1958, pp. 7-21, p. 20.

3. See the brilliant interpretation in Michael Geyer, Vom massenhaften Tötungshandeln, oder: Wie die Deutschen das Krieg-Machen lernten, in: Peter Gleichmann/Thomas Kühne (eds), *Massenhaftes Töten. Kriege und Genozide im 20. Jahrhundert*, Essen: Klartext 2004, pp. 105-42; see also Ziemann, Chemin des Dames.

> They don't know what war is. This makes those of us from the front terribly proud, blindly so at times no doubt, but we have a right to feel proud.[4]

This mechanism, which tended to minimise the consequences of difference in rank, was, however, effective only during deployment on the front line. Even there, it worked only if immediate superiors dealt with the dangers involved in the mission in exemplary fashion, which was not always the case.[5] In the back area, the hierarchical divide between officers and ordinary soldiers, along with the associated hardships, remained as significant as ever. 'The word "comradeship" only has any meaning now directly at the front. The officers and soldiers in field grey uniform shake hands more often there. But away from the front there's usually no comradeship, that is, none between these two groups.'[6]

As between officers and ordinary soldiers, comradeship among the latter was also 'determined above all by the mission'. During the fighting and particularly in situations of great danger, members of a unit did everything they could to help one another.[7] Soldiers had to serve together in the same unit for a certain amount of time, however, if they were to develop a subjective sense of belonging together in the group beyond deployment at the front. This happened quite rarely under conditions of war. The high turnover rate among the troops was significant even among the base army and encouraged mutual indifference in comparison to peacetime:

> In peacetime, the feeling of belonging together is rooted in the camaraderie of those sharing the same quarters. You can even see this in the expression 'my quarters-mate' [*Zimmerkamerad*] invented by the men themselves. This important factor has lost its meaning in the war because men move from one unit to another so often, because the barracks are so full and because it is hard to keep them warm, particularly in winter. The men do not feel at home in the barracks and head for the tavern as soon as they are off-duty.[8]

Heavy losses in the field, mainly among the units subject to the most intense fighting, often meant that soldiers lost comrades they were used to interacting with on an everyday basis; they were constantly coming

4. Excerpt from a war letter, 23.9.1917: BSB.
5. Ulrich/Ziemann, *Frontalltag*, p. 124.
6. Josef [surname unknown], 16.7.1916, to Verband der Bergarbeiter Deutschlands: BArch, 92, 271, fol. 274.
7. Cron, *Studentendienst*, p. 44.
8. Liaison officer, E./R.I.R. 12, 11.12.1917: BHStA/IV, stv. GK I.AK 2378.

'across lots of unknown faces' in their unit.[9] The Bavarian army's best-known combatant experienced this. In early December 1914, after receiving the Iron Cross Second Class, he wrote to an acquaintance: 'Of course, almost all my comrades, who deserved it [such a decoration] too, are dead.'[10] It was not only the turnover rate among units that hindered the development of comradely bonds. Various observers confirmed that wherever the sense of comradeship, which generally diminished during the course of the war, still pertained, it was mostly self-interested.[11] The living conditions of the troops rapidly worsened as the war progressed. This sidelined the kind of idealistic comradeship which may have arisen among enthusiastic soldiers during the first months of the war. What is more, it forced every soldier to focus first and foremost on satisfying his own basic needs for food, drink, quarters and clothing, generating a widespread 'spirit of selfishness'. This was manifest, for instance, in countless cases of theft from comrades.[12]

Furthermore, ordinary soldiers had little prospect of moving up the ranks. Regulars and reservists thus tended to differentiate themselves from territorial reservists and substitute reservists, and vice versa.[13] Student volunteers faced hostility from conscripts because they had better prospects of promotion. The latter sometimes subjected those who embraced the war with 'high spirits' to physical abuse and intimidation.[14] Aversion could turn to maliciousness if a volunteer's 'comrades' suspected him of being of poor character as well. When three soldiers of the 32nd Infantry Regiment were taken prisoner while on patrol, one soldier noted in his diary:

> The captured bandsman had the biggest mouth in our company and was the filthiest swine as well. The French must have had a good laugh. They didn't need to send out a patrol and knew which unit was on the other side anyway. We couldn't stop laughing that day, everyone was so pleased because the volunteer Gesicht had been taken prisoner. The French are very decent - there was no curtain fire from them.[15]

9. Richert, *Beste Gelegenheit*, pp. 158 (quote), 176, 323.

10. Adolf Hitler to Joseph Popp, 3.12.1914, quoted in Joachim C. Fest, *Hitler. Eine Biographie*, Frankfurt/M., Berlin: Propyläen-Verlag 1991, p. 103.

11. Cron, *Sekretariat*, pp. 14, 26.

12. Jacob Weis, 'Feldseelsorge bei den Truppen u. im Feldlazarett der Front im Stellungskrieg', n.d. [Easter 1916]: AEM, NL Faulhaber 6776.

13. Cron, *Sekretariat*, pp. 14–15.

14. Ulrich, Desillusionierung, pp. 118–19.

15. War diary of Georg Schenk, 4.5.1917: BHStA/IV, HS 3410.

In addition, subjective factors hampered identification with the social reality of the armed forces. Soldiers subject to the kind of socialisation that was unavoidable as long as the war lasted had no choice but to cooperate with one another in order to fulfil their duties. Units were cobbled together from men of all classes and age groups, who lived together in cramped conditions. In such circumstances, friction was bound to arise among 'comrades'. Many soldiers hid their fear and uncertainty behind an unimpressed exterior and rough manner, which inevitably incensed those of a more sensitive nature:

> I used the pillow you sent me yesterday for the first time and it was so soft to sleep on, but my first tears also fell upon it. My dear Bettl, during the day, among all these different types of unknown people (and you have no notion, thank God, what kind of rascals and characters are among them), you can't show your feelings or you'll be laughed at and mocked. But at night as I lay alone on the pallet and looked at the lovely photograph of you, I felt such sorrow and tears welled up in my eyes.[16]

Other soldiers, meanwhile, were from the outset disinclined to show those serving alongside them the same degree of consideration generally required in everyday life, because of their character or the manners typical of their home milieu:

> There are lots of things that people don't like at all about military life. Your comrades are your biggest problem, apart from the few that you get along with very well. But the youngsters, especially lads from the country, are very hard to cope with. They think they can take all kinds of liberties with us older men. For most people, these young lads have nothing. They've brought nothing but their peasant's arrogance with them and their callous way of talking. It really makes me angry at times. The so-called comradeship exists only on paper. Nowhere have I seen as much selfishness as in the armed forces.[17]

Given these tendencies, which hindered the emergence of comradely relations, many soldiers naturally developed close bonds only with a small number of their fellows whom they felt they could rely on come what may. The more individual peculiarities and character traits came to the fore over the course of time, the more likely such people were to become friends. The importance of these relationships, which did not depend solely on serving together, was particularly apparent in the

16. Reservist M.E., 21.2.1915: BfZ, Slg. Schüling vol. 63.
17. Excerpt from a letter by a soldier from Augsburg, 12.7.1917: BSB.

bitterness felt after the death of a good friend, usually referred to as one's 'best mate [*Kamerad*]':

> I'm in reasonably good shape but the offensive has really taken it out of me. Thank God I made it OK. But I really thought I would be taken prisoner. Or blown to pieces at any moment. I've never experienced shelling like that. A lot of men bit the dust again. My best mate was buried alive and when he was dug out he was already dead. He was married, has a wife the same age as you and a girl of six. It is awfully sad how families are being torn apart. And for what? Everyone in the trenches moans about and curses this mass murder.[18]

In the field, soldiers from rural areas relied above all on personal relationships which developed with work colleagues and friends from their local area. They were less than happy to find themselves among 'lots of unknown comrades' or when 'no friends' served in their company.[19] Farmers were particularly pleased to meet relatives or friends from their village or the surrounding area among their fellow soldiers and made much of such encounters in their letters or memoirs.[20] Interaction with such people was smooth and inspired a sense of familiarity otherwise rare in the field. One could exchange news about the fate of friends or relatives. Generally speaking, therefore, farmers could identify with their fellow soldiers to the extent that they could pick up on the network of relations to which they were already accustomed in civilian life. In the early stages of the war, many young soldiers in fact hoped to see something of the 'world' during the campaign. Did such hopes lead these men to view their involvement in the war positively? In 1915, for example, when his company was about to be transferred, one miner expected his wartime experience to endow him with undefined knowledge of much value in civilian life:

> I for my part will be pleased if I can move up the ranks a little so I can see and learn as much as possible. You can put what you learn here to good use later on. The war can't last for ever, it's got to end sooner or later. If I can do the same job afterwards as I did before, a good deal of what I've seen, heard and observed here will come in useful.[21]

18. Excerpt from a letter, 6.5.1917: BSB.
19. Stefan Schimmer, 26.10.1914: BHStA/IV, Amtsbibliothek 9584.
20. Christoph Erhardt, 20.5.1917: BfZ, Slg. Knoch.
21. K. Grüttner, 6.8.1915: BArch, 92, 271, fol. 54.

Some farmers mention impressive sights such as imposing churches or cities larger than any they had seen before. They thus took advantage of the opportunities for 'tourism' presented by their stint in the field.[22] Their encounter with the realities at the front, however, pushed this aspect of wartime experience into the background. 'I remember Fritz saying it was good that I had to get out into the "wide world". He imagined it would be "an enrichment" and lovely things like that. Oh there have been plenty of negative things, but good ones? Heavens above!'[23] In 1917, a young soldier noted that men of his age were annoyed at having to spend their 'best years ... uselessly' in the field, rather than working to advance their careers.[24] At the beginning of the last year of the war, some front-line soldiers expressed their indignation at having to live 'like a gypsy' all the time.[25] Servants and farmers who had served at the front for a long time generally wished for peace and the chance to return to their village as soon as possible: 'Dear Kathrine, I have been in this dreadful country for nearly six months now and have seen more than enough. If only this swindle would come to an end.'[26]

The desire to return home draws attention to a perceptual model whose significance was already apparent in relation to the desire for furlough and to how the prevailing atmosphere among the troops developed over time. Going home referred not only to a geographical goal that soldiers hoped to live long enough to see again. Its meaning was anchored in the network of social relations which linked the soldier with a particular place. The longing to return home was thus directly connected with homesickness. As one army chaplain working in a field hospital on the Western Front put it, this was an 'illness ... which has infected us all'.[27] The concept of homesickness, first discussed in depth in the medical and psychiatric debates of the eighteenth century, was later used primarily in a romantic way as a literary symbol of the pain of separation. Both strands of the discussion focused on a figure that

22. Hans Spieß, 14.10.1916: BHStA/IV, Kriegsbriefe 340.

23. Excerpt from a letter, 28.4.1918: BSB.

24. Letter by Ludwig Schröder, 23.11.1917: WUA, vol. 5, p. 275.

25. Excerpts from letters in the postal surveillance report for the 5th Army, 10.1.1918: BA/MA, W-10/50794, fol. 41f.

26. Christoph Erhardt, 30.10.1917: BfZ, Slg. Knoch.

27. Anton Gulielminetti, *Heimweh und Heimkehr. Ein Feldbrief an die heimwehkranken Kameraden*, Munich: Tuch 1916, p. 4.

embodied the feeling of loss associated with leaving home before the days of industrialisation: the soldier.[28]

Minus its romantic patina, from 1914 on conscripts also used this concept as an interpretive model. Most front-line troops made a constant effort to prevent ties with their civilian identity and families from being severed. This depended on a constant stream of information and interpretations reaching the field by means of the armed forces' postal service. Should the post fail to arrive, soldiers sometimes felt moved to reflect upon the hopelessness of their situation:

> If no letters arrive on Sundays, I can't help feeling put out. It's very easy to feel put out by the way. Only half of you is here. The other [half] is always at home. In a way, you live here in bits. You only take in half of everything, because your soul is always making its way home. Hopefully this unbearable double life will soon be at an end.[29]

Farmers were mainly interested in the state of the economy back home and in how their relatives were getting on in the fields. Letters by soldiers from a farming background tend to contain a litany of discussions on livestock prices, how the crops were doing, the slaughtering weight of pigs, and so on. The letter-writers thus documented their ongoing emotional ties with the civilian contexts from which they came.[30] It may be objected that there were other reasons for concentrating on this group of themes. Farmers, after all, were well used to dealing with such matters, and they could thus avoid describing the extreme reality of war, which was hard to get across in words. Many soldiers in fact hesitated to tell their relatives about moments of particular danger, or sometimes even injuries, because they wished to avoid 'making [their] loved-ones' hearts even heavier'.[31] In evaluating this factor, we should bear in mind that only the minority of soldiers who identified positively with the events of the war tended to produce detailed descriptions of fighting and of their own achievements in battle.[32] It was above all young soldiers with an academic education who waxed lyrical about the theatre of war, on the basis of

28. Ina-Maria Greverus, *Auf der Suche nach der Heimat*, Munich: C.H. Beck 1979, pp. 106–48.

29. Soldier from Warsaw, 6.1.1918: BSB.

30. Jakob Eberhard, 26.5.1915: private possession.

31. Günther Simroth, 25.12.1914: WUA, vol. 5, p. 262.

32. See the letters written by one such individual in Ulrich/Ziemann, *Frontalltag*, p. 85.

their enthusiasm for battle and their ability to express themselves in writing. When farmers wrote their brief depictions of battles, they tended to consider the destructive consequences, the 'horrific devastation'.[33] Their intention here was not to idealise their role as soldiers. A farmer's son wrote to the 'peasant doctor' Georg Heim, who was a pivotal figure in the Christian Peasants' Association, in 1917: 'I also think it vital that school books, the next time they publish new ones, stop praising and idolising the soldiers, and instead present them as despicable, a disgrace and murderers, because that is exactly what war is.'[34]

Some soldiers were aware of the sharp contrast between their own perceptions and the way letters published in newspapers stylised the heroic life of the soldier.[35] Ultimately, though, fighting was just one - admittedly highly problematic - aspect of everyday life at the front. Soldiers' anxiety about satisfying their basic daily needs often pushed it into the background.[36] In any case, soldiers from a farming background did not refer to life back home only through formulaic queries. Farmers in fact remained closely connected with their farms and gave their wives detailed instructions on how to carry out the necessary work. Some, however, had to face the fact that, after a long period in the field, they had lost some of the necessary knowledge and competence and could no longer intervene by means of letter:

> I've had nothing since your letter of the 23rd. Is something amiss at home or, dear Babet, do you have no time? Or have you forgotten me with all that work? I don't give a damn about the work, I'd rather you looked after yourself and the children and think of me as well from time to time - as for other things and things that need doing at home, leave the fields as they are, as long as you all have enough to eat! How far have you got with the harvest and with the threshing, do you have everything at home? Just do what you can, my dear, and what is of use to you - I can't do anything![37]

Farmers were constantly preoccupied with the fate of their farms and often went home on leave. This intensified their longing to return to their families as soon as possible. Married farmers suffered particularly badly from the feeling of homesickness, which worsened as the war dragged

33. Stefan Schimmer, 18.10.1914: BHStA/IV, Amtsbibliothek 9584.
34. Michael Kitzelmann, n.d. [1917]: StaA Regensburg, NL Heim 1316.
35. Ulrich/Ziemann, *Frontalltag*, p. 144.
36. Klemperer, *Curriculum Vitae*, p. 401.
37. L.R., 7.8.1917: BfZ, Slg. Schüling vol. 5, no. 83.

on. They perceived this forced separation from their familiar civilian milieu as one of the least palatable consequences of deployment at the front. As one farmer wrote in March 1917, most had 'felt homesick for a very long time'.[38] The desire to return home during periods of sowing and harvesting, which was bound up with homesickness, was particularly strong. At such times, farmers felt their dissatisfaction with military life and the futility of the time spent in the armed forces with painful intensity:

> The work will be starting up again at home. Oh, how, how I would like to be at home and help out from early in the morning until late at night, and go without every pleasure, if I could be with my loved ones. Never in my life would I have imagined that I would end up in such a wretched situation. But hopefully things will get better soon. I haven't taken off this uniform for four months. If only this war would come to an end, you can't even call it a war, we have a quite different word for it. I would much prefer not to be alive at all any more, I wish I had never been born.[39]

The rhythms of farming life, reflecting the passage of the seasons, had become deeply ingrained in some farmers' perceptual models. It sometimes took no more than an improvement in the weather to make such men feel intensely homesick.[40] Thoughts of home could, however, have a soothing effect on some soldiers or even make them more willing to face further exertions. For as long as one fought in the land of the enemy, the villages and towns of home were spared the destruction of buildings and land, at least that visible in the war zone. This motivated farmers primarily in relation to their own property and community.[41] Government propaganda and sermons by army chaplains, meanwhile, attempted to use or strengthen this motivation, with an added nationalistic flavour, to encourage men to stay the course.[42]

Homesickness was thus connected with men's working lives. Apart from this, it revolved around seeing one's closest relatives again, one's wife and children. Around Easter, Whitsun and Christmas, men longed for their families with particular intensity. This had much to do with the

38. Josef Beigel, 20.3.1917: BHStA/IV, Militärgericht 6. Ldw.-Div. B 11.

39. Letter by a soldier in the field, 7.3.1917: BSB.

40. Christoph Erhardt, 15.8.1917: BfZ, Slg. Knoch.

41. O.K., 2.11.1917: BfZ, Slg. Schüling vol. 110.

42. Albrecht, *Landtag*, p. 205; Johann Klier, *Von der Kriegspredigt zum Friedensappell. Erzbischof Michael von Faulhaber und der Erste Weltkrieg*, Munich: UNI-Druck 1991, p. 109.

fact that at such times, when soldiers were usually off-duty, there was no daily work routine to distract them from mulling over their own situation. Attending church and religious festivals also caused religious soldiers to remember their home areas.[43] In the replacement army, every Sunday might inspire painful thoughts of one's family. Farmers' sons did not suffer as badly from homesickness as married soldiers. They too, however, harboured the desire to see their nearest and dearest again in a peaceful, civilian context.[44]

Soldiers from a rural background, particularly married farmers, were concerned mainly with the contexts of their civilian life even during deployment at the front. It is at present impossible to determine precisely the strength of homesickness and the desire for a civilian life among units made up of other social classes. Soldiers from an urban background, however, certainly felt the desire to 'see each other again in [their] home town'.[45] Soldiers from a farming background were, however, the only ones to link a longing for their families with a longing for civilian work and its seasonal rhythms, endowing homesickness with a particular intensity. This was rooted in the fact that the farming family moulded and shaped its members to an extraordinary degree. It was at once an economic unit, the site of social reproduction and the hub of emotionally significant relations.

Soldiers thus felt terribly homesick, while camaraderie diminished over the course of the war. Together, these factors left little room for an interpretation of the self geared towards the symbols of a militaristic identity, such as comradeship, heroism or the cult of the warrior. In their interpretation of the war as a whole, soldiers from rural areas adapted elements of political ideologies which few of them had previously embraced. Such soldiers, however, fell back on different models to process their own circumstances. Bolstered by structural mechanisms such as frequent furlough, they tended to conceive of their time at the front as a merely temporary removal from their accustomed domain of action. The power of the - however idealised - notion of *Heimat* to structure the self-perception of rural soldiers diminished only partially, even when they were in the field for long periods. Traditional models of identification, such as being with one's family and working on one's own farm, were of

43. Entries in the diary of Jakob Eberhard from 28.3.1915 and 3.6.1915: private possession.

44. Hans Spieß, 13.12.1916, 16.6.1918: BHStA/IV, Kriegsbriefe 340.

45. August Horn, 22.9.1917: BHStA/IV, Militärgericht 6. Ldw.-Div. H 31.

central significance. Soldiers aimed to achieve these things; at the same time they served as symbols of a life back on track after the return home. This casts doubt on the oft-repeated claim that soldiers felt increasingly alienated from their home. The topos of the alienated front-line soldier is largely rooted in the perception of soldiers with nationalistic leanings, determined to stay the course at all costs. While on leave and especially once the war was over, such men inevitably became aware of the widespread mood of political radicalism and rejection of the war.[46]

One possible factor leading to conflict between front-line soldiers and their wives was the issue of extra-marital relations on either side.[47] Stories about the affairs of soldiers' wives unsettled front-line soldiers and inspired them to send admonitory letters home.[48] The extra-marital sexuality of soldiers at the front was, however, a far more serious problem for public debate, because it was closely linked with discourses about population policy and social hygiene. The military authorities took steps to prevent venereal diseases among soldiers, the post-demobilisation situation weighing heavily on their minds in this regard. Due to the possible demographic consequences of promoting artificial contraceptives, however, such plans were pursued only to a limited degree.[49]

The back area, which featured a large number of brothels sanctioned and supervised by the military authorities, was the key setting for sexual encounters. The establishments open to regular soldiers were neatly separated from those created especially for officers. The military authorities thought it unwise to abolish these 'for disciplinary reasons'.[50] Soldiers also took advantage of opportunities arising beyond the regulated brothels, in part because prostitutes were expensive relative to their salary, costing between two and ten marks.[51] Girls living among the civilian population that remained in the area of operations made themselves available; some were so poor that they sold their bodies for a loaf of bread.[52]

46. Martin Bochow, *Männer unter dem Stahlhelm. Vom Werden, Wollen und Wirken des Stahlhelm, Bund der Frontsoldaten*, Stuttgart, Berlin, Leipzig: Union 1933, p. 20.

47. Cron, *Sekretariat*, p. 38.

48. Excerpt from a letter by a soldier at the front, 29.5.1917: BSB.

49. Daniel, *Arbeiterfrauen*, pp. 139–44.

50. Chief of the field sanitary services, 11.6.1918: WUA, vol. 11/1, p. 161.

51. Ulrich/Ziemann, *Frontalltag*, p. 138.

52. Klemperer, *Curriculum Vitae*, p. 387.

The age distribution of soldiers who contracted a venereal disease for the first time during the war provides us with a general indication of differences between men in terms of how willing they were to take advantage of opportunities for sexual contact in the field. Almost 60 per cent of these men were 30 years of age or younger, the vast majority of them unmarried.[53] A thorny subject of this kind was hardly likely to be dealt with openly in letters. Nonetheless, evidence shows that married Catholic farmers condemned other soldiers' extra-marital sexual relationships as an offence against moral conceptions of a religious nature:

> My dear wife! You can't imagine how much I love you. As soon as I get a letter from you, I put everything down. I just have to read your letter. If only the war was over at last. The next time you send me tobacco, do me a favour and pop in that rosary you bought me. I'm keen to find out whether there will be peace during the month of Marian worship. The war's a punishment from God of course and the people are unwilling to change their ways. Our soldiers are also a cross to bear. A lot of them, including the married ones, behave dreadfully; if they come back for a couple of days, or those sent to the front months ago, it's unbelievable. In Duaige more than 300 men are in the field hospital (with venereal diseases). Isn't that sad? And men like that want peace? My dear wife, I would rather die than be unfaithful to you, we love each other so much. I'd much rather get one of your letters. Hopefully we'll see each other again quite soon, it would be wonderful. We just need to have faith in the Mother of God and everything will turn out all right.[54]

Young, unmarried men were more willing to break the bounds of Catholic social morality. The control of sexuality was one of the 'central axes of Christian socialisation' within popular Catholicism.[55] At the front, and amid the anonymous hustle and bustle of the garrison towns back home, the threshold for offences against the normative religious code sank during the war. Conditions were particularly ripe for such offences around barracks. In Munich the wives of many conscripts were 'particularly inclined to surrender their bodies to soldiers' even without payment.[56] Men could now indulge in sexual contact free of the influence of parents and gossiping neighbours. Above all, the disciplining influence of the local

53. *Sanitätsbericht*, p. 166.
54. Johann Baptist Blehle, 8.5.1915: StAA, Amtsgericht Immenstadt E 29/1920.
55. Mooser, Volksreligion, p. 156.
56. Police headquarters Munich, 25.9.1915: BHStA/IV, stv. GK I.AK 2278; Daniel, *Arbeiterfrauen*, p. 143.

priest, anchored in confession, died away.[57] Army chaplains noted that uncontrolled sexual relationships reduced the effectiveness of religious disciplining. Such relationships should be considered as one of the factors underlying the change in the behaviour of male farm labourers apparent after the war.[58]

4.2 Religious Stabilisation

Of the rural population of southern Bavaria at the beginning of the twentieth century, Catholics made up around 90 per cent in Swabia and almost 100 per cent in other areas. Religiosity was their primary means of 'interpreting the world and helped guide them through life'.[59] Popular piety rested on a densely woven web of organisations rooted in the local milieu, such as religious associations and congregations; it was closely bound up with the rhythms of everyday rural working life in the liturgical forms of cultic piety and the wide variety of popular customs. Apart from regions in which many people were members of the Bavarian Peasants' League, priests enjoyed much prestige as opinion leaders among the rural population. They came up against the limits of their influence, however, whenever they attempted to stem the magical-superstitious elements so fundamental to this form of religiosity, especially in rural areas.

The sources impose a number of constraints on any discussion of the significance of religiosity for soldiers from rural backgrounds. Reminiscent of the legendary character of some traditions from the pre-war period, many accounts and publications by priests tend to stylise and overdraw the piety of soldiers, and many of these were produced long after the war was over.[60] Surviving periodic accounts by military pastors and the local village clergy, however, paint a fairly unvarnished picture of the symptoms of crisis. The first type of source does not allow us to pin down the social background of supposedly pious soldiers with any precision.

57. Michael Mitterauer, Religion in lebensgeschichtlichen Aufzeichnungen, in: Andreas Gestrich *et al.* (eds), *Biographie-sozialgeschichtlich*, Göttingen: Vandenhoeck & Ruprecht 1988, pp. 61-85, pp. 76-9.

58. Buchberger, *Seelsorgsaufgaben*, p. 59.

59. See Blessing, Kirchenfromm; idem, *Umwelt*, pp. 13-14 (quote); Mooser, Volksreligion.

60. Explicit mention of the symptoms of crisis can be found in Erhard Schlund (O.F.M.), Aufgaben der Volksmission nach dem Kriege, *Theologisch-praktische Monats-Schrift* 29 (1919), pp. 51-9; this contrasts with the later apologetic depiction: idem, *Die Religion im Weltkrieg*, Munich: Knorr & Hirth 1931.

Some observers, however, underlined the particular religiosity of farmers at the front.[61]

It is likewise unclear precisely to what extent soldiers took in theological arguments and what impact these had on them. To focus on such subtleties is, however, to miss the point. The popular Catholicism created and organised in the nineteenth century under the influence of ultramontanism did not necessarily require its adherents to have a thorough intellectual grasp of contentious issues of dogma. It in fact tended to 'encourage and reward' the publicly 'visible demonstration of faith'.[62] To bolster their pastoral success, the Jesuits had directly encouraged such a 'superficial' model of piety in the pre-war period. The military chaplains were faced with the consequences. One remarked critically in 1916 that of the soldiers from Altbayern 'many [seemed] heavy-handed, lacked education and had a mechanistic approach to religion'.[63] Another military pastor stated that, for soldiers from Altbayern, God was first and foremost a 'helper in times of need', their prayers were 'prayers of supplication and He proved His value by answering them'.[64]

The intensity of soldiers' religious engagement depended first of all on the conditions under which the military clergy's pastoral activities at the front took place.[65] In contrast to Prussia, there was no exempted military pastoral care in Bavaria in peacetime; troops were included in the parish in which their garrison was located. During the war, the Archbishop of Munich and Freising, Cardinal Franz von Bettinger, took over the post of military chaplain of the Bavarian army and thus overall control of Church matters. Military chaplains, higher-ranking military officials with the rank of officer, wore a uniform. Previously, their duties were hardly regulated at all and thus depended heavily on their personal commitment. In carrying them out, they relied on the divisional commander, as the military authorities were responsible for organising pastoral care.

61. War chronicle by the priest Karl Lang, p. 13: ABA, NL Karl Lang. In his chronicle, composed in 1934, Lang goes into detail about his experiences as chaplain of the 11th Infantry Division.

62. Mooser, Volksreligion, p. 148.

63. Jacob Weis, Feldseelsorge bei den Truppen, Ostern 1916: AEM, NL Faulhaber 6776.

64. Franz-Xaver Eggersdorfer, Felderfahrung und Heimatseelsorge, *Theologisch-praktische Monats-Schrift* 27 (1917), pp. 576–81, 631–43, quote p. 634.

65. Arnold Vogt, *Religion im Militär. Militärseelsorge zwischen Kriegsverherrlichung und Humanität*, Frankfurt/M., Berne: Peter Lang 1984, pp. 260–82, 466–74, 504–19; Klier, *Kriegspredigt*, pp. 68–72.

Pastoral care on the front line was makeshift in the extreme. Troop movements, the sometimes irregular oscillation between front line and billet, the existence of a large number of small, isolated units and above all the length of front for which a particular division was responsible made it difficult to hold regular services, which were possible only every two to three weeks at most.[66] Particularly during the first months of the war, but also later on, many pious soldiers complained that they had no opportunity to attend a service for weeks or months at a time.[67] Only soldiers stationed in the back area for long periods, such as farmer Jakob Eberhard, were able 'to go to church every day' and 'to receive Holy Communion every Sunday, which I like most of all'.[68]

Before examining the meaning of their religious engagement for soldiers and the tendencies hampering it, we trace the fluctuations in its external intensity evident over the course of the war. We are aided in this task by a series of observations and assessments. These diverge on specific points but may be fitted together to form a clearly recognisable trend. Contemporary observers took it for granted that the war would contribute to a religious renewal and would inevitably intensify the need to create meaning through religion, especially for combatants. The wave of religious interest that began during mobilisation confirmed this supposition.[69] The trend continued during the first months of the war. Large numbers of men attended services and prayers on the front line. Many took up the opportunity to attend confession, and many a soldier found his way back to his faith. Numerous soldiers' letters from this period show that prayer was a common practice among Catholic troops.[70]

Initially as early as 1915, and then on a fairly large scale from 1916, the combatants' religious fervour and the frequency with which they attended mass and received the sacraments diminished. At the beginning of September 1916 a deputy officer serving in the 14th Reserve Infantry Regiment reported that there was no longer 'any sign of prayer' among the soldiers; only six men in an entire company had taken the chance to attend the Sunday confessional.[71] General remarks on such signs of crisis

66. Eggersdorfer, Felderfahrung, pp. 578–81.

67. Bishopric of Regensburg, 12.12.1914: BZAR, OA 1328.

68. Jakob Eberhard, 26.5.1915: private possession.

69. Ulrich/Ziemann, *Frontalltag*, pp. 109–10.

70. Cron, *Sekretariat*, p. 40.

71. Quoted in Helmut Weck, Herr Expositus, wie lange wird der Krieg noch dauern? Die Kriegsjahre 1916–1918 im Spiegel der Chronik des Miltacher Expositus Karl Holzgartner, *Beiträge zur Geschichte im Landkreis Cham* 2 (1985), pp. 289–324, p. 319.

by military chaplains confirm these dates. In July 1916, at a conference of military clergy, a divisional priest stated that the initial religious 'zeal' had 'gradually diminished as a result of positional warfare and because the war has gone on for so long'.[72] A few months later, alongside the general 'waning of religious zeal', another priest complained about cases in which soldiers had 'begun to have agonising doubts about their faith, and even to lose it entirely'.[73] In one battalion, about a quarter of which was made up of Catholics, only five soldiers went to confession in the final quarter of 1916. In one sickbay occupied by 5,500 men during the same period, no more than eighty on average could be assembled to attend mass.[74]

The crisis of piety among soldiers, widespread from 1916, did not alter fundamentally during the rest of the war. Only during the spring offensive of 1918 - in line with the general improvement in soldiers' mood during this period - did some begin to receive the sacraments once again, having failed to do so for a number of years.[75] Towards the end of the war, soldiers waited in front of the church, although they were obliged to attend mass.[76] Apart from pastoral reports by military chaplains, which have survived only in fragments, accounts by village clergy also confirm the negative consequences of serving in the war for the religiousness of soldiers, which struck them while such men were home on leave. Many stayed away from mass, indulged in faithless and blasphemous talk and thus increased the number of 'doubters' grumbling about God in the village. As priests frequently stated, however, these symptoms of crisis were only ever to be seen among a limited number of soldiers on leave.[77] Some local priests explicitly mentioned that a good number of soldiers continued to conscientiously perform their religious duties until the end of the war and showed no signs whatever of incipient doubts about their faith; some of them even took the opportunity to go on a pilgrimage to Altötting.[78]

Taken as a whole, this evidence shows that it was only some soldiers who felt less attached to the Church and grew less inclined to interpret the world through a religious lens. Many held onto their religious attitudes

72. Protokoll der Konferenz der katholischen Feld- und Etappengeistlichen der Armeeabteilung A, 4.7.1916: AEM, NL Faulhaber 6776.

73. Divisional chaplain Gregoire, 6. Ldw.-Div., 26.9.1916: AEM, 'Ordinariat 310'.

74. Michael Drummer, 7.2.1917: AEM, Akten des DK Buchberger.

75. Pastoral report by Michael Schaumberger, 3.4.1918: BZAR, OA 1328.

76. War chronicle by Karl Lang, p. 106: ABA, NL Karl Lang.

77. Sulzbach parish office, 12.6.1916: ABP, DekA II, Fürstenzell 12/I.

78. Ulbering parish office, 30.6.1916: ABP, DekA II, Pfarrkirchen 12/I.

until the end of the war. All soldiers' fundamental beliefs about the world were subjected to an extreme test of endurance by life on the front. Their views of religious matters became polarised. Differences in the intensity of faith, which existed even before the war, came to the surface. These had previously been concealed by the religiosity firmly entrenched within the Catholic milieu. Now, however, many soldiers openly articulated their doubts about religion. The emerging crisis, apparent in the behaviour of individuals and in collective forms of religious activity, was expressed with an intensity which seemed threatening to army chaplains. Some evidence suggests that for almost half of combatants religious convictions had become less significant as a means of mental orientation and stabilisation.[79]

An overview of the forms and distribution of the religiosity practised by soldiers shows that for them the Catholic faith was of significance primarily in grappling with a specific, particularly precarious aspect of everyday life at the front. Most front-line soldiers had to live with the fear of serious injury and the possibility of their own death. Many of them suppressed the latter possibility. For religious soldiers, meanwhile, religion had the potential to help them come to terms with this existential risk which applied to all those in the line of fire, was impossible to predict and contingent in nature. This highlights the fact that the 'instruments of grace' which the Church had to offer were valued particularly 'in the face of death'. It also indicates that vestiges of the concept of 'tamed death' (Philippe Ariès), which acknowledged it as part of human life and thus made it easier to bear, persisted among soldiers from rural backgrounds.[80] 'Impending death', as Swabian priest Karl Lang put it on the basis of several years of experience at the front, was a 'great ally' of the army pastor.[81] Services and prayers, as forms of a religiosity carried out and experienced collectively, were of considerable importance to pious soldiers.[82] The following analysis, however, is limited to religious practices carried out by individuals, because it is impossible to determine precisely whether soldiers' attendance at services was anchored in a serious religious conviction, as attendance was generally compulsory in the armed forces.

79. Schlund, *Religion*, p. 36.

80. Wiebel-Fanderl, Todesbewältigung; quote in Buchberger, *Seelsorgsaufgaben*, p. 7.

81. War chronicle by Karl Lang, p. 113: ABA, NL Karl Lang.

82. War diary of Jakob Eberhard, 28.3.1915: private possession.

Differences in the intensity of religious activity among the various units point to the importance of faith to coping with extreme situations. Troops less exposed to enemy fire, such as those in supply units and the artillery, particularly munitions columns, were markedly less inclined to attend mass than infantrymen.[83] Before troops departed to engage in particularly severe fighting, such as that which occurred on the Somme in the summer of 1916, up to five times as many men made their way to confessionals manned by military chaplains as at quieter times. According to one such clergyman, this showed the soldiers' 'true state of mind in matters of faith'. At times of 'crisis and danger', 'faith [had to be] taken off the shelf'. Afterwards, it was 'banished to its former position'.[84]

The key means deployed by pious soldiers to obtain supernatural assistance was unremitting prayer. The individualisation of prayer made little headway in the rural society of the Alpine region until well into the twentieth century, though more individual forms of 'ensuring salvation' did gain some ground within the context of the Sacred Heart Apostolate of Prayer. The traditional form of family prayer, however, continued to hold sway.[85] This state of affairs came to an abrupt end during the war. Collective prayer appears to have been a rarity on the front line. One army chaplain mentioned rosary prayers in 1915 during which one soldier led the prayers within a fairly small group. The chaplain made a point of mentioning that men placed 'boundless faith in the intercession' of the Virgin Mary and tried to 'pray away the winter campaign' by invoking it.[86]

Front-line soldiers wrote to their relatives reminding them how essential it was to pray and vice versa; they were still integrated into familial religious practices. Family members wrote to their relatives serving in the war expressing the hope that God would protect them or assuring them that they would pray to the Mother of God or saints such as St Joseph to shield them from harm. This reinforced pious soldiers' belief that they had not been 'abandoned' by their relatives while in the field.[87] Their letters mentioned that they were continuing to pray dutifully. In return, they urged relatives and friends to keep on praying that they (the combatants)

83. Pastoral report by Michael Drummer, 7.2.1917: AEM, Akten des DK Buchberger.

84. Pastoral report by Balthasar Meier, 7.2.1917: AEM, Akten des DK Buchberger.

85. Busch, *Katholische Frömmigkeit*, pp. 283-90, quote p. 289.

86. Norbert Stumpf (O.M.Cap.), 17.10.1915: AEM, NL Faulhaber 6779.

87. Georg Maier, 14.11.1914: AEM, Kriegschronik Altenerding B 1837.

be saved and for their safe return home: 'Pray as much as you can. I say a rosary three or four times a day. I pray almost day and night that my life shall be saved by the grace of God.'[88] In certain circumstances, even soldiers whose memoirs otherwise contain no evidence of much piety glanced heavenwards and said a quick, heartfelt prayer or begged the saints to assist them. Others vowed to pray regularly in future, should they be spared: '25 August [1914]. Remember us as long as we are alive, many lives have been lost on both sides not to mention all the injured. I promised to say a rosary every day at home or to have one said if I return home safe and sound from the campaign.'[89]

Intensive prayer, supplemented from time to time by paying to have a mass said, reinforced pious soldiers' faith that they could be sure of God's mercy and protection. This build-up of prayers also featured a strong focus on what one could expect after death. To the extent that it seemed possible to influence this positively by saying prayers constantly, this made the fear of death less unbearable: 'If I am shot, you can rest assured that I was well prepared. I pray day and night. I am also sending a two-mark note. Use it to have a mass said.'[90] Though most likely limited to a few extreme cases, hopes of increasing God's mercy through fervent prayer and an awareness of the unfathomable nature of divine Providence could lead to a highly stoical attitude. In his memoirs, Victor Klemperer alludes to the reaction of a very pious peasant's son when Klemperer leapt to one side to dodge a shell which had suddenly fallen from the sky but proved to be a dud. His comrade remained where he was and amiably rebuked him: 'Don't be angry with me, but what's the jumping aside all about? God takes your life or protects you as he sees fit. I am very calm.'[91]

Penance done in prayer and through confession was not, however, aimed solely at saving the individual believer at a time of great danger. Even before the war, popular Catholicism had come to stress the the problematic nature of modern society and the de-Christianising impact of industrialisation. Through their prayers, the mass of pious worshippers could and should stop the symptoms of decline.[92] The faithful believed that the war had laid bare the catastrophic consequences of such societal development. It thus seemed natural to many inhabitants of rural areas to

88. Stefan Schimmer, 4.11.1914: BHStA/IV, Amtsbibliothek 9584.
89. War diary of Georg Schenk, 25.8.1914: BHStA/IV, HS 3410.
90. Stefan Schimmer, 10.12.1914: BHStA/IV, Amtsbibliothek 9584.
91. Klemperer, *Curriculum Vitae*, p. 407.
92. Mooser, *Volksreligion*, pp. 154-5.

embrace the view propagated by bishops and theologians that the war was God's punishment. As a farmer from Swabia shows in his diary, one's own prayers were thus placed in the context of resisting the 'secular spirit'. The fact that he dedicates this passage to his wife, whom he calls 'Mother', clearly shows that this idea constituted his last wishes:

> But the great World War had to come because the people have been too wicked and are still too wicked. There are still wicked elements who do not believe in God, in whom the seducer world spirit is present and through whom he enters the world; but many have returned to our dear God and have obtained His mercy. My dear Mother I go to church every day and say a rosary whenever I can. This is the truth and if I should never return home, the book will come home and that should comfort you, because I am under the protection of the dear Mother of God because I pray every day to the Virgin Mary and to God to protect me.[93]

In the context of soldiers' piety, prayer had a primarily stabilising function, particularly in relation to the extreme experience of a serious injury or possible death. Furthermore, prayer practices carried out while in the field also provide us with information about the extent to which people accepted various types of cult. Because of its semi-official character within the Church as a specific 'cult for coping with the war', devotion to the Sacred Heart of Jesus achieved considerable popularity among soldiers in the field. The stylisation of the Sacred Heart as a 'guarantee of victory', which was bound up with this, inevitably reduced its appeal drastically, however, as the prospect of victory came to seem more distant and the more indifferent the troops felt about it as a goal.[94]

Meanwhile, the Marian rosary dominated the cultic preferences of southern Bavarian soldiers, as a number of quotations have already shown. In late 1915 one army chaplain emphasised that the rosary was one of 'the best pastoral gifts for soldiers in the field'; 'many blackened soldiers' hands' were always held out as the priest distributed them. He also alluded to a practical reason why the rosary, which he stereotyped as a traditional phenomenon, was so dominant, by pointing to the fact that one needed no light to say rosaries during the long winter nights.[95] Troops preferred Marian prayers above all because of the Marian tenor of the popular piety which traditionally prevailed in Bavaria, as is apparent,

93. War diary of Jakob Eberhard, 26.2.1915: private possession.
94. Busch, *Katholische Frömmigkeit*, p. 108, pp. 110–14.
95. Pater Christ (S.J.), 18.12.1915: AEM, NL Faulhaber 6777.

for example, in the huge influx of around 300,000 visitors to the pilgrimage church in Altötting each year. Moreover, the rosary was commonly considered a helpful prayer, particularly at times of crisis, both before and after the First World War.[96]

Another way of assuring oneself of divine assistance involved doing or vowing to do something which proved one's status as a person of a particularly pious nature. One farmer therefore volunteered to help recover the body of a dead soldier at night despite the dangers involved, as this seemed to him a 'work of spiritual compassion'.[97] Should they return home safe and sound from the campaign or make it out of a dangerous situation, soldiers promised to go on a pilgrimage to one of the sacred sites in southern Bavaria after the war. As the numerous votive plaques in pilgrimage churches in Altbayern show, many veterans did not content themselves with pledges but made good on their word.[98] Finally, to prepare for the possibility of death, the remission of the temporal punishment for sins by means of an indulgence was an essential precondition. A sudden death without receiving the final sacraments was one of the prospects that most horrified the Catholic population.[99] In April 1918 army chaplain Karl Lang witnessed how a heavily injured young soldier 'cried out and confessed his sins' in a casualty station.[100] Droves of soldiers in front-line units thus made their way to confession, especially before departing for a heavily contested position. If there was insufficient time for all the soldiers to make their confession, the mass absolution performed instead was 'accepted very gratefully'.[101]

Penitence and the Church's instruments of mercy could convince a pious soldier that he was sufficiently prepared for the extreme realities of everyday life at the front. The scale and once-and-for-all nature of the

96. Michael Mitterauer, 'Nur diskret ein Kreuzzeichen.' Zu Formen des individuellen und gemeinschaftlichen Gebets in der Familie, in: Andreas Heller/ Therese Weber/Oliva Wiebel-Fanderl (eds), *Religion und Alltag. Interdisziplinäre Beiträge zu einer Sozialgeschichte des Katholizismus in lebensgeschichtlichen Aufzeichnungen*, Vienna, Cologne: Böhlau 1990, pp. 154-204, pp. 181-8.

97. Stefan Schimmer, 6.12.1914: BHStA/IV, Amtsbibliothek 9584.

98. Rudolf Kriss, *Volkskundliches aus altbayerischen Gnadenstätten. Beiträge zu einer Geographie des Wallfahrtsbrauchtums*, Augsburg: Filser 1930, pp. 52-3, 104-5, 133.

99. Wiebel-Fanderl, Todesbewältigung, p. 220.

100. War chronicle by the priest Karl Lang, p. 85: ABA, NL Karl Lang.

101. Pastoral report by the priest Josef Holzner, 1916: AEM, Akten des DK Buchberger.

threats facing them caused many combatants, especially those without links to the Church but also many of the faithful, to seek general forms of insurance capable of keeping them safe. A range of devotional objects of a superstitious-magical character, as used in previous wars, thus became highly popular among soldiers; their main, immediate aim was to provide protection from injury. These included, first of all, the prayer chains circulating among soldiers in the field and the *Schutzbriefe* and *Himmelsbriefe* (letters with prayers supposedly protecting the soldier from injury and death) which they took with them to the front.[102]

Such things were also popular among the rural population. A village priest complained in 1915 that he had been rewarded with nothing but 'hate and persecution' in the community after reproaching from the pulpit a farmer's wife who had provided every departing soldier with a *Schutzbrief*.[103] As surviving *Schutzbriefe* attest, the prayers they contained were usually of a Christological flavour. Jesus was claimed to have 'rendered harmless' all 'swords' and other weapons by means of his 'Five Holy Wounds' and the blood that flowed from them; anyone carrying such a letter was thus protected from all dangers.[104] While not all of these devotional objects had the Church's seal of approval, the scapular was an official Roman Catholic amulet. This was a consecrated pendant of cloth adorned with various indulgences, particularly common among adherents of the Sacred Heart cult and also popular among soldiers in the field during the war.[105]

Religious patterns of understanding the world had ambivalent consequences, though. Faith helped those who appear to have maintained their prayer practices until the war was over to deal with existential dangers, above all the possibility of death. It also made it easier to fit men into the system of military subordination, in that the religious conviction that God would 'make everything fine again' made the demands of military service seem easier to bear.[106] One of the most widespread 'forms of expression' of soldiers' religiosity was a pronounced 'fatalism' *vis-à-vis* the strains of everyday life on the front line.[107] It was not only soldiers' hopes that they as individuals would be saved which were linked with

102. Hanns Bächtold, *Deutscher Soldatenbrauch und Soldatenglaube*, Strasbourg: Trübner 1917, pp. 14-25.

103. Neuhofen parish office, 13.6.1915: ABP, DekA II, Pfarrkirchen 12/I.

104. *Schutzbrief* sent from Augsburg in April 1917: BSB.

105. Busch, *Katholische Frömmigkeit*, pp. 308-9.

106. Georg Meier, 24.1.1915: AEM, Kriegschronik Altenerding B 1837.

107. Cron, *Sekretariat*, p. 42.

God. Devout soldiers also believed that the war as a whole was solely the result of divine Providence. The decision to continue or end the war seemed to them part of a divine plan of salvation removed from human influences. In line with Catholic wartime sermons, most of them assumed that God would assist only their own side.[108]

Catholic faith clearly functioned to stabilise the soldiers mentally. It is, however, equally clear that there were limits to the diffusion and persuasiveness of such interpretive models. First, a mechanism of social adaptation ensured that direct advocacy of pious convictions or loyalty to the Church rarely met with much success. In September 1915 one soldier described to Bishop Michael von Faulhaber the resistance he encountered when he attempted to hold to account 'lapsed and half-hearted Catholics', who even bragged about their 'filthy talk'. Though he was rewarded with nothing but 'scorn and derision', he found consolation in contemplation of the 'Holy Archangel Michael', the 'Defender' of the Faith.[109] The pressure among soldiers to conform socially and the extremely rough manner that they cultivated as a result put pious soldiers off carrying out religious activities in public.[110] Many soldiers of a religious frame of mind were often 'afraid of other people', as army chaplains confirmed. As a consequence, mockers, who were condescending about the devoutness and religious activities of their comrades, tended to gain the upper hand among the troops over the course of the war. They expressed their disbelief vociferously, fuelling the religious doubts of even many convinced Catholics.[111]

Furthermore, the war went on for longer than expected and the fighting tended to intensify, while the number of casualties mounted rather than diminished. Soldiers increasingly began to doubt the efficacy of divine Providence. The course of the war made the notion that God's plan of salvation underpinned it seem absurd in the eyes of ordinary soldiers. A lengthy war thus brought the problem of theodicy to the forefront. What is more, the conviction that a just and 'all-gracious God' would surely 'not sit back and watch such murder' caused more and more men to doubt that God existed in the first place.[112] Even a military chaplain had to admit in retrospect that in 1916, taking in the many dead in a

108. Jakob Eberhard, 26.5.1915: private possession.

109. Franz St. Buscher, 28.9.1915: AEM, NL Faulhaber 6774.

110. Schlund, Aufgaben, p. 52.

111. Buchberger, *Seelsorgsaufgaben*, p. 57.

112. Georg Baumgartner, *Feldpostbrief an Mitglieder und Freunde des katholischen Burschenvereins*, Passau 1916, p. 9.

casualty station at Verdun, he had thought: 'The tempter is assailing me. "Can there be a God".' In his despair he begged God: 'O Lord increase my faith! You did not want any of this to happen!'[113] The military pastors sometimes responded to questions about God's influence by underlining the unfathomable nature of God's plan of salvation. Others tried to endow suffering with meaning by referring to Providence until the end of the war.

Soldiers also had to suffer the fact that their prayers went unanswered. This was particularly destructive of people's faith in the meaningfulness of religious engagement because this faith was often underpinned by a highly mechanistic conception of religion. This applied both to soldiers from rural areas of Altbayern, traditionally accustomed to such practices, and to those who sought security in prayer for the first time due to the pressures of war:

> Dear Franz, who would have believed in 14 that it would go on for 3 years and still no end in sight, I would have been better off if those two shots at Wytschaete in 14 had finished me off, rather than coming to grief in this hell. If only it would rain gunpowder for three days and then lighting would strike, so that everything was wiped out, then even a sacrilege can be a pious wish, if it led to peace in the world, then it would please God, but where is God now? I learned to pray from May to August 15 in the fighting at the Loretto Heights, but that's all over now, and you curse enough to make a peasant proud, and yet it's still better than ruining your nerves. I've had it up to here, sacrificing 5 years of your life to the Fatherland is really too much to expect, not to mention the three bullets which I'll have in my body.[114]

Ultimately, the pastoral activities of military chaplains inspired criticism, especially if they reflected propaganda urging soldiers to stay the course. From the very beginning, Church office-holders as well as organised and political Catholicism had seen the war as an opportunity to finally remove from Catholics the persistent stain of national unreliability and to achieve recognition as equals *vis-à-vis* the established political forces. The Church was unconditionally willing to do its national duty, make sacrifices and recognise the military authorities.[115] Clergy in the field and behind the lines included warnings to this effect in their sermons. The

113. War chronicle by the priest Karl Lang, p. 36: ABA, NL Karl Lang.

114. Letter by a soldier at the front, 3.8.1917: BSB.

115. See Wilfried Loth, *Katholiken im Kaiserreich. Der politische Katholizismus in der Krise des wilhelminischen Deutschlands*, Düsseldorf: Droste 1984, pp. 278-89.

nationalistic emotionalism of 'homiletic ammunition' reached its apogee in the notion advocated by the military chaplain of the Bavarian armed forces, Cardinal von Bettinger, that for the 'devout Christian' his 'superior' was the 'representative of God in this sphere of influence'; to follow his orders was to 'fulfil God's will'.[116] In addition, mainly at the beginning of the war, many military chaplains cultivated a 'military tone' when interacting with the troops.[117]

Catholic army chaplains, whose sermons had the character of 'spiritual tirades worthy of a veterans' association', urging soldiers not to waver and to uphold their oath of allegiance, met with the aversion of the war-weary troops. They described such priests as 'warmongers'.[118] The military chaplains' privileging of the nation and their association with the military system helped devalue their achievements as pastors in the eyes of the soldiers. However, the increasing realisation that 'continually stirring up patriotic feelings' in sermons was bound to seem 'repulsive' to the troops made a number of army chaplains rethink their approach. To avoid further damaging the pastoral care of soldiers, during the second half of the war they emphasised the 'problem of the hereafter' and the 'inner value of suffering' in their sermons.[119]

Apart from this, as religious interpretive models increasingly failed to persuade soldiers, the individual priest's personal engagement became more and more important to the success of pastoral activities at the front. One divisional chaplain stated in early 1917 that army chaplains, rather like officers, were 'valued to the extent that' they visited the troops in the front-line trenches and talked to them.[120] The great esteem felt for Father Rupert Mayer (a Jesuit) in the 1920s in Munich and beyond was anchored in large part in the ceaseless dedication he showed as

116. See Richard von Dülmen, Der deutsche Katholizismus und der Erste Weltkrieg, in: idem, *Religion und Gesellschaft. Beiträge zu einer Religionsgeschichte der Neuzeit*, Frankfurt/M.: Fischer Taschenbuch-Verlag 1989, pp. 172–203; Karl Hammer, *Deutsche Kriegstheologie 1870–1918*, Munich: Deutscher Taschenbuch-Verlag 1974; Missalla, quote p. 104–5; Klier, *Kriegspredigt*, pp. 164–8, 208–12. Bishop Keppler of Rottenburg published a collection of military sermons which he described as 'homiletic ammunition': ibid., p. 148.

117. War chronicle by Karl Lang, p. 112: ABA, NL Karl Lang.

118. J. Weis, Seelsorge bei den Truppen, Easter 1916: AEM, NL Faulhaber 6776.

119. Document on the conference of military chaplains in divisions A and B, 26.9.1916: AEM, 'Ordinariat 310'.

120. Pastoral report by Norbert Stumpf (O.M.Cap.), 6.2.1917: AEM, Akten des DK Buchberger.

the army chaplain closest to the front line; he suffered serious injury in December 1916. In 1918, in remarks on the 'personality of the pastor in the field', Mayer himself emphasised that one must 'guard' against 'acting the officer'. The priest should see 'unflagging enthusiasm' during 'pastoral care of individuals' in the trenches as the true 'quintessence of pastoral care for soldiers in the field'.[121] Catholic pastoral care in the armed forces thus confirmed the validity of a notion which had already moulded the relationship between lay people and clergy in the nineteenth century. This suggested that clerical 'milieu managers' were of key importance to the content of the religious activities of the faithful and how intensively they carried them out.[122]

4.3 National Identity?

> I'm not going to risk life and limb for the damned Prussians and big capitalists any more.[123]

As with religious interpretive models, the political convictions of the soldiers also had consequences for their willingness to stay the course, as the opening quotation attests. The troops in general were increasingly unmoved by explanatory models anchored in the nation. Yet the nation was still the be all and end all for government departments and the press. Soldiers were expected to stay the course for the nation and to willingly sacrifice their lives on the 'altar of the Fatherland'. The contrast in attitudes inevitably generated a counter-movement among combatants which impaired their motivation in battle. Changes in the troops' political attitudes provoked by their experiences on the front line and their reaction to wartime political movements are, moreover, of general interest to a history of mentalities and experience. Apart from the transformation of soldiers' political views, the key question is how differentiated these were and how coherent they were in terms of content and political programme.

Southern Bavarian farmers and servants did not enter the war in a spirit of patriotic exuberance. Yet they were swayed by the monarchical cult of the Wittelsbachs. This cult communicated values summed up like a rallying cry in the formula 'with God for King and country'; combatants

121. Quote in Buchberger, *Seelsorgsaufgaben*, pp. 85-8; see R. Bleistein (ed.), *Rupert Mayer S.J. Leben im Widerspruch*, Frankfurt/M.: Knecht 1991.

122. Busch, *Katholische Frömmigkeit*, pp. 232-43.

123. Letter by building fitter Otto Biegner, 12.8.1917: BHStA/IV, MilGer 3524.

felt it was worth staying the course for the sake of these values. Soldiers initially assumed that their own side was waging a purely defensive war and were thus ready, as 'Bavarians', to defend their *Bayerland* without question.[124] A special aura surrounded the monarch, visible with particular clarity when he took the salute at parades in person. This was a tremendous honour for those present. The hopes that soldiers in the field initially placed in the Bavarian king are apparent in a rumour widespread in 1916 in Upper Bavaria and the Bavarian Forest region. It suggested that Ludwig III had broken off his friendship with the Kaiser because he wished to drastically cut the number of men in a Bavarian regiment. This regiment was supposed to have turned against Prussian troops, for whom it had to retake a position several times at Verdun.[125]

Alongside the monarchical cult, high-ranking generals were also popular figures with whom soldiers could identify, though only partially, as long as they were successful and did not have a reputation for needlessly endangering the lives of the troops under their command. Because of the military victories on the Eastern Front, Paul von Hindenburg was surrounded by the aura of a successful army commander in the minds of Bavarian soldiers, even before he became Supreme Commander in 1916. As the inspectors of correspondence noted, the Supreme Command was 'beyond all criticism' even in subsequent years, in contrast, for example, to the Imperial government. As with the divisional commanders, to whom soldiers therefore often complained, this may have been due in part to the notion that the Supreme Command bore no responsibility for the dire conditions in the army and did not know about them.[126] As defeat loomed, however, and the numbers of those killed for no obvious purpose increased rapidly during the final months of the war, soldiers were no longer willing to give their leaders the benefit of the doubt. In the final stages of the war, the troops labelled Hindenburg a 'mass murderer' and 'butcher'.[127]

Notions demonising other countries as the enemy and the stereotypes bound up with them failed to sway how soldiers from rural areas interpreted the war. Only Italy's decision to enter the war on the side of the Allies in the spring of 1915 provoked outrage. This, though, had less to

124. B.G., 12.2.1915: local authority of Kochel.

125. Account by a high-ranking military police official, 31.8.1916: BHStA/IV, MKr 2335.

126. Postal surveillance report, 5th Army, 10.1.1918: BA/MA, W-10/50794, fol. 35f.

127. Liaison officer, II. E./4. Feld-Art.-Rgt., 29.8.1918: BHStA/IV, stv. GK I. AK 1980.

do with a clearly defined and firmly anchored anti-Italian stereotype than with the fact that a former member of the Triple Alliance had switched sides. This was interpreted as a betrayal in a personalised way: 'On 24 May 1915 the miserable, faithless Italians declared war on Austria. But out there in the field, the fury is mounting.'[128] As the war dragged on, nationalistic interpretive models increasingly failed to persuade even those soldiers who initially harboured no doubts about deployment at the front, believing they were serving their Fatherland in a just cause. The perceptions underlying this development probably explain why the experience of war failed to make farmers and small farmers serving in the army more inclined to accept nationalistic ideologies. First, soldiers observed that national and bourgeois circles were by no means motivated to get involved in the war primarily by ideal notions of the Fatherland, according to which the German mission was mainly a matter of fighting for an inward-looking 'culture'.[129]

Claims to the contrary were repudiated in their eyes by the fact that, alongside those who definitely benefited from the war such as black marketeers, many big industrial and trading firms rapidly increased their profits. The living standards of relatives back home, in contrast, fell. Soldiers' poor wages made it impossible for them to improve their lot even to a minor degree. National convictions thus tended to be a concern only of those who were able to profit from the war. This connection was expressed pithily in the slogan: 'If the wages were better, there would be plenty of patriotism to go round.'[130] At the same time, the notion of a social contract based on a relationship characterised by mutual recognition is apparent here. This contract would have rewarded citizens and soldiers appropriately for carrying out their duties, but this did not happen in the war. As the postal surveillance office of the 6th Army stated in September 1918, many soldiers were motivated to reject concepts that privileged the national for precisely such reasons:

> A certain number [of letter-writers] state that it is vital to stay the course, and some lines demonstrate, alongside the many who express their ill-humour and dissatisfaction, loyalty to the King and unwavering love for the Fatherland, which is worth all the sacrifices. The number of letter-writers who openly wish death on the Fatherland is, however, not much smaller. Almost none of

128. War diary of Jakob Eberhard: private possession.

129. Ay, *Entstehung*, pp. 77-80.

130. Liaison officer, Reserve Hospital Munich H, n.d. [November 1917]: BHStA/IV, stv. GK I.AK 2403.

> the letter-writers expresses a feeling of love for the Fatherland. The overall impression created by monitoring the letters almost seems to suggest that soldiers would feel a certain sense of shame merely by putting thoughts of the Fatherland into words. Some letters are anchored in the view that 'Anyone showing robust faith in the Fatherland has a vested interest in the war and will benefit and profit from it'.[131]

Second, the officers' condescending treatment of the regular soldiers devalued national interpretive models, insofar as these had been underpinned by the notion of a camaraderie transcending rank in the army. In fact, many officers were plainly concerned first and foremost with personal gain, viewing the war as a means of enriching themselves. This inspired soldiers to turn away from nationalistic ideas, as reliably attested in the letters of members of the Deutschnationaler Handlungsgehilfen-Verband (German National Association of Business Clerks), a nationalistic interest group with an elaborate *völkisch* ideology.[132] Around 100,000 members of this association had been conscripted, and most mentioned perceptions similar to those expressed by a letter-writer in May 1917:

> In my opinion the problem lies with the lack of comradeship shown by the officers towards the regular soldiers. Exceptions, which are truly rare, merely prove the rule. The most crass, unbridled egotism is taking hold and is even being encouraged by those at the top. On the third day of mobilisation, I went into the field as a territorial reservist, full of ideals, in accordance with my membership of the German national forces. My experience of our officers over the course of time has, however, long since destroyed my idealism. The war is simply regarded as good business, and everyone tries to profit from it as much as possible.[133]

Soldiers sharply and openly rejected arguments rooted in extreme nationalism. This rejection became especially virulent from September 1917. In response to the peace resolution passed by the Imperial Diet,

131. Report by postal surveillance office of the 6th Army, 4.9.1918: Thimme, *Weltkrieg*, pp. 268–9.

132. Fricke, *Lexikon*, vol. 2, pp. 457–75.

133. Walther Lambach, *Ursachen des Zusammenbruchs*, Hamburg: Deutschnationale Verlagsanstalt 1919, p. 59, figure p. 24. In early 1918 a back area soldier wrote: 'Germany's powerful are greater enemies than the Frenchman, but because of minor disagreements they're going to lead us [the people] to the slaughtering block.' Postal surveillance officer at field post office 46, 4.2.1918: SHStAD, Kriegsarchiv (P) 21133, fol. 98.

those in favour of continuing the war banded together in the German Fatherland Party, which aimed to achieve extreme annexationist goals.[134] The Fatherland Party's decisive advocacy of a 'Hindenburg peace' had a polarising effect, which far exceeded the new party's achievements in mobilising support. The opposing political standpoints on the aims of peace thus finally became clearer in the minds of soldiers from the autumn of 1917. Widespread rejection of the Fatherland Party among the troops was usually linked with the conviction that its supporters, most of whom had supposedly been recalled from the front to work in war industries, and the representatives of capitalist interests would quickly abandon their boundless aims if forced to do a stint in the trenches. A farmer's son wrote in April 1918 to Georg Heim:

> The biggest traitors of the Fatherland are the members of the Fatherland Party. The leaders of these rascals belong in prison. By opening their big mouths and making their demands, they are ruining the courage of the soldiers at the front. All the soldiers believe that no part of our Fatherland should be lost. But the gentlemen with the big money have the governments in their pocket in every country, and these then make demands which are impossible to achieve through negotiation. They want to expand the national territory, compensation and all sorts of other things. If only these people had to get by on 70 pfennigs a day and could see shell splinters flying past, a lot of things would be different.[135]

Given that the regular soldiers felt this way, the fact that a number of officers joined the Fatherland Party must inevitably have impaired the legitimacy of military rule. The representative for educational work in the replacement battalion of an infantry regiment stated that one of the questions asked most often by the regular soldiers was: 'Why are the officers not forbidden from joining the Fatherland Party? How long will the "pan-Germans", who after all have a vested interest in extending the war, be allowed to stuff themselves full?'[136] The vociferous propagation of ambitious annexationist aims by nationalistic groupings inevitably shook troops' faith in the necessity of fighting on; they had after all gone into battle believing that Germany was defending itself.[137] On the whole, soldiers' experiences at the front failed to prime them to accept more readily attempts to push nationalistic perspectives or to embrace

134. Fricke, *Lexikon*, vol. 2, pp. 391-403.
135. Michael Kitzelmann, 21.4.1918: StaA Regensburg, NL Heim 1316.
136. Liaison officer, II. E./3. I.R., 1.12.1917: BHStA/IV, stv. GK I.AK 2403.
137. Thimme, *Weltkrieg*, p. 205.

nationalistic interpretive models. Fighting together with units from other contingents of the army was just as ineffective in terms of integrating Bavarian soldiers more deeply into the nation state. Regional antagonisms in fact increasingly shaped how troops interpreted reality; the authorities could do nothing to keep this under control.

Soldiers from different regions had difficulties understanding one another simply because they spoke different dialects. Even within the Bavarian units, the relationship between soldiers from the Rhenish Palatinate and those from Altbayern, Swabia and Franconia was hampered by mutual incomprehension. Soldiers from the Palatinate were regarded as morally inferior by the 'real' Bavarians and felt themselves isolated in units recruited mainly from those areas of Bavaria to the right of the Rhine: 'Otherwise nothing much has changed here. Of course it's not nice being a half-French native of the Palatinate in a German-Bavarian regiment. If you love your Fatherland, you soon learn to hate it here.'[138]

The 'hatred of Prussia' common among Bavarian soldiers was, however, a far more serious problem. From 1916, and more extensively from 1917, resentment against Prussia had become a key factor affecting the mood of the civilian population of Bavaria, one which proved impossible to keep in check. The anxious authorities discussed and identified a wide range of possible reasons for this development. Prussian attempts to weaken the federal structures of the Empire were taken into account, as were Bavaria's economic disadvantages, particularly in terms of food supply; the generous catering provided for north German visitors to the tourists sites of Bavarian Allgäu and in Upper Bavaria were another factor.[139] It was apparent here that the stories told by soldiers on furlough reinforced the hatred of Prussia among the civilian population.[140] In August 1916 one observer of the popular mood in the Miesbach area summed up the view which prevailed there: 'We're going to become French after the war. But that's better than being Prussian, we've had our fill of that, every soldier returning from the field tells us that.'[141]

At the front, rumours that Bavarian units were being discriminated against by their Prussian counterparts underpinned the hatred of Prussia, which became rampant. In 1915 'petty jealousies and teasing' also marked

138. Jakob Hoock from Altrig (BA Ludwigshafen), 2.3.1916: BHStA/IV, Militärgericht 6. Ldw.-Div. H 49.

139. Ay, *Entstehung*, pp. 134–48.

140. Stimmung zwischen Nord und Süd. Memorandum, 23.6.1918: BHStA/II, MA 97566.

141. Karl Alexander von Müller, 31.8.1916: BHStA/IV, MKr 2335.

the relationship between different units within the Bavarian army and were inspired by the movement to the west of units from the Eastern Front, as these felt superior to the units already stationed there.[142] As early as June 1916, the military authorities were confronted by proliferating rumours of 'discord' between soldiers in different contingents.[143] Subsequently, soldiers from Bavarian and Prussian units frequently got into fights in the field.[144] Some Bavarian soldiers noted at an early stage that Prussian soldiers always took credit for the successes of others.[145] From late 1915 many believed that Prussian commanders in the field used Bavarian units to retain sections of the front at particular risk for Prussian units or to carry out difficult offensive manoeuvres. Front-line soldiers home on leave disseminated the view that they had to pull 'the chestnuts out of the fire for Prussia'; this was reflected in rumours about the numbers of casualties in Bavarian units, which were far higher than for Prussian troops.[146]

In the final stages of the war, Rhinelanders, Hanoverians, Hessians and even Silesians joined soldiers from Bavaria and Baden in grumbling about the 'Prussians'.[147] This points to the fact that the 'hatred of Prussia' common among Bavarian soldiers took on a significance which cannot be explained solely by the reactivation of parochial models of identification or the perception of supposed injustices. The articulation of anti-Prussian resentment in fact functioned to provide a popular interpretive model. Within this framework, the reasons why a war which the troops found increasingly pointless was still being fought could be summed up pithily in one concept. The 'Prussians' met with opposition from Bavarian troops primarily because they saw German politics, dominated by Prussian power interests, as one of the main reasons why the war was still going on. In August 1917 a plain-clothes policeman keeping trains under surveillance noted a conversation between soldiers and an NCO:

> Soldiers longed above all for the war to end soon and mentioned that Germany also bore some of the responsibility for the continuation of the war.

142. GK I. bayer. AK, 27.2.1915: BHStA/IV, 2. Inf.-Div. Bund 97.

143. Ulrich/Ziemann, *Frontalltag*, p. 76.

144. Liaison officer, E./20. I.R., 24.8.1918: BHStA/IV, stv. GK I.AK 1980.

145. Matthias Meier, 16.10.1914: AEM, Kriegschronik Altenerding B 1837.

146. Anonymous petition from 4.6.1916 to King Ludwig III: BHStA/II, MA 97566.

147. Postal surveillance report, 5th Army, 31.8.1918: BA/MA, W-10/50794, fol. 79.

> They suggested that Germany had made specific plans and was determined to implement them. As long as Bavaria was with Prussia, there would be war, because the Prussians with their big mouths had been involved in every war.[148]

As an explanatory framework within which warmongering political interests could be placed, references to 'the Prussians' were not associated with a political programme. The focus tended to be Prussians' flawed character and therefore generally remained vague. However, during the second half of the war an increasing number of soldiers linked this notion with interpretations which generally presented the war as guided by the interests of socially influential groups. This inspired more and more soldiers to accept the anti-war arguments put forward by the Minority Social Democrats and the radical leftists organised in the Spartacus group. The weakening of the traditional political loyalties of many combatants was bound up with this development. This applied even to soldiers from rural areas of Bavaria, who had tended to support the Centre Party; as a major change of attitude, this received a great deal of attention. Front-line members of the Sekretariat Sozialer Studentenarbeit, an association of Catholic students, stated: 'In particular, it was evident that Bavarian farmers and industrial workers had swung suddenly to the left as a result of the war. The technique applied successfully in one Bavarian unit, of shutting up the noisiest ones by decorating them, obviously failed in the long term.'[149]

Alongside the profits that major industrial firms were making from the war, this change of attitude, apparent from 1916, was anchored in the debate on war aims. In the spring of 1915 the leading industrial associations presented their war aims in a submission to the *Reichstag*, the first time they had done so in such a direct and vigorous manner. Various groups demanded, with increasing fervour, that the war produce major benefits for Germany. Imperial Chancellor Bethmann-Hollweg publicly advocated this position in the *Reichstag*, though in more moderate form than the industrialists. Such demands culminated in November 1916 in open discussion of war aims in the press. Annexationist demands were clearly rooted in the class interests of business and big industrial firms. This fuelled the conviction of civilian workers and others that the war was being prolonged solely to further the interests of the 'rich and powerful'.[150]

148. Report by the Bavarian police HQ, 10.8.1917: BHStA/IV, MKr 11484.
149. Cron, *Sekretariat*, p. 21.
150. Kocka, *Klassengesellschaft*, p. 69.

Such views were also common at the front, showing that civilians and troops agreed on many points in their interpretation of how the war was going. Resentment towards the capitalist system and the idea that the war was being prolonged only to serve the interests of 'capital' were initially popular among working-class soldiers in particular.[151] Soldiers from a farming background also soon came to believe that those groups within society that managed to enrich themselves during the war must have triggered it and kept it going. In July 1915 one farmer expressed such ideas in a letter to his sister-in-law as follows:

> The people who have brought this misery upon the world don't have to fight to the last man. They are making so much money that they don't know what to do with it. None of them knows what it's like to hear a bullet whistling past, and the poor devils are being shot for such people. It's impossible to imagine anything more unjust than this war. I mean, it makes no difference to us whether our Fatherland is this large or half as large, we have to pay the price whether we win or lose; it is terrible.[152]

Many regular soldiers agreed with notions of this kind, which soon took on concrete expression in attacks on 'big capitalists'; they were also shared by many soldiers from a rural background. In June 1916 the general secretary of the Bavarian Christian Peasants' Association, Sebastian Schlittenbauer, drawing on his own frequent observations and what he heard within his organisation, stated that the inhabitants of rural areas were being 'directly stirred up' in taverns by soldiers on leave. In conversations with civilians, the soldiers presented the 'war as a battle on behalf of the big capitalists'.[153] The postal surveillance offices concluded that 'the view that the war was continuing solely to serve the interests of our big capitalists appears to be widespread in the army'. Critical comments on 'capitalists', 'fat cats' and 'profiteers' were 'the order of the day' in soldiers' letters.[154]

The minority within the SPD opposed to the war and the leftist radicals who later banded together in the Spartacus group publicly accused Germany of waging a war of conquest dominated by capitalist interests; they stepped up such attacks from the spring of 1915.[155] The military

151. Cron, *Studentendienst*, pp. 50, 52.

152. Johann Bätz, 7.7.1915: BHStA/IV, Amtsbibliothek 9584.

153. Sebastian Schlittenbauer, 5.6.1916: BHStA/II, MInn 66327.

154. Report by postal surveillance office 40, 25.8.1917: BHStA/IV, 6. Inf.-Div. Bund 81.

155. Kruse, *Krieg*, pp. 208-14.

authorities were worried that such views might be disseminated among the troops by means of targeted propaganda. When transferring and assigning soldiers, Bavarian replacement units were instructed in 1918 to inform the new unit in writing which soldiers had been identified as 'supporters' of the USPD to prevent them from being given 'positions of trust'.[156]

After the war, the claim that the USPD had specifically tried to gain soldiers' support for revolution was at the heart of the 'stab-in-the-back' thesis. Contemporary observers such as Sebastian Schlittenbauer, meanwhile, insisted that interpretive models of this kind were for the most part spread 'systematically by means of word-of-mouth agitation'.[157] This thesis is closer to reality, since conscripted workers who were members of the SPD or of trade unions endeavoured to inform other soldiers of their views. Their opportunities to do so were, however, limited by their distrustful and suspicious superiors, who kept an eye on any soldiers they knew to be Social Democrats.[158] Discussions between soldiers surely contributed to the dissemination of the idea that the war was chiefly a means of serving capitalist interests. There was plenty of material on which to base views of this kind in soldiers' perceptions of their own circumstances and those of relatives back home. This is clearly apparent in a number of soldiers' letters. Some soldiers thus adopted specific interpretive elements characteristic of the Social Democratic minority or the Spartacus group and repeated them as slogans. By no stretch of the imagination, however, did this necessarily involve subjecting these groupings' political programmes to purposeful examination, as becomes obvious when reading their letters. In any case, even many soldiers who had joined the SPD clearly 'had no idea of their party's basic aims and justified their membership solely by referring to problems of an economic and political nature.'[159]

As one volunteer, the son of a Social Democratic couple, stated in autumn of 1915, 'soldiers' shift towards Social Democracy [was] to a large degree negatively' motivated and consisted chiefly of 'rage at the whole rotten bourgeois society'.[160] Apart from the longing for peace, this 'rage' was not associated with any clearly defined progressive or socialist

156. K.M., 4.5.1918: BHStA/IV, stv. GK I.AK 593.
157. Sebastian Schlittenbauer, 5.6.1916: BHStA/II, MInn 66327.
158. Wilhelm Platta, 19.5.1915: BArch, 92, 271, fol. 196.
159. Cron, *Sekretariat*, pp. 19–20.
160. Otto Braun, 12.9.1915: WUA, vol. 11/1, p. 345.

aims, which were in any case hardly likely to win many converts among farmers. It was in fact fed by a widespread sense of dependence and powerlessness in relation to the war and its consequences.

A range of differing perceptions and interpretations underpinned soldiers' aversion to 'big capitalists'. First, it seemed obvious to them that the general desire for peace among both front-line soldiers and the civilian population was being ignored. The soldiers blamed the 'powerful' or the 'masters' for this. By this they may have meant the Imperial government or the ruling elites of the 'top ten thousand'. It was characteristic of the armed forces that regular soldiers lacked influence and had little opportunity to express their opinions freely. This brought home to them the clash between the goals of ordinary people and those of the powerful in particularly painful fashion: 'My only hope now is that the war comes to an end this year and you can say what you think, because as long as you have on the slave's clothes you can't speak the truth. Of course everyone knows, even those who are not soldiers, how we are oppressed. The war has made everyone a social democrat.'[161] Apart from this, it was above all the rapidly worsening living conditions experienced by those at the front and their relatives back home that fuelled soldiers' certainty that the war would benefit a tiny minority only. The following letter was sent in November 1916 by a territorial reservist and married basket-maker from rural Swabia to his wife. It brings into sharp relief how soldiers' perceptions of their individual situation and their analysis, which doubled as a kind of rallying cry, of how society as a whole was developing were inextricably linked:

> What a misery you are going to have when you come to the [child-]bed later this month and I won't be with you, no help apart from the children. And the devils' swindle is still not done, I don't have any counsel what to begin from all what I learn about you, dear wife Rosina. That bunch of whores is always writing in [to him or into the countryside?] you are helped and you are getting so much [help] the swindlenazion. Dear wife it can go as it wants, I am fed up I stayed several days longer with you and now I have earned two months in prison. It makes no difference dear wife Rosina, I know my thoughts. I have told them already in the trial I want to be relieved, I want nothing more to know about this misery. That would be the remuneration for the years spent protecting the big cap[it]alists, their

161. Excerpt from a letter in the postal surveillance report for the 5th Army, 31.8.1918: BA/MA, W-10/50794, fol. 89.

> stuff they should protect it themselves and not those who have to search for their advancement out there in the world[.] I don't have received anything from them and I also want nothing but to return home to you, now it's been more than two years that you and the children have hardship and misery and myself. I have nothing to defend now, I want out, I want to earn my stuff myself, I need nothing from them except hunger and hardship to guzzle, they don't give us anything else apart from Koulash, but that's just potatoes and the rest guzzle those who are behind us [in the back area]. ... If there was a Lord he would have sorted it out a long time ago but there isn't one we can imagine that.[162]

This letter-writer clearly had no need of party political or enemy propaganda to conclude that the representatives of the prevailing order in the field wanted to 'pull the wool over the eyes of the soldiers'.[163] This letter and others like it also demonstrate that soldiers' close emotional ties with their relatives tended to hamper rather than encourage the politicisation of the contrast between themselves and the social elites. The 'wailing letters' from their wives failed to inspire soldiers to reflect on how society might be organised more justly. Combined with the widely felt sense of homesickness, they in fact made soldiers even more keen to get on with 'advancing' themselves, pursue their own plans and acquire the material basis necessary to do so once they returned home.

In a related development, because large numbers of people saw the basis of their economic subsistence being destroyed over the course of the war, another interpretive model emerged, described as 'astonishing' by one inspector of correspondence. This asserted that the war had been 'instigated' in order to 'eradicate' working people.[164] According to this view, the loss of huge numbers of soldiers from an 'ordinary' background enhanced the ability of elites to wield power. The ruled would find it more difficult to resist, if there were fewer of them. This notion expresses the intense sense of powerlessness which soldiers felt with respect to how society was developing during the war. Many believed that the war not only reinforced social inequality but also eliminated possible resistance to

162. Peter Hammerer to his wife Rosina on 3.11.1916: BHStA/IV, Militärgericht 6. Ldw.-Div. H 5. Hammerer, born in 1878, had six children. He had exceeded his leave by six days. According to his statement, he did so to alleviate the material hardship suffered by his wife by weaving baskets. His punishment was two months in prison.

163. Ibid.

164. Thimme, *Weltkrieg*, pp. 268–9.

this development by means of mass casualties among front-line soldiers. In general, highly pessimistic views of the war and its social consequences were thus associated with attacks on 'big capitalists'. Such views featured a certain affinity with analyses produced by the Social Democratic minority, but had little in common with their political programme. Soldiers from a rural background found the Social Democratic manifesto, and indeed that of the MSPD, attractive only because they were in favour of peace, as became clear in 1917.

The year 1917 brought far-reaching international and domestic political changes, intensifying the interest in political matters at the front. The United States entered the war in April 1917 and Russia was gripped by revolution, transforming global power structures. The domestic political dispute over the question of peace was, however, a more important factor in the perception of the combatants. This dispute was becoming increasingly heated and was being fought out openly between the political parties, while the Imperial Diet was increasingly in the public eye as the key forum for discussion. As the parliamentary debates on peace approached their zenith in early July 1917 with the creation of the Interparty Committee (*Interfraktioneller Ausschuß*), one very patriotically inclined soldier wrote:

> 'For what' have we put up with everything and 'for what' are we still putting up with things and going without? And who has more right to ask this question than us who have been in the field for three years? How have we been rewarded for our sacrifices? I for my part - bloody injustice. It's all the fault of our government, with its old-fashioned system from the year dot. There is of course a clamour in our *Reichstag* at the moment and a decision - one way or the other - seems about to be made. A recruit who couldn't give a damn about politics now knows what he wants and needs after six months on active duty. Everyone is brimming over with resentment and bitterness.[165]

The efforts of the representatives in the Imperial Diet to achieve peace as soon as possible peaked with the passing on 19 July of the peace resolution, which advocated a peace of understanding, with the support of the Progress Party (Fortschrittspartei), the Centre Party (Zentrum) and the Majority Social Democrats. Most front-line soldiers supported the resolution.[166] It was, however, subject to dispute within the Centre Party. Matthias Erzberger performed impressively before the Budget

165. Letter by a soldier from Munich, 8.7.1917: BSB.

166. Cron, *Sekretariat*, p. 46.

Commission (*Haushaltsausschuß*) of the Imperial Diet, presenting overwhelming evidence that the submarine war had failed.This convinced most within the party to support the pursuit of a peace of understanding. The chairman of the parliamentary Centre Party in the Bavarian Diet, however, rejected the resolution shortly before it was passed, as did the newspapers close to him. Bavarian Centre Party politicians had pushed annexationist demands as early as 1916. The agrarian wing of the party had spoken out strongly in favour of radicalising the way in which Germany was fighting the war by giving free reign to submarine warfare.[167] Soldiers in the field inevitably concluded that the Centre Party in Bavaria was unlikely to work wholeheartedly to make a political reality of their desire for peace:

> It saddens me deeply that many deputies are still against peace, even Centre Party ones. Anyone that wants this war to go on belongs at the front. Deputy Erzberger has all the soldiers on his side, we are very grateful to him. If it wasn't for the Church, I would be in favour of revolution too. You can't help but feel ashamed before the Lord as a human being. Wild animals are saints compared with our peoples. I beg you, if possible, please do what you can to ensure that our Centre Party deputies push for peace as soon as possible, there's enough misfortune as it is.[168]

The stance of the Bavarian Centre Party made the position of the Majority Social Democrats on the issue of peace attractive even to soldiers from a rural background. Previously, the party majority had refrained from openly opposing the Imperial government in pushing its demands for peace.The collection of signatures carried out in autumn 1916 in support of ending the war quickly made no explicit mention of giving up annexations and remained 'embedded' in the strategy of Bethmann-Hollweg, which involved underlining the Reich's willingness to embrace peace without alluding to concrete conditions. Following the establishment of the USPD in April 1917, however, the majority felt forced to publicly express opposition to the Reich leadership, to prevent the increasingly intense longing for peace from bolstering support for what had formerly been a competing group within the same party. By adopting the formula produced by the Petrograd Soviet of a peace 'without annexations or reparations' on 19 April 1917, the MSPD launched a propaganda offensive intended to have a mass impact. With the help of a media campaign, the

167. Albrecht, *Landtag*, pp. 157-72.
168. Michael Kitzelmann, 26.9.1917: StaA Regensburg, NL Heim 1316.

MSPD succeeded in presenting itself as a political force for peace *vis-à-vis* the USPD and in making the term 'Scheidemann peace' synonymous with a peace of understanding.[169]

It was soon apparent that this skilful approach had had an enormous impact on soldiers in the field among others. In May 1917 the *Kölnische Volkszeitung* (Cologne People's Daily), close to the right wing of the Centre Party, called on its readers to sign up to a resolution advocating a 'Hindenburg peace'. Towards the end of the month, the *Münchener Post* (Munich Post), affiliated with the Majority Social Democrats, addressed its readers, including those on the front line, with an appeal for 'immediate peace'.[170]

The response was overwhelming. Within a very brief period of time several thousand letters of support flowed in from the field, some bearing the signatures of up to 200 men. A number of companies signed collectively, including the NCOs. Other units made it clear that only a lack of paper or superiors' attempts at intimidation were preventing larger numbers of men from taking part. The military authorities in the field sometimes also tried to stop the military post offices from transporting the letters to Munich. As the press officer at the War Ministry noted, it was 'striking' that 'the inhabitants of rural areas make up a particularly large proportion of signatories'. As a result, as he accurately stated: 'The letters probably reflect the views of large numbers of soldiers.'[171] A number of surviving excerpts from the accompanying letters show that support for the Social Democratic peace offensive was anchored in deep disappointment at the behaviour of the Centre Party and the other bourgeois parties. It is just as clear, however, that soldiers turned to the SPD primarily because it represented their 'last hope' as far as peace was concerned. Apart from this, some soldiers saw the party as the representative of democratic 'rights', 'to which the lower classes are also entitled'.

The final year of the war saw no domestic political events with the same power to mobilise soldiers politically as the SPD's support for a peace of understanding. It is thus impossible at present to pin down other possible changes in their political loyalties. This overview of how

169. Boll, *Frieden ohne Revolution?*, pp. 194-221, quote p. 202.

170. Deist, *Militär*, pp. 778-9.

171. Memorandum by War Ministry press officer von Sonnenburg, 15.6.1917: BHStA/IV, MKr 2332; here also the letter excerpts sent by the *Münchener Post*, quoted below. The reference to the rural population was probably based on the then common practice of adding one's profession when signing one's name.

the general mood developed over time has shown that the goal of a peace of understanding continued to enjoy support. So, ultimately, did peace at any cost. However, the prospect of a 'final blow', which had existed since the winter of 1917, pushed political considerations into the background, as the soldiers' ambivalent reaction to the January strike laid bare. On the whole, we should avoid overstating the degree of politicisation among the troops, even in the second half of the war. When the domestic political dispute approached its zenith in September 1917 after the appointment of a new chancellor, the peace resolution and the establishment of the Fatherland Party, a postal surveillance officer noted: 'Of all the letters, we have not found a single one in which the writer tackles the political issues currently so hotly disputed in Germany. Other observations made by the military surveillance offices have also shown that soldiers have little inclination to deal with the political issues of the day.'[172]

The value of such evidence should not be exaggerated. Soldiers took censorship into account, often waiting until they were home on leave to discuss political matters. It is impossible to know exactly what the postal surveillance offices meant by 'political issues of the day'. We can also assume that the military authorities had a vested interest in stylising the prevailing attitude at the front as stoic, non-political fatalism. Yet we have other evidence that soldiers in the field, chiefly concerned with their material living conditions, were not hugely interested in political matters or debates.[173]

A survey was carried out in November 1917 on 'frequent questions' raised in the context of the Patriotic Instruction programme in the replacement army. This provides information on a range of fundamental political convictions held by most soldiers during the last two years of the war. As far as political matters are concerned, the survey revealed not questions but answers which the instructors were compelled to note without being able to exert much influence. The view that Germany was chiefly to blame for the war because of its armament programme - also apparent in the large number of its enemies - was mentioned, as was the popular notion that the war was being waged solely to further the interests of big capitalists and 'high finance'. Soldiers showed no interest whatever in Alsace-Lorraine remaining in the Empire, while the

172. Postal surveillance report for the 5th Army, 28.9.1917: BA/MA, W-10/50794, fol. 28.

173. Report on the mood in the 2nd Infantry Division, 3.10.1917: BHStA/IV, MKr 2335.

notion that empires and kingdoms were 'outdated' led many to call for a republic.[174]

The fact that Ludwig III had publicly advocated annexationist aims since 1915 was the main reason why soldiers rejected the monarchy.[175] Its standing was severely damaged amid the maelstrom of anti-annexationist and anti-Prussian resentment felt by so many soldiers, who saw the king as assisting Prussian power interests; this is why he was called 'half-Prussian'. In August 1917 an officer responsible for issues of agricultural economics reported that many rural soldiers on furlough thought 'that the same thing should happen here as in Russia; we too can do without an emperor or king, then the war would surely be over soon'.[176] During the second half of the war, many soldiers on furlough publicly indulged in *lèse-majesté*. In one reserve unit the drastic view was expressed that 'the emperor and king should be shot dead'.[177]

Given that the cult of the monarchy was in full swing when the war started, it is evident that the war changed the political attitudes of soldiers from a rural background remarkably. At the end of the war, they entered the new republican state having accepted Social Democratic peace proposals and a republican system; they had an analytically underdeveloped yet strong awareness of how vested political interests had caused the war and the social inequality which it had brought in its wake. They had known defeat was inevitable. Many thought revolution imminent; the old elites were largely discredited, alerting many to the inevitability of political transformation. Beyond these basic political insights, however, soldiers' notions of the character and content of the new political order were generally sketchy. The liaison officer for Patriotic Instruction in a territorial reserve battalion mainly made up of farmers told his superiors in June 1918:

> With reference to the dogma lurking in many heads that the war will be followed by revolution, I informed the men of the horrors of the French Revolution and present conditions in Russia, where no one is safe. It seemed to me that, though many soldiers believe revolution imminent, most people have absolutely no idea what revolution actually involves. When I asked

174. Liaison officer, Grenzschutz-Aufsichtsbezirk Reutin, 4.12.1917: BHStA/IV, stv. GK I.AK 2404.

175. Albrecht, *Landtag*, pp. 154–7.

176. Head Economic Officer, 14.8.1917: BHStA/IV, stv. GK I.AK 2762.

177. Liaison officer, II. E./Feld-Art.-Rgt. 4, 26.9.1918: BHStA/IV, stv. GK I. AK 1981.

> them about this, they replied: 'the big baiting', and in my opinion this is most soldiers' idea of revolution.[178]

A small proportion of the troops of urban origin became increasingly radicalised and willing to pursue revolutionary goals, if necessary through violent means.[179] Among the overwhelming majority of the troops, as late as the autumn of 1918 it was, however, merely rhetorical radicalism that prevailed. This is apparent in the words of a Bavarian soldier one year earlier:

> If only this war was over at last, but all the grumbling and talk of revolution doesn't get us anywhere. I have even prayed about this, but it all seems to be in vain. Now though I do have real hopes that the Pope will act as intermediary. Unless our arrogant scoundrels make excessive demands, I'm quite convinced we'll have peace soon. But if they try to annex half the world again, they ought to be hanged, these scoundrels have had it coming for a long time.[180]

Many soldiers, moreover, delayed coming to terms with the social evils they had observed until after the war. Given the realities of military life, coloured by censorship and subordination, they saw little scope for action; achieving peace was, for the time being, uppermost in their minds. The troops' main concern, in general and in a political sense, was with peace; they were in fact obsessed with it. This is a key reason why, very soon after the armistice, the political momentum of the soldiers' movement failed to match the intensity of the radicalism that had accumulated during the war at the front.

178. Liaison officer, E./Ldst.-Btl. I B 18, 20.6.1918: BHStA/IV, stv. GK I.AK 2410.

179. Ulrich/Ziemann, *Frontalltag*, pp. 207–8; see the different interpretation by Kruse, Klassenheer.

180. Excerpt from a letter by a soldier serving in the Bavarian 15th Infantry Division, 28.9.1917: BA/MA, W-10/50794, fol. 34.

5

Village Communities, 1914–23

War and inflation marked a profound turning point for village society and its economy. Women workers were the group initially most affected. The experience of married peasant women and their husbands who returned home in 1918 was moulded above all by the controlled economy (*Zwangswirtschaft*) in agriculture which existed until 1923. The period from 1919 to 1923, increasingly dominated by inflation, also saw an 'illusory boom' in the agricultural economy.[1] There were short-term economic benefits. At the same time, farmers as a group developed a growing awareness of their estatist qualities (as the literal translation of the German term *Standesbewußtsein* must go, although it is hardly possible to convey in English the sense of genuine distinctiveness that the term *Stand* implies). These factors made it possible for veterans to reintegrate into society relatively smoothly and for memories of the negative aspects of their wartime experience to slip rapidly to the back of their minds. The soldiers' return, on the other hand, intensified protests against agricultural policies. In a context changed profoundly by the revolution of 1918/19, it also made farm labourers more willing to fight for their interests.

5.1 Peasant Wives, 1914–18

Rural society faced an entirely new situation during the war. Conscription removed a significant proportion of the male population from the villages for several years. This chapter probes the consequences for women working in agriculture - primarily peasant wives. The key focus is on how such women interpreted the war and the changes it brought with it. The analysis here first spotlights their work as agricultural producers and changes in the gendered division of labour. It then scrutinises conditions

1. Friedrich Aereboe, *Der Einfluß des Krieges auf die landwirtschaftliche Produktion in Deutschland*, Stuttgart: Deutsche Verlags-Anstalt 1927, p. 108.

within peasant families.[2] Did their husbands' absence influence how peasant women understood their role? Did it affect their emotional relationship with their husbands?

These issues were closely linked in peasant women's subjective perception. They mirror the structures of the peasant family economy, in which there was very little space for an 'ideal notion' of male and female roles 'separate from working life'. Men and women were basically expected 'to carry out certain tasks.'[3] Beyond this, however, gender relations were also embedded in a moral order. Offences againt the rules of this order that occurred during the war show that peasant women, at least to some extent, were protected by their emplacement within the patriarchal structure of the farm. In exploring these issues, we have fewer sources at our disposal than for life in the army. This applies especially to war letters by peasant women. This is in part because only a few soldiers held on to the letters they received or brought them back while on furlough. The letter excerpts collected by Adolf Schinnerer, intended to be representative, help make up for the lack of private materials.

The figures relating to Bavaria in the census of 1916 help us to determine how many men running their own farms were called up, indicating a 36.3 per cent decline in self-employed male agricultural workers. As this occupational survey, unlike others, was carried out during winter, when there was less work to do, this decline is not fully reflected in the increase in the number of female farm heads. If we assume that the number of self-employed farmers was the same as in 1907, around 44 per cent of all farms were headed by a woman in 1916.[4]

A large proportion of the remaining male workers consisted of youths and elderly men. According to the census of 1916, almost 27 per cent of male agricultural workers were younger than 16 and a good 16 per cent were older than 60. The main means of making up for the labour shortage, increasingly pressing from 1915 on, was the deployment of prisoners of war in agriculture. In late 1916, 46,305 POWs were working in Bavarian agriculture. In the spring of 1917 this had climbed to around 62,000.[5] Farmers preferred POWs to urban women or *Hilfsdienstpflichtige*, those

2. Daniel, *Arbeiterfrauen*, pp. 127-39.

3. Michael Mitterauer, Geschlechtsspezifische Arbeitsteilung und Geschlechterrollen in ländlichen Gesellschaften Mitteleuropas, in: Jochen Martin/Renate Zoepffel (eds), *Aufgaben, Rollen und Räume von Frau und Mann*, Freiburg, Munich: Alber 1989, pp. 819-914, p. 819.

4. Kriegs-Volkszählungen, pp. 185-6.

5. Ibid., pp. 278-9.

liable under the Auxiliary Service Law of 1916, because they generally worked hard and were relatively cheap, costing a total of three to four marks a day. The latter groups, moreover, were suspected of being mainly interested in improving their diet.[6] Prisoners sometimes took precedence over farm labourers as well, particularly if the latter were likely to be called up.[7] POWs did not, however, come close to replacing all the conscripted men, particularly given that the number of Russian prisoners declined rapidly following the end of the war with Russia in 1918.[8] Large farms heavily dependent on non-family labour were worst affected by the labour shortage. For small and medium-sized farms of up to 20 hectares, which had in any case employed more women than men before the war, men on leave from the replacement army helped balance things out.[9]

Peasant women's workload had been huge even in peacetime.[10] The dearth of male workers during the war meant that they had to do more than ever and take on a greater range of tasks. Traditionally, depending on the size of the farm and how many non-family workers were employed on it, men were largely responsible for the demanding work involved in the cultivation of the fields, especially ploughing and reaping. Women had to work in the fields only on smallholdings, on farms mainly growing root crops or during the busiest period of the grain harvest.[11] During the war they were forced to work constantly in the fields:

> We brought in the hay and corn with great effort. Things aren't looking too good with the summer cereal because of the long dry spell we had here, but there are lots of potatoes and cabbage. Once again, there will be enough, though we're not allowed to use too much. But we always eat our fill, dear sister. I have to do Josef's work as well of course. It's hard for me sometimes. The ploughing for instance isn't going too well and having to do all the driving [of a harnessed team]. You yourself know what a farmer's life is like. Just imagine, when there's no man around, all the things you have to do. We've already finished sowing, now we're busy spreading manure for the winter, then we start planting the potatoes. You really do nothing but work, which I don't much like, always stuck with the worldly side of things, where you can't

6. Grundsätze für die Beschäftigung der Kriegsgefangenen in Industrie, Handwerk, Landwirtschaft, n.d. [1917]: BHStA/IV, stv. GK I.AK 2772.

7. WB BA Dachau, 28.4.1917: BHStA/IV, stv. GK I.AK 1952.

8. München-Nord Economic Office, 21.8.1918: BHStA/IV, stv. GK I.AK 1968.

9. Rosenheim Economic Office, n.d. [May 1917]: BHStA/IV, MKr 17166.

10. Rosa Kempf, *Arbeits- und Lebensverhältnisse der Frauen in der Landwirtschaft Bayerns*, Jena: Fischer 1918, p. 108, pp. 119–23.

11. Ibid., pp. 94–109.

> stay anyway. I treasure solitude and keeping company with God more than anything else. I trust God to take care of my destiny. He'll do what's best.[12]

The remaining male workers also had to work more as a result of conscription. At harvest time it was not unusual for people to work from 3 a.m. until 9 p.m. in the fields. In the spring of 1915 one farmer was shocked to discover that his wife was able to write to him only at around 11 p.m.[13] The women not only had to cope with increased outdoor work, which would have been more or less impossible if the men's absence had not caused the birth rate to fall rapidly, reducing the need to look after small children.[14] They also had to do their usual work in the animal pens and in the house. Peasant women were thus subject to intense physical strain. Forced to manage without adult male help, their mood was highly despondent: '3 years of working alone like a huge brute, people can't take it any more. We've already done a lot for God, and no end in sight. We had enough work to do before the war but no human being would have believed it would get as bad as this.'[15]

The subjective perception of injustice further sharpened the sense of being overstretched. Married peasant women fitted their extra work into the context of restrictions in production and consumption brought about by the controlled economy. Urban dwellers were frequently the subject of comparison. These were believed to benefit from agricultural policies. Industrial workers were not thought to work enough to justify such special treatment, especially in comparison to their rural counterparts. The impression took hold that one's own efforts were of benefit only to city folk: 'How are you? Like us perhaps. We have nothing left to eat at all, just a lot of hard work. They take from us and give to the urban people. Now they've taken our entire harvest. I'm doing no more, even if we end up starving.'[16]

After three years of war, more and more peasant women managing alone suffered from abdominal pains and miscarriages as a result of the constant physical overexertion. Towards the end of the war, their capacity to work declined rapidly.[17] Mortality in rural regions, however, increased

12. Farmer's wife from Erdenwies, 23.9.1917: BSB.
13. Stefan Schimmer, 13.5.1915: BHStA/IV, Amtsbibliothek 9584.
14. Mitterauer, Arbeitsteilung, pp. 822-3, 891.
15. Letter to a POW from Grünbach (Lower Bavaria), 7.6.1917: BSB.
16. Letter by a farmer's wife from Kissing, 8.7.1917: BSB.
17. Weilheim Economic Office, 18.1.1918: BHStA/IV, stv. GK I.AK 1961.

less than in the cities because rural dwellers were better fed.[18] Women struggled not only with the greater amount of work, but also with tasks previously reserved to men. Training and driving the teams of horses and other draught animals was a task left to the men within the usual division of labour. In the case of horses, this was due to the great prestige associated with owning and working with them, but also to the great strength and skill it took to drive them.[19] It was particularly hard to do without the men in this respect.[20] Traditionally, men were also responsible for business management tasks such as dividing up the individual plots of land in line with the desired crop rotation and determining the dates to sow and harvest and for buying and selling cattle and horses. Here, too, peasant women were generally dependent on advice from their husbands, given in detailed written instructions from the field.[21]

These realities cast doubt on the notion that peasant women made progress towards becoming the 'equal partners' of their husbands during the war by running their farms.[22] Peasant women managing alone were dependent on the help and advice of their husbands and had great trouble disciplining farm labourers, though most were still youths. Neither could the women count on any special consideration from the remaining male farm owners. These were clearly not prepared to accept the changes in women's sphere of activities made necessary by the war. One early anonymous complaint referred to their 'heartless tyranny' *vis-à-vis* the 'women left behind', expressed among other things in the enticement of farm labourers.[23] Often, in meeting their delivery quotas, soldiers' wives were ultimately powerless in the face of the constraints imposed by the male personnel of district authorities as well as mayors: 'am very pleased, we've produced a lot of corn. But you can't take pleasure in it because you're only allowed to work and they do what they want with the results. You have to do it whether you like it or not. We feel like slaves, we become desperate how they treat the peasant people.'[24]

18. Mattes, *Bauernräte*, pp. 51–2.
19. Mitterauer, Arbeitsteilung, p. 846.
20. Letter by a farmer's wife in Swabia, 13.3.1917: BSB.
21. Mattes, *Bauernräte*, p. 54; Mitterauer, Arbeitsteilung, pp. 866–9.
22. Harald Winkel, Die Frau in der Landwirtschaft (1800–1945), in: Hans Pohl (ed.), *Die Frau in der deutschen Wirtschaft*, Stuttgart: Steiner 1985, p. 98.
23. Anonymous submission by the 'wives of the *Landsturm*' to King Ludwig III from January 1915: BHStA/IV, MKr 2822.
24. Letter by a farmer's wife from Thundorf (Lower Bavaria), 11.9.1917: BSB.

As well as maintaining and managing agricultural production, peasant women coping on their own were subject to heavy strains with respect to their personal ties to family members at the front. The most palpable and profound effect of the war was the death of husbands and sons. Casualty reports quickly brought about an intense longing for peace.[25] Women who had lost a relative relied mainly on the empathy of family members as they coped with their sorrow. Within the village, the even greater losses suffered by neighbours made one's own loss easier to bear. In any event, the conception of the kingdom-come associated with the Christian interpretation of death offered consolation. Religious conviction also strengthened the patience of soldiers' widows:

> Dear Anna, it is surely painful for both me and you that the children have lost their father so early, but we must remember that it was God's will. Dear God will continue to look after us. He is our best father, who takes care of widows and orphans. We must pray to Him every day asking that he does not abandon us. No one who has sought refuge in Him has ever been turned away. We must trust in God, and everything will be all right.[26]

According to one parish priest, only a few of the wives of the fallen in his parish 'grumbled', while the others 'meekly [bore] their fate'.[27] Even extreme personal and economic stress was 'borne' by peasant women in the name of the 'holy will of God'.[28] The Sacred Heart of Jesus cult, which became increasingly popular in rural communities during the war, propagated a 'self-sacrificing mentality' characterised by 'humility' and 'self-denial'. Its practitioners were mostly women.[29] In the case of the many missing soldiers, women could not even be sure whether their relatives might still be alive. Particularly among the peasants of southern Bavaria, rumours circulated about relatives long reported missing who had supposedly been hidden away by the military authorities in 'secret hospitals' due to their terrible injuries.[30] Peasant women also showed

25. WB BA Kaufbeuren, 11.12.1915: StAA, Regierung 9762.

26. Letter by a widow from Obergermaringen, 22.5.1917: BSB.

27. Parish of Unteriglbach, 30.6.1916: ABP, DekA II, Fürstenzell 12/I.

28. Letter by a farmer's wife from Cham, 28.5.1917: BSB.

29. Norbert Busch, Die Feminisierung der ultramontanen Frömmigkeit, in: Irmtraud Götz v. Olenhusen (ed.), *Wunderbare Erscheinungen. Frauen und katholische Frömmigkeit im 19. und 20. Jahrhundert*, Paderborn: F. Schöningh 1995, pp. 203–19, pp. 205, 209.

30. Sonthofen district court, 17.6.1917: BHStA/IV, stv. GK I.AK 1723.

a willingness to suffer, embedded in religious notions, in relation to the increasing problems they faced in disciplining their children in the absence of paternal authority:

> Regarding our children. They do as they are told all right with the help of the cane, especially Jakob. They need to be told what's what. They're still children of course. All of them are scared of having too much to do, even Hans. The more you have the more difficult it is. They're always fighting. Hans and Mari would try the patience of a saint. I could tell you a thing or two, but I'll hold my tongue. I have my cross to bear and no doubt I've earned it.[31]

Unlike the men who remained at home, whose participation in communion generally declined markedly in the second half of the war, women's religious zeal remained largely unchanged.[32] Peasant women were reinforced in their extremely passive attitude to the strains of the war by their expectation of a peace that could ultimately be delivered only through divine Providence. This religiously inspired interpretation of the war was bound up with the notion of a social order grounded in morality, based on a just division of burdens. However, this religious interpretive model, common at both the fighting front and the home front, became less and less persuasive as time went by.[33] For such hopes to be fulfilled people had to behave impeccably in both religious and moral terms; it was essential for them to embrace repentance and penitence. The moral decline apparent in the most varied realms of society, however, seemed to make hopes of divine assistance increasingly obsolete.[34] If 'people [became] ever lower and worse', the efforts of the virtuous would be all for nothing.[35] The collapse of the moral order of society thus also affected those who continued to believe in this ideal. Commenting on the affairs pursued by soldiers' wives, an Upper Bavarian peasant woman regretfully stated: 'The German women are getting worse and worse. Now God must deny peace even to the good women.'[36]

It no longer made sense to interpret the war, as did the priests in their sermons, as 'God's punishment', when war profiteers were able

31. Anna Eberhard, 19.10.1914: private possession.

32. Reports on wartime pastoral care, parish of Biessenhofen, 1.8.1919: ABA, DA 6, Karton 13.

33. Letter from Kolbermoor, 29.6.1917: BSB.

34. Letter by a woman from Nuremberg, 8.4.1917: BSB.

35. Letter by a farmer's wife from Bimwang, 3.12.1917: BSB.

36. Farmer's wife from Mühldorf am Inn, 23.8.1917: BSB.

to enrich themselves at the expense of the public good with a clear conscience.[37] Peasant women's forbearance reached its limits when their relatives lost their lives, and this was reflected in their behaviour. Like some soldiers, more and more people at home came to believe that the war was being pursued by the powerful only in order to decimate the working population: 'People are now saying openly what they once only whispered in secret, that the war is happening so that there are fewer people and the powerful have more power over the poor again.'[38] Some peasant women came to straightforward conclusions in the light of the death, at the hands of the 'powerful', of the sons they had raised with such effort, becoming increasingly willing to practise birth control.[39]

The question of whether the long separation emotionally alienated peasant women from their husbands and caused them to feel released from the ties of matrimony is as important as it is difficult to answer.[40] Several pieces of evidence suggest that this was not the case. First, communication by letter was of great importance to women, as it was to their relatives in the field. The constant exchange of letters helped bolster emotional stability. Letters from the field were also evidence of their husbands' freedom from bodily harm: 'My dear husband, I'm happy to work again now because I've had another sign of life from you. I can't describe the joy we felt, which was great indeed.'[41] Separation from one's husband eventually became an oppressive normality. Conflicts sometimes arose, when men tried to make decisions relating to farm business from afar by letter. These required the women to have a minimum of self-confidence. On the whole, however, they suggest that the long separation from their husbands was causing women to lose confidence and thus to become increasingly unsure of how to behave.[42]

Rather than making the women feel increasingly alienated from their husbands, separation generally made them 'long boundlessly for peace and their husbands' return', a feeling which intensified with time.[43] This

37. Excerpt from a letter by a woman from Upper Bavaria, 24.3.1917: BSB.

38. Letter from Rosenheim, 17.6.1917: BSB.

39. Memorandum by the War Ministry Press Office, 19.9.1916: BHStA/IV, MKr 233.

40. Daniel, *Arbeiterfrauen*, pp. 150-1; see the critique in Ziemann, *Geschlechterbeziehungen*.

41. Excerpt from a letter by a farmer's wife from Bavarian Swabia, 27.2.1917: BHStA/IV, stv. GK I.AK 1979.

42. Letter by a farmer's wife from Upper Franconia, March 1917: BSB.

43. Commander of the 11th Infantry Division, 15.12.1915: BHStA/IV, MKr 2330.

desire was rooted in the peasant women's conviction that there was nothing good about being on one's own.[44] They wished for the return both of a qualified labour force and of the person with whom they had the closest emotional connection. Securing the economic stability of the farm was the dominant motive here.[45] Sometimes, however, peasant wives were simply worried about the well-being of a familiar individual with whom they had shared a home for so long: 'Dear Christoph, today is the Whitsun festival. How much longer will you be away? You may never come home, and if you should never come, what am I to do then and how will I cope? I would rather be with you, along with the children. There would be nothing left for me in this world'.[46]

The relationship between peasant spouses thus throws the limits of a purely economic interpretation of the peasant family economy into particularly sharp relief. Even the few women who felt satisfaction at having coped well with their enforced independence longed for their husbands.[47] Peasant women's actions in relation to the deferral of military service and furlough also show that their soldier husbands were not solely of interest as labourers whose shoes could be filled by any random male. It was thus far from unusual for workers or POWs to be turned away 'in order to prove that deferral or discharge was necessary' and thus 'bring their relative home from the field'.[48]

Women were as keen to see their husbands again as the latter were to get home, key evidence that spatial separation did not lead to emotional alienation. Whether peasant women felt that their husbands' habituation to warfare might threaten the future peace and civility of married life is hard to judge.[49] However, their sympathy for the burdens borne in the field is likely to have been uppermost in their minds.[50] The opportunity to have relationships with other men did, however, represent a threat to peasant marriages, particularly when husbands were away for a long time. It was primarily the profound moral disgrace of an illegitimate relationship that disciplined peasant women in this respect. A letter to a POW from 1917 lays this bare:

44. Anna Eberhard, 11.2.1916: private possession.

45. See letters by Stefan Schimmer, 21.12.1914, 2.1.1915, 13.1.1915: BHStA/IV, Amtsbibliothek 9584.

46. Katharine Erhardt, 19.5.1918: BfZ, Slg. Knoch.

47. Letter by a farmer's wife from Münchsdorf (Lower Bavaria), 20.4.1918: BSB.

48. Stv. GK I.AK 28.4.1917: BHStA/IV, stv. GK I.AK 2768.

49. Daniel, *Arbeiterfrauen*, pp. 150-1.

50. Christoph Erhardt, 3.8.1917: BfZ, Slg. Knoch.

> I have to tell you that there's plenty of amour going on in R., and not just among the young girls but the married women too. There are three of them in the village putting on such a performance that it's a disgrace for the whole community, you won't be surprised to hear that the first is the wife of St.-Schorß. It's lucky for her that Schorß has been taken prisoner, so at least she is safe. Frankl was in play before, then he had to report for duty. Now she has a sergeant. He even bought her a ribbon for her hair. Then there's F. Nandl and the wife of O. Heinrich, there was a terrible commotion there one night, they had their door smashed, all sorts of insults will be flying there. I can't begin to tell you all the things that are going on and how bad people are becoming. This war hasn't improved anything. I'm always being held up as an example by various people, because you've been away for such a long time, and no one has heard the slightest thing about me. Not that I have a high opinion of myself, it is of course my holiest duty, but you are just happy to have a clear conscience and be seen by others as a proper person. In any case I could never do that to my dear little man.[51]

Unmarried maids were not significantly concerned about their standing in the eyes of the village public when pursuing their flirtations. The moral constraints which affected farm owners because of their need to preserve their vested property did not apply to them. Other than dismissal by their employers, there was no effective means of controlling them.[52] This is probably one reason why maids entered into sexual relations with POWs working on farms more often than married peasant women. Of the latter group, it was mainly those whose husbands had died or were missing who had such relationships, despite the risk of moral and legal condemnation.[53]

Another factor which made illegitimate relationships downright inviting was the rapidly falling number of marriages during the war. The decline was even more dramatic in rural communities than in the cities. This was because, first, more recalled soldiers lived in the cities than in the country. Second, rural dwellers were generally cautious in this regard. This is particularly apparent in the fact that in 1914, in towns with a population of 20,000 or more, and to an even greater extent in major cities, the number of marriages per 1,000 of the population lay above that of 1913. In communities of less than 2,000 inhabitants, meanwhile, there was a rapid decline as early as 1914. This points to the fact that a wave of 'war weddings' in August and September of 1914 failed to occur in the

51. Letter to a POW in Rottau (BA Traunstein), 29.5.1917: BSB.
52. Schulte, *Dorf*, pp. 142–53.
53. Parish of Haiming, 14.7.1918: ABP, DekA II, Burghausen 12/I.

countryside. Clearly, rural dwellers wished to wait 'until the uncertain political and personal situation [had been] resolved' before deciding to marry, a decisive turning point in the life of the peasant.[54]

Increasing numbers of farmers' daughters and maids entered into relationships with POWs despite threats of punishment by the Deputy General Command; these often came to light only when the girl became pregnant.[55] The names of these women were printed in the official gazette to discourage such behaviour. Priests warned against moral offences from the pulpit and threatened to take action.[56] POWs in the villages, however, were monitored only very superficially. Because their labour input made them indispensable, most were thoroughly integrated into the peasant household.[57] People sometimes refrained from reporting such incidents out of fear that the prisoner would be taken away.[58] In the light of the prevailing public climate, in which relationships with POWs were condemned as shameless and as a dereliction of national duty, anonymous informers took the opportunity to blacken the name of neighbours with whom they had fallen out or to avert imminent affiliation cases.[59] Despite the heightened sensitivities of 'national' circles, POWs generally integrated smoothly; they worked closely together with maids on a daily basis. These were favourable conditions for the development of intimate relations. These young women fell in love easily and sometimes even wished to marry a prisoner. If such relationships resulted in pregnancy, however, maids and farmers' daughters often found out how difficult it was for someone in their social position to have a baby. Many then attempted to abort the pregnancy by taking easily available substances such as soapsuds, gunpowder or hot red wine.[60]

Peasant women's predicament during the war was characterised primarily by extreme overwork and profound anxiety over the lives of their loved ones. Their temporarily expanded sphere of action offered them little scope for boosting their egos. There is no evidence that taking on men's work helped them attain the prestige traditionally associated with it. The precarious reality of peasant women managing on their own was

54. *ZBSL* 51 (1919), pp. 90–5, quote p. 92.

55. Daniel, *Arbeiterfrauen*, pp. 145–6.

56. WB BA Neu-Ulm, 15.12.1917: StAA, Regierung 9764.

57. WB BA Eggenfelden, 3.12.1917: BHStA/IV, stv. GK I.AK 1960.

58. Liaison officer of the E./Ldst.-Btl. Passau, 26.4.1918: BHStA/IV, stv. GK I. AK 2408.

59. *Münchener Post*, 31.7.1917.

60. StAL, Rep. 167/2, 1093, 1094, 1120, 1122, 1128.

apparent not only in their overwork, but also in their inability to defend themselves against the patriarchal behaviour of the remaining men and the authorities. Religiously motivated forbearance reinforced married peasant women's willingness to put up with even extreme economic and personal strains. Many people began to lose hope that the war would bring about a moral renewal; a whole range of symptoms of declining social and religious morality coalesced, causing some to believe that the war had triggered the collapse of the moral values which had formerly held sway.

5.2 Agrarian Economy and Inflation, 1914–23

As in other areas of the Empire, agriculture in southern Bavaria faced numerous obstacles to production during the war. Alongside the serious labour shortage, the number of draught horses, the farmer's most valuable tool, fell by a third as young horses were taken by the armed forces. The supply and thus consumption of artificial fertiliser, particularly the nitrogen-based varieties mainly imported from abroad before the war, dropped by roughly 40 per cent. In addition, because there were fewer animals, the amount of animal dung produced fell by around half. From 1913 to 1918 the number of pigs fell by 55 per cent. The notorious 'pig killing' of 1915 in Bavaria caused only a negligible drop in numbers, as it was mainly smallholders who raised pigs there. The disruption to the supply of animal fodder from abroad led to a dramatic reduction in the quantities available on the state-controlled fodder market and put a stop to intensive milk production. Because Bavarian agriculture was not heavily mechanised, the difficulty in procuring agricultural machines, which increased in price far in excess of the manufacturer's price, was of relatively minor significance. The lack of fuel, however, made threshing by machine, among other things, more difficult.[61]

These problems caused crop yields to fall significantly during the war, though they reached their lowest level only in 1919. In Bavaria in 1919 the winter wheat yield per hectare was 25 per cent lower than in 1913. The figure for winter rye was 30 per cent, summer barley 26 per cent, oats 30 per cent and potatoes 38 per cent lower. The transition to extensive agriculture is also reflected in changes in the area under cultivation. In 1923 the figures for wheat and rye were only around 89 and 75 per cent

61. Franz Achter, Die Einwirkungen des Krieges auf die bäuerliche Wirtschaft in Bayern, PhD dissertation, Munich 1920, pp. 64–90.

respectively of the level in 1914, while clover and alfalfa had climbed to around 124 and 148 per cent of the 1914 level.[62]

The impact of the loss of capital suffered during the war and the over-exploitation of labour, soil, machinery and equipment continued to be felt for several years after the war, though it is very difficult to determine the conditions of production during this period. The return to more intensive farming was hindered by the high, fluctuating and thus hard to calculate prices for concentrated feed and artificial fertiliser. The exhausted soil regained its former fertility only very gradually.[63] Yields per hectare for all vegetable products were thus still lower in 1923 than before the war. A major crop failure made matters worse in 1922. However, we need to bear in mind that, because of the delivery quotas set by the state during and after the war, farmers were notorious for understating their crop yields and area under cultivation. We cannot be sure of the extent of this deception.[64]

Lack of farm accounts forces us to make a rough, global estimate of the objective profitability of farms during and after the war. The sale of horses to the armed forces, the rising prices of agricultural products on the officially administered and, above all, the black market and the restrictions on farm expenditure on investment produced a growing surplus of money capital even during the war. This was apparent in the increase in savings deposits made at the agricultural *Zentralgenossenschaften* (cooperative societies).[65] The *de facto* ban on imports of agricultural products, brought about by the depreciation of the currency, stabilised producer prices above the world market level. As a result, the surplus of liquid capital increased again in the post-war period. Most farmers, however, made little use of the opportunity this presented to enhance their working capital or did so too late. It was not until the spring of 1922 that large numbers of farmers began to take refuge in physical assets. In many districts new buildings were erected, while stables, other animal enclosures and farm buildings were renovated; many farms were provided with electricity.[66] A stabilisation crisis set in during the transition to the *Rentenmark* in 1923, which was intended to overcome inflation. Falling producer prices

62. Calculated on the basis of the *Statistisches Jahrbuch für den Freistaat Bayern* 16 (1924), pp. 41-2.

63. Achter, Einwirkungen, p. 127.

64. *Statistisches Jahrbuch für den Freistaat Bayern* 16 (1924), p. 42.

65. Achter, Einwirkungen, pp. 115-44.

66. HMB RP Schw., 20.3.1922: BHStA/II, MA 102147.

quickly made it plain that farms had benefited superficially from inflation as a result of increased profits. Yet the general failure to invest these profits quickly enough or on a large enough scale generated structural weakness. From this perspective, the period of inflation featured a merely 'illusory boom'.[67]

The outbreak of war was a key turning point for agricultural policy. For farmers, economically speaking, it defined the entire period from 1914 to 1923. Since the passing of the tariff legislation of 1879, agriculture had enjoyed comprehensive protection from foreign imports of cereal and meat. This shielded the domestic market from the price pressures of imports, the world market prices being markedly lower. It also allowed agricultural producers to boost their profits at the expense of consumers.[68] This privileged position was shaken by the switch to a 'consumption-oriented food policy' in the autumn of 1914. This way of putting it may seem astonishing given the catastrophic food crisis during the second half of the war. Yet the lack of food was mainly due to the obstacles to production described above and the fact that the Empire met around a fifth of its needs through imports of food and animal feed, to which the Allied blockade put an end.[69] To manage this shortage and limit the increase in prices for consumers, a controlled agricultural economy was created with the initial support of the agricultural interest groups. This encompassed until 1917 almost all food products as well as animal fodder.[70]

This complex set of measures, whose intricacies we will not be exploring further here, was set in motion in October 1914 with the introduction of maximum producer prices for the wholesale trade in bread-making cereals. Fodder cereal and potatoes, among other things, were soon subjected to the same kind of price restrictions. From January 1915 on, stocks of cereals for bread making and flour were confiscated. At the local level, the acquisition of cereals and all the other products later subject to state control, seizure of stocks, checks to ensure that farmers delivered everything they were supposed to, occasional expropriation and, finally, storage were the responsibility of the municipal syndicates (*Kommunalverbände*). Generally, these were created by the

67. Aereboe, *Einfluß*, pp. 113-23, quote p. 108.

68. Wehler, *Gesellschaftsgeschichte*, vol. 3, pp. 648-53.

69. Schumacher, *Land und Politik*, p. 271; figure: Daniel, *Arbeiterfrauen*, p. 183.

70. Schumacher, *Land und Politik*, pp. 33-69.

kreisfreie Städte (self-administered towns) and the *Bezirksämter* (district authorities).[71]

It was soon apparent that these administrative measures were chronically insufficient. On the production side, this was because, among other things, farmers immediately responded to the imposition of a price ceiling for a particular product by withholding it. The later maximum prices were introduced, the higher they were. As a result, the relationship between the price of cereals and that of pigs or cattle, whose prices were laid down only towards the end of 1915 and in March 1916, became particularly skewed. Despite the imposition of a ban from October 1914, this led to more bread-making cereals being fed to animals. An attempt in the fiscal year 1917/18 to rectify the price structure by increasing the price of cereals to the disadvantage of the pigs failed; rather than officially supervised slaughter, more were simply slaughtered at home. With the compulsory delivery of milk, introduced throughout Bavaria in December 1916, and the compulsory cattle quotas from March 1916, which were to be supervised by livestock delivery committees run by the local authorities, the administrative system was largely complete.[72]

The crisis-hit political situation, the meagre food supply and the demands of both wings of the SPD ensured that the controlled economy continued after the end of the war. However, because the controls had largely failed and as a result of the skilful politics pursued by Andreas Hermes, Imperial Minister for Food from 1920, a far-reaching political consensus gradually took hold that they should be phased out. State controls on pigs, cattle and potatoes were removed from August to October 1920, and on milk in 1921. In the case of cereals for making bread, especially important to satisfying consumers both physically and psychologically, controls were retained in the modified form of apportionment (*Umlageverfahren*) from 1921 until the spring of 1923. Subsequently, a certain quantity of cereals had to be surrendered to the local authorities at a reduced price; this was determined annually and was shared out between the *Länder* in line with former average crop yields. Farmers could sell the remainder at the market price.[73]

The controlled economy had a constant, massive impact on farmers' ability to plan ahead and take economic decisions. Peasants had been

71. Achter, Einwirkungen, pp. 27–32.

72. August Skalweit, *Die deutsche Kriegsernährungswirtschaft*, Stuttgart: Deutsche Verlags-Anstalt 1927, pp. 99–114, 187–96.

73. Schumacher, *Land und Politik*, pp. 130–86.

economically privileged before 1914. Ceaseless and at times unpredictable state intervention in the market for agricultural products and the shifting relationship between the prices of individual products, especially the restrictions on officially allowable profits, made them feel that the interests of consumers, now being represented by the government, were taking precedence. The collective front which producers as a whole adopted *vis-à-vis* urban consumers was more important than variations in the intensity with which specific groups of peasants were affected by the controlled economy. State controls ultimately caused the state's legitimacy and authority to diminish rapidly in rural areas and the agricultural associations to protest ever more vigorously; in this they had the support of their disgruntled members, rapidly growing in number.[74]

This thesis, first developed using the example of farmers in Westphalia and the Rhineland, has placed the traditional interpretation of the distributive effects of inflation in a different light. Farmers, along with other owners of physical assets, are generally counted among the winners from inflation because the progressive currency depreciation made it possible to pay off existing mortgage debts easily.[75] Yet, as farmers' representatives argued at the time, with apportionment the government had created a 'special tax afflicting a single class' (Sebastian Schlittenbauer), in that it prevented farmers from making as much profit on the open market as they would otherwise have done. From this perspective, state intervention to set the prices of agricultural products, which continued even after the war was over, meant that farmers were able to view themselves as losers from inflation, regardless of the debt relief that it entailed as far as cereals were concerned.[76]

This line of argument no doubt captures significant aspects of peasants' perceptions and how they came to terms with the controlled economy, as well as the political response to these developments. This view is underpinned by an exemplary notion of the peasant economy which assumes it to have been determined largely by the rational calculation of economic interest, which now showed the balance shifting to the disadvantage of farmers, at least to some extent. However justified a purely economic calculation of distributive effects may be, it is limited. This applies especially to post-war inflation, the impact of which demands

74. Moeller, *Peasants*, passim.

75. Franz Eulenburg, Die sozialen Wirkungen der Währungsverhältnisse, *Jahrbücher für Nationalökonomie und Statistik* 122. (1924), pp. 748-95, 763-4.

76. Sebastian Schlittenbauer, 29.3.1922: BHStA/II, ML 1069; see Moeller, Losers.

analysis beyond the spectacular crises of 1923. First, we cannot simply take for granted that the members of a social group responded to inflation primarily, and in uniform fashion, in accordance with means-end rationality. Second, inflation destroyed social structures along with the overarching moral norms which lent them legitimacy.[77]

In what follows, we shall therefore be concentrating on the differences among the peasantry produced by the controlled economy and inflation, and probing peasants' moral interpretive model, which integrated economic and social problems. We will discover that many farmers had a very positive view of their economic situation, regardless of the interference in the agricultural market. The large number of complaints made by peasants about their economic position in the weekly reports of the district authorities and other sources are a good place to begin. Farmers were already well known for complaining incessantly about their economic problems in the Imperial era.[78] Nonetheless, by classifying peasants' complaints about the controlled economy, we can obtain a helpful overview of which aspects of interference in the peasant economy were perceived as especially unwelcome and who felt most affected by them.[79]

First of all, farmers suffered restrictions on their freedom of disposal not only as producers but also as consumers of agricultural products. Once bread-making cereals had been confiscated, they, their family members and permanently employed non-family workers were granted for their own use a 'self-sufficiency ration' (*Selbstversorgerration*) of nine kilograms of cereal per capita per month, along with similar quantities of other products. Grinding certificates helped the authorities monitor the rationing system; these were signed at mills to confirm receipt of the required quantity of cereals. From 1916 home slaughtering could be carried out only with the approval of the local authority.[80]

77. Jens Flemming/Claus-Dieter Krohn/Peter-Christian Witt, Sozialverhalten und politische Reaktionen von Gruppen und Institutionen im Inflationsprozeß. Anmerkungen zum Forschungsstand, in: Otto Büsch/Gerald D. Feldman (eds), *Historische Prozesse der deutschen Inflation 1914-1924. Ein Tagungsbericht*, Berlin: Colloquium-Verlag 1978, pp. 239-63, pp. 242-3.

78. Hans-Jürgen Puhle, *Agrarische Interessenpolitik und preußischer Konservatismus im wilhelminischen Reich 1893-1914*, Bonn-Bad Godesberg: Verlag Neue Gesellschaft 1975, p. 242.

79. Moeller, *Peasants*, pp. 53-7.

80. This regulation was retained for bread-making cereals until the introduction of apportionment in 1921. *Die öffentliche Bewirtschaftung von Getreide*

There is no doubt that farmers generally enjoyed an adequate and secure food supply by urban standards; they were allowed to consume more than city dwellers.[81] It was also easy to get round the grinding-certificates system with the help of the millers, who kept a substantial quantity of corn in return for their assistance. This made many farmers appear the true beneficiaries of the controlled economy. Some farmers switched over from the flour-based foodstuffs typical of Altbayern to alternatives. The *Selbstversorgerration* in itself, however, represented profound interference in an aspect of peasant autonomy otherwise taken for granted, the freedom to do with one's own produce as one wished. Married peasant women in particular objected bitterly: 'and if the war drags on for a long while yet, what will happen then? Even now we're not allowed to harvest a single potato before 15 September. We'll have no choice but to steal from ourselves. No one's come up with any regulations about hoeing - we were allowed to do that ourselves.'[82]

Given how hard they had to work, peasants found official restrictions on food particularly unfair.[83] Fines imposed by the courts for proven offences against the regulations governing grinding certificates and home slaughtering made them yet more bitter. This source of discontent was sometimes placed in the context of the idea of a comprehensive conspiracy against the peasants:

> The stupid peasant has to pay until he has nothing left to give as well as work, and then the rules tell you that you can eat 100 grams of bread today. If those who are not working, who have no regulations to follow, don't have enough, then you only get 50 grams of bread, and if you eat 51 you get a 1500M fine. The papers are full of it. Someone ate a pound too much and either faces six months in jail or a fine of 1500M. Another dared to slaughter a pig he himself had raised - 1500M fine, and a 300M reward for whoever told on him. Now that the harvest is beginning and we're about to start threshing, six or seven men come and stand around and count every little grain of corn that falls from the sheaf. They know how much that is those doing no work, and there will soon be nothing left for the peasants. There are too many people sitting around trying to work out how to ruin the peasantry as quickly as possible. Whoever can do it quickest is greatly rewarded. They don't mind sending the

---

und Mehl in Bayern, Munich: Statistisches Bureau 1923 (Beiträge zur Statistik Bayerns, 103), pp. 3, 35–42.

81. Skalweit, *Kriegsernährungswirtschaft*, p. 210.
82. Letter by a farmer's wife from Pfaffenhofen, 3.8.1917: BSB.
83. Michael Melchner, 20.6.1916: BHStA/IV, MKr 2330.

> peasant estate [*Bauernstand*] to war, there's no one else out there [at the front], because it's only fair, for we have so little work otherwise and don't have enough to do. That's why they cannot stop fighting. The others have to stay at home, otherwise there would be no one to take everything from our women. People are always saying the peasant is to blame and so on.[84]

Together with a number of other letters written by peasant women, this letter elucidates a specific aspect of peasant mentality, namely their tendency to perceive society in a holistic manner. Peasants did not analyse their individual hardships separately from the social problems lying beyond their own sphere of interest. They were understood within a narrow framework and were subject to moral generalisation. The main reason for this was the low level of role specialisation characteristic of farmers' working lives and life-world. Farmers tended to ascribe central significance to their own work or, during the war, overwork. Peasant outrage at state controls was thus not solely motivated by the straightforward perception of their disadvantaged economic position. These controls in fact became a problem because they were interpreted in the context of a deeply rooted peasant working morality which received very little recognition during the war. This may explain why peasants were so vexed by an issue such as self-sufficiency rations, which was of relatively minor significance within the overall context of state controls.

For the same reason, when the self-sufficiency ration for cereals, which had already been reduced in 1916/17, was lowered again to 6.5 kilograms towards the end of March 1918, the restrictions on consumption ultimately became caught up in the fraught opposition between urban and rural areas.[85] Farmers were particularly indignant about these measures because workers in areas of industry important to the war were given extra pay for heavy or very heavy work. The War Food Office (Kriegsernährungsamt), however, did not consider agricultural workers to be doing very heavy work, and only a few local authorities considered them to be doing heavy work. Farmers saw this as scandalous discrimination, particularly while working hard to till their fields in spring and given the scant regard for the work being done shown by their industrial counterparts.[86] In the immediate post-war period as well, 'farmers' bitterness about the controlled economy [was] mainly' down to

84. Letter by a farmer's wife from Altomünster, 30.6.1917: BSB.
85. Skalweit, *Kriegsernährungswirtschaft*, pp. 211–12.
86. WB BA Eggenfelden, 2.5.1918: BHStA/IV, stv. GK I.AK 1965.

the self-sufficiency ration, which they considered too little.[87] A meeting of the mayors of the district of Landau in August 1919 placed the demand for the abolition of grinding and slaughtering certificates at the top of its list of complaints about the controlled economy.[88] As with consumption, restrictions on the freedom of disposal affecting production, which constituted major interference in the peasant autonomy, caused much bitterness.[89] Peasants were especially critical of delivery quotas because they had so much work to do themselves:

> The producers have it no better. The officials waste no time in confiscating cattle, poultry, cereals, potatoes, hay and straw. They work it out in such a way that you get the most meagre quantity possible. We're left with just six centners of oats for two horses until harvest. They've left us with too few seeds per daily task [*Tagwerk*]. We in agriculture have to slave away and worry ourselves sick in order to feed all. Yet you're still now and later the stupid peasant.[90]

As a letter written by a farmer in October 1917 lays bare, people began to wonder if there was any point in continuing to farm as large an area as possible given all the restrictions on production: 'It really is time that this terrible war came to an end, because we have to put up with all kinds of restrictions. Everything is confiscated, everything we grow. The fruit, the cereals, the potatoes, the cattle - in short, everything we have. But they haven't confiscated the work yet, that we're allowed to do, but we're not to eat much, despite bringing in a good harvest again.'[91] Thus, regardless of price-fixing for specific products and the loss of income which resulted, farmers felt that state controls seriously disadvantaged them compared with other groups, particularly city dwellers.

Farmers who conscientiously handed over all they were supposed to began to doubt that their honesty made sense and was being respected. This was in part because of the inspections of cereals stocks carried out by the local constabulary and military commando on all farms. There were also many reports in the press and statements made in the *Landtag* in which 'the tardiness of the producers was generally criticised'.[92]

87. WB RP Ndb., 11.8.1919: BHStA/II, MA 102139.
88. MdL Mayer, 25.8.1919: BHStA/II, ML 1497.
89. Letter from resident of Upper Bavaria, 26.2.1917: BHStA/IV, stv. GK I. AK 1979.
90. Letter by a farmer's wife from Amendingen, 23.12.1917: BSB.
91. Letter by a peasant from Steinling, 4.10.1917: BSB.
92. RP Schw., 27.6.1917: BHStA/II, ML 1353.

Shortly after the war, an amnesty was declared on fines imposed on those who had failed to meet their delivery quotas. So those who had 'done their duty' and would have 'welcomed' such penalties in their community felt that they were not receiving the recognition that they had expected for their 'good behaviour'.[93]

Generally, the farmers who suffered most economically from the various price adjustments and incentives undertaken by the authorities were those who had initially been willing to supply produce at the maximum prices originally imposed. Those agricultural producers who had been faithful to the controlled economy from the beginning thus felt disadvantaged mainly because of the way in which prices were assessed rather than because of the measures as such. Inevitably, these farmers too became increasingly unwilling to meet the obligations required by the authorities. These peasants were, however, not only critical of the state, which had initiated the unsuccessful measures. They also felt that farmers who had been reluctant to deliver the due amounts from the outset and had sold their products on the black market instead had done better than them. Farmers who had done as they were told and handed over to the local authorities fatstock, whose price had been set too low compared with productive livestock, thus complained that they had suffered worse financial losses than those who had broken the rules and sold it to other traders for a better price.[94]

This conflict within the peasantry frequently came to the attention of the general public. Admonitory articles in the press addressed those farmers who 'profiteer like the meanest caftan Jew', and 'right thinking peasants' thus became more likely to favour the vigorous persecution of such 'greedy behaviour'.[95] In January 1920 the newspaper of the Christian Peasants' Association deployed symptomatic rhetoric to assail farmers who sold their cereals on the black market rather than delivering it, 'as an honest Christian must do'. Even before maximum prices were introduced by the government and advocated by the SPD, this particular element of their own social group was blamed for the disadvantages suffered by those farmers willing to deliver their due. The latter were repeatedly urged to exercise 'self-control' and to report their fellow peasants.[96]

However, it proved impossible to effectively stop people from getting round the delivery quotas. Some districts experimented with committees

93. WB BA Donauwörth, 20.12.1918: StAA, Regierung 9765.

94. WB BA Augsburg, 3.5.1919: StAA, Regierung 9766.

95. *Amper-Bote*, 10.5.1919.

96. *Bayerisches Bauernblatt*, 27.1.1920.

organised by the local priest. These were meant to encourage people to deliver their produce and denounce farmers selling to hoarders (*Hamsterer*). Such efforts largely failed because, within the confined milieu of the village, denunciations featuring precise information were bound to reflect back upon those making them, and no one wished to 'make an enemy' of his neighbour.[97] During the war, the only effective means of ensuring that farmers met their requirements was to deny harvest furlough to farmers reported by the local authority for gross failure to deliver the due amount.[98]

Because controls were ineffective, during the course of the war the vast majority of farmers began to sell products regularly on the black market to individuals hoarding on behalf of their families or to commercially active black marketeers.[99] Contemporary estimations assumed that around one-third of food in total found its way to the consumer outside the official market.[100] In the last two years of the war, most products sold on the black market for about twice as much as the official maximum price. Some evidence suggests that cereals and cattle eventually cost up to three times as much in the post-war period.[101] The sale of products on the black market was not, however, a purely rational economic decision taken immediately by all farmers in response to the higher prices.[102] Those farmers initially willing to hand over the required amount to the local authority without question needed to experience the inherently disadvantageous maximum-price system on numerous occasions before following the example of their tardy colleagues. Officials in some districts noted that farmers who had been trustworthy hitherto only became interested in boosting their profits during the second half of the war because of the high prices fetched by hoarded produce. They justified their actions by pointing to the profits to be made from such trade or claimed that, given that the war was a great 'swindle', it was necessary 'to lie now'.[103]

97. WB BA Aichach, 25.9.1920: StAM, LRA 99497.

98. Passau Economic Office, 23.7.1918: BHStA/IV, stv. GK I.AK 3193.

99. Ay, *Entstehung*, pp. 160–5.

100. Kocka, *Klassengesellschaft*, p. 34.

101. WB BA Freising, 29.9.1917: BHStA/IV, stv. GK I.AK 1957. From 1914 until the harvest of 1920, maximum prices climbed somewhat less than the currency depreciated; *Bewirtschaftung*, pp. 101–2.

102. Robert G. Moeller, Dimensions of Social Conflict in the Great War. The View from the German Countryside, *Central European History* 14 (1981), pp. 142–68, p. 154.

103. Parish of Triftern, n.d. [1917]: ABP, DekA II, Pfarrkirchen 12/I.

No doubt many farmers held back from evading the rules of the controlled economy mainly because they traditionally felt an obligation to obey the authority of the state. Beyond this, it is also possible to identify religious obstacles to such behaviour, which appears consistent from an economic point of view. Within Catholic morality, profiteering was viewed as the 'exploitation of one's neighbour's hardship to obtain impermissible profit'. This was an offence against fundamental moral principles according to which commodity prices must not exceed purchasing costs. Priests and the Christian Peasants' Association thus also condemned income from hoarding as 'accursed money'.[104] Imbued with such rhetoric, one Lower Bavarian farmer's wife confessed to her parish priest in 1918 that she could take 'no pleasure' in the 'blood money' acquired through sales to hoarders. Priests asserted that only some farmers - albeit a growing number - in their parishes were trading on the black market. In some villages all the farmers adhered to the official regulations.[105]

Over the long term, however, religious-moral conceptions could not stop farmers from engaging in 'profiteering', even during the war, particularly in the light of the collapse of moral values generally confirmed by married peasant women. Their husbands' return from the front in 1918, moreover, caused a massive increase in the refusal to deliver the required amounts.[106] In the end, as the head of the district of Swabia noted in September 1919, the 'profiteering spirit' spread 'to the remotest village', 'a spirit which means using one's time and circumstances to the full and, like all too many role models in industry, commerce and trade, earning as much money as possible'.[107] This view, aired time and again in subsequent years, reflects one consequence of the general rise in prices, which intensified significantly once inflation began to gallop in the autumn of 1919. Most farmers responded by consistently taking full advantage of the profits attainable on the black market and by immediately raising the price of their products whenever the income of urban and rural employees and civil servants went up. Thus, by 1920 most farmers had accumulated large quantities of cash, sometimes running to six-figure sums.[108]

104. Franz-Xaver Eberle, *Katholische Wirtschaftsmoral*, Freiburg/Br.: Herder 1921, pp. 83-9, quote p. 86.

105. Parish of Engertsham, 20.6.1918: ABP, DekA II, Fürstenzell 12/I.

106. WB RP Schw., 18.11.1919: BHStA/II, MA 102145.

107. WB RP Schw., 9.9.1919: BHStA/II, MA 102145.

108. WB BA Aichach, 6.10.1919: StAM, LRA 99497.

Following the abolition of most aspects of the controlled economy and in the light of the depreciation of the currency, which accelerated rapidly in 1922, the activities of large numbers of traders caused the prices of most products to shoot up even further. In Lower Bavaria in 1922, buyers from Saxony and northern Germany mainly bought cattle being sold off eagerly by farmers 'at any price' because of the dearth of animal feed.[109] A clear trend towards speculative economic practices emerged from the end of the period of relative stabilisation in the late summer of 1921 and to an even greater extent once hyperinflation took hold in the summer of 1922. Some farmers engaged in large-scale speculation with cereals or dollars acquired for this purpose. Some even tried their luck on the stock exchange. One priest expressed the view that those seeking consolation no longer read the Bible but the 'stock exchange list' instead.[110]

Even during the course of the war, the controlled economy had undermined to some extent the traditional moral order of rural society by rewarding those who ignored moral norms and punishing those who stuck to the rules. As well as making people feel economically disadvantaged, this caused quarrels and jealousy within village communities, which sometimes crossed the usual group boundaries separating smallholders and big farmers. If people initially refrained from such 'immoral' behaviour, inflation quickly changed the minds of most farmers. By accumulating cash, peasant business practices geared towards selling as dearly as possible, and frequently speculative in nature, could clearly be highly profitable; they washed away moral and legal reservations even in the intimate sphere of peasant families.

One example is provided by 'even rich peasant women' from Lower Bavaria, who bought up eggs, butter and lard and then smuggled them into Czechoslovakia in 1923.[111] In Swabia farmers' sons even stole cereals from their parents' farm, then sold them on.[112] Another example of the moral and political confusion produced by the 'profiteering spirit' is recorded for the district of Miesbach. In March 1923, at a rally of the Communist Party (KPD), a young peasant generally known to favour keeping milk prices high stepped forward. He 'stirred up' the crowd against two landowners who had failed to increase their milk prices as

109. HMB RP Nbd., 18.10.1922: BHStA/II, MA 102140.
110. HMB RP Schw., 18.11.1921: BHStA/II, MA 102147.
111. HMB RP Ndb., 18.3.1923: BHStA/II, MA 102140.
112. HMB RP Schw., 21.11.1922: BHStA/II, MA 102147.

recently stipulated, by voicing his suspicion that they were providing their workers with no milk at all.[113]

The Christian Peasants' Association, the Peasants' League and the *Bauernkammern* (peasants' trade associations) frequently urged peasants to content themselves with the set prices and to take a stand against profiteering among peasants. Farmers were urged not to succumb to the temptations of the many buyers, who were presented as most to blame for driving up prices. Such admonitions rarely failed to mention the risk that the poor might be 'driven [onto] the streets to improve their lot' and that this might ultimately lead to a 'new revolution'.[114] Some farmers distanced themselves from the actions of most of their fellows, emphasising that they were not 'war profiteers' and had 'acted with nothing but honesty during the current period of hardship, and had not engaged in profiteering'.[115] In 1920 the Bavarian government under Gustav von Kahr chose the populist route of passing anti-profiteering legislation, tightening up the price auditing measures already put in place during the war in order to stem the 'price boosting' practised by traders and producers.[116] This approach met with the approval of some representatives of peasants' interests who regretted the fact that 'all the honest peasants are being blamed [for the] misdemeanours of a few profiteers'.[117] The new measures, however, were geared mainly towards trade and had little impact.[118]

Some peasants were willing to help rein in price increases, particularly during the period of relative currency stabilisation in 1920/21.[119] Farmers in some districts repeatedly stated that they would consider smaller profit margins entirely sufficient, when the price of products no longer subject to state control was increased. This applied to potatoes, for instance, in the autumn of 1920. Many Swabian peasants were satisfied with 20 marks for a centner of potatoes, while others, given the hoarder prices, which had sometimes already been paid, would not consider selling for less than 25-30 marks. Such willing restraint was due in part to farmers' satisfaction with the economic situation and the profits they had already made. It is

113. HMB RP Obb., 24.3.1923: BHStA/II, MA 102136.

114. *Neue freie Volks-Zeitung*, 12.8.1921.

115. Michael Holzmann, 12.6.1921: StaA Regensburg, NL Heim 2305.

116. Geyer, Teuerungsprotest, pp. 198-206.

117. WB BA Memmingen, 6.11.1920: StAA, Regierung 9767.

118. Report by the senior public prosecutor at Oberlandesgericht Munich, 1.2.1922: BHStA/II, ML 1426.

119. WB RP Ndb., 20.9., 1.11.1915: StAL, Rep. 168/5, 1117.

also explained by an announcement made by the agriculture minister that those selling at more than 20 marks per centner risked being reported to the anti-usury authority (*Landeswucherabwehrstelle*).[120] A few farmers could thus still be moved to refrain from maximising profits through the application of moral pressure, even during this period. The massive price hikes following the general unfreezing of cereals prices in the summer of 1921, however, also provoked fears in Swabia that consumers might take direct action to improve their lot, leading many farmers to declare themselves entirely 'satisfied' with the old maximum prices.[121]

When hyperinflation set in during the summer of 1922, it became obvious that money had finally lost its role as stable intermediary in social and economic relations. The price of agricultural produce was now increasingly geared towards the strength of the dollar.[122] In the autumn of 1922 rural artisans, millers, doctors and vets began to demand that farmers pay their bills in quantities of cereals, which they then sold on themselves.[123] When inflation peaked in October and November 1923, the farmers finally withheld almost all of their produce 'to protect themselves from the depreciation of the currency'. They were willing to part with such produce only in direct exchange for goods necessary on the farm or if they urgently required means of payment. Some even demanded payment in gold marks.[124]

The consequences of the controlled economy and inflation were ambivalent for the peasant economy. Continuing intervention in the agricultural market seemed to farmers to favour consumers' interests. They came to feel this not directly because of the economic disadvantages they faced, but because they interpreted these against the background of the heavy peasant workload. For the peasants, the real injustice lay in the fact that they were supposed to work, deliver their due and restrict consumption, while urban dwellers, they felt, failed to appreciate their efforts and were unwilling to countenance similar restrictions. The maximum-prices system, moreover, frequently penalised the very thing it was meant to achieve, namely delivery of the full complement of produce on time. This, and to an even greater extent inflation, undermined the moral order upon which the peasant economy and its social foundations rested. A rigid form of social control traditionally prevailed in rural communities.

120. WB RP Schw., 28.7., 5.10., 12.10.1920: BHStA/II, MA 102146.
121. HMB RP Schw., 23.7.1921: BHStA/II, MA 102147.
122. HMB RP Ndb., 18.10.1922: BHStA/II, MA 102140.
123. HMB RP Ndb., 18.11.1922: BHStA/II, MA 102140.
124. HMB RP Ndb., 3.10.1923: BHStA/II, MA 102140.

Each farmer's way of life and economic activities were normally subject to unceasing appraisal by the community. Deviation from norms soon featured in the omnipresent 'gossip' in which villagers engaged; they quickly formed an opinion about it. Villagers were 'harsh and unsparing' in matters of morality. A family tainted by scandal was often judged for generations by the misdemeanours of its forefathers.[125] After the war, resistance to inconsistent and speculative economic practices, which was anchored in this system of norms, began to dwindle. The immorality of the 'profiteering spirit' made headway in the villages. Despite their sometimes hard-fought battle against the allocation of cereals (*Getreideumlage*), farmers may be described, in line with how they saw themselves, as overall 'winners' from inflation. This generalisation is, however, only half true. Exchange rate fluctuations and the declining capacity of money to function as the intermediary of economic relations rendered an economics rooted in stability and calculability impossible. This not only tempered the economic gains made by farmers but, as we shall see, triggered a wave of political irrationality.

5.3 Agrarian Mobilisation: Protests and Politics

The switch to agricultural policies mainly geared towards the needs of consumers during the war also set in motion the politics of peasant interests. At the plenary session of the *Landtag* and within the Advisory Board on Food (*Ernährungsbeirat*) created by the Bavarian Ministry of the Interior in 1916, the clash between the SPD, championing consumer interests, and peasants' advocates led to heated debates. Representatives of the agrarian Centre Party, particularly Deputy Sebastian Schlittenbauer, protested against alleged discrimination against Bavaria in agriculture, which they claimed was due to the centralisation of decision-making authority in the war economy bodies (*Kriegsgesellschaften*) in Berlin. Representatives of the Peasants' League, meanwhile, attacked the Bavarian authorities, whom they accused of flagrant discrimination against peasants. Friedrich Lutz and Karl Gandorfer were particularly radical and increasingly critical opponents of the government's policies on food.[126]

The Christian Peasants' Association, on the other hand, only ever criticised the details of pricing policy, not the system of state controls as

125. W. Latten, Das Dorf als Lebensgemeinschaft, in: Leopold v. Wiese (ed.), *Das Dorf als soziales Gebilde*, Munich, Leipzig: Duncker & Humblot 1928, pp. 71-7, quote p. 75.

126. Albrecht, *Landtag*, pp. 119-24, 140-53, 214-19.

a whole. Backed up by letters from members of his organisation, Georg Heim expressed pointed criticism of individual maximum-price measures in the Association's publications, provoking a lengthy dispute with War Ministry censors. On the other hand, Heim repeatedly called on farmers to meet their delivery quotas.[127] The Peasants' Association's commitment to the principle of the monarchical state limited the extent to which farmers' discontent could be translated into action. It was thus the only such organisation which failed to increase its membership during and after the war.[128] A number of municipal syndicates, moreover, had transferred their management to the Central Cooperative of the Peasants' Association based in Regensburg and its warehouses as commission agent. Georg Heim was director of the Cooperative.[129] As a consequence, Heim came under fire from critics of the syndicates' business practices. Rumours circulating on the front and in a number of districts of Lower Bavaria in 1917 suggested that Heim had been arrested because the Cooperative had been exporting pigs to England.[130]

In the autumn of 1918 war weariness, scarcity of food and price rises had built up a potential for protest in the cities that the state authorities – which had lost their legitimacy and in the replacement army had themselves been mobilised for revolution – was no longer able to rein in. The MSPD could no longer channel this potential to its own ends. The USPD around Kurt Eisner took the opportunity to bring about revolutionary change. Beginning in Munich on 7 November, this quickly reached the provinces. As social protest and political mobilisation interacted, the revolution in Munich and many smaller cities took on increasingly radical forms. The two resulting, short-lived KPD-dominated soviet republics established in April 1919 were overthrown only after armed conflict.[131]

127. Friedrich Münch, Die agitatorische Tätigkeit des Bauernführers Heim. Zur Volksernährungsfrage aus der Sicht des Pressereferates des bayerischen Kriegsministeriums während des Ersten Weltkrieges, in: Karl Bosel (ed.), *Bayern im Umbruch. Die Revolution von 1918, ihre Voraussetzungen, ihr Verlauf und ihre Folgen*, Munich, Vienna: Oldenbourg 1969, pp. 301–44.

128. Osmond, Peasant Associations, p. 187.

129. Eberl, *Wirtschaftsmoral*, p. 105.

130. StaA Regensburg, NL Heim 207.

131. Martin H. Geyer, Formen der Radikalisierung in der Münchener Revolution, in: Helmut Konrad/Karin M. Schmidlechner (eds), *Revolutionäres Potential in Europa am Ende des Ersten Weltkrieges*, Vienna, Cologne: Böhlau 1991, pp. 63–87.

Peasants initially approved of the revolution, believing it would make an armistice and the return of the soldiers more likely. This belief was soon replaced by a more sober assessment. Rural dwellers were uneasy about the increasingly radical nature of the revolution in the cities. They wanted speedy elections to the National Assembly, hoping that the transition to political business as usual would defuse political tensions.[132] Events in Munich were thus of little relevance to most peasants. There a Central Peasants' Council (*Zentralbauernrat*), formed by the left wing of the Peasants' League around Karl Gandorfer, cooperated with the Eisner government within the framework of the Provisional National Council. In any case, farmers in the Christian Peasants' Association, particularly in the Franconian districts and the Upper Palatinate, opposed the Central Peasants' Council from the outset. Even in the Peasants' League, however, the left wing around Gandorfer and Konrad Kübler, which supported the concept of soviets, had been isolated since the formation of the government under Prime Minister Johannes Hoffmann in mid-March 1919.[133]

The establishment of local peasants' councils, announced by the Eisner regime in late November 1918, thus often progressed at a slow pace. Frequently, the establishment of councils at the borough level was rejected outright or a peasants' council was formed only for the sake of appearances or to prevent interference from workers' councils. Many peasants' councils concentrated on issues of marginal political import such as reducing the length of Sunday sermons to one hour or restricting the consumption of 'luxury automobiles'.[134] This last, however, at least had a moral and generational underpinning. Particularly in the light of the prevailing dearth of fuel, older farmers were outraged by the often 'very young people' to be seen driving through the countryside in civilian and military vehicles, to no useful end in their opinion, during the revolutionary turmoil. This lays bare once again the crucial significance of the division of work and leisure to farmers' conception of society.

Workers' councils frequently turned up to register food supplies in the villages, while the peasants' councils largely failed to tackle black marketeering for fear of provoking the 'enmity and discontentment' of their neighbouring villagers, or because their members were themselves involved.

132. WB BA Aichach, 24.11.1918: StAM, LRA 99497.
133. Mattes, *Bauernräte*, pp. 66-87, 114-20, 143-95.
134. *Bayerisches Bauernblatt*, 26.8.1919.

Rural areas were thus clearly out of sync with the urban councils' movement, which represented the interests of the workers in matters of food supply. On the whole, such councils were an ephemeral phenomenon in the countryside. Overall, the peasants failed to make an impact during the revolution as an autonomous political force.[135] First and foremost, farmers expected the revolutionary regime to remove state controls as comprehensively as possible.[136] Once such hopes had been disappointed, many of them took spontaneous, direct action to improve their lot in the weeks and months following the revolution, in order to avert interference in their freedom of economic disposal. They were aware that, following the revolutionary changes and the 'collapse of the army', the authorities were having a hard time ensuring that people obeyed the regulations governing agriculture.[137]

Even in the final stages of the war, the staff of the Meat Supply Authority responsible for acquiring cattle and the mill inspectors were subjected to 'physical intimidation' by soldiers home on leave.[138] Immediately after the soldiers had returned home for good, it became clear that they were prepared to protest actively on a massive scale. Veterans openly admitted that they would resist the delivery quotas and would switch over to the black market. One farmer told the authorities that he was 'not as foolish as his wife, who had delivered cereals to the Municipal Syndicate for four years. He would come first, and only then other people.'[139] During stable controls, former soldiers subjected inspectors to 'physical attacks on a daily basis and the coarsest of insults'. Some threatened them with the weapons distributed to the paramilitary citizens' militias (*Einwohnerwehren*).[140] Alongside such acts of violence by individuals, numerous acts of collective protest occurred in 1919, sometimes involving all the farmers in a community. Mill inspectors or officials of the War Anti-Usury Authority (*Kriegswucheramt*) sometimes found a crowd of people wielding dung-forks and other tools barring their way at the village entrance.[141] In one village in Lower Bavaria in January 1919, official inspectors were first driven from a property by two young men

135. WB BA Erding, 21.12.1918: StAM, LRA 146315.
136. Mattes, *Bauernräte*, p. 91.
137. WB BA Augsburg, 28.12.1919: StAA, Regierung 9766.
138. K.M., 29.9.1918: BHStA/IV, stv. GK I.AK 557.
139. WB BA Zusmarshausen, 8.2.1919: StAA, Regierung 9766.
140. WB RP Ndb., 25.11.1918: StAL, Rep. 168/5, 1116.
141. WB BA Markt-Oberdorf, 15.10.1919: StAA, Regierung 9766.

with wooden cudgels, before being chased out of the village by a menacing crowd that assailed them with spades and hoes, including women and children.[142]

Such concrete forms of protest were common only in the first few months following demobilisation. For a short time, the potential for protest which had accumulated because of the absence of men, the only actors able to engage in political activities in the village, was released. This occurred with reference to the 'new freedom' generated by the revolution and offered an alternative to the politically meaningless peasants' councils.[143] Soldiers' return to their villages also boosted the membership of all the peasants' interest groups, with the exception of the Christian Peasants' Association. The Peasants' League increased its membership sevenfold compared with the pre-war period; the League of Farmers (*Bund der Landwirte*) had two and a half times as many members, and a new organisation was established, the Free Peasantry (*Freie Bauernschaft*). Anti-clerical resentment had clearly built up in the Peasants' Association, among other places. After the war, farmers everywhere took up positions as regional functionaries that were formerly occupied mainly by clergy.[144]

The Peasants' Association had to take into account the competing interests of the workers being pursued within the BVP. It therefore advocated dismantling state controls only gradually. The left wing of the BBB, meanwhile, in whose election rallies in early 1919 illegal slaughtering and grinding of corn were presented as the self-evident rights of peasants, vigorously advocated the immediate removal of controls and threatened to organise a strike taking in both farming and the supply of produce. This was in response to pressure from most local members, whose 'stubborn refusal' to accept further constraints was comparable 'with the state of many sections of the army' in October 1918. The moderate wing of the Peasants' League around Georg Eisenberger, meanwhile, called on farmers to conscientiously meet their delivery quotas.[145]

After most state controls were abolished in 1920, the associations focused on the struggle against the cereals apportionment. The Peasants' League came under pressure from its own members, since the head

142. Verdict of the Landshut Land Court relating to eight of those involved: StAL, Rep. 167/2, 1156.

143. WB RP Ndb., 18.11.1918: StAL, Rep. 168/5, 1116.

144. Osmond, Peasant Associations, figures p. 187.

145. WB BA Erding, 23.8.1919: StAM, LRA 146315.

of the Imperial Ministry of Food and his counterpart at the Bavarian Ministry of Agriculture were drawn from the ranks of the League at the peak of the wave of agitation in 1922. Particularly in the League's strongholds in Lower Bavaria, the Free Peasantry and its members, mostly wealthy farmers with large farms, used this fact with a good deal of success for political agitation featuring populist attacks against the state and constant threats of a delivery strike. Such action only ever delayed the delivery of the cereals apportionment, but never stopped it entirely. Most farmers were interested mainly in increasing the price of the apportionment, which they felt was too low. They also complained that only cereals producers had to suffer, while industry and farmers mainly producing cattle, milk or hops had no special 'tax' to pay.[146] In 1921 the apportionment was delivered on time even in Lower Bavaria, as many farmers feared arson attacks from enraged consumers.[147]

Following the harvest period of 1921/2, many small farmers complained that they were disadvantaged by apportionment; they often farmed such small areas of land that they were left with very little to sell on the market.[148] The radical tone struck by the various interest organisations at their rallies and in their announcements also addressed the interests of small farmers in order to stop them from leaving the associations.[149] A smaller group of 'insightful' farmers saw their own economic position as good. As some had done with respect to the earlier state controls, these farmers fully acknowledged the need for the apportionment; they merely felt that the absence of maximum prices for industrial products was unfair. In these circles, as recorded at a meeting of the Free Peasantry, some farmers thus talked 'disparagingly' about interest group politics featuring no-holds-barred rhetoric. Support for this rhetoric among the peasantry was thus limited; the moderate forces within the associations gained ground. The advocacy of extreme agricultural policy positions thus largely reflected the needs of farmers eager to 'earn boundless amounts of money'.[150]

Anti-Semitism grew in the post-war period among peasants and – with the exception of the Peasants' League – their associations; it was bound up with the struggle to have state controls slackened. Inflation thus had

146. HMB BA Aichach, 15.10.1922: StAM, LRA 99497.

147. HMB RP, 17.9.1921: BHStA/II, MA 102139; on the Free Peasantry see Osmond, *Rural Protest*.

148. HMB BA Neuburg, 31.3.1922: StAA, BA Neuburg 6971a.

149. *Bayerisches Bauernblatt*, 16.5.1922.

150. HMB BA Landshut, 23.8.1922: StAL, Rep. 164/10, 2008.

momentous consequences for the political culture in rural areas over the long term. During the second half of the war, supply problems and price increases had unleashed a wave of anti-Semitic resentment among the urban middle classes. This intensified further after the war under the pressure of the waves of inflation and became a set component of the rhetoric of price increases. People suspected that the many Jews supposedly employed at the various organisations created to administer raw materials and food both in Bavaria and in federal institutions were simply pursuing their own interests and were thus bringing 'disaster' upon 'Christian mankind'. One resident of Munich insisted as early as 1917 that these 'scoundrels' should have swung from the 'gallows a long time ago'.[151] During the war, according to reports by the district authorities, only a few peasants were affected by this increase in anti-Semitism. At the front, too, only a few soldiers expressed such antipathy. Only towards the end of the war do accounts from Upper Bavaria suggest that people were of the opinion that the 'Jews' in the war economy bodies in Berlin had made enough money and therefore now wanted a cease-fire.[152]

The revolution brought about further change. Jewish politicians on the radical left, denounced by the *völkisch* right and by the Christian Peasants' Association, played a prominent role in the revolution. It was this, above all, that convinced rural dwellers that Jews were among the 'most outstanding beneficiaries of the war and the revolution'.[153] During the period of inflation, however, it was economic motives which generally triggered the increased prominence of anti-Semitic sentiment, which became virulent when state controls on leather were abolished towards the end of 1919 while farmers' produce was subject to continued restrictions. The price of shoes and leather goods increased massively. Some peasants responded by demanding that state controls be reintroduced in this area.[154]

This measure triggered a wave of anti-Semitic resentment, which built on anti-Jewish prejudices already present among the Catholic population that soon spread to a large proportion of the peasantry, especially in Swabia and Upper Bavaria. Jews' involvement in trade, particularly in cattle, brought them into personal contact with farmers. Jews traditionally made up a disproportionately large number of company owners in this

151. Letter by a resident of Munich, 20.9.1917: BSB.

152. Report by an agricultural expert from Upper Bavaria, 21.9.1918: BHStA/IV, stv. GK I.AK 1969.

153. WB BA Nördlingen, 13.12.1919: StAA, Regierung 9766.

154. Bergmann, *Bauernbund*, p. 179.

branch of the economy.[155] The unfreezing of the price of leather was thus described as a 'Jewish sham'. The Imperial government's refusal to reintroduce state controls on leather, as the peasants demanded, reinforced many farmers' conviction that the government was dependent on capitalist circles and particularly Jews.[156] Throughout 1920 the involvement of Jewish-owned trading firms in the business activities of the local authorities also came in for mounting criticism from peasants, as did the acquisition by Jewish traders of cattle and horses to be surrendered to the victorious powers.[157] In August 1921 in Memmingen a Jewish cheese merchant was dragged across the market square to the prison and beaten by a crowd of people outraged at the increase in the price of milk and stirred up by a doctor known for his anti-Semitic views. Rural areas were, however, free of acts of violence of this kind. As one report emphasised, 'local' Jews were largely excepted from criticism in the countryside.[158]

The factors underpinning this heightened anti-Semitism show that among peasants the sense of their own disadvantaged economic position as a result of state controls was linked with the traditional accusation that Jews were avaricious profiteers.[159] The rhetorical connection between 'Jewish' and 'capitalist' also points to the fact that it was chiefly the profound sense of insecurity about the crisis-prone fragility of the capitalist economy which made rural dwellers increasingly likely to embrace anti-Semitism during the era of inflation. In the district of Dillingen people began to make 'anti-Semitic statements' when rumours of imminent state bankruptcy and reports of the speculative purchase of gold coins were doing the rounds in early 1920, as they did in many parts of Swabia.[160] Michael Melchner, director of the Christian Peasants' Association in Upper Bavaria, instrumentalised such fears for the purposes of agitation. In 1920 he informed a gathering of peasants in Dachau that the Jews would exploit the hardship of the population. The workers, he opined, would eventually realise that they were nothing but the 'slaves of the Jews'. He

155. Heinz Reif, Antisemitismus in den Agrarverbänden Ostelbiens während der Weimarer Republik, in: idem (ed.), *Ostelbische Agrargesellschaft im Kaiserreich und in der Weimarer Republik*, Berlin: Akademie 1994, pp. 379-411, p. 398.

156. WB BA Altötting, 27.9.1919: BHStA/IV, stv. GK I.AK 3920.

157. WB RP Schw., 14.9.1920: BHStA/II, MA 102146.

158. WB BA Nördlingen, 13.12.1919: StAA, Regierung 9766.

159. Walter Zwi Bacharach, Das Bild des Juden in katholischen Predigten des 19. Jahrhunderts, in: Manfred Treml/Josef Kirmeier (eds), *Geschichte und Kultur der Juden in Bayern*, vol. 1, Munich: Saur 1988, pp. 313-19.

160. WB BA Dillingen, 1.2.1920: StAA, Regierung 9767.

claimed that it was vital for agriculture 'to help itself in order to detach itself from international big capitalism'.[161]

Following an initial wave in the 1890s, the Christian Peasants' Association again constantly deployed anti-Semitic discourse in its political propaganda from the closing stages of the war onwards.[162] The leaders of the socialist and communist labour movement, along with war profiteers and 'big capitalists', were all denounced as Jews. Accordingly, the struggle between capital and labour was interpreted as a mere 'sham'. At the same time, the Jews were portrayed as an influential interest group whose bidding the government in Berlin was obliged to follow. Slogans decried 'Jewish black marketeers' said to wear 'diamond rings' and 'fur coats', which unlike livestock no one had counted. Propagandists thus made use of prejudices about traders' profits, making them out to be the true profiteers from the controlled economy. This was, however, a discordant argument of limited application. However many 'honest' farmers there may have been, large numbers of people believed peasants to be the true profiteers. It was thus necessary to distance oneself simultaneously from those farmers who had already been 'possessed by the Jewish profiteering spirit'.[163]

The *Bayerisches Bauernblatt*, a newspaper catering to Bavarian peasants, tackled the unfreezing of leather prices, which had triggered the burgeoning rural anti-Semitism, through a discourse that was at once political and economic in nature. The policy was blamed on the 'Spartacists' and portrayed as the cause of the supposedly tightened delivery quotas for other products. Memories of the 'soviet Shangri-La' of the workers' parties were linked with references to their leaders, '80 per cent' of whom were claimed to be Jews. Finally, the author of the article described the Jewish 'proletarian leaders' as 'people who have studied but who have no interest in doing any work', a highly populist phrase given peasants' experiences of the war.[164]

Aggressive anti-Semitic stereotypes privileging race do not feature in the publications of the Peasants' Association, which instead tended to pick up on the political and economic resentment towards Jews that was such a common feature of the post-war political debate. This appears to have involved matching the mood of the rank and file, rather than

161. *Amper-Bote*, 28.2.1920.

162. See, for example, *Bayerisches Bauernblatt*, 12.2.1918, 25.5.1920, 17.1.1922.

163. HMB RP Ndb., 18.11.1922: BHStA/II, MA 102140.

164. *Bayerisches Bauernblatt*, 13.1.1920.

instrumentalising anti-Semitism in order to mobilise members. At the general meeting of the Peasants' Association in 1920, where Georg Heim expressed outrage about the 'Jewish dwarves in Berlin', a 'strong trend towards anti-Semitism' was apparent 'among the ranks of the members'. At a rally in Rosenheim in early 1923 the peasants attending found Heim's comments on the 'Jewish question' too 'mild and hesitant'. They felt a 'certain amount of disappointment'.[165]

No other event was to trigger such an outpouring of anti-Semitic sentiment as the unfreezing of leather prices, though many peasants no doubt continued to hold such views long after this event, as became apparent when inflation peaked in 1923. Plans considered by General State Commissioner von Kahr in autumn 1923 to expel eastern European Jews were thus not only popular among the *völkisch* right, but were also 'welcomed' by many Lower Bavarian peasants. In fact, their failure to get off the ground due to Imperial intervention caused much disgruntlement.[166] During the same period a speaker at a meeting of the Free Peasantry ridiculed Imperial Chancellor Stresemann and Social Democrat Finance Minister Rudolf Hilferding as 'Jewish international scoundrels'. This organisation cooperated openly with the *Volk*-centred bloc from 1924.[167]

The well-known political crises of 1923, culminating in the turmoil of the Hitler putsch in November,[168] finally brought the NSDAP (Nazi Party) some peasant support as well. A sample of members who joined between September and early November 1923 revealed that farmers and farmers' sons in southern Germany made up 12 per cent, and 20.4 per cent in rural areas, the first time this group was represented in the party to any significant degree. Those of up to 23 years of age, who had thus not been called up, made up almost half of members both among farmers and in general.[169] Even in 1923, however, the NSDAP failed to persuade most peasants, especially because the two largest peasant organisations warned them against the party. Thus in the aftermath of the attempted

165. *Bayerisches Bauernblatt*, 10.2.1920.

166. Gendarmerie-Station Achdorf, 1.11.1923: StAL, Rep. 164/10, 2008.

167. HMB BA Rottenburg, 15.9.1923: StAL, Rep. 164/16, Fasz. 38, No. 198.

168. See Harold J. Gordon, *Hitlerputsch 1923. Machtkampf in Bayern 1923-1924*, Frankfurt/M.: Bernhard & Graefe 1974; Ernst Deuerlein (ed.), *Der Hitler-Putsch. Bayerische Dokumente zum 8./9. November 1923*, Stuttgart: Deutsche Verlags-Anstalt 1962.

169. At the beginning of 1923, the party had a total of 15,000 members and about 55,000 by late 1923. Michael Kater, Zur Soziographie der frühen NSDAP, *Vierteljahreshefte für Zeitgeschichte* 19 (1971), pp. 124–59.

putsch, country people generally approved of von Kahr's actions, in part because they remained 'distrustful' of the 'non-Bavarian leader[s]' of the party and of Ludendorff in particular.[170] By as early as 1924, however, the *völkisch* movement had managed to attract a number of farmers and agricultural workers. Subsequently, the NSDAP was particularly successful in those areas in which the Peasants' League was the dominant political force and political participation had thus been detached from the Catholic milieu.[171]

5.4 Social Conflicts

> A terrible, contradictory time. Certain people fell to their knees to plead for mercy from the Almighty while in the same breath caring nothing for those eking out a wretched existence. (Max Bauer, then working as a farmhand, on farmers during the period of inflation)[172]

Rural society was no peaceful idyll. While the mentality of the property-owning peasants and the rural lower classes featured certain fundamental commonalities anchored in working life and the rural setting, their social reality was quite different and marked by opposing interests. Conflicts existed above all between farmers and the farm workers and day labourers working for them, though the latter had practically no opportunity to openly articulate their demands, let alone collectively pursue them, in the pre-1914 period. Alongside this traditional opposition, another conflict moulded rural experience during the war and after it, particularly during periods of increasing inflation. By turning the normal, ceaseless process of ensuring the supply of food via calculable markets 'upside down', war and inflation intensified the otherwise secondary conflict between the producers and consumers of agricultural products.[173] Peasant producers thus came into clear and at times palpable conflict with those entitled to receive food; most consumers lived in the cities, though the rural districts were home to some.[174]

Peasants as a group became increasingly aware of their estatist group identity (*Standesbewußtsein*) through the conflict between urban and

170. HMB BA Neuburg, 14.11.1923: StAA, BA Neuburg 6971a.

171. Gordon, *Hitlerputsch*, pp. 501-2.

172. Bauer, *Kopfsteinpflaster*, p. 66.

173. Tenfelde, Stadt und Land, pp. 55-6.

174. Provisional Economic Plan for the Harvest Year of 1917, 7.1.1918: BHStA/II, ML 1039.

rural areas and through their efforts to resist the new republic's social achievements from 1918 on. Their new awareness fused a desire to defend their prosperity, fuelled by temporarily favourable economic conditions, with indifference to the social hardships faced by other sections of the population. This *Standesbewußtsein* is not understood here as a consequence of special rights to which peasants alone were entitled or as an 'honour of estate' reflecting a traditional Christian morality. As some articles in Catholic Peasant Association publications complained in 1921, 'peasant pride', which had long been transfigured by conservative circles, had in any case declined dramatically as a result of the 'profound selfishness' of many farmers.[175] Here *Standesbewußtsein* will denote the peasants' knowledge that they were materially advantaged by their ownership of land, generally unattainable by other social groups; it also includes peasants' efforts to differentiate themselves from those not privileged in this way. This consciousness was important because it was not merely an ascription applied by outside observers living in quite different social circumstances, but clearly constituted a form of *self*-awareness. During the war, farmers came into conflict with city dwellers mainly as a result of worsening food shortages, which constantly preoccupied the authorities and led to the first hunger riots in the cities as early as 1916.[176] Mainly during the second half of the war, shortages forced city folk of every type to go on 'hoarding trips' (*Hamsterfahrten*) to the countryside in order to supplement their meagre rations.[177]

Particularly at weekends, rural districts were inundated by hundreds of hoarders arriving by train. Farmers were 'pleased' if railway station controls and other police measures stemmed the tide of city dwellers, at least some of the time.[178] When hoarders were turned away, they often cursed the peasants in 'words not to be repeated' or threatened to set alight to fields or buildings. The peasants may have expected that people wishing to obtain from them scarce commodities at almost any price would approach them with a suitably subservient air. Because of the extreme hardships they faced, city dwellers in fact behaved in a way which demonstrated their belief that they had a right to food. This 'hardened further' the already 'harsh sentiments of the peasants'.[179] Some

175. *Bayerisches Bauernblatt*, 19.4.1921.
176. Albrecht, *Landtag*, pp. 147-53, 238-42, 326-31, 343-8.
177. Daniel, *Arbeiterfrauen*, pp. 215-26.
178. WB BA Ebersberg, 11.3.1917: BHStA/IV, stv. GK I.AK 1951.
179. WB BA Augsburg, 2.12.1916: StAA, Regierung 9763.

farmers used their rifles to drive away men working in the coal-mining towns of Upper Bavaria, who brandished knives at them in an effort to force them to hand over food.[180] Soldiers' wives managing on their own were particularly badly affected by the hoarders' aggressive behaviour. They frequently had to look on helplessly, while the hoarders succeeded in literally 'requisitioning' food from them.[181] Despite the profits it brought them, the flow of hoarders convinced farmers that they were being exploited by city dwellers. Peasants showed little understanding of the very real material hardship that forced the urban population to hoard.[182]

Some farmers even thought it might be possible to make city dwellers step up their protests and take direct action to bring the war to an end by refusing to provide hoarders with food:

> and I go to the countryside a lot. I'm going on Sunday to get some food before this misery brings us to our knees. Then you have to put up with the peasants talking the biggest load of rubbish. Last Sunday we visited five villages and got nothing, not even a piece of bread. The peasants think that if they stop giving the poor people food, the war will come to an end. They say that then the people would do something and that would stop the war.[183]

The farmers' unwillingness to part with their produce and patchy food supply provoked a fair number of thefts from fields, especially near industrial areas, from 1916 on. Even the local constabulary was unable to put a stop to this. In 1918 cattle were stolen and slaughtered on the spot in the mountain pastures. It was mainly these waves of thievery, which increased towards the end of the war, that inspired peasants to form the paramilitary *Einwohnerwehren* to protect themselves. The protagonists on one side of the urban-rural social conflict were armed.[184]

Those living in the countryside but not working in agriculture and dependent on food tokens had to look on powerlessly as urban hoarders, for some of whom money played 'no role', went about their business, while the 'rural poor' got very little indeed.[185] During the war, the potential for conflict accumulated in line with the bitterness people felt

180. WB BA Weilheim, 20.10.1917: BHStA/IV, stv. GK I.AK 1958.
181. WB BA Freising, 5.5.1917: BHStA/IV, stv. GK I.AK 1953.
182. Letter by a man from Munich detailing a hoarding trip, 19.4.1917: BSB.
183. Letter by an Augsburg resident, 13.6.1917: BSB.
184. WB BA Miesbach, 24.9.1916: BHStA/IV, stv. GK I.AK 1945.
185. Letter by a woman from Oberndorf, 9.9.1917: BSB.

about peasants' unwillingness to give some of their produce to those rural inhabitants entitled to state food aid. The stereotype of the peasant interested in nothing but his own material enrichment became firmly established everywhere: 'I read the Bible constantly, but you never hear peasants saying the Lord's Prayer. They go to bed cursing and curse again when they rise in the morning. These people think only of worldly matters. I've got to know what peasants are like. They have no soul. All they think about is how can I get money and how can I make lots of money.'[186]

As we have already seen in many statements by peasant wives, peasants were indifferent to the hardships suffered by city dwellers in part because they felt that urban workers were failing to match their great exertions. Such resentment was reinforced by the restrictions on production and strikes in the cities, such as those in January 1918. Peasants began to ask 'what would happen if the peasants stopped working and delivering produce'.[187] The sight of city dwellers taking a leisurely stroll through the countryside at harvest time made peasants feel that they had a right to a better food supply:

> I think there will be plenty of food for the city this year. Of course us country people have never had any reason to complain. You know those animals I told you about in my last letter? They weren't really ill at all, that was just fake by the farmers to have their roast. I always have enough food when I go away, but the city folk aren't too pleased to see this because they reckon the country people are a lot better off than them. It's true that it's hard to find butter or ham in the city and we eat a lot of both at harvest time. When we're working hard under a hot sun to bring in the harvest and see city people strolling along, we often say, 'we're certainly not going to be sparing'. We go out of our way to eat heartily, which unlike them we've earned the right to do.[188]

While peasants felt indignant about the self-sufficiency ration, which they considered paltry given how hard they had to work, subsistence agriculture ensured that farmers, as one married peasant woman affirmed in 1917, 'never need go hungry'.[189] Given the dramatic decline in city dwellers' rations and the hunger they suffered as a result, the rural population was profoundly privileged in this regard. This had a pacifying

186. Letter by a man from Munich, 6.7.1917: BSB.
187. WB BA Eggenfelden, 4.2.1918: BHStA/IV, stv. GK I.AK 1962.
188. Letter by a farmer's daughter from Weibletshofen, 30.9.1917: BSB.
189. Farmer's wife from Haidlfing, 22.4.1917: BSB.

effect in rural areas, while city folk were out for 'revenge', considering the situation 'unjust'.[190] During the war, change was also apparent in another sphere. This was probably even more important to how peasants saw themselves before 1914 than the countless attempts to turn supposedly stable and 'natural' peasant culture into a conservative bulwark against bourgeois modernity and democracy.[191]

This change in perception, anchored in the civilisational distinction between town and country, has not yet been studied in depth. It is, however, clearly apparent in subsequent critiques.[192] The difference in living standards in urban and rural areas, which became increasingly dramatic at least from the turn of the century onwards, meant that peasants no longer seemed backward to urban folk in a purely economic sense. The clothing, manners and intellectual horizons of peasants encountered on the market square or during trips to the country no longer corresponded to urban standards. The Attic comedy of the fourth century BC had featured similar imagery, though under quite different circumstances. Peasants were aware that city folk thought less of them than of 'dogs', because they seemed 'stupid', usually smelt of animal excrement and were forever 'rooting about' in the fields.[193] In a 1923 retrospective, the newspaper of the Allgäu Peasants' Association emphasised that the peasant had formerly been denigrated as a 'figure of fun', mocked on account of his 'clumsiness' and 'course manners', while now he was considered a 'profiteer and shark'.[194]

During and after the war, however, it became patently obvious to farmers that the food shortage had pushed this perception into the background and moved them into a privileged position, so that even city people whose clothing clearly marked them as well off had to court their favour:

> We'll have a foal by mid-June. I've already sorted out the mare. That will be tremendous fun – a foal, the hay harvest and no man in the house. You'd be

190. Letter by a Kempten resident, 17.5.1917: BSB.

191. Wolfgang Kaschuba, Dörfliche Kultur. Ideologie und Wirklichkeit zwischen Reichsgründung und Faschismus, in: Jacobeit, *Idylle*, pp. 193–204.

192. Heide Wunder, Der dumme und der schlaue Bauer, in: Cord Meckseper/Elisabeth Schraut (eds), *Mentalität und Alltag im Spätmittelalter*, Göttingen: Vandenhoeck & Ruprecht 1985, pp. 34–52.

193. Heinrich Rothenbücher from the Spessart region, 1.7.1917: BHStA/II, ML 1353.

194. *Allgäuer Bauernblatt*, 3.2.1923.

> better off with nothing at all. You do nothing but slave away and when you do have something, you have to hand it over and you're supposed to go without enough food. The peasant has become nothing more than an ox which has to work so the others can have a good laugh at him. They always used to say that the filthy peasants should eat their potatoes themselves. But now the fine ladies and gentlemen in the town would be pleased to get anything from the filthy peasant. We're also supposed to provide city children with board and lodging, but that's one honour I can do without. If all our wishes were granted, there would be millions fewer people in the world, but I think the devil has gone, or he would have carried off whole handfuls already. There are plenty of people going around with the same fat belly as in peacetime. No sign of hunger there. But they're very keen to make sure that we don't suffer from obesity. They know from experience that it makes it harder to move about and work.[195]

This malicious fantasy of annihilation aimed at city dwellers lays bare how profoundly frustrated and thus resentful peasants had become as a result of the civilisational backwardness of their working lives and life-world. The reference to having to work like an ox also reveals why the *Standesbewußtsein* of the peasants, rooted in a rising income and adequate food supply, was unable to develop fully during the war. In the case of peasant wives, it was also hampered by separation from their husbands and sons and the pain they suffered, should their loved ones die at the front. Peasants' negative experience of how city people had tended to denigrate them, however, then made them feel even more justified in putting their prosperity on display during the inflation period.

The transition to the republic soon frightened farmers as the revolution took on increasingly radical forms in Munich and other major towns, leading to battles redolent of civil war in the spring of 1919. Though the extent to which peasants identified with the counter-revolutionary activities and the large number of paramilitary groups has frequently been overstated, there is no doubt that peasants' initial support for the new state gave way to a more sober view. Farmers came into open conflict with the republic insofar as it entailed significant social welfare measures for workers. Shortly after the revolution began, country people had assumed that the new 'People's state' would focus on 'advancing the lot of the working classes'.[196] Peasants were first directly affected by

195. Letter by a farmer's wife from Swabia, 9.3.1917: BSB.
196. WB BA Wolfratshausen, 23.11.1918: StAM, LRA 40945.

the abolition of the farm labourers' working rules (*Gesindeordnung*). In addition, peasants formed a united front against the urban working classes that picked up on their heavy wartime workload, which had diminished to normal pre-war levels after the soldiers' return. However, the key point of reference in judging one's own situation, the workload of the urban working classes, had changed substantially. They now worked an eight-hour day, one of the 'crucial material achievements of the November Revolution'.[197] Rural workers, for whom the Provisional Regulations on Farm Work (*Vorläufige Landarbeitsordnung*) continued to prescribe longer working hours, also wanted a shorter working day.[198]

A shared sense of disadvantage *vis-à-vis* city dwellers was, however, stronger than this new point of contention between rural employers and employees, as farmers working small and medium-sized farms and their labourers were used to long working hours. During the labour-intensive harvest period, the contrast could be experienced directly, when labourers working on the sewerage system provoked the men and women working in the fields on their way home by shouting that they were 'dolts' to slave away for 'so long'. Such incidents made farm labourers and farmers angry that they had 'to work to provide food for "idlers"'.[199]

Peasants generally considered city folk to be work-shy pleasure-seekers. In early 1919, for instance, farmers were 'infuriated' by the 'goings on' in the cities, the 'dancing entertainments and pleasures of every kind'. The fact that homecoming celebrations for soldiers and festive weddings were being held all over the countryside at the same time may not, given the emotionally loaded opposition between town and country that had already taken hold during the war, have tempered such views.[200] Such complaints about urbanites' 'pleasure-seeking' and unwillingness to work were among the traditional topoi of peasants' urban critique.[201] The advantages of the new welfare state for the working classes, such as the eight-hour day and unemployment benefit, reinforced and institutionalised the impression that the values central to the morality of work that traditionally held sway in rural areas were being systematically undermined in the cities. Farmers thus came into conflict

197. Detlef J.K. Peukert, *Die Weimarer Republik. Krisenjahre der klassischen Moderne*, Frankfurt/M.: Suhrkamp 1987, p. 128.

198. WB BA Aichach, 8.11.1919: StAM, LRA 99497.

199. WB BA Mühldorf, 9.8.1919: StAM, LRA 188445.

200. WB RP Schw., 6.5.1919: BHStA/II, MA 102145.

201. Letter by Johann Menhard, 26.2.1917: StaA Regensburg, NL Heim 1630.

with the republic because of these factors, so important to how peasants understood themselves.[202]

The conflict over food supplies remained intense even after the war. Following a temporary improvement in 1920 and 1921, which nonetheless failed to come close to pre-war levels, the period of hyperinflation saw things get a lot worse for those entitled to state food aid. Urban protests were initially directed against rising prices, then the food supply system fell apart during the crisis of 1923.[203] Thus, few complained of large numbers of urban hoarders in the countryside in 1920 and 1921.[204] But from early 1923, as the impoverishment of the urban population gained pace and food shortages reached catastrophic proportions, hoarding occurred on an even greater scale than during the war. Until the autumn of 1923 hoarders increasingly resorted to begging. Alongside the many cases of theft from fields, some engaged in the collective looting of farmland. 'Hordes' of young men now streamed through the countryside. On many farms, hot meals or loaves had to be kept ready each day in order to 'move on' as quickly as possible the up to 200 city dwellers who turned up asking for a donation.[205]

The peasant producers, however, remained unmoved by the material problems of the working and middle classes reliant on food purchases. The 'fears and hardships' of the poorer members of society, reported an official from Lower Bavaria in 1922 on the basis of daily conversations with peasants, were not causing the latter to 'lose any sleep'. All that mattered was 'that you yourself have money and hope to earn more'.[206] In the autumn of 1923 one Swabian farmer in a village inn expressed the drastic view that the 'factory workers' should spread 'cow dung on their bread instead of butter'.[207] Peasants' longing for the restoration of the old order, which was bound up with their failure to grasp the social crisis unfolding at the time, was apparent in 1921 in the Lower Bavarian District Peasants' Trade Association, where a motion from the district of Griesbach met with unanimous approval. This proposed placing restrictions on marriages among those lacking 'sufficient income' and the necessary 'moral qualities'. If this could no longer be achieved through the right of residence as in the nineteenth century, the local authorities and housing

202. Bergmann, *Bauernbund*, pp. 249-53.
203. Geyer, Teuerungsprotest.
204. HMB RP Schw., 19.5.1921: BHStA/II, MA 102147.
205. HMB BA Neuburg, 31.1.1923: StAA, BA Neuburg 6971a.
206. HMB RP Ndb., 2.6.1922: BHStA/II, MA 102140.
207. HMB RP Schw., 8.9.1923: BHStA/II, MA 102147.

departments should at least be urged to refrain from providing 'such people' with material support.[208]

Peasants not only showed a complete lack of understanding for others' hardship during the inflationary period, despite the growing bitterness this inspired among consumers of food in cities and villages. Their stance was in fact enmeshed with the desire to exhibit their own prosperity. In this way, peasants wished to document their awareness that they were now the economic winners. At homecoming celebrations for soldiers and many peasant weddings in 1919, with their concomitant illegal slaughtering and banquets, peasants had already demonstrated their food surplus without embarrassment.[209] They showed no restraint in their approach to cultivating memories of the war. Veterans' associations managed to quickly find sums of 30,000 marks and more for war memorials even in communities formerly considered impoverished. Some peasants spent up to 1,000 marks in one evening in the tavern - more than twice the daily wage of a miner in 1922. Collections for the needy, meanwhile, produced meagre results.[210]

Another indication of peasants' *Standesbewußtsein*, rooted in their prosperity, was the fact that some of the sons and daughters of even small farmers, who normally went to work on the farms of others, remained on their parents' farms after the war. The money they could make under another employer seemed too little and could in any case be disregarded given how much they could make at home. Moreover, one did not have to work so hard on one's parents' property.[211] Some sons of wealthy farmers did well-paid casual work constructing roads to supplement their basically secure livelihood. As the authorities correctly noted, the oft-repeated claim that agriculture was suffering a 'labour shortage' was thus disproved. What peasants were really complaining about was the rising cost of non-family labour.[212]

Ultimately, when peasants took 'refuge in physical assets' as currency depreciation accelerated, their efforts went beyond acquisitions useful to the peasant economy. Imposing luxury items such as pianos and motorbikes found a place in peasant households; bicycles, sewing machines, luxurious materials, clothes and shoes were acquired in large

208. Meeting of the District Peasants' Trade Association of Lower Bavaria, 18.3.1921: StAL, Rep. 168/1, Fasz. 949, Nr. 7432.

209. WB BA Erding, 15.2.1919: StAM, LRA 146315.

210. HMB BA Ebersberg, 15.5.1921: StAM, LRA 79889.

211. WB RP Schw., 30.12.1919: BHStA/II, MA 102145.

212. WB BA Zusmarshausen, 8.5.1920: StAA, Regierung 9767.

quantities. Rural artisans were inundated with requests to refurnish peasant sitting rooms.[213] In 1922, in the district of Kaufbeuren, farmers even began to acquire furniture and other dowry items for daughters who, at between ten and twelve years old, were still of school age. As the local official remarked critically, they were well aware of the fact that large numbers of people were unable to buy even the most essential articles of underwear and had to go hungry.[214]

Peasants' inconsiderate behaviour, given workers' difficulties, not only led workers in provincial towns, and some small farmers reliant on purchasing food, to despise wealthy farmers.[215] The pent-up rage erupted in physical altercations for the slightest of reasons. In the late summer of 1921, in the district of Ebersberg, the local constabulary prevented a violent clash between farmers and angry workers only with great difficulty, after producers had temporarily demanded 30 pfennigs more per litre of milk. In the district of Zusmarshausen and elsewhere, meanwhile, members of the KPD, trying to push their political views among farm labourers and small sharecroppers (*Häusler*), were violently driven from the villages by farmers.[216] People sometimes shot at each other in the fields, as happened for example in Freising, where a farmer's son shot a woman gathering potatoes in a neighbour's field.[217]

Officials, worried about public safety on account of such clashes, repeatedly issued peasants with warnings and managed to keep things from 'getting out of hand'. They did not, however, manage to 'awaken [the peasants'] social conscience'.[218] Why, given the meagre supply of food and rising prices, were there no massive demonstrations or consumer protests in the smaller provincial towns?[219] One reason is that in the post-war period farmers refrained to some extent from charging the poor in their own communities and the surrounding areas the same price for food as they did urban hoarders. Farmers tended instead to claim that they had nothing left to sell.[220] They were clearly aware of the social obligations

213. HMB BA Mindelheim, 15.2.1923: StAA, BA Mindelheim Abgabe 1941, Nr. 45.

214. HMB RP Schw., 7.6.1922: BHStA/II, MA 102147.

215. HMB RP Obb., 23.5.1922: BHStA/II, MA 102136.

216. WB RP Schw., 28.7.1920: BHStA/II, MA 102146.

217. HMB RP Obb., 10.10.1922: BHStA/II, MA 102136.

218. HMB RP Obb., 10.10.1922: BHStA/II, MA 102136.

219. On the situation in Munich see Tenfelde, Stadt und Land, pp. 49–52.

220. HMB BA Aichach, 1.8., 15.12.1922: StAM, LRA 99497.

existing within the village community and its immediate surroundings. Even inflation did not entirely obliterate this awareness.

Farmers' willingness to accommodate the needs of people living in the rural provinces is also apparent in another fact that explains the lack of protests. Following the abolition of most state controls in 1920/21, and under pressure from the authorities and sometimes of their own accord, farmers sold food at a reduced price to the poorer families in the district. In 1921 the Bavarian Agricultural Chamber (*Landesbauernkammer*) organised a 'Bavarian Farmers' Relief Programme', from which the local district authorities benefited far more than the major towns. In Swabia, which achieved the best results of the three southern Bavarian districts, almost 12,000 centners of cereals and 15,000 centners of potatoes were sold off to local people or provided free of charge; towns benefited to the tune of 3,000 and 5,000 centners of each. Milk to a nominal value of 1.3 million marks was sold at a reduced price. With 'a few centners of rye and wheat', stated the local press to encourage farmers to take part, the peasant could deprive 'the revolutionary forces of their most dangerous instrument', slogans decrying 'rising bread prices'.[221] In October 1923, in the district of Dingolfing, cut-price potatoes were sold off in direct response to protests by workers at an engineering works angry at increased bread prices. The head of the district authority also provided a quantity of flour at a reduced price through the local authority.[222] The relief programmes were a short-term tactical concession to 'calm down consumers'.[223]

Farmers were intensely aware that the general population was more dependent on their produce than ever. This awareness was reinforced by the palliative relief programmes, as one man's critique of his fellow farmers' attitudes lays bare. In a 1921 letter to Georg Heim, this farmer from the district of Krumbach, a member and representative of the Christian Peasants' Association, castigated those farmers who harboured the conceit that they were doing 'good deeds' when they contributed a few potatoes to collections for city folk. They ought to realise that this was 'their holiest duty' because they had 'already taken' the savings of the supposed beneficiaries. This isolated admonisher also mentioned the concomitants of the obsession with making money, a phenomenon which was bound to 'elicit a furious response from the hungry' and

221. *Traunsteiner Nachrichten*, 7.9.1921.
222. HMB BA Dingolfing, 31.10.1923: StAL, Rep. 164/3, 2641.
223. HMB RP Obb., 6.9.1921: BHStA/II, MA 102136.

ultimately satisfy his wish for the 'hour of revenge'. Farmers would, he stated, spend the 'whole evening' in the tavern drinking wine, hold extravagant family celebrations that inevitably 'provoked the ire' of poorer folk and splash out on jewellery, luxury goods and dowry items. He warned that the rich would soon face punishment, citing a passage in the New Testament (James 5:1-4):

> 'Come now, you rich, weep and howl for the miseries that are coming upon you. Your riches have rotted and your garments are moth-eaten. Your gold and silver have corroded, and their corrosion will be evidence against you and will eat your flesh like fire. You have laid up treasure in the last days. Behold, the wages of the labourers who mowed your fields, which you kept back by fraud, are crying out against you, and the cries of the harvesters have reached the ears of the Lord of hosts.'

However, the farmer added that the 'leather Jews' and 'factory owners' had also robbed the poor of their money.[224]

It was not solely farmers' eagerness to make money which made them unreceptive to the needs of others. The general economic and legal uncertainty caused by constant state intervention and money's demise as a stable intermediary of social and economic relations also played a role. If 'conscientious' farmers initially willing to deliver their quotas regarded their social conscience as expressive of certain values dear to them, frequent increases in maximum prices not only made such values economically irrational, but also undermined them. In the post-war period, a moral 'respectability' rooted in continuity and stability 'discredited' those who continued to practise it 'because it could not control the law of the jungle that prevailed within an inflation-ravaged society'.[225] Despite hopes expressed by the Lower Bavarian district head in early 1923, even the Church, the only institution with any 'real authority' among the peasants, was unable to exercise any 'improving influence' in this regard.[226]

Farmers, moreover, used this opportunity to break out, at least for a time, of their civilisational backwardness, which had caused city folk to regard them as 'stupid' in former times. Farmers made up for this experience through their prosperity, which, for example, transformed peasant living rooms. To the extent that their experience was moulded

224. Farmer Michael Fischer, 7.12.1921: StaA Regensburg, NL Heim 2305.
225. Peukert, *Krisenjahre*, p. 76.
226. HMB RP Ndb., 18.2.1923: BHStA/II, MA 102140.

by constant work and overwork, it generated a defensive, reactionary politics *vis-à-vis* significant achievements of the republic. On the whole, however, farmers, or at least those with large or medium-sized farms, were aware that they were among society's winners during periods of extreme inflation. In 1922 the mayor of a village in Swabia thus produced a maxim which adapts the language of the labour movement in a way that may seem strange to the modern reader: 'All the stomachs stand silent, still, if that be our strong hands' will.'[227]

Farmers have been complaining about the failure of agricultural servants (*Dienstknechte*) to work hard enough and their tendency to run away for as long as this particular employment relationship has existed. This indicates that in general such workers identified with their work only to a very limited degree, whatever the patriarchal ideology of the peasants might imply. In the pre-1914 period, however, servants and maids, most of whom were young, had few real opportunities to improve their lot, other than by moving to the cities. Farm workers who squandered their good reputation by failing to work enough or suddenly running off at harvest time had a hard time finding a good job.[228]

In what follows, the factors determining farm workers' social predicament during the war are examined. Between 1914 and 1919 this group's wages increased by an average of 121 per cent in Upper Bavaria, 156 per cent in Lower Bavaria and 135 per cent in Swabia.[229] Comparing the cash wage with the changing price of the typical 'basket of commodities' makes little sense, as farm workers got their board and lodging free. The rapidly increasing cost of clothing and shoes was, however, a problem.[230] Maids and servants traditionally saved most of their wages. These savings formed the basis of their dowry or were used for the acquisition or expansion of a house and the land attached later in life.[231] Until early 1919, wage increases still offset the mark's depreciation against the dollar. Rural workers lagged far behind the nominal wage increases achieved by Bavarian industrial workers from 1914 to April 1919 of 332 per cent

227. Mayor Josef Bürle from Bayerdilling, 16.6.1922: StAA, BA Neuburg 8025. 'All the wheels stand silent, still/If that be your strong arms' will' is a line from the party anthem (*Bundeslied*) of the *Allgemeiner Deutscher Arbeiterverein*, the Social Democratic Party founded by Ferdinand Lassalle in 1863.

228. Schulte, *Dorf*, pp. 46, 135.

229. G. Klier, Die Lohnverhältnisse der Landwirtschaft in Bayern während des Krieges, *ZBSL* 52 (1920), pp. 615-23.

230. WB BA Dachau, 3.2.1918: BHStA/IV, stv. GK I.AK 1962.

231. Schulte, *Dorf*, pp. 137-8.

for skilled workers, 354 per cent for women and 369 per cent for young workers.[232] This contrast, however, paints a skewed picture. Because the cost of food rose so dramatically, the real wages of urban workers, who had to spend more than 50 per cent of their money on food, fell significantly during the war.[233]

From a comparative perspective, the key factor is thus how much income was spent on food. A survey carried out by the Bavarian Agricultural Council from 1918 estimated the value of food as higher than that of the wage for most types of worker.[234] Two district authorities put the monetary value of one day's food at around 1.40 or 2 marks on average in early 1919.[235] Taking these more convincing figures as our yardstick, farm workers' payment in food almost matched their money wage.[236] While urban workers obtained only paltry quantities of food, reflected only partially in their actual wages because of the collapsing market in foodstuffs, farm workers enjoyed a more plentiful supply. This appears to have been a significant factor, beyond its monetary value, in maintaining their living standards during the war at around the same level. Considering the demoralising effect of insufficient food, rural workers in fact enjoyed a high degree of security.[237]

Food was of course of central importance, and battles over its quantity and quality were key to the disputes between farm workers and farmers during the war, as they had been before it.[238] It was reported from Lower Bavaria as early as 1915 that farm workers receiving less food because of the self-sufficiency ration threatened to leave the farm or did less work.[239] This continued over the next few years, some workers switching to another farm where their new employer was willing to meet their demands.[240] On dairy farms the workers drank some of the milk while

232. Calculated on the basis of average hourly earnings for all branches of industry. See *ZBSL* 53 (1921), p. 34.

233. Kocka, *Klassengesellschaft*, pp. 32–6.

234. *Statistisches Jahrbuch für den Freistaat Bayern* 14 (1919), p. 107.

235. WB BA Rottenburg, 21.2.1919: StAL, Rep. 164/16, Fasz. 38, Nr. 198.

236. Klier, Lohnverhältnisse, pp. 621–5.

237. Ludwig Weissauer, Lohnbewegung in der bayerischen Landwirtschaft im Laufe eines halben Jahrhunderts, 1870–1924, PhD dissertation, Munich 1926, p. 90.

238. Georg Ernst, *Die ländlichen Arbeitsverhältnisse im rechtsrheinischen Bayern*, Regensburg: Verlag der Zentralstelle der christlichen Bauernvereine Bayerns 1907, pp. 58–78.

239. WB RP Ndb., 1.3., 8.3.1915: StAL, Rep. 168/5, 1117.

240. Garrison Eldest Passau, 31.7.1916: BHStA/IV, stv. GK I.AK 1944.

milking the cows. In Alpine pastures they sold some of the butter to forestry workers.[241] Given the severe labour shortage, most farmers were compelled to accede to the demands of the newly 'assertive' farmhands, sometimes juveniles.[242] Peasant wives managing on their own were particularly affected by such assertiveness. They often lacked the ability and authority to discipline the labourers:

> I've had just about enough, it seems to me that people are getting worse and worse the longer the war goes on. The young people have gone completely wild. The servants are so cheeky, they don't accept any advice from a peasant woman and demand higher wages. A maid now gets up to 500M, and lads just finished school make 6M a week. My servant boy (*Dienstbub*) will be finishing elementary school next spring and gets 180M a year. Still, the main thing is that he does as I tell him. People have become valuable. If only the men could be home by spring.[243]

During the war, moving to the city was therefore not the only way nor, given the shortages there, necessarily the most sensible way for farm labourers to improve their lot. A decree issued in 1915 required such workers to obtain permission from their employers, should they wish to move to a new area during harvest time.[244] Despite this, farmers complained that workers were still leaving the countryside, suggesting just how valuable every worker was because of the overall shortage of labour. Farmers' laments mainly referred to maids, who made their way to the towns more often than their male counterparts.[245]

The revolution brought major changes for agricultural workers; these were the 'most significant effect' of the political transformation in rural areas.[246] When the Council of People's Representatives abolished the *Gesindeordnungen*, the regulations governing what farm labourers could and could not do, they no longer faced penal prosecution for breach of contract. Agricultural workers now enjoyed the unrestricted right of freedom of association and the right to strike. The membership of all three agricultural workers' organisations grew substantially compared with the pre-war period, as did that of trade unions as a whole. Membership peaked in 1919, before it began to decline rapidly between 1921 and

241. WB BA Miesbach, 19.8.1917: BHStA/IV, stv. GK I.AK 1956.
242. Kempten Economic Office, 19.1.1918: BHStA/IV, stv. GK I.AK 1961.
243. Letter by a farmer's wife from Bimwang, 3.12.1917: BSB.
244. Stv. GK I.AK, 18.3.1915: BHStA/IV, stv. GK I.AK 1097.
245. WB BA Dachau, 11.3.1917: BHStA/IV, stv. GK I.AK 1951.
246. Bergmann, *Bauernbund*, pp. 100-9.

1924.[247] The Social Democratic German Agricultural Workers' Association (DLV) trade union had 48,118 members in Bavaria in 1919, the Christian 'Central Association of Agricultural Workers' had 18,462 in 1920 and the Catholic Rural Labourers' Association 30,241 in 1920. The membership of the DLV and the Central Association was made up mainly of workers on the few large estates; labourers on smaller farms rarely joined.[248] The Provisional Regulations on Farm Work issued by workers' and employers' organisations towards the end of 1918 established the framework for collective labour agreements and provided for a regular working day of eight, ten or eleven hours during each four-month period of the year. The trade unions and the Bavarian Association for Employers in Agriculture and Forestry, founded in November 1919, created a task force to regulate collective wage issues at district and *Land* level.[249]

We shall not be looking at collective wage agreements in detail here, as they were of little relevance to the actual working conditions and pay rates of the farm labourers (servants and maids) who made up the bulk of the non-family labour force. This was due to the fact that few farm workers or peasant employers were members of any kind of labour organisation.[250] What is more, farmers were generally able to pay more than the collectively agreed wage because they were making a good income. The DLV confirmed in 1923 that 'most agricultural labourers already receive a wage significantly higher than the collectively agreed figure'.[251] Apart from this, farmers often felt compelled to pay this group of workers more because they were now more willing to take industrial action, as we shall see.

Collectively agreed wages do not therefore enable us to pin down farm labourers' living standards up to 1923 with any precision. Even if the wages such workers received were in fact several times higher than the collectively agreed figure, this could not make up for the depreciation of the currency, at the very latest once hyperinflation took hold in the summer of 1922.[252] From 1923 on, agreements thus laid down how much free corn, potatoes, milk and wood workers were to receive in addition

247. Weissauer, Lohnbewegung, pp. 99–102.

248. BA Wolfratshausen, 12.7.1919: BHStA/IV, stv. GK I.AK 3920.

249. Heinrich Schrader, *Landarbeiterverhältnisse in Niederbayern und Oberpfalz*, Straubing: Beck 1925, pp. 103–6, 113.

250. WB BA Ebersberg, 14.12.1919: StAM, LRA 79889.

251. Deutscher Landarbeiter Verband, Gau Oberpfalz/Ndb., 28.5.1923: BHStA/II, MArb 401.

252. Weissauer, Lohnbewegung, pp. 104–6

to their wages. By selling these at the current market price or exchanging them for other goods, the diminishing value of their regular wage could be offset, at least to some extent.[253] In many districts, farm labourers received free items far more valuable than the collectively agreed wage, which practically constituted payment in kind. In addition, male farm labourers sometimes received bicycles and maids sewing machines. As a result, by 1923 farm labourers' incomes had generally stabilised at a high level.[254] While it is true that such workers enjoyed a secure food supply for the duration of the post-war period, it should be borne in mind that they had no opportunity to accumulate assets of lasting value. This made it hard for older labourers to settle on their own farms; as mentioned above, it was one reason why so many took up jobs in industry.[255]

Farm labourers' notably improved legal position, together with the need to constantly adjust wages to match the depreciation of the currency in the post-war period, triggered a new attitude towards industrial action among rural workers. Workers frequently threatened to take collective strike action during harvest time in some communities or districts. The disputed wage issues were then resolved in negotiations between the workers and farmers. The willingness to strike sometimes waned even without negotiations, or employers raised wages to deter strikes.[256] In the district of Ebersberg in 1922, all the labourers working for one farmer appeared in his bedroom at four o'clock one summer's morning. Should he fail to pay them almost four times the collectively agreed weekly wage, which had just been negotiated, they would down tools immediately. In the light of the poor harvesting weather, the farmer agreed.[257]

Wage increases, of course, also depended on farmers' willingness to respond to farm labourers' demands. Events in the district of Zusmarshausen in the summer of 1920 demonstrate how dependent the farm labourers' struggle to improve their lot was on their employers in highly individual employment settings. In May farm labourers held a meeting to discuss possible wage demands. While some farmers were prepared to agree to their demands for a pay increase of up to 25 per cent 'of their own free will', others declared that they would rather fire their farm labourers than do so. Shortly afterwards, the workers on some farms and at a meeting of employers and employees threatened to go on strike

253. Ibid., pp. 103–4, 137–8.
254. Ibid., pp. 106–7.
255. Achter, Einwirkungen, p. 114.
256. HMB BA Dingolfing, 16.7.1921: StAL, Rep. 164/3, 2641.
257. HMB BA Ebersberg, 15.9.1922: StAM, LRA 79889.

before the hay harvest. The majority of farmers responded by threatening to dismiss striking farm labourers. Some workers then refused to work during the harvest, which generally resulted in their sacking.[258]

Agricultural workers sometimes carried out their threats to take strike action in pursuit of their demands. Official statistics reveal that no agricultural strikes took place in 1919 in the three southern Bavarian *Regierungsbezirke*. In the 1920-22 period four are recorded.[259] The statistics are, however, beset by significant shortcomings. The weekly reports, only fragments of which have survived, provide a good deal of evidence of strike action not covered in the statistics and thus of a tactic rarely employed by agricultural servants. Farm labourers went on strike in the district of Fürstenfeldbruck in 1919 during the harvest. In Aufkirchen, the most affected village, all the farm labourers and maids downed tools and demanded 30 per cent more pay or an eight-hour day. They soon returned to work after a 10 per cent rise.[260] On 18 August 1919 thirteen of the seventeen male farm labourers in the village of Tandern went on strike demanding a 40 per cent pay raise. None of the maids whom they had urged to join them the day before did so. Because it was harvest time, the farmers agreed to provide extra pay and the men went back to work the same day. Several farmers, however, stated their intention never to re-employ the strikers. The farm labourers in the district of Aichach stopped work again in 1921, just in time for the start of the hay harvest, in pursuit of higher wages.[261] In 1922 similar events occurred in the districts of Dachau and Kaufbeuren.[262]

In the light of the massive wave of strike action by agricultural workers east of the Elbe from 1919 on, such occasional strikes were not especially remarkable.[263] Agricultural work in southern Bavaria, however, was dominated by the family. In this context, the strikes were a clear signal that farm labourers, few of whom had ever questioned their subordinate position within the farmer-centred patriarchy, were now willing to take direct action to obtain higher wages as a result of the war. The generally short duration of the strikes does not undermine this argument, because the pressures of harvest work generally led farmers to quickly agree to most of the labourers' demands. The strikes took in most workers in the

258. WB BA Zusmarshausen, 15.5.1920: StAA, Regierung 9767.
259. Bergmann, *Bauernbund*, pp. 103–4.
260. WB BA Fürstenfeldbruck, 27.7.1919: BHStA/IV, stv. GK I.AK 3920.
261. HMB BA Aichach, 30.6.1921: StAM, LRA 99497.
262. *Amper-Bote*, 3.8.1922.
263. Schumacher, *Land und Politik*, pp. 296–309.

respective villages, and farm labourers who downed tools faced the threat of dismissal forthwith or in the foreseeable future. It is therefore clear that, regardless of the quite different working conditions on individual farms, farm labourers were aware of their common interests and had thus developed a fair degree of solidarity. Many farm labourers now found the 'courage' to stand up 'for a civilised' and more tolerable existence, the 'prerequisites' for which had previously been lacking.[264]

On the whole, the lot of rural farm labourers during the war and the period of inflation was ambivalent. On the one hand, currency depreciation made obsolete the otherwise typical effort to save up enough to get married and acquire a small property. On the other hand, the labour shortage during the war, the changed legal framework from 1918 and emancipatory tendencies in the religious sphere, probably resulting from experiences at the front, created new opportunities for male farm labourers to articulate their interests. Rural dwellers had enough food to eat throughout this period, whatever the differences in working conditions between areas. This was a crucial factor in their social situation, particularly in comparison with urban workers. The son of a small sharecropper, who gave up working in agriculture in 1925 and took a job in a quarry, summed up the years he had spent working for various farmers: 'The years gone by were positive in the sense that I had enough to eat during the worst years of food shortages. Otherwise, I gained nothing materially from my seven years as an agricultural servant.'[265]

264. Bauer, *Kopfsteinpflaster*, p. 57.
265. Ibid., p. 82.

6

Veterans, 1918–23

'The lucky ones were killed right away.'[1] Five days after Stefan Schimmer bitterly summed up his front-line experience in a June 1915 letter to his wife, he himself was killed in action. After nine months of horrors and strain, knowing he might die at any time, his stark appraisal is understandable. In July 1918, when the German units had already begun to withdraw in the face of a superior enemy, Hans Spieß expressed a very different attitude towards his own life: 'I always convince myself that things aren't so bad if you make it through in one piece.'[2]

Those soldiers who did finally 'make it through' and lived to see the armistice on 11 November 1918 began to conceive of their wartime experience in a fundamentally new way. From now on, such survivors took for granted that they were among the most privileged of former combatants. This was a momentous shift.[3] It made it possible to gradually forget the suffering and the injustices of army life and to retrospectively transfigure their own wartime past. Soldiers might also suppress their experiences and busy themselves making the most of the new opportunities that had opened up as a result of the war. The lack of biographical sources stretching beyond the end of the war, however, makes it very difficult to determine how many men chose this route. A soldier's letter from July 1917 shows that some soldiers had planned to do just that:

> Unfortunately I can no longer tell you – everything – that burdens me. Perhaps we'll find a chance to talk about it later on. Then again, later – there will be no point, we've come through it and will have to see that we banish all unpleasant memories of these terrible times from our minds. Let us live only for the future, which will hopefully be a happy one for us.[4]

1. Stefan Schimmer, 17.6.1915: BHStA/IV, Amtsbibliothek 9584.
2. Hans Spieß, 3.7.1918: BHStA/IV, Kriegsbriefe 340.
3. Elias Canetti, *Masse und Macht*, Frankfurt/M.: Fischer Taschenbuch-Verlag 1994, pp. 249–50.
4. Letter excerpt from 25.6.1917: BSB.

Both types of attitude to the post-war period, involving either the fading of memories or their transfiguration, were equally common among rural ex-servicemen. Before they could liberate the conception of their own lives from the wartime past, however, such men had to reintegrate into a changed civilian society.[5] It is apparent from the processes of demobilisation and reintegration up to 1921 that the veterans sought to return to civilian normality as quickly as possible. As the events of the war receded into the past, military experiences were endowed with new meaning and pacified more often than they were transfigured. Transfiguration was most obvious in the specific ways veterans sought to transfer their war experience to public activities and traditions. The self-image and structure of the associations created by veterans and victims of the war and the forms of cult of the fallen which they fostered help elucidate these matters.[6]

6.1 Demobilisation, 1918–21

When the armistice came into effect on 11 November 1918, the key war aims of most soldiers were achieved: an end to the fighting and the certainty that they would return home soon.[7] The task now facing the military authorities was to move the troops back to east of the Rhine within 31 days as stipulated in the armistice. They were aided in this by the fact that the troops could 'think of only one thing': 'we want to be at home for Christmas', as Quartermaster-General Wilhelm Groener put it.[8]

5. Bessel, *Germany*.

6. Nothing comparable to the classic study by Prost, *In the Wake of War*, has been produced for Germany. We are limited to a number of works on the politics of the veterans' associations: James M. Diehl, The Organization of German Veterans, 1917-1919, *AfS* 11 (1971), pp. 141-84; idem, Germany. Veterans' Politics under Three Flags, in: Stephen R. Ward (ed.), *The War Generation. Veterans of the First World War*, Port Washington: Kennikat Press 1975, pp. 135-86; Elliott, Organisations; idem, The Kriegervereine in the Weimar Republic, *Journal of Contemporary History* 10 (1975), pp. 109-29; Cohen, *The War Come Home*; Whalen, *Bitter Wounds*.

7. Jetty von Reitzenstein, *Lieb Heimatland. Dorfskizzen aus den Tagen des Krieges*, Munich: Schick 1931, p. 60.

8. Telephone conversation between Groener and Ebert, 5.12.1918, quoted in: Lothar Berthold/Helmut Neef, *Militarismus und Opportunismus gegen die Novemberrevolution. Das Bündnis der rechten SPD-Führung mit der Obersten Heeresleitung November und Dezember 1918, Eine Dokumentation*, Berlin: Rütten & Loening 1958, p. 59.

As a result of the defeat, the plans for gradual demobilisation drawn up from 1916 on were no longer worth the paper they were written on.[9] In many units, discipline slackened and sometimes dissolved entirely. As a result, despite firm warnings from the Supreme Command, soldiers demobilised on their own initiative as soon as they reached the German borders. The 'urge to return home' now made itself felt 'with elemental force in the Western army as well'.[10] On 1 December 1918 the number of men travelling alone or who had lost contact with their unit was calculated for the Western army at one million, of a total strength of around 3.2 million.[11] Information and assembly points were erected at border railway stations and in the interior of the country to supervise, feed and – if requested – immediately discharge these soldiers. The great majority of the individual returnees, however, streamed past these points in uncontrolled fashion.[12] Alongside the military authorities, the soldiers' councils were also keen for combatants to return home as quickly as possible and thus tried to maintain discipline as they marched along. The soldiers' council of the Bavarian 30th Reserve Division issued the following appeal to soldiers on 16 November: 'The sole priority of the soldiers' council is to get our comrades back home as quickly as possible, give them back their old jobs and let them contribute to the People's Republic. All of us must stand together. Be united! Maintain order! Follow the orders given by your superiors, who we will be checking up on.'[13]

In line with the discharge regulations drawn up towards the end of November 1918, only soldiers from 20 to 23 years of age were obliged to remain in their units. Modified regulations of late December required only those born in 1899 to do so. This overhasty action, however, made it impossible to uphold all regulations, particularly because the soldiers 'were pushing [for] immediate discharge'.[14] Most soldiers from rural districts had thus returned home by late December 1918.[15] This happened both because soldiers were demanding a swift return home and because

9. Bessel, *Germany*, pp. 49–70.

10. Colonel Reinhardt at a meeting with the demobilisation commissioners on 18.12.1918: BHStA/II, MH 16166.

11. Representative of the Ministry for Military Affairs at the Prussian War Office, 7.12.1918: BHStA/II, MH 16155.

12. Ministry for Military Affairs, 15.11.1918: BHStA/IV, stv. GK I.AK 800.

13. Statement by the soldiers' council of the 30th bayer. Res.-Div., 16.11.1918: WUA, vol. 11/1, p. 420.

14. WB BA Aichach, 15.12.1918: StAM, LRA 99497.

15. Zorn, *Bayerns Geschichte*, p. 156.

a large number of them were serving in the replacement army and were thus already on home ground.[16]

Initially, the returnees were mainly preoccupied with 'having [at last] made it home safely'.[17] The fact that they had been defeated and that their own exertions as soldiers had thus been for nothing was unable to mar their joy at having returned at last to their nearest and dearest. People were so taken up with seeing each other again that they were 'unaware' of the alleged 'disgrace' of defeat, as one police station reported: 'Happy that the war is over, people are currently living for the moment rather than thinking about the future.'[18] Returning soldiers craving revenge would in any case have had little prospect of finding anyone interested in their views.

In the autumn of 1918 the political views typical of rural civilians generally chimed with those of most front-line soldiers hailing from the countryside. Even peasants who had backed the monarchy 'absolutely' threw their convictions 'overboard' and voiced support 'for the republic'.[19] The desire for peace at any price was also widespread among the rural population; in contrast to city dwellers, people in the countryside were 'indifferent towards all consequences, even of a peace of subjugation'.[20] It was well known that the 'soldiers on the Western Front were being drawn back'. Those on the home front approved of this as a 'means of bringing about peace quickly'.[21] Soldiers and civilians with similar views were thus reunited, making it easier to reintegrate the former. Peasants' desire to 'till the earth once again', and their relief at the soldiers' return, initially made them more accepting of the revolutionary transformation.[22] In the first few weeks after the armistice, a 'large majority' of rural people voiced support for the 'men of the revolution', because they had striven to bring the fighting to an end and thus made it possible for the soldiers to return home in the first place.[23]

In southern Bavaria, moreover, as a consequence of Austria's armistice with the Allies of 3 November, Allied occupation seemed possible. Given

16. Dieter Dreetz, Rückführung des Westheeres und Novemberrevolution, *Zeitschrift für Militärgeschichte* 7 (1968), pp. 578-89, p. 588.

17. *Bayerische Staatszeitung*, 26.11.1918.

18. Simbach police station, 27.2.1919: StAL, Rep. 164/14, 8724.

19. Passau Economic Office, 19.11.1918: BHStA/IV, stv. GK I.AK 1971.

20. Standortältester Miesbach, 22.10.1918: BHStA/IV, stv. GK I.AK 1971.

21. WB BA Altötting, 19.10.1918: BHStA/IV, stv. GK I.AK 1970.

22. WB BA Augsburg, 26.10.1918: StAA, Regierung 9765.

23. Catholic parish of Egglham, 1.4.1919: StAL, Rep. 164/14, 8724.

the possibly imminent threat to farms and farmland, the steps taken to secure the borders led to panic, particularly in the Upper Bavarian border region, though they were meant to be kept secret. People clamoured to seek assurances from savings banks that they would keep securities safe; cash was hoarded. The armistice was thus greeted with particular relief in southern Bavaria, inspiring some peasants to support the revolution.[24] Rural folk thus remained unimpressed by the anti-Semitic agitation in the publications of the Christian Peasants' Association, which blamed both the war and the defeat on Jews serving in the revolutionary government.[25]

The joy felt at the soldiers' safe return found institutional expression in the celebrations welcoming them home which took place throughout the countryside. Such festivities had been encouraged by the Bavarian Council of Ministers in November 1918.[26] In most rural communities such celebrations of welcome thus took place in January and February of 1919. They usually involved decorating the houses and the village entrance with festoons and banners of welcome. As well as a service of thanksgiving, a homecoming celebration was arranged, featuring a procession of ex-soldiers through the village; speeches were given; banquets and dances were organised.[27]

It was impossible to avoid a rhetoric of gratitude in Christian garb on such occasions. Even the mining community of Penzberg, most of whose inhabitants were SPD supporters, welcomed its veterans with the motto 'God bless your arrival!'[28] For the soldiers, such festivities were primarily welcome opportunities to recuperate after the privations and strains of the war. In the secular element of the events they could try to make up for what they had missed during the war, taking part in community celebrations and other entertainments.[29] Even in the semi-official part of the celebrations, the joy felt at returning home and the fact that the strains of war were now a thing of the past were more important than issues of victory or defeat, as the rhetoric of festive speeches reveals. One priest, reading from letters written by members of the community lost in action, recalled in detail the suffering of the soldiers and the social injustices of

24. BA Traunstein, 31.10.1918: StAM, RA 57942.

25. *Bayerisches Bauernblatt*, 19.11.1918.

26. Decision by the Ministerial Council on 18.11.1918: Franz J. Bauer (ed.), *Die Regierung Eisner. Ministerratsprotokolle und Dokumente*, Düsseldorf: Droste 1987, p. 42.

27. Head teacher Schaller from Triftern, 12.2.1919: StAL, Rep. 164/14, 8724.

28. Tenfelde, Proletarische Provinz, p. 104.

29. Parish of Mering, 26.6.1919: ABP, DekA II, Burghausen 12/I.

army life in his sermon. After remembering the dead, he urged the congregation to be happy the privations were now over.[30] In Hartpenning in Upper Bavaria a master baker declared in the name of the veterans: 'Demobilisation is complete and the soldiers have returned home. The return home, the aim of our most fervent wishes, of our most heartfelt efforts, has now, after a time both long and hard, been realised.'[31]

If the soldiers' endurance was acknowledged, it was because they had prevented their home country from being laid waste by enemy forces.[32] The notion that soldiers were 'undefeated in the field' and the stab-in-the-back myth promoted by the nationalist right found no expression in the way returning rural soldiers were honoured.[33] The stab-in-the-back myth was in fact publicly criticised, particularly by the left wing of the Bavarian Peasants' League. The military defeat was instead blamed, among other things, on the 'scandalous behaviour of many officers at the front and in the back area'.[34]

Most front-line soldiers, who had experienced the disintegration of the army and the inevitability of defeat first hand, were in any case dismissive of the stab-in-the-back notion. This is apparent from comments in their memoirs and a wealth of pamphlets published in the first few years after the war, mainly by members of the SPD and USPD, intended to remind people, from a partisan perspective, of the soldiers' republican potential.[35] The fateful consequences of this fake history probably lay less in its effect on those directly concerned at the time than in how it moulded over the long term a conception of history conveyed by historical accounts and textbooks.[36]

30. 'Sermon on the reception of returning soldiers' by priest Felix Fischer on 26.12.1918: AEM, Kriegschronik der Gemeinden Riedering und Neukirchen B 1830, pp. 245-53.

31. Speech at a celebration on 26.1.1919, quoted in Josef Bichler, *Chronik der Gemeinde Hartpenning*, Hartpenning: Post Holzkirchen 1927, p. 87.

32. *Oberbayerische Landeszeitung. Traunsteiner Nachrichten*, 18.1.1919.

33. Bessel, *Germany*, pp. 85-6.

34. WB RP Ndb., 29.12.1919: BHStA/II, MA 102139.

35. ABA, Pfarrarchiv Osterbuch, Chronik von Osterbuch, p. 321; compare Bernd Ulrich, Die Perspektive 'von unten' und ihre Instrumentalisierung am Beispiel des Ersten Weltkrieges, *Krieg und Literatur/War and Literature* 1, No. 2 (1989), pp. 47-64.

36. P. Jardin, La 'legende du coup de poignard' dans les manuels scolaires allemands des années 1920, in: Jean-Jacques Becker/Jay M. Winter/Gerd Krumeich/Annette Becker/Stéphane Audoin-Rouzeau (eds), *Guerre et cultures 1914-1918*, Paris: Armand Colin 1994, pp. 266-77.

Once military personnel had been fully demobilised, the problems thrown up by Germany's defeat found expression mainly in disputes over what form peace would take, until the conclusion of the Versailles Treaty on 28 June 1919. The Allied peace terms and the Treaty, finally accepted after an Allied ultimatum, were accompanied by a wave of rejectionist sentiment, reinforced by propaganda and embracing all parts of the political spectrum with the exception of the USPD. This response was focused above all on the so-called 'war guilt lie' disseminated by the Allies.[37] In the countryside, in line with the attitude expressed in the autumn of 1918, no importance was attached either to the peace terms or to the campaign against them. In the weeks following their safe return home, farmers were mainly interested in returning to their normal, prewar civilian lives, as far as possible, following the turmoil of war and revolution. Country folk in fact ignored the start of the peace conference. They were simply 'happy that they [could] again devote themselves peacefully to their accustomed activities'.[38] Following the announcement of the peace terms in May 1919, the Lower Bavarian district chief was forced to conclude that 'with a few exceptions' people were 'not particularly concerned' about the 'terrible consequences' of the planned 'peace of tyranny'. Most people were 'apathetic' when it was concluded in June.[39] When rural Bavarians expressed any explicit view of the peace treaty at all, it was generally positive. The fact that one no longer risked losing one's relatives and friends and could get on with one's work in peace without interruption carried more weight than the harsh terms of the treaty.[40]

Despite the revolutionary turmoil and clashes in the spring of 1919, reminiscent of civil war, demobilisation was dominated by the desire to return to everyday normality as soon as possible. After a transitional phase of recuperation from the war and military service, the ex-servicemen's highest priority was to savour agricultural work free from outside interference. The military defeat and peace terms thus failed to mould people's lived experience. None the less, beyond the fixed point of the rural family economy, the soldiers' return caused unrest in

37. Ulrich Heinemann, *Die verdrängte Niederlage. Politische Öffentlichkeit und Kriegsschuldfrage in der Weimarer Republik*, Göttingen: Vandenhoeck & Ruprecht 1983, pp. 22-53.

38. WB BA Augsburg, 18.1.1919: StAA, Regierung 9766.

39. WB RP Ndb., 26.5.1919/23.6.1919: BHStA/II, MA 102139.

40. WB BA Vilsbiburg, 22.7.1919: StAL, Rep. 164/19, 3296.

the villages and threw up the problem of their reintegration into the narrow confines of rural social morality.

The experiences of serving at the front and in the garrisons and the collapse of the monarchical order generally diminished the willingness of rural veterans to insert themselves back into traditional structures of authority. In the first few weeks and months following demobilisation, priests, constables and local authority officials, representatives of the traditional order in the countryside, complained that the ex-soldiers fancied themselves as 'barons' and were unwilling to 'fall into line'.[41] Particularly with respect to the state controls governing the agricultural economy, ex-soldiers felt no need to obey 'any regulations' and resisted them with growing militancy.[42] Army-issue rifles brought back from the field offered good prospects for poaching, practised on a large scale everywhere in the first few weeks after the end of the war.[43]

The soldiers' return, however, also impacted on social and religious life, as pre-war standards of behaviour came undone for a time. Rural soldiers had become increasingly critical of the war and had undergone palpable politicisation, at least in rural terms. They began to find the SPD appealing. The party found favour with 'young people [who had] returned home from the army' in the immediate post-war period, in the country as well as the towns.[44] After the election, one observer in Palling in Upper Bavaria was surprised that there had not been more votes for the SPD in rural communities, as he had 'read, in letters written by decent soldiers, that everyone would vote SPD after the war'.[45]

Front-line soldiers, increasingly critical of the war, voted SPD not so much because they agreed with its policies, but because doing so allowed them to register their dissatisfaction. Soldiers had come to reject the monarchy. This laid the ground for them to support the SPD and the Peasants' League as the parties responsible, in the popular imagination, for ending the war.[46] Two priests serving at Augsburg cathedral expounded a similar view in an analysis of the revolution and its consequences for the Church published in late November 1918. The element of the revolutionary movement made up of soldiers, they opined, wanted nothing more than the 'war to end and peace at any price' and were acting 'out

41. Ering police station, 30.1.1919: StAL, Rep. 164/14, 8724.
42. WB BA Aichach, 19.1.1919: StAM, LRA 99497.
43. WB RP Ndb., 25.11.1918 and 9.12.1918: StAL, Rep. 168/5, 1116.
44. WB BA Wertingen, 11.1.1919: StAA, Regierung 9766.
45. *Oberbayerische Landeszeitung. Traunsteiner Nachrichten*, 18.1.1919.
46. Parish of Raitenhaslach, 30.7.1919: ABP, DekA II, Burghausen 12/I.

of justified displeasure' at the 'excesses and shortcomings' of life in the armed forces. Such men turned to the socialist parties only 'to express their displeasure at the old system of government and the excesses of militarism'.[47]

Beyond qualitative evidence, the shift to the SPD, anchored in soldiers' anti-war views, can be shown only indirectly in quantifiable successes in the elections of 1919. On average, during the Weimar years, ex-soldiers made up more than one quarter of the electorate. Their votes must therefore have had a substantial influence on the results.[48] Separate counting of the votes in a number of barracks and field hospitals, carried out during the elections to the Bavarian *Landtag* in 1919, underlines the general support for the SPD in the army at the time. The figures in Table 6.1 reveal the strong support for the SPD among soldiers. They also elucidate once again the political milieu in which peasant soldiers had moved during the war. The results of this separate count tell us very little, quantitatively speaking, about rural areas as such, because the great majority of rural soldiers had already returned home when the election was held. They were thus under-represented among voters in the barracks. The meagre vote for the Bavarian Peasants' League should also be understood in this light. The number of votes for the USPD, meanwhile, only slightly higher

Table 6.1 Voting in elections to the Bavarian *Landtag* on 12 January 1919 in special constituencies established for barracks and field hospitals (% of valid votes)

	SPD	*USPD*	*DDVP*	*BBB*	*BVP*	*BBU*
Upper Bavaria	72.5	7.0	3.8	0.8	5.3	10.3
Lower Bavaria	67.0	0.9	9.2	-	20.2	2.7
Swabia	71.3	3.0	6.6	3.4	8.9	6.7
Bavaria	68.0	4.9	6.7	0.8	8.0	10.7

Note: *BBU* = *Bund der Berufsunteroffiziere* (League of Professional NCOs).
Source: *ZBSL* 51 (1919), pp. 881–3. The total number of voters was 73,944 and of valid votes 39,452.

47. Heinz Hürten, *Die Kirchen in der Novemberrevolution. Eine Untersuchung zur Geschichte der Deutschen Revolution 1918*, Regensburg: Pustet 1918, pp. 85–9.

48. Bessel, *Germany*, pp. 270–1.

than its overall result of 2.5 per cent, demonstrates that soldiers were unmoved by radical notions of a new political order.

A number of accounts, however, show that the BVP and the priests urging people to vote for it were sharply criticised in rural communities.[49] This confirms the assessment of one rural priest. In his pastoral report to the Passau ordinariate (*Ordinariat*, the central administration of a Catholic bishopric) in the summer of 1919, he stated with the benefit of hindsight: 'The socialist training in the trenches and back area was often manifest in distrust, and sometimes spitefulness towards priests and in the demonstrative exhibition of "unbelief".'[50] This is a key indication that ex-soldiers' religious 'waywardness', which so unsettled the priests and Church authorities, was closely bound up with the erosion of traditional political loyalties among these men.

Compared with the separate count in the barracks, electoral tallies according to gender offer even more compelling evidence that in 1919 the SPD succeeded in making inroads into the previously dominant form of political Catholicism among soldiers. Generally, following the enfranchisement of women in the Weimar Republic, women tended to vote for the Christian and conservative parties, while the SPD counted a disproportionate number of men among its voters.[51] The results of separate counts in Bavaria in the 1920s confirm this picture. Strikingly, at the *Landtag* election of 1919, the SPD managed to become the strongest party among male voters, with 42.6 per cent, while the BVP received only 32.7 per cent. By the *Landtag* elections of 1920, the BVP had regained its lead among men as well with 34 per cent - compared with just 21.2 per cent for the SPD.[52]

These counts do not, however, tell us exactly how many rural soldiers went over to supporting the SPD. A glance at election results in the rural districts clearly shows that this trend applied to the countryside significantly less than the cities. We should, however, note that among peasant voters in southern Bavaria the Bavarian Peasants' League benefited most from the potential for protest that had built up as a result of front-line experiences and the war economy. Its involvement in the revolution allowed it to appear as the 'SPD of the flat country'; it thus managed

49. Priest of Neuhofen, 24.6.1919: ABP, DekA II, Pfarrkirchen 12/I.

50. Parish of Heiligkreuz, 17.8.1919: ABP, DekA II, Burghausen 12/I.

51. Gabriele Bremme, *Die politische Rolle der Frau in Deutschland. Eine Untersuchung über den Einfluß der Frauen bei Wahlen und ihre Teilnahme an Partei und Parlament*, Göttingen: Vandenhoeck & Ruprecht 1956, pp. 68–71.

52. Figures from *ZBSL* 51 (1919), pp. 874–9; *ZBSL* 53 (1921), pp. 348–51.

Table 6.2 Results of elections to the Bavarian *Landtag* on 12 January 1919 in self-administered towns and districts (% of valid votes)

	BVP	*SPD*	*BBB*	*USPD*	*DDVP*
Districts in Upper Bavaria	44.6	24.1	24.8	0.5	0.2
Towns in Upper Bavaria	26.9	46.6	0.4	4.7	18.2
Districts in Lower Bavaria	37.3	23.8	34.5	0.4	3.9
Towns in Lower Bavaria	46.7	33.0	2.3	0.5	15.7
Districts in Swabia	42.8	17.3	31.7	0.6	7.0
Towns in Swabia	31.6	41.3	1.3	1.7	22.1
Districts in Bavaria	39.6	27.8	13.1	1.6	10.2
Bavarian towns	25.0	44.1	0.4	4.5	22.3
Bavaria (total)	35.0	33.0	9.1	2.5	14.0

Source: *ZBSL* 51 (1919), pp. 665–75.

to gain votes primarily as a possible alternative to the BVP, which had dominated these regions before the war.[53]

Despite these qualifications, the elections to the *Landtag* and to the National Assembly in 1919 seem to have been extreme protest votes, which brought the Peasants' League and SPD rural votes on a scale never seen before. The elections of 1920 confirm that the 1919 results reflected a passing mood which arose immediately after the end of the war. In the districts, where far fewer voters took part in the elections to the *Landtag*, the SPD lost 14.5 per cent of its support over 1919, though the socialist camp as a whole suffered a loss of only 7.4 per cent thanks to a much improved showing by the USPD.[54] The issue of who could be

53. Bergmann, *Bauernbund*, p. 19.
54. *ZBSL* 53 (1921), p. 347.

considered to have tried to extend the war or bring it to an end, a still pressing matter immediately after the war, had probably become less significant to voting behaviour as people became increasingly weary of politics and political parties.[55] The majority of farmers, moreover, had no time for the radicalisation of the revolution in the form of the two short-lived soviet republics of April 1919. There was therefore fertile ground for the anti-socialist and anti-Bolshevist propaganda disseminated by the BVP and Christian Peasants' Association from the start of the revolution onwards.[56] In the wake of these developments, the political influence of rural returnees, always limited at best, quickly lost its cohesion.

The after-effects of this short-term shift to the SPD and Peasants' League, anchored in the anti-war critique that took hold at the front, were also palpable in the convulsion that overtook religious life after demobilisation. More and more rural folk felt fed up with religion from 1916 on, a shift fuelled primarily by front-line soldiers home on leave; priests were subject to mounting criticism. These were serious symptoms of crisis. Priests and Church authorities were already aware towards the end of the war that the return of the soldiers would create even greater problems for pastoral care. The ordinariate of Munich-Freising put dealing with veterans on the agenda of the first pastoral conference of the year in April 1918. Taking military chaplains' negative experiences as the starting point, the participants discussed ways of strengthening people's ties to the Church and approaching the expected upheavals in Christian family morality. Within the framework of the male apostolate (*Männerapostolat*), ex-soldiers were to begin attending communion again regularly. Missions aimed at the masses and active efforts by priests in the veterans' associations were to strengthen the Church's influence on them.[57]

The evidence of the first few months after the war with respect to the 'religious waywardness' of ex-servicemen confirmed the pessimistic expectations: 'The community is horrified at the waywardness of many of our soldiers. Not only are many young people brutalised, but many married men have also gone wild.'[58] This gloomy conclusion by a former military chaplain is broadly confirmed in pastoral reports. The most striking symptom of religious indifference among veterans was their lack

55. WB BA Donauwörth, 27.1.1920: StAA, Regierung 9767.

56. Parish of Raitenhaslach, 30.7.1919: ABP, DekA II, Burghausen 12/I.

57. Buchberger, *Seelsorgsaufgaben*, pp. 21–5, 46–50.

58. H. Mekes (O.F.M.), Wie soll die Frau den religiös verwilderten Mann behandeln?, *Ambrosius* 33 (1919), pp. 1–6, p. 1.

of participation in public forms of community life. Given that religiosity was still firmly entrenched, the refusal to take part in Easter communion, incumbent upon all Catholics, was a spectacular declaration of dissent by a small number of ex-soldiers only. More often, priests noted that they tended to stay away from mass and attended confession less often. Younger soldiers were especially likely to exhibit such behaviour.[59] In their reports, priests pointed out that the trust in Church interpretations and the confidence that religion could provide answers had been shaken above all by how the Church and its representatives had justified the war. Pastors, some of whom received anonymous threats, confirmed that the following slogan was doing the rounds: 'The Church and clergy are to blame for all the misery of the lost war'.[60]

Alongside the waning faith of veterans in the political authority of the clergy, their moral 'aberrations' also occasioned concern, notably the so-called 'abuse of marriage', in other words birth control, which clashed with the Church dogma that reproduction was the highest aim of marriage. Reinforcing the insights gained by women during the war, many men brought a heightened awareness of the advantages of birth control back home. As early as 1918, soldiers on furlough had stirred up opinion in favour of a reduction in the number of children. 'The clerics are a smart lot, they don't have any children'; this was the reproach heard by some priests in the confessional.[61] Peasants on furlough had learned about the methods and purpose of contraception through contact with soldiers from an urban background.[62]

Despite the admonitions expressed in the confessional and the threat of refusing absolution, an increasing number of ex-servicemen continued to adhere to their newly won insight that 'you can't feed as many children as you could before, so you're justified in having fewer of them'.[63] As a consequence of this attitude, in an analysis of pastoral reports the ordinariate of Regensburg came to the conclusion that 'the plague of abuse of marriage' was beginning to 'wreak havoc among the country people'. We have no evidence that it accelerated the trend towards having fewer children in rural areas.[64] Even if it involved no more than the

59. Parish of Birnbach, n.d. [1919]: ABP, DekA II, Pfarrkirchen 12/I.

60. Parish of Triftern, 18.8.1919: ABP, DekA II, Pfarrkirchen 12/I.

61. Parish of Sulzbach, n.d. [1918]: ABP, DekA II, Fürstenzell 12/I.

62. T. Stadler, Der Krieger und unsere Friedensarbeit, *Katechetische Blätter* 45 (1919), pp. 241–7, pp. 243–4.

63. Parish of Triftern, 18.8.1919: ABP, DekA II, Pfarrkirchen 12/I.

64. *Oberhirtliches Verordnungsblatt für die Diözese Regensburg*, 1920, p. 105.

demonstrative expression of intentions, however, attentively noted and probably overstated by observers, this attitude demonstrates how ex-soldiers disregarded the moral norms of the Church.

Priests attempted to counter the new religious indifference and critiques of the Church by stepping up their pastoral work. In the light of the wartime symptoms of crisis apparent on the home front, people's missions (*Volksmissionen*) were deployed, as they generally had been every ten years in the pre-war period. These events were an extraordinary means of spreading the Word, above and beyond the clergy's efforts during mass and in the veterans' associations. Carried out by monks over the course of a week, they were intended to mobilise the faithful with intensive prayer and sermons calling for repentance, and were rounded off with general confession and communion.[65] The ordinariate of the archbishopric of Munich-Freising suggested to pastors that they prepare missions as 'one of the most important tasks' of the post-war period.[66] The people's missions carried out by Redemptorists in the bishopric of Passau, however, achieved only limited success.[67] Traditional peasant crises such as the outbreak of foot-and-mouth disease in 1920 were more likely to lead to religious intercession, as the priest of Osterbuch stated with reference to the failure of the missions carried out in the area: 'The livestock epidemic which raged throughout Bavaria in 1920 had more effect than the *Volksmission*. The peasants desisted from dancing and took part in Rogation processions and pilgrimages.'[68]

As it was mainly younger soldiers whose lack of interest in religion was noted by priests, the latter's pastoral efforts surely formed only one element in the restoration of traditional religious practices. Far more significant was the change in status brought about when these young men founded a family, as many did in the immediate post-war period. The number of marriages rocketed immediately after the completion of demobilisation in early 1919, reaching more than twice the pre-war level for a short period in rural areas as elsewhere.[69] The integrating effect of

65. Mooser, *Volksreligion*, p. 147.

66. *Amtsblatt für die Erzdiözese München und Freising*, 1918, pp. 173–5, p. 175.

67. Parish of Sulzbach, pastoral report 1921 [n.d.]: ABP, DekA II, Fürstenzell 12/I.

68. Priest Friedrich Schwald, Chronik von Osterbuch: ABA, Pfarrarchiv Osterbuch, Chronik, p. 325.

69. Bessel, *Germany*, pp. 228–42.

marriage was based on becoming established in village society, a process bound up with taking over a farm.

As a result of these developments, as statements by priests reveal, religious engagement soon increased. By 1920 or 1921 ex-servicemen were attending services as often as their fellows.[70] Naturally enough, priests did not analyse this return to normality in detail, as they had the symptoms of the crisis. The brief intensity of the critique by ex-servicemen and the fact that it abated in parallel to the election results of 1920, however, suggests that it was aimed primarily at the Church's support for the war as a temporary political aspect of Catholicism. This is apparent in a letter written by one such ex-soldier to the priest of his home village of Aretsried in March 1919, his emotional words profoundly influenced by the events of the revolution:

> You see how it is, the Church didn't teach people to 'Protect your neighbour's life and property'. All through the war it told people 'It is your holiest duty to go to war, subjugate people, who are after all our neighbours, burn villages and towns and kill people' who have done us no harm. This was the Christian teaching. The Church has stopped at nothing to force on the people a load of lazy, good-for-nothing, insane kings and princes, who have bled the people white.[71]

We have no evidence that the fundaments of popular Catholicism were seriously damaged over the long term by processes of secularisation. Nonetheless, this brief period of religious indifference, bound up with a temporary realignment of political allegiances, was significant with respect to long-term continuities. It demonstrates that at times of crisis even the proverbially religious Bavarian peasant no longer took it for granted that religion was the sole means of understanding the world. As its power to convincingly explain things dwindled, it had to be supplemented by elements of secular ideologies.[72]

Taking up their old jobs again was a process of central importance to how quickly and smoothly soldiers reintegrated into civilian life. Farmers were more worried that there would be a labour shortage rather than surplus after demobilisation. In addition to losses suffered during the war, they feared that many rural soldiers would look for work in the

70. Parish of Kirchberg, 12.7.1920: ABP, DekA II, Pfarrkirchen 12/II.
71. Letter from 8.3.1919: ABA, Pfa 6/I.
72. Mooser, *Volksreligion*, p. 151.

cities.[73] Farmers themselves expected to 'fit painlessly' into the local economy.[74] Following the labour shortage and excessive workload during the war, peasant farms declared themselves willing to re-employ former workers who had been discharged from the army. Though manpower requirements at the time were in fact modest, all returning intra-family workers and farmhands were re-employed smoothly immediately following demobilisation towards the end of 1918.[75] This situation, so different from the severe labour shortage affecting agriculture east of the Elbe, was due mainly to the structure of the agricultural labour force in Bavaria. The return was made easier by the fact that so many rural soldiers were farm heads or worked within the family.[76]

The reintegration of rural soldiers was thus unhampered by unemployment. Their smooth absorption into peasant farms did not, however, mean that manpower requirements for the spring cultivation had definitely been met. The state of the rural labour market became clear only on 2 February, the traditional day on which farm labourers changed employer. The demobilisation authorities were aware that the figures provided by the employment offices on the numbers of those seeking work and the jobs available did not convey an accurate picture of labour supply and demand, especially in the agricultural economy. Farmhands in Bavaria very rarely found work by perusing information on vacant positions. At Candlemas 1919 the State Commissioner for Demobilisation therefore instructed the district authorities to estimate, on the basis of their local knowledge, how far the need for farm labourers was being met.[77] Their surveys indicated that the demand for permanent employees was being 'sufficiently met' in 60 of 77 districts for which evidence was available. In the remainder, 50–80 per cent of positions were occupied.[78] Only the district of Neuburg an der Donau reported an extreme labour shortage. Here, however, as in other places, this was due not to a general lack of workers but to the unwillingness of some farmers to meet the 'demands for increased wages'.[79]

73. Bessel, *Germany*, pp. 198–9.

74. Liaison officer E./1st I.R., 27.10.1918: BHStA/IV, stv. GK I.AK 2412.

75. WB RP Ndb., 16.12.1918: StAL, Rep. 168/5, 1116.

76. WB BA Wolfratshausen, 23.11.1918: StAM, LRA 40945.

77. State Commissioner for Demobilisation, 7.2.1919: StAL, Rep. 164/13, 10394.

78. Kurt Koenigsberger, Die wirtschaftliche Demobilmachung in Bayern während der Zeit vom November 1918 bis Mai 1919, *ZBSL* 52 (1920), pp. 193–226, p. 214.

79. WB BA Neuburg, 25.1., 15.2.1919: StAA, Regierung 9766.

Complaints by priests and local authority officials about the religious degradation and consumption-intensive entertainments typical of demobilisation reflected the deep sense of insecurity felt by the traditional rural authorities in the wake of the changes brought about by the revolution. They were shaken by the transformation of the political system and by the fact that peasants, strongly committed to the royal house of the Wittelsbachs before the war, initially welcomed the republican order. The rural elites' longing for the restoration of the old moral and political order, however, involved idealisation of the comparatively intact society that had existed before the war.[80] When people talked about the symptoms of crisis, the behaviour of ex-soldiers was top of the list. Whether in terms of their political attitudes, engagement in religious life or how they approached the command economy in agriculture, the return of the soldiers brought an element of unrest and criticism of prevailing realities to the villages in a number of ways. It is, however, vital to recognise that these effects were of limited duration. Soldiers were basically keen to get back to their familiar working lives, as they had stated so often during the war. As unemployment did not stand in their way, ex-servicemen no longer constituted a distinct group within the public life of the villages by 1921.

6.2 Defensive Mobilisation: Paramilitary Groups, 1918–21

At its constituent meeting on 19 November 1918, the peasants' council in Lindau discussed ways of protecting the community from 'roaming, plundering soldiers and civilians'. A unanimous decision was reached to establish a 'security force', whose members would wear a blue and white armband, in every community in addition to the police; these forces were to bring suspicious individuals without ID before the peasants' council, which would then ensure that they were handed over to the soldiers' council in Lindau.[81] Peasant support for the preventive detention of 'suspects' by specially created civilian forces shows how threatened they felt.

After the armistice, there was a further increase in the number of thefts from fields, robberies, break-ins and other offences against property, all of which had already been on the up during the war. Urban hoarders

80. Bessel, *Germany*, pp. 220–53.

81. Minutes of the meeting of the Lindau peasants' council, 19.11.1918: StAA, BA Lindau 3972.

were the main perpetrators.[82] Particularly during the months of the revolution, until the spring of 1919, a period of frequent demonstrations and much unrest in the cities, peasants became increasingly concerned about security in the countryside. The possible threat from the underfed unemployed unsettled them and raised the prospect of city dwellers coming to rural areas to loot.[83]

The local constabularies, few in number and heavily depleted by conscription during the war, were unable to stem the tide of criminality.[84] Self-defence through armed vigilante groups thus seemed all the more appealing. In a number of districts, such local forces had been established by December 1918. With the approval of the Social Democrat Minister of the Interior, Erhard Auer, they armed themselves with handguns.[85] When the urban movement of revolutionary workers' councils became more radical in March and April 1919, peasants became increasingly afraid that 'Bolshevist bands might descend upon the flat country'. To defend themselves against this possibility and the risk of robbery and looting, people felt an urgent need for armed protection.[86] Before a local property defence force was created in the shape of the citizens' militias (*Einwohnerwehren*), however, people waited to see if the military response to the two soviet republics founded in rapid succession in April would be successful. From its refuge in Bamberg, the government formed on 17 March under Prime Minister Johannes Hoffmann (MSPD) tried to assemble a military force to defeat the revolutionary centres in southern Bavaria.[87]

This was achieved by reorganising, merging and regrouping a large number of military units. The key distinction here was between the *Volkswehr* and the *Freikorps*. On 14 April the Hoffmann government called on citizens to establish a people's militia (*Volkswehr*). This gathered newly recruited volunteers around the organisational core of units in the old army. The plan to set up *Volkswehr* councils was intended to avoid

82. Individual accounts in Swabian district authority weekly reports: StAA, Regierung 9766.

83. WB BA Aichach, 24.11.1918: StAM, LRA 99497.

84. Bessel, *Germany*, pp. 243–4.

85. WB BA Nördlingen, 21.12.1918: StAA, Regierung 9765.

86. WB RP Schw., 24.4.1919: BHStA/II, MA 102145.

87. Ulrich Kluge, Die Militär- und Rätepolitik der bayerischen Regierungen Eisner und Hoffmann 1918/1919, *Militärgeschichtliche Mitteilungen* 13 (1973), pp. 7–58, pp. 50–4.

the impression of a 'White Guard'. Some officers, meanwhile, joined the *Freikorps* on their own initiative for pay.[88]

In the *Regierungsbezirk* of Swabia, attempts by district authority officials to get people to sign up for the *Volkswehr* at local meetings failed to sway the rural population despite support from the peasant lobby.[89] The clergy were no more successful in procuring volunteers. They were cautious, having disgraced themselves among the general population for promoting confidence in victory and encouraging people to subscribe for war loans.[90] There were a number of reasons why men were unwilling to sign up for the *Volkswehr*. The aversion felt by many former soldiers to involvement in another military force was palpable; they had after all borne the exertions of the war with anything but enthusiasm: 'If the desire to fight the external enemy was already dwindling among country folk, there is now no sign at all that they are prepared to join a defence force to fight their own countrymen.'[91]

Rural people did support the Hoffmann government's overthrow of the soviet republic (*Räterepublik*) without reservation. Until the local militias were allowed weapons, however, as had been demanded on numerous occasions, most rural residents were unwilling to actively intervene in the fighting. Few signed up for the *Volkswehr*. Promotional campaigns were successful only in a small number of districts, where some communities offered a lump sum for joining.[92] We lack documents detailing how the promotional campaigns for the *Volkswehr* unfolded in Upper and Lower Bavaria.[93] However, more people probably joined there than in Swabia. The same goes for the Chiemgau, one of the centres of counter-revolutionary activity. The Chiemgau was also the centre of efforts to attract *Freikorps* soldiers in southern Bavaria. None of the countless paramilitary organisations established after 1918 is as surrounded by legend as the *Freikorps*. The ideologues of the SA and NSDAP, and some historians, thought them the true embodiment of the spirit of the front-line soldier in the post-war period. Roughly 250,000 men in the Empire served in the *Freikorps*; many of them, especially

88. Karl-Ludwig Ay (ed.), *Appelle einer Revolution. Dokumente aus Bayern zum Jahr 1918/19*, Munich: Süddeutscher Verlag 1968, Anlage 93.

89. WB RP Schw., 29.4.1919: BHStA/II, MA 102145.

90. WB BA Donauwörth, 4.5.1919: StAA, Regierung 9766.

91. WB BA Neuburg, 26.4.1919: StAA, Regierung 9766.

92. WB BA Markt-Oberdorf, 10.5.1919: StAA, Regierung 9766.

93. Bergmann, *Bauernbund*, p. 113.

high-school and university students, had never taken part in the war. It is now recognised that only a radical minority of veterans was involved.[94]

In Bavaria the Hoffmann government initially refused to allow recruitment to the *Freikorps* units and, as late as March 1919, expelled the *Freikorps* recruited by Colonel von Epp at the request of Prussia.[95] Only after it had fled to Bamberg on 7 April, and in the light of the general failure to recruit men to the *Volkswehr* and the defeat of troops loyal to the government by the 'Red Army' of the soviet republic at Dachau, did the government call for the establishment of purely voluntary units. The first Bavarian *Freikorps* units were then created, particularly in northern Bavaria.[96] Ultimately, alongside units from Prussia and Württemberg, *Volkswehr* and *Freikorps* units from Bavaria with a strength of around 19,000 men helped overthrow the Munich soviet republic.[97] A number of southern Bavarian *Freikorps* units also took part in the fighting, these consisting mainly of farmers' sons and farmhands, most of them youths. Some 550 inhabitants of the district of Memmingen signed up for the Swabia *Freikorps* founded on 21 April 1919.[98] The Aibling *Freikorps* gathered together 700 peasants from the area around Tuntenhausen, and the Wasserburg *Freikorps* recruited 600 residents of the district of the same name.[99] A total of around 3,000 peasants was mobilised in April and May of 1919 within the framework of the *Freikorps* in order to overthrow the soviet republics in southern Bavarian cities.

We cannot attribute sophisticated ideological motives or a '*Freikorps* spirit' to members of the rural *Freikorps*, particularly given that most researchers who have considered this issue have been restricted to studying subsequent myth-making.[100] It seems plausible that peasants were willing to join the *Freikorps* primarily in order to combat the soviet republic, of which they strongly disapproved. Their willingness was anchored in their political goal of 'peace and order'.[101] Moreover,

94. Bessel, *Germany*, pp. 256–9.

95. Hagen Schulze, *Freikorps und Republik 1918–1920*, Boppard: Boldt 1969, pp. 90–4.

96. Ay, *Appelle*, Anlage 94.

97. Large, *Law and Order*, p. 15.

98. WB RP Schw., 19.5.1919: BHStA/II, MA 102145.

99. *Die Niederwerfung der Räteherrschaft in Bayern*, Berlin: Mittler 1939, p. 208.

100. Schulze, *Freikorps*, pp. 54–69.

101. Fenske, *Konservativismus*, pp. 56–7; Christa Landgrebe, *Zur Entwicklung der Arbeiterbewegung im südostbayerischen Raum. Eine Fallstudie am Beispiel Kolbermoor*, Munich: C.H. Beck 1980, p. 156.

Freikorps wages, at five marks a day, were extraordinarily high compared with what the young agricultural workers or farmers' sons were earning. This sometimes made it seem lucrative to sign up for a period of military service which - unlike the fighting in the Baltic region, for example - looked likely to be of limited duration.[102] The progress made in putting together the *Freikorps* and *Einwohnerwehren* in the Chiemgau in particular was largely down to a generous advance, supposedly of half a million marks, which Rudolf Kanzler, *Landtag* deputy for the Centre Party until 1918 and leader of the *Einwohnerwehr* in Rosenheim, received from the ministers Martin Segitz and Ernst Schneppenhorst to build up militias in April.[103] Although peasants were clearly opposed to the soviet experiment, outside of the Chiemgau they could only be mobilised against it for brief periods of time. Protecting the villages against possible attacks by organising armed militias took priority. Ex-soldiers frequently declared that they were tired of new military activities.

Attempts to establish and merge local militias were beset by similar difficulties.[104] Especially in the districts of Rosenheim and Wasserburg, with the financial support of the Hoffmann regime ambitious militia leaders built up a dense network of local militias under their command. Rudolf Kanzler in Rosenheim, Franz Schneider in Wasserburg and Georg Escherich in Isen managed to organise solid militias in their districts by mid-May 1919. Escherich had a particular talent for exploiting the fear of further unrest. Through skilful lobbying, he managed to gain the support of the leading lights of the Bavarian Group Commando 4 of the *Reichswehr* and the Ministers of the Interior and Armed Forces for his plan to consolidate and organise the *Einwohnerwehren*.[105]

On 17 May 1919 these Social Democrat ministers had called on the administrative authorities to support the creation of militias, conceived primarily as a self-defence force supplementing the police. In the case of a mobilisation, however, they were to be assigned to units of the regular army. So-called 'defence commissioners' were also appointed by the district authorities for a transitional period. They were officers tasked

102. WB BA Markt-Oberdorf, 14.6.1919: StAA, Regierung 9766.

103. Horst G.W. Nusser, *Konservative Wehrverbände in Bayern, Preußen und Österreich 1918-1933, mit einer Biographie von Forstrat Escherich*, Munich: Nusser 1973, pp. 87, 196.

104. Erwin Könnemann, *Einwohnerwehren und Zeitfreiwilligenverbände. Ihre Funktion beim Aufbau eines neuen imperialistischen Militärsystems (Nov. 1918-1920)*, Berlin: Deutscher Militärverlag 1971.

105. Large, *Law and Order*, pp. 16-19.

with organising equipment and arms for the militias on behalf of the government. The commissioners opposed Escherich's plan to define the *Einwohnerwehren* under civil law, fearing a loss of state control. In the light of the disarmament provisions in the Versailles Treaty, it proved possible, particularly through the efforts of Gustav von Kahr, district chief of Upper Bavaria, to dispel opposition within the government to detaching the militias from the state. With the support of the Armed Forces Ministry, the government finally accepted the organisation of the militias on a private basis in the shape of the '*Land* leadership' for all of Bavaria, chaired by Escherich as '*Land* Captain' (*Landeshauptmann*), created in late September 1919.[106]

More significant than the organisational consolidation of the *Einwohnerwehren*, however, is the issue of what motivated peasants to join them. Peasants sometimes rejected the *Einwohnerwehren* because they felt secure again now that the fighting had abated and believed that the 'Spartacist threat ha[d] been fully dealt with.'[107] Rural communities that had to come to terms with a large minority of Social Democratic industrial workers sometimes shied away from provoking them by creating a local militia. Because workers were opposed to the militias - those belonging to left-wing political parties were in any case barred from joining - artisans and merchants also feared financial losses, should they join. In such communities farmers showed no interest in joining. They expected further unrest in the event of a confrontation involving the militias and wished to avoid 'being arrested by the Red Guardists.'[108] Farmers were, however, very interested in the militias' efforts to organise the defence of local property. The distribution of weapons to the militias by the Armed Forces Ministry, beginning in November 1918, was the key factor here.[109] The peasants' associations also supported the militias' property-protection activities. For the Christian Peasants' Association, they also performed a political function as a counterweight to workers' organisations.[110]

Yet there were clear limits to mobilisation. These were linked with the wartime experiences of militia members, most of whom were former soldiers. Escherich's plan provided for a division of the militia

106. Ibid., pp. 20-4.
107. WB BA Ebersberg, 29.6.1919: StAM, LRA 79889.
108. BA Wolfratshausen, 12.7.1919: BHStA/IV, stv. GK I.AK 3920.
109. Large, *Law and Order*, pp. 29-33.
110. Bergmann, *Bauernbund*, pp. 114-19.

organisation into units of varying capacity. The local militias, and a '*Gau* contingent' available within the *Gaue* whose borders matched those of the districts, were to act as a self-defence force. Apart from this, so-called *Landfahnen* were planned, which would operate throughout Bavaria. The establishment of a powerful strike force in the shape of the *Landfahnen* was one of the key aims of the *Land* leadership around Escherich, which was made up of many former officers who were eager to expand these mobile units directly under their command into a reserve army ready for deployment at all times.[111]

When the militias were expanded in the summer of 1919, however, it rapidly became obvious that local units would not generally be deployable beyond the local area. A number of local officials, called on to support and become personally involved in the militias, came to the conclusion that the militiamen were 'egotists concerned only with protecting their own farms or communities and cannot bring themselves to make sacrifices in the interests of all'.[112] Key figures in the overall organisation feared that obliging the militias to deploy beyond their communities would cause them to break up. The aversion to any obligation to serve beyond the local community, associated with signing up for the *Landfahne*, also applied in the heartland of the *Einwohnerwehren* in rural Upper Bavaria:

> In general, it may be stated that the purely peasant population is also concerned solely with defending its own property. Constant efforts are required simply to make people submit to deployment within the district. It has so far proved impossible almost everywhere to make a clear division between local and *Land* contingent. Many people still believe the *Einwohner-Wehr* is a kind of continuation of military service obliging one to fight everywhere. What is certain is that the vast majority is totally averse to taking part in possible fighting against Munich; no one has any time whatsoever for any obligation to fight beyond the district.[113]

Only in the former areas of action of the military leaders Escherich and Kanzler did attempts to establish *Landfahnen* meet with much success. In May 1920 the *Landfahnen* of the Chiemgau alone comprised 1,600 men, those of the districts of Traunstein and Isengau 1,000 each. Of the 15,000 members of the *Landfahnen* in Bavaria in February 1921, Upper

111. Fenske, *Konservativismus*, pp. 84–9.

112. WB BA Memmingen, 7.6.1919: StAA, Regierung 9766.

113. Report by the *Wehrkommissar* for Upper Bavaria, Major Schnitzlein, 4.8.1919: BHStA/IV, stv. GK I.AK 3895.

Bavaria accounted for 8,800, Lower Bavaria only 1,220, Swabia 990 and the Allgäu a mere 335.[114] In the case of *Landfahnen* organised in rural areas, moreover, the *Land* leadership assumed that they would be available for action only outside of the peak period of field cultivation.[115] Ex-soldiers' aversion to the militias' military-style structure, meanwhile, hampered the expansion of the *Einwohnerwehr* organisation. The loss of legitimacy suffered by the system of military discipline among soldiers affected attitudes beyond the end of the war. The resulting potential for criticism made it more difficult to develop paramilitary organisations. This was apparent when attempting to get people to join the local militias, as the *Wehrkommissar* for Swabia concluded after a journey through the districts of Füssen, Kempten, Kaufbeuren, Markt Oberdorf and Neuburg in June 1919: 'The people are ready to defend their village and home area, the district, against all threats, but very few are prepared to take part in expeditions further afield. The aversion to even the slightest hint of a military organisation is tremendous, most of the relevant men having already been in the field for a lengthy period. They want to be left in peace.'[116]

After initial contact with the civilian authorities, the General Command of the 1st Army Corps also established that 'nothing is so harmful to the progress of the *Einwohnerwehren* than even the slightest hint that "militarism" is behind the organisation'. The General Command therefore recommended that military terms such as 'commando' or 'battalion' and the use of officers as local militia leaders be avoided.[117] The Ministry of the Interior also urged the avoidance of military pomp and suggested that drills be carried out only when strictly necessary.[118] Nonetheless, some militiamen refused to sign the membership form, as it was considered a military document in disguise obliging them to perform military service.[119] Some local militias broke up. In one Lower Bavarian community this happened because people perceived the commitment not to leave once the militia had been called to arms as a 'silent revival of conscription'.[120]

114. Rudolf Kanzler, *Bayerns Kampf gegen den Bolschewismus. Geschichte der Bayerischen Einwohnerwehren*, Munich: Parcus 1931, pp. 164–72.

115. Monthly report by the *Land* leadership, 7.5.1920: BHStA/IV, Einwohnerwehr, Bund 3.

116. *Wehrkommissar* for Swabia and Neuburg: BHStA/IV, stv. GK I.AK 3895.

117. GK I.AK, 28.6.1919: BHStA/IV, stv. GK I.AK 3895.

118. MInn, 26.7.1919: BHStA/IV, stv. GK I.AK 3895.

119. *Wehrkommando* Wasserburg, 4.2.1921: StAM, LRA 184297.

120. Monthly report by the *Land* leadership, 7.9.1920: BHStA/IV, HS 920, S. 372, 353.

Yet these obstacles to mobilisation in rural areas did not ultimately stop the militias from spreading extensively. The number of members in Bavaria was 264,439 in January 1920, passed 300,000 in May 1920 and had reached 348,273 shortly before disbandment in April 1921. At this time there were 73,224 militiamen in Upper Bavaria (without Munich), 37,513 in Lower Bavaria, 32,440 in Swabia and 23,696 in the Allgäu.[121] In terms of numbers, the militias were strongest in rural areas, while urban workers rejected them. Workers in the MSPD and USPD were in any case banned from membership. In Munich it proved possible to attract no more than 30,000 members.[122]

The aim of providing property with armed protection secured the militias plenty of support. The last thing the *Land* leadership had in mind, however, was an exclusively defensive force supplementing the police. Through the state funding for the *Einwohnerwehr* and contributions from wealthy businessmen, the organisation at *Land* level had rapidly developed a massive bureaucracy, with 467 paid employees when it was dissolved in 1921.[123] The leadership's vision also went beyond developing the militias along military lines as a potential supplement to the *Reichswehr*. They were used to threaten the government under Social Democrat Prime Minister Johannes Hoffmann within the domestic political power struggle. While some restraint had initially been exercised, as the militias were dependent on the organisational and financial support of the government, the leadership sharpened its tone in early 1920. The Kapp putsch provided the opportunity for direct action against the government. When the general population found out about the putsch on 13 March, the *Einwohnerwehren* were mobilised to perform guard duty and carry out patrols. Some 80,500 militiamen were called to arms in Bavaria, concentrated in cities such as Munich and Augsburg. In rural Upper Bavaria 7,500 men were mobilised.[124]

The leadership of the *Einwohnerwehren* had substantial influence within the political intrigues of the time. Escherich in particular, along with the district chief of Upper Bavaria von Kahr and Munich's chief of police Pöhner, pressured the Bavarian *Reichswehr* commander, General von Möhl, to demand executive powers. The threatening noises coming from the *Reichswehr* and *Einwohnerwehr* compelled Prime Minister Hoffmann to resign. The *Einwohnerwehr* was thus a key player in Bavaria,

121. Kanzler, *Einwohnerwehren*, pp. 161-2.
122. Nusser, *Wehrverbände*, pp. 114-21.
123. Ibid., p. 107, pp. 144-50.
124. BHStA/IV, HS 920, p. 255, pp. 334-5.

the 'stronghold of order', now under newly elected Prime Minister von Kahr.[125]

The leadership at *Land* level was able to pursue such activities without having to justify itself to the local militias; the rural population certainly approved of the change of regime, as the election results of 1920 attest. The attempted coup d'état at Imperial level, however, met with disapproval. The peasants of the district considered the general strike organised in Memmingen by the USPD and MSPD in protest against the putsch unnecessary. As they approved of the tenor of the strike, however, they refrained from engaging in a suppliers' strike threatened by the peasants' associations, which some locals had initially considered.[126] In the local militias, the fact that those in higher leadership positions were always appointed, rather than elected as the articles of association stipulated, was already a source of discontent.[127] Several pieces of evidence from the district of Miesbach reveal criticism of the political ambitions of militia leaders. As early as December 1919, the *Regierungsbezirk* chief's response to a report by the local authority shows that the people were not interested in plans that went beyond self-defence. According to him, it would be wrong to impute 'subversive endeavours' to the militias, as some voices in the Miesbach area were clearly doing. The 'organisational union of the militias', which had inspired this notion, was intended only to 'secure order, peace and work'. Popular aversion to the militaristic structure of the militias and their conjoining for major military undertakings is also evident in the *Regierungsbezirk* chief's response.[128]

Because peasants were keen on the militias' policing function, such criticisms of the *Land* leadership's actions did not lead to open tensions or organisational restructuring. People continued to resist the paramilitary expansion of the militias, however, as the Miesbach district authority concluded in April 1921:

> That I conveyed the real mood of the people perfectly accurately in my numerous earlier reports, however, is clearly apparent in the fact that the bourgeois members [of the district assembly] underlined that the people,

125. Large, *Law and Order*, pp. 35-40.

126. Franz Schneider, Geschichte der Einwohnerwehren des Inngaues, p. 88: BHStA/IV, Einwohnerwehr, Bund 14, Akt 4.

127. State Minister of the Interior, 10.12.1919: BHStA/IV, Einwohnerwehr, Bund 3.

128. RP Obb., 9.12.1919: StAM, RA 3788.

> particularly the peasants, far from approving of the military organisation too often evident throughout the country, in fact strongly disapprove of it. They want the *Einwohnerwehr* only as a defensive institution with policing functions and do not regard these festive shooting events and flag consecration ceremonies as appropriate, but as unseemly provocation.[129]

In criticising the superfluous 'festive shooting', the farmers had pointed up a key component of the efforts to anchor the local militias organisationally. In his history of the *Einwohnerwehren*, Rudolf Kanzler reveals that the leadership was counting on the expansion of the property-protection system. Once the political situation had calmed down and new attempts by the workers to overthrow the regime had become more and more unlikely during the course of 1919, many peasants felt that it would have been enough to ensure the security of farms 'if every man had a rifle at home'. Reference to the Spartacist threat was no longer enough to 'maintain the organisation'. This is why the militias were organised rather like the marksmen associations (*Schützenvereine*). It proved possible to engage new militiamen beyond the original core of members interested in self-defence by constructing shooting ranges and appealing to their 'joy of shooting'.[130]

The *Land* leadership also tried to instrumentalise the marksmen activities in presenting the militias as a powerful force. From 26 to 28 September 1920 it organised a '*Land* shooting event' for the *Einwohnerwehren* in Munich in which 40,000 militiamen took part, and at which von Kahr and Escherich emphasised the importance of the militias to the stability of Bavaria as a 'stronghold of order'.[131] In the district of Donauwörth, however, a number of militiamen refused to participate in the event, fearing a coup d'état and thus immediate return to the barracks. An anonymous observer from a *Reichswehr* background concluded that 'particularly rural, very conservative minded circles' among the ranks of the militias 'objected to these "gala events", as they were called'.[132]

In their everyday practice, the rural militias behaved as an organisation of the propertied class and those peasants whose priority was peace and order. They were thus involved in policing the 'gypsies' in the district.[133] When urban workers went on strike, the militias were ready to intervene

129. BA Miesbach, quoted in HMB RP Obb., 20.4.1921: BHStA/II, MInn 66139.
130. Kanzler, *Einwohnerwehren*, pp. 183–4.
131. Nusser, *Wehrverbände*, pp. 128–9.
132. Anonymous account, 6.10.1920: BHStA/IV, RwGruKdo 4, 176.
133. WB RP Schw., 11.8.1919: BHStA/II, MA 102145.

if need be.The local militias also organised patrols to tackle the increasing number of thefts from fields and of grazing cattle and to deter urban looters. Finally, the militiamen tried to curb black marketeering.[134] The government was called upon to formally back the militias, and thus those members of the general public in favour of active intervention to stabilise the economy, in the battle against black marketeering.[135] The demand for official backing as a form of 'insurance' shows that peasants' interest in the militias had reached its limits. Many peasant militiamen clearly felt a sense of 'moral conflict', impeding the militias in the battle against black marketeering. Many farmers were themselves involved in such activities and would thus have had to persecute themselves or their neighbours.[136]

Rural workers thus criticised the *Einwohnerwehren* for arming the very farmers involved in profiteering. In a common submission towards the end of 1919, the workers' organisations of the community of Büchlberg underlined that, with the distribution of weapons to the Leoprechting *Einwohnerwehr*, the worst local black marketeers, those most unreliable in meeting their delivery quotas, would be armed and the workers powerless against them.[137] Against the background of the emotionally loaded conflict between producers and consumers, the peasantry protested against repeated demands by the Entente from March 1920 onwards that the *Einwohnerwehren* be disbanded and disarmed, fearing that this would diminish security in the countryside.[138] In the spring of 1921 the militias themselves finally began to come round to the idea of disbanding, in part because members feared denunciation by informers, should they fail to hand over their weapons.[139]

In any case, the dissolving of the *Land* leadership and the surrender of heavy weapons in late June 1921, carried out in response to the London Ultimatum of 5 May, did not mean the end of all armed organisations.[140] Some weapons and members - via the secret 'Pittinger Organisation' - were transferred to the 'League for Bavaria and the Empire' (*Bund*

134. Monthly report by the *Land* leadership, 5.1.1920, 3.3.1920: BHStA/IV, HS 920, pp. 201-4, 235-9.

135. WB RP Schw., 9.3.1920: BHStAA/II, MA 102146.

136. Swabian *Einwohnerwehr* district office: BHStA/II, MA 102146.

137. Protest by Free Trade Union, Christian Association of Quarrymen, SPD, USPD and workers' and peasants' council of Büchlberg, 19.11.1919: BHStA/II, MInn 66135.

138. WB BA Augsburg, 10.4.1920: StAA, Regierung 9767.

139. HMB BA Kempten, 30.5.1921: StAA, BA Kempten 6224.

140. Large, *Law and Order*, pp. 73-5.

Bayern und Reich). In July 1923 it had 56,715 members in Bavaria, many of them in Swabia and Upper and Lower Franconia. The extent of its popularity in the countryside is, however, unclear.[141] Rural inhabitants did not support right-wing organisations' attempts to stage a coup, as the Miesbach district authority stated in the autumn of 1921: 'A few hundred men from the Chiemgau, etc. led by Kanzler and his supporters are not the whole *Land*. The peasants tell me at every opportunity that all that matters at the moment is ensuring domestic peace, quiet and order and that we must wait until the economy has recovered and become stronger before deciding which type of state is best.'[142]

The crises of 1923 brought the 'League for Bavaria and the Empire' some more peasant members.[143] Yet even these organisational endeavours were aimed more at improving the security situation, which had become much worse as a result of hyperinflation, than overthrowing the political order. In June 1923, as a result of the solid 'distrust of the pro-Fatherland associations', the 'Free Peasants' and Citizens' Militia' was founded, its presence strongest in the districts of Miesbach, Tölz and Wolfratshausen. It specifically described its raison d'être as straightforward defence of property.[144] The frantic domestic and foreign policy developments of autumn 1923 provoked rumours of imminent armed clashes with France, although 'anything but a warlike atmosphere' prevailed among the peasants. On the other hand, against the background of religious decline among male farm labourers and the hordes of mainly youthful beggars, farmers came to the conclusion that the reintroduction of military service might help discipline the youth.[145] Nationalistic sentiments developed during the war were, however, central neither to such views nor to peasant involvement in the militias.

Farmers' attitude to the occupation of the Ruhr can be considered a litmus test that reveals the extent to which they embraced nationalistic resentment in 1923. Much of the population was swept up in a wave of nationalistic outrage, reinforced and instrumentalised to foreign policy ends by the Battle for the Ruhr announced by the Imperial government.[146] Meanwhile, the three southern Bavarian district chiefs were all regretfully

141. Nusser, *Wehrverbände*, pp. 215–55.

142. HMB RP Obb., 6.9.1921: BHStA/II, MA 102136.

143. HMB RP Obb., 23.6.1923: BHStA/II, 102136.

144. HMB BA Miesbach, 6.7.1923: BHStA/II, MInn 73441.

145. HMB BA Kempten, 14.8.1923: StAA, BA Kempten 6224.

146. Hans Mommsen, *Die verspielte Freiheit. Der Weg der Republik von Weimar in den Untergang 1918–1933*, Berlin: Propyläen 1989, pp. 141–5.

forced to conclude that the 'country folk [looked on at] the events apathetically' and were interested solely in the fact that they were likely to drive up the prices of agricultural produce.[147] Apart from that, propagandistic reports of the 'black disgrace' supposedly represented by black French soldiers and the occupiers' brutality awoke rural dwellers' memories of the 1914-18 period. In February 1923 a woman travelling by train in Lower Bavaria declared that tales of atrocities by the French in the Ruhr were as false as official reports from the front during the war; most of her fellow passengers agreed. The real 'war criminals' were the Germans. To prove the point, she handed out photographs of the destruction in the Belgian and northern French war zone.[148]

A large number of paramilitary organisations were founded after the war. Through their political activities, numerous armed clashes and acts of violence, they endowed Weimar political culture with an extremely violent character. Attempts to explain this phenomenon generally stress continuities with the lived experience of the front.[149] The difficulties involved in getting the rural *Einwohnerwehren* off the ground, however, demonstrate that front-line service did not necessarily generate the potential for violence. The militiamen were in fact tired of fighting, and their armed engagement was largely reactive and defensive. The theory that the *Einwohnerwehren* contributed to the militarisation of their members is equally dubious.[150] Former soldiers in fact disliked the militaristic form of the militias. In contrast to the widely held view, the wartime experiences of the veterans set limits to paramilitary mobilisation rather than underpinning it.

6.3 Veterans' Associations

Within the *Einwohnerwehren*, ex-soldiers were involved in post-war social conflicts and urban-rural antagonism. Their wartime experience

147. HMB RP Ndb., 3.2., 18.2.1923: BHStA/II, MA 102140.

148. BA Pfarrkirchen, 5.3.1923: StAL, Rep. 168/5, 501.

149. Bernd Weisbrod, Gewalt in der Politik. Zur politischen Kultur in Deutschland zwischen den beiden Weltkriegen, *Geschichte in Wissenschaft und Unterricht* 43 (1992), pp. 391-404, p. 392; see Gerd Krumeich, Kriegsgeschichte im Wandel, in: Gerhard Hirschfeld/Gerd Krumeich (eds), *Keiner fühlt sich hier mehr als Mensch ... Erlebnis und Wirkung des Ersten Weltkriegs*, Essen: Klartext 1993, p. 18, who speaks of an 'incomplete psychological demobilisation' with respect to the militias. See the discussion in Ziemann, Violent Society?

150. Diehl, *Paramilitary Politics*, p. 38.

was apparent only as a rather implicit motive which did not ultimately hamper the formation of the militias. Since the nineteenth century, the veterans' associations (literally warriors' associations, *Kriegervereine*) had offered a setting for ex-soldiers' public self-presentation, which was firmly anchored in the life of the village.This did not change after the First World War. However, the associations within the Bavarian Veterans' and Soldiers' League (*Bayerischer Veteranen- und Kriegerbund*) lost their sole claim to represent the interests of soldiers, and the league itself had to 'fight for survival' after 1918.[151] The crisis of the veterans' associations was apparent both within the local branches and in their relations to the umbrella body. It demonstrates that, in the first few years after the war, attempts to transform soldiers' experience of the front into a tale of heroism succeeded only to a limited degree at best.

The local veterans' associations had been stagnating since the beginning of the war, and meetings had become few and far between. This was due above all to the large number of members who had been called up, reported to be 175,000. During the war itself membership declined rapidly, probably due in the main to soldiers leaving. In any case, the number of members in Bavaria fell from 346,229 in 1913 to only 278,927 in early 1918.The second figure, however, excludes both passive members and the small number of honorary members. We may assume that the membership of a significant number of conscripts merely lapsed during the war.[152]

Even at this time, however, there was no escaping the fact that aversion to the veterans' associations was mounting along with war-weariness and anti-war sentiment. Many soldiers ceased to regard them as the natural advocates of their interests.[153] There was now pressure from competitor organisations keen to represent the interests of disabled ex-servicemen. In April 1918 the League of German Veterans and Disabled Servicemen (*Bund deutscher Kriegsteilnehmer und Kriegsbeschädigter*) was founded in Munich. Close to the Christian trade unions and aimed at the

151. Eugen Roth, *Festschrift zur Halbjahrhundertfeier des Bayerischen Kriegerbundes, 1874-1924*, Munich: Knorr & Hirth 1924, p. 58. Because of the dearth of archival material (see Karl Führer, Der deutsche Reichskriegerbund Kyffhäuser 1930-1934. Politik, Ideologie und Funktion eines 'unpolitischen' Verbandes, *Militärgeschichtliche Mitteilungen* 36 (1984), pp. 71-2), the newspaper *Bayerische Krieger Zeitung*, designed for the rank-and-file members, is the main source for the veterans' associations after 1918.

152. Fricke, *Lexikon*, vol. 3, p. 333.

153. Soldier's letter, February 1918: BA/MA, W-10/50794, Bl. 66.

working classes, its key focus was pursuing the interests of war invalids, represented personally by the deputy chairman, Rupert Mayer.[154] Under pressure from the authorities, particularly the Ministry of the Interior, which was keen to avoid fragmentation of the non-socialist veterans' organisations, the new grouping merged with the existing association, which was renamed the Bavarian Veterans' League (*Bayerischer Kriegerbund*), in September 1918.[155]

The revolution plunged the umbrella organisation of the *Kriegerbund* into a severe crisis from which it recovered only slowly after 1923. This happened because the main pillars of its political ideology vanished with the abdication of the monarchs in Bavaria and the Empire. In the pre-war period, the veterans' associations' much evoked 'loyalty' was also a demonstrative oath of allegiance to the ruling houses and the political system they represented.[156] Once soldiers had lost faith in Ludwig III and the monarchy in general, as happened on a massive scale in the second half of the war, and the leaders of the armed forces began to cooperate with the new rulers, it was unthinkable that they should continue to declare their loyalty to the old order. As early as November 1918, the chairmanship of the league called on members to place themselves at the disposal of the new 'People's state' in the interests of public order.[157] Of those who had got involved in the associations only as a means of achieving 'titles and medals', which had now become useless, many lost interest and some left, while others grew 'weary'.[158] During the revolutionary period, when emotions were running high, the veterans' associations came in for severe criticism as supporters of the monarchy. Attacks on the associations' 'militarism' mounted. Some even suggested that they bore some responsibility for the war. In 1919 rumours spread that the Allies planned to demand their disbandment.[159]

The national leadership responded quickly to the new situation by changing the articles of association. Instead of 'cultivating the idea of the monarchy', the aim was now to 'strengthen loyalty to the German Fatherland, love of the Fatherland and national consciousness'. Alongside the traditional goals of promoting comradeship and interring comrades who

154. *Bayerische Krieger Zeitung*, 25.9.1918.
155. Document on the meeting of 24 September 1918: BHStA/IV, MKr 11511.
156. Rohkrämer, *Militarismus*, pp. 194–203.
157. *Bayerische Krieger Zeitung*, 20.11.1918.
158. Ibid., 15.7.1919.
159. Ibid., 20.8.1920.

had died, the associations were to provide more help to war invalids.[160] Their interests were represented above all by Rudolf Schwarzer, *Reichstag* deputy for the BVP and General Secretary of the Association of Southern German Catholic Workers' Organisations, who was elected the third chairman of the league at a sitting of the general assembly on 21 September 1919.[161] Despite these measures, the links between the league leadership and local associations proved extremely loose and fragile between 1918 and 1923. Declarations of loyalty to the nation were hardly likely to appeal to Bavarian soldiers utterly disenchanted with the nation as a result of their wartime experiences. One symptom of the internal problems was the dearth of communication between the leadership and local branches, apparent in the circulation figures for the newspaper of the league. This was received by a mere 16,000 members; only in 1920 did the figure rise to 30,000 for a brief period.[162] The newspaper was read mainly by the chairmen of local associations, who did not necessarily pass it on to the members. Communication was largely a one-way process. Requests for a large number of copies were made only when reports on the local association appeared.[163]

The leadership was thus aware that the Veterans' League involved 'large numbers but little contact between its individual parts'.[164] The problem of connecting the branches to the centre intensified dramatically when the executive board (*Bundesführung*), to secure its finances, decided to increase the annual amount deducted for the league from the membership fees. The general assembly convened in autumn 1919 had approved an increase from 20 pfennigs to one mark per member for 1920.[165] This measure alone caused a total of 383 associations containing 40,000 members to leave the league by late 1920.[166] Yet this was a smaller amount than that paid for membership of an individual association. In addition to a joining fee of 1.50 to 3 marks, there was an annual contribution of between 2 and 6 marks.[167]

160. Ibid., 23.3.1919.
161. Ibid., 1.10.1919.
162. Ibid., 1.9.1919.
163. Ibid., 5.7.1922.
164. According to the third chairman of the League, Rudolf Schwarzer: ibid., 20.4.1920.
165. Ibid., 1.10.1919.
166. MA, 12.1.1921: BHStA/II, MInn 73033.
167. Statutes of a number of veterans' associations, in: StAM, LRA 134332.

The remaining associations were slow to pay the increased membership fee. The national leadership put this down to disinterest in the work of the league and its central office,[168] to which some associations simply reported lower membership figures.[169] To cover the budget for 1920, the decision was finally made to impose a national emergency levy of one mark and to double the membership fee in line with inflation.[170] This provoked heated debates at the general assembly in 1921. It was apparent here on several occasions that rural branches were particularly resistant to additional payments. The representative from the district of Aichach, for example, explained that many associations were already financially stretched by the holding of flag consecration ceremonies (*Fahnenweihen*), each costing up to 15,000 marks. The additional fees and a further inflation-related adjustment for 1922 were none the less passed.[171]

Those present at the general assembly responded to references to expensive flag consecration ceremonies with some indignation. This shows that the dispute over the emergency levy was largely symbolic. Rural members were mainly interested in local self-representation. The leaders of the organisation, meanwhile, were regarded as superfluous accessories. Criticism was frequently directed at the expense involved in administering the league. One district in the Upper Palatinate sent back its emergency levy forms because the chairmen and members felt that the administration was bloated and did too little.[172] Here, as elsewhere, people were especially dissatisfied with the district secretariats established in 1919, whose full-time heads spent most of their time advising local branches on benefits and welfare issues. Such work was hampered by the general lack of interest in the associations, which wanted to stick with tried and tested activities. However, the executive board of the *Kriegerbund* also came under fire, mainly because of the many officers in its ranks.[173] Sporadic calls were made for improved representation of rural areas.[174] A 1923 discussion of the state of the organisation found that many associations felt that: 'The league unites the veterans' associations in the most loose and informal way possible - now that the factors

168. *Bayerische Krieger Zeitung*, 5.8.1920.
169. Ibid., 20.4.1921.
170. Ibid., 5.11.1920.
171. Ibid., 5.6.1921.
172. Ibid., 20.5.1921.
173. Ibid., 20.6.1921.
174. Ibid., 20.4.1921.

holding it together in the days of the monarchy no longer apply – to one end: to return the deductions for the league in the form of benefits.' For many, the executive board's remit was limited to this function and giving speeches of welcome on festive occasions. Interference in the autonomy of associations and districts, meanwhile, was rejected as 'militarism' and 'ordering us about'.[175]

The crises of the post-1918 period also found expression in the membership flows of the Bavarian Veterans' League. We lack data for the difficult years immediately after the war. If the *Bundesführung* was able to gain an overview at all, it was not prepared to publish accurate figures, at least not at that time.[176] It instead produced fictional statistics far in excess of the real membership strength.[177] While the available figures must be treated with much caution, it is clear that pre-war membership levels had not been matched even by 1924. In 1921 there were 260,120 paying members (excluding the Palatinate), and in 1922 288,675. If we add the 1922 figures for the Palatinate, where the veterans' associations came under considerable pressure as a result of the French occupation and many were dissolved, we reach a figure of 303,247 members. Together with belated notifications and the 18,626 honorary members which existed in 1922, the total membership towards the end of 1922 was 325,189. This was still around 20,000 less than in 1913. No major changes had occurred by 1924; on 1 April, excluding the Palatinate, there were 309,195 members.[178]

This finding is all the more remarkable given that the First World War had produced 1.4 million Bavarian conscripts and thus potential members. None the less, the veterans' associations had the most members of all such organisations in Bavaria until the late 1920s, as the 'Steel Helmet, League of Front-Soldiers' (*Stahlhelm*) failed to make headway in Bavaria.[179] Yet it proved possible to mobilise veterans only to a modest degree. By no means all members had served in the war; as late as 1929 no more than 66 per cent of those in Bavaria had done so.[180] Only about one in every six Bavarian soldiers who had served in the First World War was thus a member of a veterans' association.

175. Ibid., 15.2.1923.
176. Ibid., 20.11.1921.
177. Ibid., 1.4.1920.
178. Ibid., 20.11.1921, 15.2.1923.
179. In the late 1920s the 'Steel Helmet' had only 3,000 members in the Coburg area: Nusser, *Wehrverbände*, pp. 289–94.
180. Elliott, Organisations, pp. 16–17; *Bayerische Krieger Zeitung*, 20.6.1920.

We have no data broken down by region on the social structure of association members during the Weimar period. We can none the less be sure that the share of members and chairmen made up by former officers, already declining before 1914, diminished further.[181] There is, however, some evidence to suggest that small farmers and sharecroppers (*Gütler*), but also veterans from the landless classes (*Söldner*), were particularly well represented in rural veterans' associations. Of the 102 paying members of the Loitzendorf association in 1919, at least 40 were small farmers or *Söldner* or their sons or fathers, the latter living on the part of the farm retained after the rest had been handed over to their successors. Six members were described as 'workers'.[182] In another Lower Bavarian village, a *Gütler* even became chairman.[183]

This does not, however, necessarily mean that those with little or no property were particularly prone to militaristic and nationalistic ideologies. In any case, researchers have as yet failed to produce convincing evidence of the degree to which members embraced the leadership's ideologies.[184] It seems more plausible to assume that the lower classes in the villages had other reasons for being interested in the associations. The estatist prestige associated with landed property was deeply important within village society. Therefore, smallholders most likely got involved primarily in an attempt to gain status and respect, which could not be denied them within the veterans' associations no matter how poor they might be. After all, men of all social classes had had to complete compulsory military service and could refer to the citizenship rights this entailed.

The lack of interest shown by most members of the Veterans' League reflected their conviction that the individual associations could achieve their goals very well without the overarching organisation. Local branches were thus able to develop in some communities despite the crisis in the

181. Elliott, Organisations, pp. 17-21.

182. The information available is minimal, as some members' occupation has not been entered. Register of income of the Loitzendorf veterans' association from September 1919: private possession. Evidence of the strong presence of the lower classes in village veterans' associations in Westphalia can be found in Michael Siedenhans, Nationales Vereinswesen und soziale Militarisierung. Die Kriegervereine im wilhelminischen Bielefeld, in: Joachim Meynert/Josef Mooser/Volker Rodekamp (eds), *Unter Pickelhaube und Zylinder. Das östliche Westfalen im Zeitalter des Wilhelminismus 1888 bis 1914*, Bielefeld: Verlag für Regionalgeschichte 1991, pp. 369-99, pp. 381-2.

183. Community of Asenham, 16.2.1923: StAL, Rep. 164/14, 8723.

184. For a critique see Ziemann, Sozialmilitarismus.

league. In rural areas, homecoming celebrations sometimes spawned new associations.[185] In Aichach, where the district chief worked particularly hard to build up the organisation, thirteen new associations (with a total of 1,000 members) affiliated to the Veterans' League were registered in 1921. Three more associations were expected to be established.[186]

The charters of both newly founded and existing groups expressed the aims typical of such associations. They provided for the cultivation of 'comradeship', the provision of welfare for needy members, within the association's financial means, and arranging the funerals of deceased members. In addition, after the war, associations also organised religious ceremonies of remembrance for members of both the associations and the community as a whole who had lost their lives in the war, which were held at least once a year.[187] At the heart of association activities after the war, however, were endeavours to build a local war memorial. This was the top priority, particularly for newly founded groups.[188] The Versailles Treaty strictly limited the extent to which associations could involve themselves in the local property guards; article 177 prohibited them from using weapons. The *Bundesführung* urged adherence to these regulations in order to prevent associations themselves from being banned.[189]

In the post-war period, association activities were moulded by the conflict between the younger ex-soldiers and the older generation. Alongside the remaining veterans of the war of 1870/1 - for the entire *Kyffhäuserbund* at Imperial level their number was recorded at 130,000 - this included pre-war reservists not called up in the First World War.[190] The chairmen of individual associations were 'too old', and a generational shift in favour of those who had served in the last war occurred only partially. A few associations even refused to accept young ex-soldiers. They referred to the charter, which required members to have completed active service in peacetime.[191] The older generation was mainly interested in traditional forms of sociability geared towards status within the village. Those recently returned from the war, meanwhile, wanted an organisation that served the interests of disabled ex-servicemen. Their efforts in this regard

185. *Bayerische Krieger Zeitung*, 1.7.1919, 5.7.1920.

186. Ibid., 20.3.1921.

187. Association statutes in: StAA, BA Neuburg 6781b.

188. *Festschrift zur 50-Jahrfeier mit Fahnenweihe*, Puchhausen 1969 (ed. by Krieger-, Soldaten-Kameradschaftsverein Puchhausen), p. 13.

189. *Bayerische Krieger Zeitung*, 20.7.1922.

190. Ibid., 5.11.1920.

191. Ibid., 5.11.1920.

were only partly successful, and there were complaints about their lack of interest in the more traditional activities.[192] With the exception of their intensive cultivation of the cult of the fallen, the rural associations in particular were not much different from those before the war. They usually met just twice a year, to hold their AGM and to take part in an evening ball. The *Vereinsmeierei* (associational sociability as an end in itself) criticised by the *Bundesführung* continued to hold sway, and people joined the associations mainly for traditional reasons: 'Because of the chairman, because of a splendid flag, because of an enjoyable ball, because of their business, because of a lovely funeral, and simply because it is customary to join the local veterans' association.'[193] The key elements of meetings in the smaller associations remained the 'tankard and tarot cards'. Chairmen keen to liven things up by engaging in political discussions quickly came up against the limits of farmers' oratorical skills. For the speeches necessary at public events such as flag consecration and founding ceremonies they could at least turn to the model texts prepared by the league.[194]

There is no evidence that the associations became politicised after the war.[195] The transfiguration of one's personal wartime past remained largely confined to events arranged by the associations, semi-public in character and largely consisting of social activities. Outside of the associations, there was clearly little enthusiasm for listening to soldiers' memories of the war in the villages. As early as 1916 the mayor of one village in Swabia alerted his son, on duty in the field, to the contradiction which prevented veterans from presenting themselves in a more assertive way after the war. His letter lamented the 'tittle-tattle neglectful of honour and duty' commonly talked by soldiers who, while complaining vociferously about the 'swindle' in their letters home, claimed that after the war ex-soldiers would all vote SPD. Assuring his son that he was 'no pious bigot or hypocrite *Augenverdreher*', he pointed out to him the consequences of such talk:

> If only such thoughtless letter-writers would think about the effects of their foolish twaddle. Don't these idiots realise that their achievements will

192. Ibid., 1.3.1919, 20.6.1921, 15.2.1923.
193. Ibid., 15.2.1923.
194. Ibid., 20.2.1922.
195. This was the incorrect opinion of Martin Broszat, *Die Machtergreifung. Der Aufstieg der NSDAP und die Zerstörung der Weimarer Republik*, Munich: Deutscher Taschenbuch Verlag 1984, p. 68.

> be valued less highly as a result? And that should they return home at last expecting honour and recognition, people will say to them: 'You yourselves said that the whole business was nothing but a great swindle and that it would have made no difference how things turned out.'[196]

Front-line service could provide grounds for political claims only if one had willingly identified with and delivered the necessary exertions. The representation of the unheroic and reluctant soldier was constrained by the discourse of 'national duty' which dominated the way soldiers were described in public.[197] As a result, the associations provided the major setting in which active members, who had stayed in the associations despite the criticism directed against them, could express the pride they felt at having successfully coped with the strains of the war. This is apparent in a decision by the veterans' associations of the district of Sonthofen. In October 1921 they refused to purchase from the *Kyffhäuserbund* 'commemorative coins' available to ex-soldiers for ten marks. They justified this by stating that because of the fee the coins could not be regarded as an 'honorary badge' (*Ehrenzeichen*). They also feared that quarrels would break out, as one had to be a league member to obtain the coins, excluding many veterans who would surely have asserted their right to such an honour.[198]

It was above all the consecration of the flag, common in the post-war period, which lent the entire community festive lustre through the participation of delegations from numerous veterans' associations, consisting of several hundred participants from the surrounding area.[199] These events also enabled people to cultivate contacts beyond the narrow horizons of the village. It was not unheard of for disputes among the often inebriated attendees to erupt into fist fights. After attending church, the young men and women involved in the consecration (*Fahnenjunker* and *Fahnenjungfrauen*) got to know each other better in the secular portion of the ceremony.[200] Though linking church services with dances in the context of flag consecration and ceremonies of remembrance for the fallen was in fact forbidden by the ordinariates, priests rarely managed to prevent it in the post-war period.[201] A tough battle often

196. Letter by the mayor of Thalhofen, J. Mayer, 12.2.1916: BHStA/IV, MKr 2330.
197. Geyer, Kriegsgeschichte, pp. 63–7.
198. *Bayerische Krieger Zeitung*, 5.12.1921.
199. *Neue freie Volks-Zeitung*, 19.5.1920.
200. *Bayerische Krieger Zeitung*, 20.7.1921, 5.9.1921.
201. Exchange of letters between a number of priests and veterans' associations and the ordinariate of Augsburg from 1921–1925: ABA, Allgemeinakten DB 362.

ensued between the chairmen of the local branches and the priests, acting as champions of discipline, over what kind of celebration lived up to the tenets of Christian morality. This shows that veterans were more self-confident in dealing with a traditionally significant authority.[202] Flag consecration ceremonies also provoked criticism from local officials, who accurately noted the disparity between the extravagant expenditure and the increasing unwillingness to give to charity. Within a few years rural communities were finding 10,000 to 15,000 marks to glorify their own achievements in the war and affirm their prosperity despite clerical opposition. Requests for charitable donations, meanwhile, were fobbed off with phrases such as 'the city folk should do some work'.[203]

As we lack source materials from the veterans' associations, we are unable to reconstruct the ideologies and world-views which prevailed there.[204] Discussions in their publications shed light on their aims. As the very survival of the associations was in doubt, however, even these texts provide no more than sporadic evidence. The associations were unable to offer their members a coherent ideology of the front-line soldier in the first few years after the war. First, people had to come to terms with the fact that the German army had by no means fought heroically to the end, many soldiers in fact allowing themselves to be taken prisoner in the summer and autumn of 1918.[205] The members of veterans' associations were thus called upon to refrain from reproaching returning POWs, including those who were 'happy to have survived', 'untroubled by a loss of self-respect':

> He who ended up a prisoner not because this was his unavoidable wartime fate, but because of his own failing courage - he has atoned for his error in the most dreadful manner. We should and must count this as his expiation. The list of debts, however, has been destroyed, the debt wiped out, and let no one consider himself entitled to count as an affront the circumstances under which anyone may have been taken prisoner.[206]

The author of this article implies that many of the ex-soldiers affected were unwilling to acknowledge their deeds, again underlining the

202. Parish of Rossbach, 19.6.1922: ABP, OA Pfa, Roßbach II, 4a.

203. HMB BA Aichach, 16.4.1921: StAM, LRA 99497.

204. To reconstruct the ideological attitudes of veterans' association members solely on the basis of membership newspapers, as does Rohkrämer, *Militarismus*, pp. 175-262, suggests a clear-cut world-view which surely never existed.

205. *Oberbayerische Landeszeitung. Traunsteiner Nachrichten*, 4.6.1919.

206. *Bayerische Krieger Zeitung*, 1.8.1919.

difficulties in representing 'reluctant' soldiers. On the other hand, this statement shows that directly after the war even 'national' circles had to grapple with the disintegration of the army, which had undeniably occurred on a massive scale.[207] Shortly afterwards, the leadership of the league emphasised that the revolution was not the doing of front-line soldiers and identified the veterans' associations as part of the front against the Treaty of Versailles.[208] Members were not, however, provided with guidelines on how to remember the lived experience of the front. Due to 'lack of space', few descriptions of battles fought by individual regiments or discussions of memoirs appeared in the association newspaper.[209]

Politically, the leadership of the *Kyffhäuserbund*, the umbrella organisation at the Imperial level, maintained a neutral stance towards the Republic, which prevented the very real reservations felt about it from becoming apparent. Because of internal problems, and in contrast to other associations in the nationalist camp, its political activities were restricted mainly to public announcements.[210] Persistent monarchist leanings among members found expression primarily in the context of festive events, at which members of the former ruling house of the Wittelsbachs often spoke.[211] In Prussia the assassinations of Erzberger and Rathenau caused the authorities to crack down briefly on the veterans' associations, whose activities could be banned by the government according to the provisions of an emergency decree issued in June 1922. Such a ban was not, however, imposed in Bavaria.[212] The Bavarian Veterans' League condemned the murder of Rathenau publicly, in part to avert state intervention. At the same time, however, in a submission presented jointly with the officers' associations, a protest was lodged against the decree removing the veterans' associations' freedom of assembly issued by Prussian Minister of the Interior Carl Severing.[213]

207. Ibid., 5.8.1920.

208. Ibid., 5.4.1921.

209. Ibid., 5.9.1922.

210. Elliott, Organisations, pp. 43, 50, 70; Werner Bramke, Die Stellung des Kyffhäuserbundes im System der militaristischen Organisationen in Deutschland 1918-1934, PhD dissertation, Potsdam 1969, pp. 47-54; Führer, Reichskriegerbund, pp. 58-62, describes the resistance to attempts by the leaders of the *Kyffhäuserbund* in 1929/30 to abandon its neutral position on the campaign for a referendum on the Young Plan among the rural associations oriented towards the BVP or Centre Party.

211. HMB BA Erding, 1.6.1923: StAM, LRA 146315.

212. Elliott, Organisations, pp. 71-4, 88-92.

213. *Bayerische Krieger Zeitung*, 5.7.1922.

Rural veterans' associations dealt with wartime experiences in an ambivalent manner.As a consequence of rural soldiers' increasingly critical view of the war and the political transformation, the transfiguration of the wartime past common before 1914 and carried out within the framework of the monarchical cult was plunged into a profound crisis.This did not have a huge impact on the life of the local associations, which was largely non-political, but did affect the overarching political representation of the veterans' associations by the Bavarian Veterans' League. This divergence was a result of the shift in rural soldiers' political views.As the monarchical system and its supporting elites, such as the officer corps, fell from grace, important elements of the political world-view of the veterans came under fire. However, the veterans' associations, mainly geared towards transfiguring ex-servicemen's time in the army, were not an appropriate setting for the organisational anchoring of a positive political vision. On the whole, veterans were successfully reintegrated into society, ensuring that the potential for critique which had developed at the front fizzled out quite soon. Meanwhile, despite the negative aspects of front-line experiences, among the core of members who remained in the veterans' associations remembrance of the 1914–18 period was soon imbued with a positive tenor. Given that few world war veterans were members of such organisations, however, this only applied to a minority of them.The majority, to some extent a 'silent' one, clearly had very little motivation to reappraise or embed their experiences within the framework of a bespoke organisation.

6.4 War Memorials

The publications of the war victims' associations sometimes described war invalids as 'living monuments' to the war to satirise the building of war memorials (literally *Kriegerdenkmäler*, 'warrior memorials'), which they found hypocritical.The emotionalism involved in honouring the dead and the amount of money spent on it, which seemed excessive given the meagre pension disabled ex-servicemen received, were contrasted with the everyday contempt shown towards disabled survivors, who 'were unlucky enough not to have stayed in the field'.[214] Such objections were, however, incapable of hindering the proliferation of public symbols of death in battle after the war.[215]

214. *Bundes-Nachrichten* No. 52 (1922).

215. For an important general argument on the symbolism and meaning of war memorials see Koselleck, War Memorials. We still lack a comprehensive treatment

The political and social dimensions of how people came to terms with the carnage at the front were obviously not exhausted by the traditional forms of mourning centred on private honouring of the dead in Christian ritual and popular customs.[216] Death in war, as a violent death suffered while doing one's duty to defend the state, demanded representation of a symbolic nature that offered surviving fellow soldiers, those left behind and indeed the entire community something with which they could identify and which helped them to make sense of violent death.[217] War memorials offered a tangible opportunity to have such needs met. They also gave those left behind a place to express their private grief and remember their loved ones, as few of the fallen were laid to rest in their home villages. Most were interred in the military cemeteries constructed behind the front line. Requests to bring back the body of a soldier killed in action during the war had a chance of success only if the body was identifiable and had not been buried in a mass grave. Even then, such requests were approved only in exceptional cases. Due to the expense involved, this was in any case an option open only to a small number of people; the authorities provided no financial support.[218] Should relatives none the less succeed, the return of the body stirred up a great deal of emotion and made the family's pain part of the community's grief, as a letter written by a resident of the district of Illertissen lays bare:

> The first fallen soldier was laid to rest here in his home village yesterday. It was the farmer of the name of August, who died in a field hospital in France.

---

of war memorials in Germany comparable to Ken S. Inglis, *Sacred Places. War Memorials in the Australian Landscape*, Carlton: Melbourne University Press 2001. A good local survey is Kai and Wolfgang Kruse, Kriegerdenkmäler in Bielefeld, in: Reinhart Koselleck/Michael Jeismann (eds), *Der politische Totenkult. Kriegerdenkmäler in der Moderne*, Munich: Fink 1994, pp. 91-128. War memorials in rural areas have generally been neglected in recent historical research.

216. Cf. Walter Hartinger, *Denen Gott genad! Totenbrauchtum und Arme-Seelen-Glauben in der Oberpfalz*, Regensburg: Pustet 1979, pp. 31-92, 125-8; Sigrid Metken (ed.), *Die letzte Reise. Sterben, Tod und Trauersitten in Oberbayern*, Munich: Hugendubel 1984. The notion that the 'decline of Christian interpretations of death' was a prerequisite for the political cult of the dead (Koselleck, War Memorials, p. 291) fails to convince. In fact, as we shall see, the latter points directly to traditional forms of remembrance; the political and the Christian were enmeshed. The official Roman liturgy was insufficient only because it could not usually be completed and because the memorial was to underline violent death.

217. Koselleck, War Memorials, p. 287.

218. Ulrich/Ziemann, *Frontalltag*, p. 208.

> His wife managed to gain permission to bring him home. The body arrived in Illertissen on Tuesday afternoon and it was in Obenhausen by seven in the evening. We had the honour of collecting him in a beautifully decorated funeral cart. The farmhand had decorated the horses beautifully. Both of them had blue and white silk ribbons on and black mourning bands at the sides. Bonifaz [a relative?] came in his new uniform, two soldiers in uniform led the horses and another twelve soldiers currently home on leave accompanied the cart. The priest fetched him from just outside the village with a cross and flags and a crowd of mourners. He spent the night in his house but unfortunately no longer alive but dead. It is a terrible thing to return home in this way. Everyone was weeping and wailing.[219]

The grief of those left behind thus generally lacked a focal point, inspiring sporadic attempts to honour the dead through permanent memorials during the war itself. Such attempts were blocked on several occasions in 1915 by the district chiefs, who pointed out that approval would not be forthcoming as long as the war was on.[220] Liaison officers were appointed in the *Regierungsbezirke* in 1917 to approve memorial designs. They were the local contact for the *Landesberatungsstelle für Kriegerehrungen*, which was set up in 1916 to give advice about how to honour fallen soldiers, and other interested parties.[221] After the end of the war, most rural communities built war memorials of one kind or another within a few years. In 1922 alone more than 1,200 such projects were approved by the authorities in Bavaria.[222] The inflationary crisis of 1923 brought the construction boom of the immediate post-war period to an end.[223] Only towards the end of the 1920s did most of the communities that had failed to realise their plans for a memorial immediately after the war finally do so.[224]

In both urban and rural areas, it was the veterans' associations that most often initiated construction of a war memorial. A memorial committee made up of association members was established, usually in consultation with community representatives and the local council. This committee attended to the selection of a design and saw the project through. Should the plan be for a memorial on or within the church, the parish usually played an active role. Particularly in such cases, but also

219. Letter excerpt, 26.4.1917: BSB.
220. RP Ndb., 29.4.1915: StAL, Rep. 164/6, 1813.
221. Correspondence in: BHStA/II, MK 14483.
222. Memorandum by the MK, 17.10.1923: BHStA/II, MK 51029.
223. RP Obb., 29.2.1924: BHStA/II, MK 51029.
224. Lurz, *Kriegerdenkmäler*, p. 28.

when the memorial was to be sited in a public place, the priest was often the driving force behind the project.[225] Plans made on the initiative or with the involvement of the priest generally resulted in the selection of a religious motif. There was general consensus that the memorial should express Christian notions and values. This consensus broke down only rarely, as in the community of Dorfbach, where the veterans' association built a memorial in the form of a soldier in contemporary uniform but with a sword and medieval helmet, against the wishes of the priest, who had proposed a design by the Society for Christian Art (*Gesellschaft für christliche Kunst*).[226]

In contrast to the cities, where disputes between different political camps frequently caused delays, within rural communities conflicts over the selection of an appropriate monument were generally rare.[227] They tended to revolve around details, while there was broad agreement over the symbolic content.[228] The memorial committee and local council in Wittibreut, for example, initially met with the citizens' disapproval solely because they proposed a simple plaque. The locals were determined to create a 'real, worthy' memorial. This could only mean a figured monument. Only when a fitting design had been chosen, did people begin to donate money on a sufficient scale.[229]

The next step towards realising a memorial was acquiring the financial means, which was generally achieved through a door-to-door collection organised by the memorial committee or veterans' association. The collected amount was usually insufficient, so the local authority topped it up from its own coffers. This generally involved about a third of the total amount.[230] In addition to money, members of the community sometimes contributed materials and labour, for example by taking on the job of carting loads.[231] Construction costs lay between 4,000 marks

225. A wealth of examples can be found in: StAA, BA Illertissen 3891.

226. Priest of Dorfbach, 28.2.1920: StAL, Rep. 164/13, 2536.

227. Sabine Behrenbeck, Heldenkult oder Friedensmahnung? Kriegerdenkmale nach beiden Weltkriegen, in: Gottfried Niedhart/Dieter Riesenberger (eds), *Lernen aus dem Krieg? Deutsche Nachkriegszeiten 1918 und 1945*, Munich: C.H. Beck 1992, pp. 344–64, p. 347.

228. HMB RP Obb., 23.5.1923: BHStA/II, MA 102136.

229. Memorial committee and community council of Wittibreut, 16.11.1921: StAL, Rep. 164/14, 8723.

230. Veterans' and soldiers' association of Attenhausen, 11.5.1922: StAA, BA Memmingen 10914.

231. Kirchdorf am Inn: StAL, Rep. 164/14, 8723.

for a glass mosaic placed in the church in Ollarzried and 120,000 marks for a memorial chapel built into the cemetery wall in Hawangen in 1922. An average of around 22,500 marks was spent on a number of memorials built in 1921 and 1922.[232] These were considerable sums for smaller communities, which were raised over a relatively short period.

If construction of the memorial was delayed, inflation could rapidly diminish the value of the money collected and scupper the project.[233] The available sum generally functioned as a constraining factor, influencing the type of monument chosen and thus its symbolic message. Due to a lack of funds for other designs, the Germanising motif of an erratic boulder (*Findling*), generally more common in northern Germany, was sometimes chosen.[234] Smaller communities in particular often made do with a simple memorial plaque.[235] The amount of money spent and the fact that the whole community helped raise it clearly shows that many rural folk felt a deep need to honour the fallen appropriately. The officials responsible for historical monuments, however, criticised the fact that major expenditure on a war memorial often served only to represent the community 'fittingly' to the wider world; its members were usually keenly interested in the memorial projects in the surrounding area. In such cases the priority was for 'the memorial to be larger and more expensive than that of the neighbouring village'.[236] For reasons of status, such 'magnificent memorials' were generally sited on a thoroughfare in a prominent location.[237]

The obstinacy generated by the status consciousness of the members of the farmers' or veterans' associations funding the memorial was one reason why efforts to gain official approval often led to lengthy conflicts. There were no Imperial regulations governing the construction of war memorials. Apart from Baden, Bavaria was the only part of the Empire to attempt to exercise some influence by means of approval procedures under the aegis of a building inspectorate.[238] The *Land*

232. This figure relates to twenty monuments for which information is available. Evidence in: StAL, Rep. 164/14, 8723; StAA, BA Illertissen 3891, BA Kempten 4715, BA Lindau 4538, BA Memmingen 10914.

233. Community of Legau, 23.1.1924: StAA, BA Memmingen 10914.

234. Lindauer Tageblatt, 7.5.1923: StAA, BA Lindau 4538.

235. Numerous examples can be found in: StAA, BA Mindelheim 3703.

236. Rudolf Pfister, Gute und schlechte Kriegerdenkmäler. Ein Wort an die Auftraggeber, *Schönere Heimat* 33 (1937), pp. 25-31, p. 25.

237. Landbauamt Memmingen, 6.5.1921: StAA, BA Illertissen 3891.

238. Lurz, *Kriegerdenkmäler*, vol. 4, pp. 114-20.

building authorities (*Landbauämter*), responsible for public construction projects, were tasked with implementing these procedures. The influence of the state was thus embodied by local officials, who, however, soon established that many rural communities were continuing to build their war memorials without state approval. In the view of the officials responsible for the preservation of historic monuments, one of the main reasons for the frequent conflicts that marked the approval process was the need to 'show-off' and the 'craving for recognition' characteristic of farmers, whose awareness of status extended to the honouring of their relatives.[239] They felt justified in making decisions about the design of the memorials free from state supervision because they were spending lots of money on them.[240]

The priority given to funding memorials highlights farmers' oft-observed tendency to seal themselves off from the social crisis of the time. On the other hand, they might interpret the loss of close relatives as a crisis in their own lives, as the wrenching loss of a social tie of outstanding significance. Representing this was a top priority shortly after the war. This illuminates how war memorials, and remembrance of the fallen generally, also had the function to represent the founders themselves and their endeavours to commemorate the dead.[241]

In realising this self-representation, the founders simultaneously formed a relationship with the dead, whose deaths were endowed with meaning by the memorials. Among farmers, this relationship took on a form directly geared towards the individual mourned relative, leading to numerous conflicts with the building authorities. In addition to the usual listing of the names of all the fallen of the community, they often wished to place photographs of the dead on the memorial plaque, particularly in churches.[242] The community of Obertürken justified this by pointing to the example of nearby Kirchberg. On the memorial plaque in the latter village, the photographs were integrated as the fruit of a stylised tree, with an illustration of the *Mater Dolorosa* at its centre.[243] Generally, however, officials responsible for the preservation of historic monuments and the

239. Regierungsbaurat Eitel, Beratungstätigkeit der Landbauämter bei Errichtung von Kriegerdenkmälern, *Süddeutsche Baugewerkszeitung* 27 (1924), No. 22, pp. 1-9, p. 1.

240. HMB BA Ebersberg, 15.5.1921: StAM, LRA 79889.

241. Probst, *Bilder*, pp. 80-4, p. 92.

242. Bezirksobmannschaft Aichach of the Bavarian Veterans' League, 20.3.1921: BHStA/II, MK 14479.

243. Community of Obertürken, 16.5.921: StAL, Rep. 164/14, 8723.

Church authorities unanimously rejected such practices, as they would profane the sacred space. They also found fault with the 'mechanical authenticity' of the photographs, which they felt were anything but artistic.[244] It was generally necessary to obtain approval from the Church authorities when building memorials in or on churches; they made a Christian motif a condition of such projects. The Church also refused to perform ceremonies or consecrate war memorials at their unveiling, should they fail to include religious symbolism.[245]

Generally, the authorities most often objected to the tendency to reinforce the 'impression of monumentality' by modifying the form of the memorial and memorial site,[246] as in the case of the design put forward for the community of Stetten. In the opinion of the *Land* building authority, it lacked 'any trace of inwardness or originality'. It was further described as 'a monstrosity with no monumental impact, more like a gravestone than a war memorial'.[247] In a submission, the memorial committee then underlined that it had consciously selected this design from a number of proposals and stated with determination:

> The idea of a 'soldier praying at the war memorial with a wreath of oak' and an 'Iron Cross on the back' matches the basic aesthetic sense of rural people perfectly. In line with the unanimous decision by the Soldiers' and Veterans' Association, the tendency to glorify the war typical of war memorials should be eliminated. It would be inappropriate to deny the aesthetic sensibilities of the people.[248]

This, however, is precisely what officials wished to do, which elucidates their stereotypical objections to the designs put forward by rural communities. The *Land* building authorities thus intervened repeatedly in memorial construction, pushing their own designs, some of which were realised. Alternatively, they mentioned the names of architects they considered qualified.[249] The authorities were ultimately obliged to grant planning permission, even if they learned about a memorial only after it had been constructed. Failure to do so was likely to provoke bitter

244. Expert report by the *Land* office for preservation of historic monuments, 11.4.1921: StAL, Rep. 164/14, 8723.

245. Jeismann/Westheider, Nationaler Totenkult, p. 42.

246. Landbauamt Memmingen, 16.7.1921: StAA, BA Memmingen 10914.

247. Landbauamt Memmingen, 7.2.1922: StAA, BA Mindelheim 3703.

248. Memorial committee of Stetten, 17.2.1922: StAA, BA Mindelheim 3703.

249. Plan drawn up by the Landbauamt Passau, 29.5.1922: StAL, Rep. 164/13, 2553.

resistance from communities.[250] While the legally permissible demolition of memorials was rarely carried out, the impact of state approval practices was quite palpable in many communities entangled in constant wrangles over modifications of one kind or another.

Depending on the initiative of the memorial founders and their financial means and the state approval practices, war memorials were created whose architectural form furnishes us with insights into how people tried to endow soldiers' deaths with meaning. After the First World War, the number of Christian motifs on war memorials increased.[251] In rural Bavaria, Christian allusions were dominant on memorials, which was hardly surprising given that they were often sited in churches and that priests played a leading role in their creation. Within this framework, the choice of a particular motif made possible varying emphases and brought out differing aspects of the Christian conception of death in battle.

Depictions of the crowned Mary with the baby Jesus as *Patrona Bavariae* must be understood within the context of the Marian piety so prevalent in Bavaria. Hovering above a soldier or being prayed to by soldiers, her image underlined the overcoming of the hardships of war. This updated the veneration of Mary as protector of Bavaria first proclaimed by Duke Maximilian I in the seventeenth century.[252] The link between piety and regional identity also received emphasis in the traditional form of the Marian column.[253] As Mary had been expressly acknowledged as protector of Bavaria in 1916 by Pope Benedict XV at the instigation of Ludwig III, such forms suggested a declaration of loyalty to the former ruling house, at least as a motive favoured by the local priests.[254] Free of religious associations, the depiction of the Bavarian lion, rare after the First World War, also served to emphasise Bavarian patriotism and soldiers' bravery.[255] In the church in Übersee, however, the lions support themselves on the beams of a cross, symbolising the notion that 'no other consolation' was available to the Bavarian people. As an 'element of consolation' for grieving relatives, a depiction of the *Mater Dolorosa* was placed under the cross.[256]

250. BA Pfarrkirchen, 24.8.1923: StAL, Rep. 164/14, 8723.
251. Lurz, *Kriegerdenkmäler*, p. 221.
252. Straßkirchen: StAL, Rep. 164/14, 8723.
253. Neukirchen: StAL, Rep. 164/13, 2532.
254. StAA, BA Memmingen 10914.
255. Neuburg am Inn: StAL, Rep. 164/13, 2542.
256. *Oberbayerische Landeszeitung. Traunsteiner Nachrichten*, 3.9.1921.

The *pietà* motif underlined the grief of those left behind. It found expression in the epitome of Christian grief, the figure of Mary cradling Jesus on her lap after he had been taken down from the Cross. The profane variant of this motif, in which a woman in contemporary dress bends down towards a dying soldier, was occasionally used, for example in a painting in the church of Schwaig.[257] Images of *pietà* were usually placed within or on the church and only rarely in the municipal area. Particularly in specially built memorial chapels, *pietà* offered those mourning at the memorial an image with which they could identify, intended to lessen the pain of their loss through religious transcendence.[258] The addition of the inscription 'See if there be any sorrow like unto my sorrow', from the Old Testament, gave this function verbal expression.[259]

The popular saints played a key role in the rural cult of the dead. This points to the belief in miracles, a major feature of popular Catholicism, and indicates from whom soldiers had expected support in exceptional circumstances during the war.[260] These ranged from St Sebastian through St Stephen to St Michael.[261] Of the female saints, St Barbara, called upon by soldiers facing death as the patron saint of the hour of death, sometimes appeared in memorial imagery.[262] St George was pre-eminent among the saints. He cropped up so often in southern Bavaria that he can be said to embody the rural war memorial. In areas such as the district of Lindau, where a number of communities mounted representations of St George on the plinth, there was the option of treading a well-worn path and simply adopting the completed design of a neighbouring community to save money.[263] The representation of St George generally chimed with the iconographic tradition, which showed him in full knightly armour astride his horse, killing the dragon at its feet with his lance.[264] Very occasionally, the memorial shows St George standing as he prepares to vanquish the dragon with his sword.[265]

From a modern point of view, the figure of St George suggests that the founders were attempting to promote nationalism, if we see the Christian

257. Probst, *Bilder*, pp. 6–26, 254–5.
258. Kirchdorf am Inn: StAL, Rep. 164/14, 8723.
259. Erlach: StAL, Rep. 164/14, 8723.
260. Mooser, *Volksreligion*, p. 148.
261. *Oberbayerische Landeszeitung. Traunsteiner Nachrichten*, 17.6.1922.
262. *Christliche Kunst* 17 (1920/21), pp. 115, 147.
263. Landbauamt Kempten, 8.3.1923: StAA, BA Lindau 4538.
264. See, for example, StAL, Rep. 164/14, 8723.
265. Frechenrieden: StAA, BA Memmingen 10914.

message as mere 'window dressing'.[266] The addition of a relief featuring the Bavarian lions, however, excludes such a reading.[267] The core of the message embodied in St George is apparent only if we relate the motif of the battle to the religious goal for which the knight struggled. According to the legend, George converted the capital city of Cappadocia through his victory over the dragon. His intercession on behalf of all those who prayed to be saved in his name made him one of the most popular saints. There were fourteen Holy Helpers in Need (*Nothelfer*), frequently called upon in times of crisis; George was the patron saint of soldiers, particularly mounted ones. In the context of rural southern Bavarian society, the dominance of the figure of George among depictions of saints was thus primarily a consequence of his importance within popular piety.[268] The specific slant of the interpretations associated with him was rooted in the notion that now that the war was over, it was vital to fight to safeguard the Christian faith with renewed vigour. This fight was naturally to be understood as the pursuit of the morally good. Wielding his lance, symbol of conversion to the true faith, St George was thus an admonitory figure promoting Christian morality, particularly among those soldiers whose behaviour after returning home showed little sign of it. The motif of urging people to uphold the Christian faith as a legacy of the fallen took on vivid form, when the memorial, as in the community of Günz, showed St George with his hands clasped in prayer.[269]

Depictions of Christ underlined various aspects of the Christian message of salvation. A common variant showed Christ bending down to bless a dying soldier with raised torso.[270] In this case, hopes of consolation and redemption for the fallen took centre stage.[271] Alternatively, the dying or already dead soldier was sometimes shown lying or sitting at the feet of the crucified Christ.[272] In addition to hopes of redemption, such a monument suggested a parallel between the soldiers' demise and

266. Lurz, *Kriegerdenkmäler*, p. 232.

267. Attenhausen: StAA, BA Memmingen 10914.

268. Oliva Wiebel-Fanderl, 'Wir hatten alle Heiligen besonders auswendig lernen müssen ...'. Die Bedeutung der himmlischen Helfer für die religiöse Sozialisation, in: Andreas Heller/Therese Weber/Oliva Wiebel-Fanderl (eds), *Religion und Alltag. Interdisziplinäre Beiträge zu einer Sozialgeschichte des Katholizismus in lebensgeschichtlichen Aufzeichnungen*, Vienna, Cologne: Böhlau 1990, pp. 55–89.

269. Günz: StAA, BA Memmingen 10914.

270. Bemmingen: StAA, BA Memmingen 10914.

271. *Amper-Bote*, 18.6.1921.

272. Lauben: StAA, BA Memmingen 10914.

Christ's sacrifice on the Cross, glorifying their death as an exemplary and altruistic act.[273] The soldiers had thus died on the field of battle to atone for the sins of the founding community.

Another variant showed one or two soldiers, their heads lowered in prayer, kneeling or standing before the crucified Christ. Here the surviving soldiers appeared as witnesses before the Cross, echoing the account of Jesus' favourite disciple in the Gospel according to St John (John 19:25-7, 35). They thus became the appointed agents and proclaimers of Christ's revelation. Should the memorial show the soldiers absorbed in prayer, this motif might also entail a note of the distress felt in the face of death. The memorial in Herrenstetten which, alongside Christ on the Cross, featured two soldiers in uniforms redolent of classical antiquity, each with a hand raised in proclamation, made the notion of proclaiming the faith explicit in the symbol of the Cross.[274] Some memorials featured the motif of the praying soldier without the link to the Crucifixion.[275]

The mainly religiously inclined interpretations characteristic of rural war memorials found visible expression in the special architectural form of memorial chapels. These were sometimes erected outside villages on or near distinctive features of the landscape. More often, they were located in cemeteries, generally inserted into the wall. In these cases, the memorial was directly associated with lamentation of the dead and functioned primarily as a proxy for the soldiers' missing graves.[276] The Iron Crosses and steel helmets added to many memorials otherwise featuring purely religious themes clarify the link to the honouring of the soldiers within the basically Christian context. At the feet of the risen Jesus, whose consoling message was verbalised in the inscription 'You will resurrect', the steel helmet with its laurel wreath found a place 'as symbol of the courage' of the fallen.[277] In association with a *Patrona Bavariae*, the Iron Cross mainly expressed the soldiers' military virtue and fulfilment of their duty, but it could also be read as a national Prussian-German symbol by the individual observer.[278]

Utterly profane depictions tended to show soldiers in contemporary uniform, generally holding a rifle. They symbolised surviving soldiers'

273. Lurz, *Kriegerdenkmäler*, pp. 222-5.

274. StAA, BA Illertissen 3891.

275. Stetten: StAA, BA Mindelheim 3703.

276. Egg an der Günz: StAA, BA Memmingen 10914.

277. Sculptor Georg Kemper from Munich, 14.1.1928: ABA, Pfa 42/2.

278. Straßkirchen, with the inscription 'To the heroes of the community of Straßkirchen': StAL, Rep. 164/13, 2553.

empathy for the fate of their fallen comrades and thus the binding nature of relationships within the armed forces beyond death and the end of the war.[279] The pain felt at the loss of comrades received particular emphasis in the figure of a soldier with his right hand placed upon his heart.[280] Memorials featuring plainly revanchist sentiments were indeed very rare in rural areas. In 1920 the community of Krün planned to build a monument with a field-grey soldier in full gear standing on an obelisk, his face turned westwards. The authorities rejected this design as it seemed too 'provocative'. The final monument showed a soldier lying at the feet of a military chaplain.[281] Abstract memorials were also few and far between in the villages. The commonest type of monument in this category featured obelisks, more ubiquitous after the war of 1870/1 as a symbol of victory,[282] and pillars topped by an Iron Cross.[283]

In the inscriptions, the founders stated more precisely or supplemented the meaning they intended for the monument. The form of language and appellative character of the inscriptions tended to curb the diversity of meanings inherent in the imagery. It is striking that the religious symbolism of the memorials, largely intended to bestow comfort and moral renewal through religion, was not replicated in the inscriptions. The figured statement was obviously considered sufficiently unambiguous, making further elaboration unnecessary. It is thus rare to come across an inscription such as 'Come to me, all who labour and are heavy laden', which in this case served to complement a depiction of Jesus caring for both victims and those left behind.[284] 'God the Lord, the strength of my salvation, thou hast covered my head in the day of battle' is another quote from the Bible that was sometimes used, expressing the certainty of salvation.[285]

Inscriptions seldom mentioned a value for which the soldiers were meant to have given their lives. The nation-centred interpretation of death for the 'Fatherland' cropped up only rarely, in contrast to urban monuments. When it did, it was never explicitly referred to as a 'German' Fatherland, at least leaving open the possibility that it was Bavaria one

279. Tussenhausen, holding a wreath, the motif being: 'Saying goodbye to his comrades': StAA, BA Mindelheim 3703.

280. Engetsried: StAA, BA Memmingen 10914.

281. Probst, *Bilder*, pp. 191-4, quote p. 192.

282. Tittling, Thyrnau: StAL, Rep. 164/13, 2543, 2548.

283. Haselbach, Praßreuth: StAL, Rep. 164/13, 2541, 2554.

284. Schwaig: *Christliche Kunst* 17 (1920/21), p. 109.

285. Wollomoos: StAM, LRA 100360.

had in mind.[286] In Frechenrieden, the fallen were expressly described as 'victims'.[287]

Inscriptions such as 'To the protectors of the Homeland [*Heimat*]', meanwhile, emphasised the soldiers' achievement in keeping the village safe from the horrors of the war.[288] It made sense in this context to list on plaques, in addition to the names of the fallen, the names of all the other soldiers from the village, as they had also rendered outstanding services to their home community.[289] The sequence of phrases ('Our dead in the World War 1914-1918. They died for us. Built by the community of Ollarzried') praised death as directly benefiting the community of the living. The latter thus had a duty to remember and documented its acceptance of this duty by erecting the monument.[290]

The fulfilment of an obligation to the dead was also emphasised in the many cases in which the community identified itself as collective founder of the memorial. These inscriptions underlined the home community as dual reference point in the honouring of the dead, a community in which both founders and fallen had their roots. In the words 'Dedicated to the fallen by the grateful community', the local context within which the village's honouring of the dead acquired its meaning was elevated to an abstract principle.[291] The frequent use of the adjective 'grateful' points implicitly to the perception described above that the war had threatened the local community.[292]

The nature of the relationship between living and dead determined the form of address used for the fallen: 'heroes', 'comrades' or 'sons'. The term 'comrades', which exclusively identified former soldiers as founders, was relatively rare. The terms 'sons' and 'heroes' were about equally common. Sometimes both terms were brought together in praise of 'heroic sons'.[293]

286. StAA, BA Illertissen 3891.

287. 'To the victims of the World War. They died for the Fatherland. Built by the community of Frechenrieden': StAA, BA Memmingen 10914.

288. Betlinshausen: StAA, BA Illertissen 3891; see *Christliche Kunst* 18 (1921/22), p. 109.

289. Boos, Frechenrieden und Lautrach: StAA, BA Memmingen 10914.

290. StAA, BA Memmingen 10914. 'Your loyalty is an example to us all' specifies this as a moral virtue: Probst, *Bilder*, p. 245.

291. Untereichen: 'Dedicated to their brave sons by the grateful community': StAA, BA Illertissen 3891.

292. Wittibreut: 'Dedicated to our loyal warriors by the grateful community': StAL, Rep. 164/14, 8723.

293. 'Dedicated by the parish of Wollomoos to its heroic sons': StAM, LRA 100360.

Calling them heroes emphasised the extraordinary and exemplary actions of the dead, sometimes specified as courage. The honoured, however, remained closely linked to the community, which documented its pride and close relationship to the dead in the simple, familiar form of words 'our heroes'.[294] The term 'sons' ultimately emphasised the individual loss which families had suffered.[295]

The periodic public displays and collective ritual acts carried out at the war memorials continued to be of key importance to conveying the meanings symbolised in them. They gave the cult of the dead concrete expression, their messages changing over the course of time, thus turning the cult into a practical guide to action.[296] Until 1923 it was mainly dedication ceremonies which played this role. Articles in the local press rarely featured verbatim accounts of festive speeches. We can thus get at the rhetoric employed only by means of individual examples. Priests generally made use of a religious triad of thanks, consolation and encouragement, which they related to the memorial in their speeches. The fallen were worthy of gratitude and remembrance because of their bravery and 'heroic Christian courage'. The relatives of the fallen were meant to find comfort in this as they reconfirmed the loss they had suffered. The memorial should serve both to encourage survivors and to urge them to keep their faith in future.[297] The teachers, veterans' association chairmen and former officers who spoke in the secular part of the ceremony struck a more patriotic note. Their speeches first praised the soldiers' heroic sacrifice for the Fatherland; the soldiers had fallen while fulfilling their duty to defend the state and nation. From the standpoint of small, isolated communities, it redounded to their honour to reinterpret soldiers' deeds, with a celebratory tone, as a patriotic act by the village and its inhabitants.[298]

Linked with this were admonitory suggestions that the soldierly spirit, which privileged comradeship, self-sacrifice and awareness of duty, ought to be regarded as exemplary in the face of a future painted as 'grey in grey'.[299] The Christian rhetoric of sacrifice, also deployed in secular contexts, was thus linked directly to contemporary circumstances,

294. Neuburg a. Inn: StAL, Rep. 164/13, 2542, 2544.

295. Arlesried: 'Our sons fallen in the World War 1914/18': StAA, BA Memmingen 10914.

296. Jeismann/Westheider, Nationaler Totenkult, pp. 43-4.

297. *Oberbayerische Landeszeitung. Traunsteiner Nachrichten*, 17.6.1922.

298. Ibid., 25.5.1921.

299. Ibid., 10.5.1922.

and emphasis was placed on the need to overcome the political and economic crises of the post-war period, which were interpreted mainly in terms of moral decline. In the light of the 'profiteering spirit' prevalent among farmers as a result of inflation, festive speeches thus featured direct appeals to Christian mercy, given the hardships faced by many city dwellers, as well as admonitory references to the terrible consequences of 'Mammon worship', 'selfishness' and food profiteering.[300] However, the 'heroic deeds' of soldiers from one's own village were also praiseworthy as acts of patriotism because they had kept the events of the war from spilling over into the homeland. The chairman of the volunteer fire brigade expressed this sentiment at the dedication of the memorial in Asbach with reference to the fallen and to the soldiers who had made it home:

> Imagine the conquered enemy countryside, flower-filled fields and meadows laid waste, peaceful villages and towns destroyed and razed to the ground, a wild chaos of rubble and ruined buildings of every kind. And the poor inhabitants, what have they been through? Many of them, surely, will never have found their way back home. Our heroes have spared our Fatherland all these horrors of war, these terrible acts of destruction.[301]

The national slant of dedication speeches was embedded in memories of one's own fears and the pride of the home community, anchored retrospectively in having successfully fended off a threat perceived as entirely realistic. The appellative aspects of the speeches offered emotive appeals to Christian-conservative morality rather than a concrete political programme.

Beyond the dedication rituals, the memorials were the setting for ceremonies of remembrance organised by the veterans' associations, which took place annually on a day of mourning. Until the end of the Weimar Republic, the national day of mourning on the sixth Sunday before Easter, held throughout the Empire from 1925 (on the fifth Sunday before Easter from 1926), did not apply in Bavaria. The Catholic Church in Bavaria rejected a date in March and insisted on holding a day of mourning within the framework of the All Souls octave in early November, traditionally devoted to remembrance of the dead.[302] From 1926 the second Sunday in November became Bavaria's day of mourning; the government supported

300. *Amper-Bote*, 23.5.1922.
301. Ibid., 5.10.1920.
302. MA, 10.2.1921: BHStA/II, MInn 72723.

it and official flags were raised. For denominational reasons, Bavaria thus pulled out, at least as far as the specific date was concerned, of the *mise-en-scène* of the National Day of Mourning (*Volkstrauertag*) arranged by the *Volksbund Deutsche Kriegsgräberfürsorge* (National League for the Maintenance of German War Memorials), a holiday reinforcing the national cult of the hero.[303]

A sufficiently large and accessible space in front of the memorial was vital if public celebrations were to be held there. Veterans' associations therefore preferred free-standing monuments rather than sites in a church or churchyard. The latter, where many rural memorials were sited, were unsuitable for such events, as the collective remembrance of the dead was bound up with the Christian ritual of mass and the requiem mass specially created for the fallen.[304] However, monuments outside of churches and cemeteries sometimes also offered a place for prayers and reflection in remembrance of relatives. Particularly for the widows and mothers of soldiers, they were a welcome refuge at times of personal distress and grief.[305] Towards the end of the Second World War, after two of her sons had been lost on the Eastern Front, one farmer's wife from the Upper Palatinate regularly visited the war memorial 'to have a good cry' after attending church. There she said a comforting prayer recommended by a woman in a similar situation, probably because it dealt with the religious doubts that burgeoned as faith was shaken by loss.[306] Women made use of the memorials as they went about this silent, certainly daily practice. The cult of the dead was thus no longer limited to the narrow group of ex-soldiers and members of veterans' associations who initially gave it impetus.

People sometimes paid community war memorials less attention after a time. In the first years after the war, their construction reflected the deeply felt need for a suitable symbol of the loss which every community

303. Fritz Schellack, *Nationalfeiertage in Deutschland von 1871 bis 1945*, Frankfurt/M.: Peter Lang 1990, pp. 204, 237–41, 269–73. On the rhetoric of the National Day of Mourning, see Karin Hausen, Die Sorge der Nation für ihre 'Kriegsopfer'. Ein Bereich der Geschlechterpolitik während der Weimarer Republik, in: Jürgen Kocka/Hans-Jürgen Puhle/Klaus Tenfelde (eds), *Von der Arbeiterbewegung zum modernen Sozialstaat. Festschrift für Gerhard A. Ritter zum 65. Geburtstag*, Munich: K.G. Saur 1994, pp. 719–39.

304. Probst, *Bilder*, pp. 63–4.

305. *Oberbayerische Landeszeitung. Traunsteiner Nachrichten*, 24.5.1921.

306. Walburga Roth, *Die Lebenserinnerungen der hundertjährigen Bäuerin Babette Roth*, Kühnhof: Selbstverlag 1990, pp. 69–72.

had suffered. After the experiences of the Second World War, historians established and in fact complained about the fact that few memorials in the Weimar Republic featured pacifist sentiments.[307] This finding, which applies to rural areas, should not, however, lead us to conclude that even memorials that underlined the religious grief felt by those left behind served only to play down the war. Such criticisms ignore the contemporary experiences which made the memorials meaningful. The location of rural memorials and the messages inscribed upon them show that they functioned mainly as places of remembrance and grief, whose significance remained linked with the importance of religion within the individual's life-world. The rural cult of the dead placed the death of members of one's own community and the possible threat faced by the locality centre stage. The political instrumentalisation of the dead was an ephemeral phenomenon. It mainly involved emphasising a loss which redounded to the country's honour and encouraging people to embrace Christian virtues in the light of contemporary notions of moral crisis. The rural cult of the dead thus served to play down the consequences of the war mainly by reducing it to the local context within which honouring soldiers made sense. It thus helped prevent people from thinking more deeply about, for example, what had caused the war.

307. Behrenbeck, *Kriegerdenkmale*, p. 367.

Conclusion

Most rural Bavarians reacted to the outbreak of war with fear, concern and uncertainty. Thus, even in the first few weeks and months of the conflict, no great wave of enthusiasm carried rural soldiers into battle. This raises the question of how they coped with such an extended period of warfare. To answer it, the present work has comprehensively analysed the social configuration of the military, which has at the same time enabled us to tease out the main components of socialisation within the armed forces.

The cohesion of the troops rested on key structural foundations. These included the security of service in the replacement army, especially palpable for farmers, zones of varying exertion at the front, the deterrent effect of military discipline and, last but not least, the 'small-scale escapes' such as furlough, which farmers were granted more often than their fellows. Together with rural soldiers' superior food supplies, this reinforced city dwellers' prejudices about 'peasant numskulls'. The urban-rural divide thus permeated the field and replacement army. From the perspective of a history of experiences, the soldiers' narrow horizon of expectations was of central importance. Though soldiers soon came to the conclusion that the war would drag on for a long time, a new turn of events could always provide grounds for hope. Practically all of them invested such hopes in offensives and peace efforts, while individual soldiers focused on their units' postings and assignments and periods of leave. The latter not only offered respite from the strains of war but was also the most important interface between front and home front. On the whole, soldiers were by no means under constant strain. Nor were they permanently subject to the extreme exertions typical of the famous battles of matériel from 1916 on, which have dominated historical memory. It was precisely during such battles that the pressures of the fighting triggered frequent acts of individual protest and scattered incidents of collective disobedience.

The experience of mass death was the most problematic aspect of front-line experience. In dealing with this danger, both menacing and contingent, rural soldiers could draw upon the repertoire of meanings offered by the Catholic religion. Though the military chaplains perceived ominous symptoms of crisis, a large number of soldiers availed themselves of this repertoire throughout the war. Even many believers, however, began to wonder if there was any point in praying, as huge numbers of their fellows were injured. This was the inevitable consequence of a highly mechanistic understanding of religion. As the war dragged on, moreover, it could no longer be interpreted as part of a divine plan of salvation. This paved the way for soldiers to embrace some of the concepts propagated by the minority current in the Social Democratic Party, which they felt provided more compelling interpretations of the war as a whole. The language used in peasant soldiers' letters took the form of a litany. In formulas which rarely varied, it lamented the misery and cruelty of the war and of life at the front, and mistreatment by 'comrades' and superiors. These it contrasted with an ideal alternative. At both front and home front, as their letters attest, this alternative vision shaped fundamentally the rhythms of peasants' lives in a unique way. It thus isolated peasant soldiers within the army. Peasant discourse revolved around the wish to return to the family, a community both of everyday life and of production, and featured a preoccupation with the customary seasonal labour on the home farm. Peasants embraced only those elements of nation-centred discourse which presented soldiers' performance of their duty and personal respectability as unquestionable values.

The front-line experience of the peasant soldiers revolved around a deeply felt sense of victimisation. They saw themselves as victims rather than perpetrators but were by no means the only ones in the German army who felt that way during the 1914-18 period. Many Social Democrats expressed the conviction that industrialists and generals were slaughtering the soldiers to economic ends. In the religious language of many Catholics and Protestants, it was God who sat idly by while the troops became victims of war. Peasants were unique in lacking any notion of how this situation might be remedied through collective action. Their descriptions of victimisation were thus grounded in a strong sense of resignation. It was in itself nothing new for soldiers to feel like cogs in the uncontrollable machinery of war. What made the First World War different, however, was that the dominant self-description as victims could be connected with the fact that soldiers were at the mercy of artillery fire, the key means of destruction. Around three-quarters of all soldiers died as a result of it, and thus through remote killing.[1] This distinguished the First World War on the Western Front from other wars before and after 1914–18, which were to a far greater extent characterised by face-to-face killing and the active violent participation of the infantrymen.

Meanwhile, 'Patriotic Instruction', into which a great deal of effort was put, and negative concepts of the 'enemy' were marginal to peasants' experiences of the front. Ideological rationales emphasising the state, the armed forces or politics had little positive impact on the cohesion of the troops. Rather than fighting *for* something, soldiers tended to fight *in anticipation of* a point in the foreseeable future that would bring them relief, at least temporarily. Only the small minority of middle-class soldiers who observed the war through a metaphysical lens required 'inner resources' in a 'predominantly metaphysical form'.[2] In any case, there were two factors that seriously undermined soldiers' willingness to hold out. First, their living conditions deteriorated substantially during the war. Second, and this was highly significant, from 1916, or 1917 at the latest, when the open advocacy of annexationist views repudiated the myth of a defensive war once and for all, it appeared increasingly obvious to the majority of rural soldiers that the war was being continued solely to benefit certain influential interest groups. This, along with the fact that those identified as supporters of the war were openly enriching themselves, triggered a shift in the political attitudes of farmers in uniform. In the light of their former adherence to the cult of the monarchy and loyalty to the Centre Party, this was a significant change. Soldiers from a rural background did not, on the other hand, come to embrace nationalist, right-wing politics.

Its advocacy of a peace of understanding in 1917 made the politics of the Majority Social Democrats more attractive even among farmers from Bavaria who had previously supported the Centre Party as a matter of course. They were, however, attracted mainly by the party's position on the peace issue, crucial to all soldiers, and had little awareness of the details of the SPD manifesto. This political shift was bound up with the decline of pro-monarchy convictions and deep disillusionment with a major pillar of the monarchical system, the officer corps. Yet most farmers interpreted officers' misconduct as a moral failure, hampering

1. See the figures in Ziemann, Soldaten, p. 157. These facts and contexts are neglected in the concept of 'war culture' developed in Audoin-Rouzeau/Becker, *Understanding*.

2. Quote in Eksteins, *Rites of Spring*, p. 205.

the politicisation of the conflict and thus helping to limit their support for the Majority Social Democrats to the issue of peace. In the autumn of 1918 the hopelessness of the war finally motivated soldiers to pursue peace through acts of individual refusal on a massive scale. It did not inspire them to embrace policies aiming at radical social and political change.

Given the political quietism of the rural milieu before 1914, these changes seemed dramatic. Yet the return of the rural veterans failed to shake the provincial countryside to the core, in part because their aims had been limited and had largely been achieved through the armistice. Moreover, farm and family had retained their crucial importance to the perception and identity of rural soldiers even at the front. The persistence of a civilian focus, moulded by the specific structures of the peasant family economy, imbued the wartime experience of rural soldiers. Their homesickness caused them to focus on returning to the familiar normality of civilian life once their stint at the front was over. When the veterans came home in 1918, their focus was thus on getting back to the normality of their pre-war lives. The present work is underpinned by the assumption that front and home front were tightly enmeshed. The fact that rural civilians adopted many elements of the anti-war sentiment common in the field, such as 'hatred of Prussia' or criticism of the shortcomings of army life, lends this assumption credence. After the war, the focus on the home village rapidly took the edge off criticism of the traditional authorities. There was in any case no prospect of an alternative to political Catholicism with the potential to win over the rural majority, as the SPD inevitably came into sharp conflict with the farmers as the representative of consumer interests.

The effects of wartime military experiences were thus apparent mainly within a field of activities specific to the veterans. The limits of paramilitary mobilisation in the *Einwohnerwehren* show that their strength was purely numerical. Peasants never truly identified with the military or political goals of the militia's leadership. After the war, the veterans' associations tried to transfigure the front-line experience, but without much success. The Bavarian Veterans' League and its organisational and political goals plunged into crisis, while the minority of veterans remaining in the associations was primarily interested in local self-representation. The cult of the dead was deeply embedded in Christian rituals, symbols and symbolic practices and integrated the civilian and former military elements of the village populace practically without a hitch. It thus appears to have been the key obligatory element of wartime experiences with an enduring impact in the countryside. It was precisely in this field that Catholicism showed its strength and got its first and best chance to recuperate from the crises of the war and post-war period. The symbolic repertoire of Catholicism was customary, nuanced and affecting, enabling the people in rural Bavaria to cope with the troubling mass experience of death and the loss of close relatives.

The 'illusory boom' (Friedrich Aereboe) in agriculture after the war made it a lot easier for veterans to reintegrate, taking the edge off potential criticism, whereas married peasant women had distinguished themselves by a more passive attitude towards the strains of war. State controls radicalised agrarian protest for a brief period after 1918 and inflated the membership figures of agrarian associations. Yet on the whole farmers could count themselves among the winners of the inflationary period. Their expressions of an estatist social consciousness (*Standesbewußtsein*) demonstrate that they indeed did so. In the wake of the agricultural boom, their hand strengthened by the wartime labour shortage, rural farm labourers stepped up their battle to assert their economic claims. During this entire period, all groups within rural society had enough to eat, a crucial fact for a history of war experiences and an important stabilising factor. 'When people are hungry, everything comes to a stop.'[3] This conclusion reached by a metalworker from Württemberg in May 1917 bears striking witness to the key difference between urban and rural war experiences, suggesting why continuity in fact prevailed in the countryside.

Taken as a whole, the wartime and post-war experiences by no means led to a radical break with traditional values and perceptions. Some elements of the peasant mentality such as monarchism were thrown overboard in the wake of the war. But this did not entail a comprehensive modernisation of rural behavioural models or norms. Most people in fact fell back on the 'traditional sources of stability' within rural society, such as the peasant family, religiosity and subsistence farming, particularly during the years of crisis from 1914 to 1923, demonstrating their ongoing significance.[4] Despite the upheaval of war and inflation, continuity outweighed change.

3. Compilation of monthly reports by the Deputy General Commands, 3.6.1917: BArch, R 1501, 12478, fol. 143.

4. See the critical remarks by Heinz Reif on the article by Werner K. Blessing, 'Der Geist der Zeit hat die Menschen sehr verdorben ...' Bemerkungen zur Mentalität in Bayern um 1800, in: Eberhard Weis (ed.), *Reformen im rheinbündischen Deutschland*, Munich: R. Oldenbourg 1984, pp. 229–47, quote p. 250. For a

Following this summary of wartime experiences in rural Bavaria during the period from 1914 to 1923, let us take up again the initial question of how the *experiences* of soldiers in particular related to the *discourse* about the allegedly 'real' front-line experience, so omnipresent in the Weimar Republic. The discrepancy between these two levels has been highlighted in historical research for a number of years.[5] Now it is possible to determine its extent more precisely. First, it is important to note that, at least until 1923, the patriotic heroism and glorification of war dominant in the discourse of the national camp failed to displace alternative representations of the front-line experience from the public sphere. This is proved by the example of rural Bavarians. The crisis-ridden Bavarian Veterans' League failed to produce a widely accepted representation of the front-line experience even in the affiliated local associations. In contrast to an established scholarly opinion, rural war memorials did not contribute to the 'glorification' of the war but focused explicitly on assigning meaning to death on a massive scale and coping with the experience of loss.[6] Other evidence points in the same direction. Ordinary soldiers' bitterness about the shortcomings of army life and the good living enjoyed by officers, and the hardships suffered by their relatives back home, were after 1918 at the centre of an intensive public discourse. This found expression primarily in numerous newspaper articles and pamphlets, and also in speeches given at war memorial dedication ceremonies. Until 1923 the conservative paramilitary groups and the *Reichswehr* battled in vain to stem this tide of publications and its 'subversive' influence on the defensive spirit of German public opinion. As the pacifist Franz Carl Endres has emphasised, the years from 1918 to 1923 were indeed a 'brief period of insight' into the grim reality of the war and the injustice within the Wilhelmine military.[7]

---

somewhat comparable argument with regard to Great Britain, see Gerard J. DeGroot, *Blighty. British Society in the Era of the Great War*, London, New York: Longman Publishers 1996.

5. See Richard Bessel, The Great War in German Memory: the Soldiers of the First World War, Demobilization and Weimar Political Culture, *German History* 6 (1988), pp. 20–34; idem, Gewalt; idem, *Germany*, pp. 254–84.

6. See chapters 5.3 and 5.4. Quoting dated literature, see Lipp, *Meinungslenkung*, p. 316.

7. Franz Carl Endres, *Die Tragödie Deutschlands. Im Banne des Machtgedankens bis zum Zusammenbruch des Reiches. Von einem Deutschen*, Stuttgart: Moritz 1924, p. 369; see Ulrich/Ziemann, *Krieg im Frieden*, pp. 60–72; Ulrich, Perspektive; idem, *Augenzeugen*, pp. 228–71. This point is again missed by Lipp, *Meinungslenkung*, p. 314.

By 1923 criticism of the war had passed its peak within public discourse. In the following years, however, the discourse on the 'appropriate' way to represent and symbolise the front-line experience was by no means dominated by one hegemonic current. The different political camps and advocates of glorifying and anti-war positions tussled over how best to remember the First World War. The nationalist right succeeded in moulding the war discourse and more or less silencing alternative ideas only after the world economic crisis began in 1928.[8] Even at this point wartime *experiences* had not disappeared, although it had become almost impossible to articulate them in the public. This applies, for example, to the anti-war critique and pacifism of the Social Democratic veterans in the *Reichsbanner Schwarz-Rot-Gold*. Together with its partner organisation for disabled ex-servicemen, the *Reichsbund*, it had the largest membership of all the veterans' organisations in the Weimar Republic.[9] Even after 1939 some managed to elude the ideological consequences of the Nazi war of annihilation. War letters from the Second World War provide evidence that soldiers from a rural Bavarian background were particularly likely to 'show aversion to the war', unlike the vast majority of *Wehrmacht* soldiers. Moulded by rural society and how it had come to terms with the experiences of the First World War, they were still 'at least partially resistant to the logic of modern, industrial war'.[10]

8. This is the main argument in Ulrich/Ziemann, *Krieg im Frieden*.

9. See Ziemann, Republikanische Kriegserinnerung. A vivid account of the wartime experiences of a rank and file *Reichsbanner* member and their ongoing effect on him during the 1920s is documented in Ziemann, Gedanken.

10. See, based on war letters written by *Wehrmacht* soldiers in Stalingrad, Jens Ebert, 'Zwischen Mythos und Wirklichkeit. Die Schlacht um Stalingrad in deutschsprachigen authentischen und literarischen Texten', PhD dissertation, Humboldt-Universität Berlin 1989, 2 vols, vol. 1, quote p. 39.

Select Bibliography

For a full list of archival and secondary sources see the appendix in my book *Front und Heimat. Ländliche Kriegserfahrungen im südlichen Bayern 1914–1923*, Essen 1997, pp. 475–508.

Archival Sources

Archiv des Bistums Augsburg

- Allgemeinakten
- Bischöfliches Ordinariat
- Pfa
- NL Karl Lang

Staatsarchiv Augsburg

- Regierung
- BA Donauwörth n.pp.
- BA Günzburg
- BA Illertissen
- BA Kempten
- BA Lindau
- BA Markt-Oberdorf
- BA Memmingen
- BA Mindelheim
- BA Neuburg
- BA Wertingen
- Amtsgericht Immenstadt: Zivilsachen E 1880–1934

Bundesarchiv Berlin-Lichterfelde

- R 1501
- R 1507
- R 3901
- R 8034 II
- 92

Sächsisches Hauptstaatsarchiv Dresden
Kriegsarchiv (P)

Bundesarchiv/Militärarchiv Freiburg
W-10

Gemeinde Kochel
War letters to Otto Freiherr v. Aufseß

Staatsarchiv Landshut
Rep. 168/1
Rep. 168/5
Rep. 164/3
Rep. 164/6
Rep. 164/10
Rep. 164/13
Rep. 164/14
Rep. 164/16
Rep. 164/19
Rep. 167/2

Archiv des Erzbistums München und Freising
Personal files of Michael Buchberger
War chronicle of the parish communities Riedering and Neukirchen B 1830
War chronicle Altenerding B 1837
NL Cardinal Faulhaber

Bayerisches Hauptstaatsarchiv München, Abt. II
MA
MInn
MK
ML

Bayerisches Hauptstaatsarchiv München, Abt. IV: Kriegsarchiv
2. Infanterie-Division
1. Reserve-Division
5. Infanterie-Division
6. Infanterie-Division
6. Landwehr-Division
Armee-Oberkommando 6
Generalkommando I. Armeekorps
Heeresgruppe Kronprinz Rupprecht
Infanterie-Leib-Regiment

Einwohnerwehr
HS
Kriegsbriefe
Militärgericht 6. Landwehr-Division
Militärgericht 1. Reserve-Division
Militärgericht 16. Infanterie-Division
Militärgerichte (MilGer)
MKr
RwGruKdo 4
stv. Generalkommando I. Armeekorps

Bayerische Staatsbibliothek München, Handschriftenabteilung
Schinnereriana

Staatsarchiv München
AG
LRA
RA
Polizeidirektion München (Pol.-Dir.)

Archiv des Bistums Passau
DekA II
OA Pfa

Bischöfliches Zentralarchiv Regensburg
OA

Stadtarchiv Regensburg
Nachlaß Georg Heim

Bibliothek für Zeitgeschichte Stuttgart
Sammlung Knoch
Sammlung Schüling

War letters and other materials: private collections
At the request of some of the private owners of war letters and diaries, the Bibliothek für Zeitgeschichte and the local administration in Kochel, the names of some of the authors of war letters and diaries have been encoded.

Published Sources

Bauer, Max, *Kopfsteinpflaster. Erinnerungen*, Frankfurt/M.: Eichborn 1981.

Bayerisches Kriegsarchiv (ed.), *Die Bayern im Großen Kriege 1914-1918*, Munich: Bayerisches Kriegsarchiv 1923, 2 vols.

Buchberger, Michael, *Seelsorgsaufgaben der Gegenwart und der nächsten Zukunft*, Regensburg: Pustet 1918.

Deist, Wilhelm (ed.), *Militär und Innenpolitik im Weltkrieg 1914-1918*, Düsseldorf: Droste 1970.

Kästner, Albrecht (ed.), *Revolution und Heer. Auswirkungen der Großen Sozialistischen Oktoberrevolution auf das Heer des imperialistischen deutschen Kaiserreichs 1917/18. Dokumente*, Berlin: Militärverlag der DDR 1987.

Klemperer, Victor, *Curriculum Vitae. Jugend um 1900*, vol. II, Berlin: Aufbau 1989.

Die Kriegs-Volkszählungen vom Jahre 1916 und 1917 in Bayern, München 1919 (Beiträge zur Statistik Bayerns, Heft 89).

Militarismus gegen Sowjetmacht 1917 bis 1919. Das Fiasko der ersten antisowjetischen Aggression des deutschen Imperialismus, Berlin: Deutscher Militärverlag 1967.

Richert, Dominik, *Beste Gelegenheit zum Sterben. Meine Erlebnisse im Kriege 1914-1918*, Munich: Knesebeck & Schüler 1989 (ed. by Angelika Tramitz and Bernd Ulrich).

Thimme, Hans, *Weltkrieg ohne Waffen. Die Propaganda der Westmächte gegen Deutschland, ihre Wirkung und ihre Abwehr*, Stuttgart: Cotta 1932.

Ulrich, Bernd/Benjamin Ziemann (eds), *Frontalltag im Ersten Weltkrieg. Wahn und Wirklichkeit. Quellen und Dokumente*, Frankfurt/M.: Fischer Taschenbuch Verlag 1994.

Ulrich, Bernd/Benjamin Ziemann (eds), *Krieg im Frieden. Die umkämpfte Erinnerung an den Ersten Weltkrieg 1918-1935*, Frankfurt/M.: Fischer Taschenbuch Verlag 1997.

Secondary Sources

Albrecht, Willy, *Landtag und Regierung in Bayern am Vorabend der Revolution von 1918*, Berlin: Duncker & Humblot 1968.

Audoin-Rouzeau, Stéphane/Annette Becker, *14-18. Understanding the Great War*, New York: Hill and Wang 2003.

Ay, Karl-Ludwig, *Die Entstehung einer Revolution. Die Volksstimmung in Bayern während des ersten Weltkrieges*, Berlin: Duncker & Humblot 1968.

Bergmann, Hannsjörg, *Der Bayerische Bauernbund und der bayerische Christliche Bauernverein 1919-1928*, Munich: C.H. Beck 1986.

Bessel, Richard, *Germany after the First World War*, Oxford: Clarendon Press 1993.

—— Politische Gewalt und die Krise der Weimarer Republik, in: Lutz Niethammer *et al.*, *Bürgerliche Gesellschaft in Deutschland. Historische Einblicke, Fragen, Perspektiven*, Frankfurt/M.: Fischer Taschenbuch Verlag 1990, pp. 383–95.

Blessing, Werner K., Disziplinierung und Qualifizierung. Zur kulturellen Bedeutung des Militärs im Bayern des 19. Jahrhunderts, *GG* 17 (1991), pp. 459–79.

—— Kirchenfromm - volksfromm - weltfromm: Religiosität im katholischen Bayern des 19. Jahrhunderts, in: Wilfried Loth (ed.), *Deutscher Katholizismus im Umbruch zur Moderne*, Stuttgart: W. Kohlhammer 1991, pp. 95–123.

—— *Staat und Kirche in der Gesellschaft. Institutionelle Autorität und mentaler Wandel in Bayern während des 19. Jahrhunderts*, Göttingen: Vandenhoeck & Ruprecht 1982.

—— Umwelt und Mentalität im ländlichen Bayern. Eine Skizze zum Alltagswandel im 19. Jahrhundert, *AfS* 19 (1979), pp. 1–42.

Busch, Norbert, *Katholische Frömmigkeit und Moderne. Zur Sozial- und Mentalitätsgeschichte des Herz-Jesu-Kultes in Deutschland zwischen Kulturkampf und Erstem Weltkrieg*, Gütersloh: Gütersloher Verlags-Haus 1997.

Cohen, Deborah, *The War Come Home. Disabled Veterans in Britain and Germany, 1914–1939*, Berkeley: University of California Press 2001.

Cron, Hermann (ed.), *Das Archiv des Deutschen Studentendienstes von 1914*, Potsdam: Reichsarchiv 1926.

—— *Kriegsbrief-Sammlung des Deutschen Transportarbeiter-Verbandes*, Potsdam: Reichsarchiv 1926.

—— *Kriegsbrief-Sammlung des Gewerkvereins der Holzarbeiter Deutschlands*, Potsdam: Reichsarchiv 1926.

—— *Kriegsbrief-Sammlung des Sekretariats Sozialer Studentenarbeit*, Potsdam: Reichsarchiv 1927.

—— *Kriegsbrief-Sammlung des Verbandes der Bergarbeiter Deutschlands*, Potsdam: Reichsarchiv 1926.

Daniel, Ute, *Arbeiterfrauen in der Kriegsgesellschaft. Beruf, Familie und Politik im Ersten Weltkrieg*, Göttingen: Vandenhoeck & Ruprecht 1989.

Deist, Wilhelm, The Military Collapse of the German Empire, *War in History* 3 (1996), pp. 186–207.

—— Verdeckter Militärstreik im Kriegsjahr 1918?, in: Wolfram Wette (ed.), *Der Krieg des kleinen Mannes. Eine Militärgeschichte von unten*, Munich: Piper 1992, pp. 146-67 .

Diehl, James M., *Paramilitary Politics in Weimar Germany*, Bloomington, London: Indiana UP 1977.

Eksteins, Modris, *Rites of Spring. The Great War and the Birth of the Modern Age*, London: Bantam Press 1989.

Elliott, Christopher James, Ex-servicemen's Organisations in the Weimar Republic, PhD dissertation, London 1971.

Feldman, Gerald D., *Armee, Industrie und Arbeiterschaft in Deutschland 1914 bis 1918*, Berlin, Bonn: J.H.W. Dietz 1985.

Fenske, Hans, *Konservativismus und Rechtsradikalismus in Bayern nach 1918*, Bad Homburg, Berlin, Zürich: Gehlen 1969.

Fricke, Dieter (ed.), *Lexikon zur Parteiengeschichte. Die bürgerlichen und kleinbürgerlichen Verbände in Deutschland (1789-1945)*, 4 vols, Cologne: Pahl-Rugenstein 1983-6.

Geyer, Martin H., Teuerungsprotest, Konsumentenpolitik und soziale Gerechtigkeit während der Inflation: München 1920-1923, *AfS* 30 (1990), pp. 181-215.

Geyer, Michael, Eine Kriegsgeschichte, die vom Tod spricht, *Mittelweg 36* 4, No. 2 (1995), pp. 57-77.

Histories of Two Hundred and Fifty-One Divisions of the German Army which Participated in the War (1914-1918), Washington: Government Print Office 1920.

Jacobeit, Wolfgang/Josef Mooser/Bo Stråth (eds), *Idylle oder Aufbruch? Das Dorf im bürgerlichen 19. Jahrhundert*, Berlin: Akademie Verlag 1990.

Jeismann, Michael/Westheider, Rolf, Wofür stirbt der Bürger? Nationaler Totenkult und Staatsbürgertum in Deutschland und Frankreich seit der Französischen Revolution, in: Reinhart Koselleck/Michael Jeismann (eds), *Der politische Totenkult. Kriegerdenkmäler in der Moderne*, Munich: Wilhelm Fink 1994, pp. 23-50.

Klein, Fritz (ed.), *Deutschland im Ersten Weltkrieg*, vol. 3, Berlin: Akademie-Verlag 1969.

Kocka, Jürgen, *Klassengesellschaft im Krieg. Deutsche Sozialgeschichte 1914-1918*, Frankfurt/M.: Fischer Taschenbuch Verlag 1988.

Koselleck, Reinhart, Der Einfluß der beiden Weltkriege auf das soziale Bewußtsein, in: Wolfram Wette (ed.), *Der Krieg des kleinen Mannes*, Munich: Piper 1992, pp. 324-43.

—— Space of Experience and Horizon of Expectation: Two Historical Categories, in: idem, *Futures Past. On the Semantics of Historical Time*, New York: Columbia UP 2004, pp. 255-75.

—— War Memorials. Identity Formations of the Survivors, in: idem, *The Practice of Conceptual History. Timing History, Spacing Concepts*, Stanford: Stanford University Press 2002, pp. 285-326.

Kruse, Wolfgang, Krieg und Klassenheer. Zur Revolutionierung der deutschen Armee im Ersten Weltkrieg, *GG* 22 (1996), pp. 530-61.

—— *Krieg und nationale Integration. Eine Neuinterpretation des sozialdemokratischen Burgfriedensschlusses 1914/15*, Essen: Klartext 1993.

Kühne, Thomas, Comradeship. Gender Confusion and Gender Order in the German Military, 1918-1945, in: Karen Hagemann/Stefanie Schüler-Springorum (eds), *Home-Front. The Military, War and Gender in 20th Century Germany*, Oxford/New York: Berg 2002, pp. 233-54.

Kühne, Thomas/Benjamin Ziemann (eds), *Was ist Militärgeschichte?*, Paderborn: Ferdinand Schöningh 2000.

Large, David Clay, *The Politics of Law and Order. A History of the Bavarian Einwohnerwehr, 1918-1921*, Philadelphia: American Philosophical Society 1980.

Lipp, Anne, *Meinungslenkung im Krieg. Kriegserfahrungen deutscher Soldaten und ihre Deutung 1914-1918*, Göttingen: Vandenhoeck & Ruprecht 2003.

Lurz, Meinhold, *Kriegerdenkmäler in Deutschland, vol. 4: Weimarer Republik*, Heidelberg: Esprint-Verlag 1985.

Mattes, Wilhelm, *Die bayerischen Bauernräte. Eine soziologische und historische Untersuchung über bäuerliche Politik*, Stuttgart, Berlin: J.G. Cotta'sche Buchhandlung 1921.

Moeller, Robert G., *German Peasants and Agrarian Politics, 1914-1924. The Rhineland and Westphalia*, London: Chapel Hill 1986.

—— Winners as Losers in the German Inflation: Peasant Protest over the Controlled Economy 1920-1923, in: Gerald D. Feldman/Carl-Ludwig Holtfrerich/Gerhard A. Ritter/Peter-Christian Witt (eds), *Die deutsche Inflation. Eine Zwischenbilanz*, Berlin, New York: de Gruyter 1982, pp. 255-88.

Mooser, Josef, Katholische Volksreligion, Klerus und Bürgertum in der zweiten Hälfte des 19. Jahrhunderts. Thesen, in: Wolfgang Schieder (ed.), *Religion und Gesellschaft im 19. Jahrhundert*, Stuttgart: Klett-Cotta 1993, pp. 144-56.

Mosse, George L., *Fallen Soldiers. Reshaping the Memory of the World Wars*, New York, Oxford: Oxford University Press 1990.

Nusser, Horst G.W., *Konservative Wehrverbände in Bayern, Preußen und Österreich 1918-1933, mit einer Biographie von Forstrat Escherich*, Munich: Nusser 1973.

Osmond, Jonathan, A Second Agrarian Mobilization? Peasant Associations in South and West Germany 1918-24, in: Robert G. Moeller (ed.), *Peasants and Lords in Modern Germany. Recent Studies in Agricultural History*, Boston: Allen & Unwin 1986, pp. 168-97.

—— *Rural Protest in the Weimar Republic. The Free Peasantry in the Rhineland and Bavaria*, Basingstoke, London: St Martin's Press 1993.

Probst, Volker G., *Bilder vom Tode. Eine Studie zum deutschen Kriegerdenkmal in der Weimarer Republik am Beispiel des Pietà-Motives und seiner profanierten Varianten*, Hamburg: Wayasbah 1986.

Prost, Antoine, *In the Wake of War. 'Les Anciens Combattants' and French Society 1914-1939*, Providence, Oxford: Berg 1992.

Rohkrämer, Thomas, *Der Militarismus der 'kleinen Leute'. Die Kriegervereine im deutschen Kaiserreich 1871-1914*, Munich: R. Oldenbourg 1990.

Sanitätsbericht über das deutsche Heer im Weltkriege 1914/1918, vol. III, Berlin: Mittler 1934.

Schulte, Regina, *Das Dorf im Verhör. Brandstifter, Kindsmörderinnen und Wilderer vor den Schranken des bürgerlichen Gerichts. Oberbayern 1848-1910*, Reinbek: Rowohlt 1989.

Schumacher, Martin, *Land und Politik. Eine Untersuchung über politische Parteien und agrarische Interessen 1914-1923*, Düsseldorf: Droste 1978.

Schumann, Dirk, *Politische Gewalt in der Weimarer Republik 1918-1933. Kampf um die Straße und Furcht vor dem Bürgerkrieg*, Essen: Klartext 2001.

Tenfelde, Klaus, Proletarische Provinz. Radikalisierung und Widerstand in Penzberg/Oberbayern 1900 bis 1945, in: Martin Broszat/Elke Fröhlich/Anton Grossmann (eds), *Bayern in der NS-Zeit*, vol. IV, Munich, Vienna: R. Oldenbourg 1981, pp. 1-382.

Ulrich, Bernd, *Die Augenzeugen. Deutsche Feldpostbriefe in Kriegs- und Nachkriegszeit 1914-1933*, Essen: Klartext 1997.

—— Die Desillusionierung der Kriegsfreiwilligen von 1914, in: Wolfram Wette (ed.), *Der Krieg des kleinen Mannes. Eine Militärgeschichte von unten*, Munich: Piper 1992, pp. 100-26.

—— 'Militärgeschichte von unten'. Anmerkungen zu ihren Ursprüngen, Quellen und Perspektiven im 20. Jahrhundert, *GG* 22 (1996), pp. 473-503.

Ulrich, Bernd/Benjamin Ziemann, Das soldatische Kriegserlebnis, in: Wolfgang Kruse (ed.), *Zivilisationsbruch und Zeitenwende. Der*

Erste Weltkrieg 1914-1918, Frankfurt/M.: Fischer Taschenbuch Verlag 1997, pp. 127-58.

Verhey, Jeffrey, *The Spirit of 1914. Militarism, Myth and Mobilization in Germany*, Cambridge: Cambridge University Press 2000.

Wehler, Hans-Ulrich, *Deutsche Gesellschaftsgeschichte*, vol. 3, Munich: C.H. Beck 1995.

Das Werk des Untersuchungsausschusses der Deutschen Verfassunggebenden Nationalversammlung und des Deutschen Reichstages 1919-1930, Vierte Reihe: *Die Ursachen des Deutschen Zusammenbruches im Jahre 1918*, 12 vols, Berlin 1925-30.

Wette, Wolfram, Ideologien, Propaganda und Innenpolitik als Voraussetzungen der Kriegspolitik des Dritten Reiches, in: Wilhelm Deist *et al.*, *Ursachen und Voraussetzungen des Zweiten Weltkrieges*, Frankfurt/M.: Fischer Taschenbuch Verlag 1989, pp. 23-208.

Whalen, Robert Wheldon, *Bitter Wounds. German Victims of the Great War, 1914-1939*, Ithaca, London: Cornell UP 1984.

Wiebel-Fanderl, Oliva, 'Wenn ich dann meine letzte Reise antrete ...' Zur Präsenz des Todes und der Todesbewältigung in Autobiographien, in: Andreas Heller/Therese Weber/Oliva Wiebel-Fanderl (eds), *Religion und Alltag. Interdisziplinäre Beiträge zu einer Sozialgeschichte des Katholizismus in lebensgeschichtlichen Aufzeichnungen*, Vienna, Cologne: Böhlau 1990, pp. 217-49.

Ziemann, Benjamin, Die Erinnerung an den Ersten Weltkrieg in den Milieukulturen der Weimarer Republik, in: Thomas F. Schneider (ed.), *Kriegserlebnis und Legendenbildung. Das Bild des 'modernen' Krieges in Literatur, Theater, Photographie und Film*, Osnabrück: Rasch 1999, Vol. I, pp. 249-70.

—— Fahnenflucht im deutschen Heer 1914-1918, *Militärgeschichtliche Mitteilungen* 55 (1996), pp. 93-130.

—— Das 'Fronterlebnis' des Ersten Weltkrieges - eine sozialhistorische Zäsur? Deutungen und Wirkungen in Deutschland und Frankreich, in: Hans Mommsen (ed.), *Der Erste Weltkrieg und die europäische Nachkriegsordnung. Sozialer Wandel und Formveränderung der Politik*, Cologne: Böhlau 2000, pp. 43-82.

—— 'Gedanken eines Reichsbannermannes auf Grund von Erlebnissen und Erfahrungen'. Politische Kultur, Flaggensymbolik und Kriegserinnerung in Schmalkalden 1926. Dokumentation, *Zeitschrift des Vereins für Thüringische Geschichte* 53 (1999), pp. 201-32.

—— German Soldiers in Victory, 1914, in: Peter Liddle/John Bourne/Ian Whitehead (eds), *The Great World War 1914-45. Vol. 1: Lightning Strikes Twice*, London: Harper Collins 2000, pp. 253-64.

—— Germany after the First World War - A Violent Society? Results and Implications of Recent Research on Weimar Germany, *Journal of Modern European History* 1 (2003), pp. 80-95.

—— Geschlechterbeziehungen in deutschen Feldpostbriefen des Ersten Weltkrieges, in: Christa Hämmerle/Edith Saurer (eds), *Briefkulturen und ihr Geschlecht. Zur Geschichte der privaten Korrespondenz vom 16. Jahrhundert bis heute*, Vienna: Böhlau 2003, pp. 261-82.

—— Le Chemin des Dames dans l'historiographie militaire allemande, in: Nicolas Offenstadt (ed.), *Le Chemin des Dames. De l'événement à la mémoire*, Paris: Éditions Stock 2004, pp. 341-9.

—— Republikanische Kriegserinnerung in einer polarisierten Öffentlichkeit. Das Reichsbanner Schwarz-Rot-Gold als Veteranenverband der sozialistischen Arbeiterschaft, *Historische Zeitschrift* 267 (1998), pp. 357-98.

—— Soldaten, in: Gerhard Hirschfeld/Gerd Krumeich/Irina Renz (eds), *Enzyklopädie Erster Weltkrieg*, Paderborn: Ferdinand Schöningh 2003, pp. 155-68.

—— Sozialmilitarismus und militärische Sozialisation im deutschen Kaiserreich 1870-1914. Ergebnisse und Desiderate in der Revision eines Geschichtsbildes, *Geschichte in Wissenschaft und Unterricht* 53 (2002), pp. 148-64.

—— 'Vergesellschaftung der Gewalt' als Thema der Kriegsgeschichte seit 1914. Perspektiven und Desiderate eines Konzeptes, in: Bruno Thoß/Hans-Erich Volkmann (eds), *Erster Weltkrieg - Zweiter Weltkrieg: Ein Vergleich. Krieg, Kriegserlebnis, Kriegserfahrung in Deutschland*, Paderborn 2002, pp. 735-58.

Zorn, Wolfgang, *Bayerns Geschichte im 20. Jahrhundert*, Munich: C.H. Beck 1986.

Index

Index

Lightning Source UK Ltd.
Milton Keynes UK
UKOW05f2028290916

284132UK00020B/491/P